D1488342

Luke's christology is carefully designed. Luke portrays the exalted Jesus as God's co-equal by the kinds of things he does and says from heaven. Through the Holy Spirit, the divine name, and personal manifestations, Jesus behaves toward people in Luke–Acts as does Yahweh in the Old Testament. His power and knowledge are supreme. As the Father's co-equal, Jesus sovereignly reigns over Israel, the church, the powers of darkness, and the world.

Luke deepens this portrait by depicting Jesus as deity who by nature behaves as servant: the earthly Jesus acted among his people as one who serves; the exalted Jesus continues serving his people by strengthening and encouraging them in their witness of him to the world.

The purpose of Luke's christology matches Paul's use of the Christ hymn in Philippians. That the believers in Acts resemble the way Jesus behaved in the Gospel means that they too are now imaging some of his servant-like character in their witness of him. The readers of Luke–Acts should pattern their lives according to the same Christ-like behavior.

SOCIETY FOR NEW TESTAMENT STUDIES

MONOGRAPH SERIES

General editor: Margaret E. Thrall

89

THE CHARACTER AND PURPOSE OF
LUKE'S CHRISTOLOGY

The character and purpose of Luke's christology

H. DOUGLAS BUCKWALTER

Assistant Professor of New Testament
Evangelical School of Theology
Myerstown, Pennsylvania

CAMBRIDGE
UNIVERSITY PRESS

Published by the Press Syndicate of the University of Cambridge
The Pitt Building, Trumpington Street, Cambridge CB2 1RP
40 West 20th Street, New York, NY 10011-4211, USA
10 Stamford Road, Oakleigh, Melbourne 3166, Australia

First published 1996

Printed in Great Britain at the University Press, Cambridge

A catalogue record for this book is available from the British Library

Library of Congress cataloguing in publication data

Buckwalter, Douglas.
    The character and purpose of Luke's christology/H. Douglas
Buckwalter.
        p.   cm. – (Society for New Testament Studies monograph series:
89)
    Includes bibliographical references and indexes.
    ISBN 0 521 56180 9 (hardback)
    1. Bible. N.T. Luke – Theology. 2. Bible. N.T. Acts – Theology. 3. Jesus
Christ – Person and offices – Biblical teaching. I. Title. II. Series:
Monograph series (Society for New Testament Studies): 89.
BT198.B83 1996
232'.09'015 – dc20   95–37960   CIP

ISBN 0 521 56180 9 hardback

CE

To Keri
Ahna, Andy, and Emily

CONTENTS

PREFACE

Without the support and assistance of family and friends, the completion of this book and subsequent revisions would not have been possible. I should especially like to thank the postgraduate community at Aberdeen, whose encouragement and insights were a stimulation and benefit to my research. I should also like to thank the Committee of Vice-Chancellors and Principals of the Universities of the United Kingdom for their financial assistance, and George McLeod, Muriel Collie, and Eileen Kuhn for their untiring technical assistance in computer matters. I owe a debt of gratitude to Dr. Max Turner, Mr. Eric Franklin, and Dr. E. W. Davies for their detailed reading and criticisms of the typescript. I am especially grateful to Dr. Margaret E. Thrall, general editor of SNTSMS, for her patience, direction, and support over the final revising stages of the project and to the staff of Cambridge University Press for their gracious and expert help. I am most grateful to my adviser, Professor I. Howard Marshall, for his numerous readings of the work, his invaluable input, and for the example he has set for me in putting the Christian faith into practice.

Special thanks are due to my parents and parents-in-law – Harold and Dolores Buckwalter and Paul and Sylvia Hollinger – for their continued prayers and encouragement along the way. Above all, I am indebted to my wife Keri, who has constantly supported me in this endeavor, and to Ahna, Andy, and "little Emily," who have helped me keep my priorities in order.

ABBREVIATIONS

A1CS	The Book of Acts in its First-Century Setting
ACNT	Augsburg Commentary on the New Testament
AnaBib	Analecta biblica. Investigationes scientificae in res biblicas
AnaGreg	Analecta Gregoriana
AncB	The Anchor Bible
ANRW	*Aufstieg und Niedergang der römischen Welt. Geschichte und Kultur Roms im Spiegel der neueren Forschung*
ASNU	Acta seminarii neotestamentici upsaliensis
AThANT	Abhandlungen zur Theologie des Alten und Neuen Testaments
ATR	*Anglican Theological Review*
ATRsup	*Anglican Theological Review supplement*
BAGD	W. Bauer, W. F. Arndt, F. W. Gingrich, and F. Danker (eds.), *A Greek–English Lexicon of the New Testament and Other Early Christian Literature*, 2nd ed., Chicago: Chicago, 1979
BBB	Bonner biblische Beiträge
BC	F. J. Foakes-Jackson and K. Lake (eds.), *The Beginnings of Christianity*. London: Macmillan, 1920–33
BDB	F. Brown, S. R. Driver, and C.A. Briggs (eds.), *A Hebrew and English Lexicon of the Old Testament*, Oxford: Clarendon, 1951
BEB	W. A. Elwell (ed.), *Baker Encyclopedia of the Bible*, 2 vols., Grand Rapids: Baker, 1988
BEThL	Bibliotheca ephemeridum theologicarum lovaniensium
BEvTh	Beiträge zur evangelischen Theologie
BHTh	Beiträge zur historischen Theologie
Bib	*Biblica*

BibKir	*Bibel und Kirche*
BibLeb	*Bibel und Leben*
Biblebh	*Biblebhashyam*
BibLit	*Bibel und Liturgie*
BibOr	*Bibbia e oriente*
BibPasBul	*Biblical–Pastoral Bulletin*
BibRes	*Biblical Research*
BIRS	Bibliographies and Indexes in Religious Studies
BIS	Biblical Interpretation Series
BJRL	*Bulletin of the John Rylands Library* (1903/8–1971/2)
BJRLUM	*Bulletin of the John Rylands Library, University of Manchester* (1972/3–)
BNTC	Black's New Testament Commentaries
BST	Biblical Studies in Theology
BTB	*Biblical Theology Bulletin*
BTS	Biblisch-theologische Studien
BU	Biblische Untersuchungen
BVC	*Bible et vie chrétienne*
BWANT	Beiträge zur Wissenschaft vom Alten und Neuen Testaments
BZ	*Biblische Zeitschrift*
BZNW	Beihefte zur Zeitschrift für die neutestamentliche Wissenschaft und die Kunde der älteren Kirche
CBQ	*The Catholic Biblical Quarterly*
CC	The Communicator's Commentary
CGTC	The Cambridge Greek Testament Commentary
ConBib nts	Coniectanea biblica, New Testament series
ConJ	*Concordia Journal*
CQ	*Church Quarterly Review*
CrisTRev	*Criswell Theological Review*
CTJ	*Calvin Theological Journal*
CTL	Crown Theological Library
CurTM	*Currents in Theology and Mission*
DCG	J. Hastings (ed.), *A Dictionary of Christ and the Gospels*, 2 vols., Edinburgh: Clark, 1908
deGrLe	de Gruyter Lehrbuch
DJG	J. B. Green and S. McKnight (eds.), *Dictionary of Jesus and the Gospels*, Downers Grove: IVP, 1992
DPCM	S. M. Burgess and G. B. McGee (eds.), *Dictionary of Pentecostal and Charismatic Movements*, Grand Rapids: Zondervan, 1988

DunwRev	*Dunwoodie Review*
EBib	*Etudes bibliques*
EDT	W. A. Elwell (ed.), *Evangelical Dictionary of Theology*, Grand Rapids: Baker, 1984
EF	Erträge der Forschung
EgTh	*Eglise et théologie*
EH	Europäische Hochschulschriften
EHPhR	Etudes d'histoire et de philosophie religieuses
EKK	Evangelisch-katholischer Kommentar zum Neuen Testament
EM	Eichsätter Materialien
EpRev	*Epworth Review*
ErThS	Erfurter theologische Studien
EThL	*Ephemerides theologicae lovanienses*
EThR	*Etudes théologiques et religieuses*
EvQ	*Evangelical Quarterly*
EvTh	*Evangelische Theologie*
Exp	*The Expositor*
ExpT	*The Expository Times*
FB bs	Facet Books, biblical series
FBib	Forschung zur Bibel
FF	Foundations and Facets
Found	*Foundations*
FRLANT	Forschungen zur Religion und Literatur des Alten und Neuen Testaments
GNC	Good News Commentary
Gnomon	*Gnomon. Kritische Zeitschrift für die Gesamt klassische Altertumswissenschaft*
GNS	Good News Studies
GorRev	*Gordon Review*
Greg	*Gregorianum*
GThA	Göttinger theologische Arbeiten
Hermeneia	Hermeneia – A Critical and Historical Commentary on the Bible
HeyJ	*Heythrop Journal*
HibJ	*Hibbert Journal*
HThKNT	Herders theologischer Kommentar zum Neuen Testament
HTR	*Harvard Theological Review*
IBC	Interpretation: A Bible Commentary for Teaching and Preaching

IBS	*Irish Biblical Studies*
ICC	The International Critical Commentary
ICT	Issues in Contemporary Theology
IDB	G. A. Buttrick (ed.), *The Interpreter's Dictionary of the Bible*, 4 vols., Nashville: Abingdon, 1962
IDBsup	K. Crim (ed.), *The Interpreter's Dictionary of the Bible, supplementary vol.*, Nashville: Abingdon, 1962
Int	*Interpretation*
IRT	Issues in Religion and Theology
ITQ	*Irish Theological Quarterly*
IVPNTCS	The IVP New Testament Commentary Series
JAAR	*Journal of the American Academy of Religion*
JAC	*Jahrbuch für Antike und Christentum*
JAOS	*Journal of the American Oriental Society*
JBL	*Journal of Biblical Literature*
JBR	*Journal of Bible and Religion*
JETS	*Journal of the Evangelical Theological Society*
JR	*The Journal of Religion*
JSNT	*Journal for the Study of the New Testament*
JSNTSS	Journal for the Study of the New Testament Supplement Series
JTC	Journal for Theology and the Church
JTS	*The Journal of Theological Studies* (1899/1900–49)
JTS ns	*The Journal of Theological Studies*, new series (1950/1–)
JTSA	*Journal of Theology for Southern Africa*
KBANT	Kommentare und Beiträge zum Alten und Neuen Testament
KEKNT	Kritisch-exegetischer Kommentar über das Neue Testament
LCL	Loeb Classical Library
LEC	Library of Early Christianity
LQHR	*London Quarterly and Holborn Review*
LThPh	*Laval théologique et philosophique*
LumVit	*Lumen vitae*
MilltSt	*Milltown Studies*
Miss	*Missiology*
MLT	Mowbrays Library of Theology
MNTC	The Moffatt New Testament Commentary
MSB	Monographien und Studienbucher
MThS	Marburger theologische Studien

NAC	The New American Commentary
NBD	J. D. Douglas (ed.), *New Bible Dictionary*, 2nd ed., Wheaton: Tyndale, 1982
NCB	The New Clarendon Bible
NCBC	The New Century Bible Commentary
NEBKNT	Die Neue Echter Bibel. Kommentar zum Neuen Testament mit der Einheitsübersetzung
NIBC	New International Biblical Commentary
NICNT	The New International Commentary on the New Testament
NIDNTT	C. Brown (ed.), *The New International Dictionary of New Testament Theology*, 3 vols., Grand Rapids: Zondervan, 1975–78
NIGTC	The New International Greek Testament Commentary
NKZ	*Neue kirchliche Zeitschrift*
NLCNT	The New London Commentary on the New Testament
NovT	*Novum Testamentum*
NovTsup	Supplements to *Novum Testamentum*
NRTh	*Nouvelle revue théologique*
NSTh	Nouvelle série théologique
NT	*Neotestamentica*
NTAb	Neutestamentliche Abhandlungen
NTC	New Testament Commentary
NTD	Das Neue Testament Deutsch
NTG	New Testament Guides
NTL	The New Testament Library
NTS	*New Testament Studies*
NTTS	New Testament Tools and Studies
ÖBS	Österreichische biblische Studien
OneChr	*One in Christ*
ÖTKNT	Ökumenischer Taschenbuchkommentar zum Neuen Testament
OTL	The Old Testament Library
PC	Proclamation Commentaries: The New Testament Witnesses for Preaching
Pers	*Perspectives in Religious Studies*
PGC	The Pelican Gospel Commentaries
PhRh	*Philosophy and Rhetoric*
PIBA	*Proceedings of the Irish Biblical Association*

PittTMS	Pittsburgh Theological Monograph Series
PJPTS	Perspective: A Journal of Pittsburgh Theological Seminary
PNTC	The Pelican New Testament Commentaries
PrinTMS	Princeton Theological Monograph Series
PRS	Perspectives in Religious Studies
PST	*The Perkins School of Theology*
QD	Quaestiones disputatae
Refl	*Reflection*
Ref Rev	*Reformed Review*
Ref T Rev	*Reformed Theological Review*
RevBib	*Revue biblique*
RevSciRel	*Revue des sciences religieuses*
RevThom	*Revue thomiste*
RevThPh	*Revue théologique et philosophique*
RivBib	*Rivista biblica*
RNT	Regensburger Neues Testament
RQ	*Restoration Quarterly*
SacDoc	*Sacra doctrina*
SacPag	Sacra pagina
SANT	Studien zum Alten und Neuen Testament
SBEC	Studies in the Bible and Early Christianity
SBFA	Studii biblici franciscani analecta
SBLDS	Society of Biblical Literature Dissertation Series
SBLMS	Society of Biblical Literature Monograph Series
SBLSPS	Society of Biblical Literature Seminar Paper Series
SBT	Studies in Biblical Theology
SBT ss	Studies in Biblical Theology, second series
SC	*The Second Century: A Journal of Early Christian Studies*
SchThu	*Schweizerische theologische Umschau*
SciEs	*Science et esprit*
ScrB	*Scripture Bulletin*
Semeia	*Semeia: An Experimental Journal for Biblical Criticism*
SESJ	Suomen Eksegeettisen Seuran Julkaisuja. Schriften der finnischen exegetischen Gesellschaft
SEv	*Studia evangelica*
SHR	Studies in the History of Religions (Supplements to *Numen*)
SJT	*Scottish Journal of Theology*

SLA	L. E. Keck and J. L. Martyn (eds.), *Studies in Luke–Acts*, Philadelphia: Fortress, 1966
SNT	Studia neotestamentica
SNTA	Studiorum Novi Testamenti auxilia
SNTSMS	Society for New Testament Studies Monograph Series
SNTU	Studien zum Neuen Testament und seiner Umwelt
SNTW	Studies of the New Testament and its World
SouBib	Sources bibliques
SPBib	Studia post-biblica
STAT	Suomalaisen Tiedeakatemian Toimitaksia. Annales academiae scientiarum fennicae, series B
StBB	Stuttgarter biblische Beiträge
StBibS	Stuttgarter Bibelstudien
SUNT	Studien zur Umwelt des Neuen Testaments
SWJT	*South Western Journal of Theology*
TAB	W. A. Elwell (ed.), *Topical Analysis of the Bible*, Grand Rapids: Baker, 1991
TBC	Torch Bible Commentaries
TDNT	G. Kittel and G. Friedrich (eds.), *Theological Dictionary of the New Testament*, 9 vols., Grand Rapids: Eerdmans, 1964–74
Them	*Themelios*
Theo	*Theology*
ThF	Theologische Forschung. Wissenschaftliche Beiträge zur kirchlich-evangelischen Lehre
ThGl	*Theologie und Glaube*
ThHNT	Theologischer Handkommentar zum Neuen Testament
ThI	Theological Inquiries: Studies in Contemporary Biblical and Theological Problems
ThLZ	*Theologische Literaturzeitung*
ThR	*Theologische Rundschau*
TS	*Theological Studies*
ThVia	*Theologia viatorum*
ThW	Theologie und Wirklichkeit
ThZ	*Theologische Zeitschrift*
TNTC	The Tyndale New Testament Commentaries
TRE	*Theologische Realenzyklopädie*
TU	Texte und Untersuchungen zur Geschichte der altchristlichen Literatur

TynB	*Tyndale Bulletin*
UBS	K. Aland *et al.* (eds.), *The Greek New Testament*, United Bible Societies, 3rd ed., New York: American Bible Society, 1975
UTB	Uni-Taschenbücher
VigChr	*Vigiliae christianae*
VTsup	*Vetus Testamentum supplement*
WBC	Word Biblical Commentary
WC	Westminster Commentaries
WEC	The Wycliffe Exegetical Commentary
WF	Wege der Forschung
WMANT	Wissenschaftliche Monographien zum Alten und Neuen Testament
WSB	Wuppertaler Studienbibel
WTJ	*Westminster Theological Journal*
WUNT	Wissenschaftliche Untersuchungen zum Neuen Testament
WUNT ss	Wissenschaftliche Untersuchungen zum Neuen Testament, second series
WW	*Word & World*
ZBKNT	Zürcher Bibelkommentare. Neues Testament
ZKT	*Zeitschrift für katholische Theologie*
ZNW	*Zeitschrift für die neutestamentliche Wissenschaft und die Kunde der älteren Kirche*
ZThK	*Zeitschrift für Theologie und Kirche*

General abbreviations

Apg.	Apostelgeschichte
Aram.	Aramaic
bib.	bibliography
bs	biblical series
cen.	century
comp.(s.)	compiler(s)
diss.	dissertation
ET	English Translation
Heb.	Hebrew
lit.	literature
LXX	Septuagint
MT	Masoretic Text
ns	new series

NT	New Testament
nts	New Testament series
OT	Old Testament
par.(s.)	parallel(s)
paren.	parenthesis/parenthetical
qual.	qualification
quot.	quotation
rev.(s.)	revision/reviser(s)
ss	second series
TR	Textus Receptus

Introduction

1

CHRISTOLOGY AND LUKE–ACTS

Introduction: the problem of ambiguity

For all of Luke's confessed concern to give his readers certainty about their knowledge of the beginnings of Christianity, it is not, perhaps, as reassuring to the modern reader. Not knowing what Luke's readers already knew, and thus the amount and kind of knowledge Luke was assuming, makes it difficult to understand Luke–Acts as his readers would have understood it.

We perhaps most sorely feel our distance from Luke in the area of christology. Luke–Acts is ultimately a story about Jesus. Luke records in his Acts preface that in the Gospel he has written about "all that Jesus began to do and to teach." This implies that Acts will continue the story. Luke details Jesus' life and career from birth to exaltation, adding in the Gospel a generous portion of dominical sayings not found in Mark and in Acts proclamation material not found in the gospel tradition. The Gospel and Acts are replete with christological titles, portraits, and descriptions. What is more, Luke professes to have given his readers a comprehensive, studied, orderly account of this two-part story to reassure them of what they had already known about Jesus and the Christian faith. But here too, in contrast to Luke's audience, the modern reader may not receive the same degree of confidence from the work itself.

We do not know enough about Luke's christological beliefs. What was his christology? How much of it did he hold in common with his readers? Were there any important christological suppositions on which he based his work but which he did not substantially develop in it, owing, perhaps, to his reasons for writing and to his belief that his readers could properly fill in the gaps?

Few would argue that Luke has given us his christology in full. But the omissions are nonetheless unsettling from our point of view. Luke makes no clear reference to Jesus' preexistence and to the believer's union with Christ, and relatively little reference to the atoning significance of Jesus' death. Was he – or were his readers – simply not aware of these teachings? Did he disagree with them? Or did he merely sense no compelling need, for whatever reason, to feature them in his writings?

The problem of ambiguity deepens in that even some of Luke's recorded christology seems confusing, if not outright contradictory. Eduard Schweizer, e.g., notes that, in contrast to Mark (and Q), in Luke's Gospel the earthly Jesus is already called Lord, but according to Acts 2:36, God does not make him Lord until the resurrection/exaltation.[1] Are we to understand Luke as merely reading *ex eventu* Jesus' Lordship back onto the Gospel account, or is there more to it for him than this? And does Acts 2, for Luke, necessarily underscore a thoroughgoing subordination of Jesus to God, or is there a better way of understanding the event within Luke–Acts? Schweizer also points out that Luke seems to present Jesus as God's Son on the basis of his birth (Luke 1:35), reception of the Spirit (Luke 3:22), Adamic descent (Luke 3:23–38), and resurrection (Acts 13:33) (p. 702). But can all of these be true? What does sonship connote for Luke? Preexistence? Adoption? Or perhaps something else altogether? Schweizer concludes that "theoretisch bleibt die Christologie unklar" ("Theoretically the christology of Luke–Acts remains unclear") (p. 702).

On the other hand, even a cursory reading of Luke–Acts leaves little doubt that theological motives had decisively influenced what Luke wrote and how he arranged the material. His unique development of the Nazareth story, travel narrative, and resurrection and ascension accounts as well as the speeches in Acts especially calls attention to this point. But opinions differ broadly on exactly how we should understand the wealth of christological material embedded in Luke's depiction of the birth of Christianity.

Stephen G. Wilson, whose comments are fairly representative in this regard, argues that:

"Luke characteristically uses diverse, and often ancient, christological materials *without integrating them into any overall scheme*."[2]

---

[1]   Schweizer, "Jesus Christus," *TRE* 16, p. 702.
[2]   Wilson, *Pastoral Epistles*, p. 69 (my italic); also, e.g., Lampe, "Lucan Portrait of

This leads to *a certain lack of uniformity, a disjunction between different strands of material which stand side by side.* Thus there is a tension between the sequence of events in Acts 1 and the statements in Luke 24.1f.; Acts 2.32–3; 5.30–1. *The use of christological titles is somewhat haphazard.* They represent the terminology of Luke's day but, in many cases, the belief of the early Church as well. Some may have had an archaic ring and were for that reason deemed appropriate to the sermons of the early Church. (p. 79, my italic)

Luke, it appears, was a *somewhat indiscriminating collector of christological traditions* who transmits a variety of traditional terms and concepts *without reflecting upon them individually or in conjunction with each other.* (p. 80, my italic)

The issue before us is whether Wilson's view best explains the evidence or whether there is a *unity* or *coherence* to Luke's christology. Our objective here is not to defend any one of Luke's christological descriptions as his main christological concern, for these may vary and change as his writing progresses. Rather it is to discern through four studies some of Luke's personal christological convictions and why he writes what he does about Christ in Luke–Acts. The net result of these studies is that they will enable us to detect Luke's writing concern, which explains the character and purpose of his recorded christology in his two-volume work according to an intended unified overall scheme.

In this chapter I shall begin by surveying briefly the proposals put forth by Lukan scholars in defense of a "controlling" christology of Luke–Acts. I shall then explain in more detail the need for this study and my method for accomplishing it.

Christ," p. 160; Robinson, "Primitive Christology," pp. 177–89; Reicke, "Risen Lord," p. 162; Wikenhauser, "Christusbild," p. 129; Creed, *Luke*, p. 73; Moule, "Christology of Acts," pp. 181–82; Kränkl, *Jesus der Knecht Gottes*, p. 212; MacRae, "Christology," p. 154; Schneider, "Christologie der Apg.," p. 332; Ernst, "Christusbild," pp. 210–11; Marshall, *Historian & Theologian*, p. 157, n. 1; Conzelmann, *Acts*, p. xlvi; Schweizer, "Jesus Christus," *TRE* 16, p. 702; Schweizer, *Challenge*, pp. 1, 47.

Proposed controlling christologies of Luke–Acts

Prior to 1950, biblical scholars by and large saw Luke–Acts as a *historical* treatise – although its reliability as a historical document was often questioned – which Luke wrote either to defend Christianity before his Roman counterparts or to defend Paul before his antagonists.[3] In describing Luke's christology, many believed that it was primitive and traditional, especially as detailed in the speeches of Acts, with Luke faithfully transmitting it to his readers, at least as he understood it.[4]

But by the early 1950s, the scholarly contributions of Philipp Vielhauer, Hans Conzelmann, and Ernst Haenchen enlarged upon the work of Martin Dibelius to spearhead the now familiar tendency to perceive Luke–Acts as primarily a *theological* treatise. Since this time much effort has gone into the study of Luke's christology.[5] In view of this theological development, we shall take the Conzelmann era as our starting point.

Our purpose here is not to discuss everything in Luke–Acts that has to do with christology, or to mention everything that commentators have said about it. Rather we shall survey the christologies which scholars contend represent Luke's *controlling* christology – i.e., a christological portrait or description which centrally affects or controls what he says christologically throughout Luke–Acts. The other christological descriptions and portraits should be understood in light of it.

By classifying the material in this way I do not mean to suggest that the differing positions are necessarily mutually exclusive, but only to point out what some believe lies at the *center* of Luke's recorded christology. To avoid redundancy, at this juncture we shall merely summarize the positions; at more relevant points in the work we shall respond to the more important of these in considerable detail.

---

[3]   See, e.g., the survey of Gasque, *Interpretation*. For more lit. on "the trustworthiness of Acts" prior to 1950, see Mattill and Mattill, *Classified Bibliography*, pp. 189–93.

[4]   See, e.g., Knox, *Acts*, pp. 72–80; Martin, *Portrait of Jesus*; Stonehouse, *Witness*; Laymon, *Portrait of Christ*; see also German and French lit. cited in Bovon, *Luke the Theologian*, pp. 122–23.

[5]   See, e.g., lit. cited in Fitzmyer, *Luke I–IX*, pp. 263–65; Rese, "Lukas," p. 2322; Bovon, *Luke the Theologian*, pp. 109–19; Schweizer, "Jesus Christus," *TRE* 16, pp. 704–705; Hultgren, *NT Christology*, pp. 253–66; Radl, *Lukas*, pp. 81–83; van Segbroeck, *Luke*, pp. 222–24.

Christologies emphasizing Jesus' humanity and exemplary functions

This relatively minor position contends that Luke concentrates on the "man" Jesus for mainly apologetic and exemplary reasons.[6]

Anti-gnostic christology

Charles H. Talbert argues for an anti-gnostic polemic as the central focus of Luke's christology and purpose in writing.[7] Talbert believes that "Luke was faced by someone who wanted to separate spirit and flesh in Jesus Christ by means of an interpretation of his baptism as the moment of the descent of a spiritual reality upon Jesus and the ascension as the moment of the spiritual reality's ascent prior to any suffering of death" (pp. 269–70).

The way Luke emphasizes the corporeality of Jesus' passion–resurrection–ascension and the eyewitness testimony of the disciples who followed him in Galilee – meaning that the Ascended One is to be identified with the one who ministered to them there – indicates, Talbert believes, that Luke was combating some docetic tendency. The continuity which Luke draws between Jesus' passion–resurrection and the ascension on the Mount of Transfiguration (Luke 9:31) and the goal of Jesus' journey to Jerusalem (Luke 9:51) he thinks further endorses this writing interest.

Luke's presentation of Jesus' baptism signals a similar concern. The corporeal character of the Spirit's descent upon Jesus in the form of a dove was meant to contradict the docetic tendency of separating the spirit and flesh in Jesus. Talbert believes that the surrounding context strengthens this idea. Luke, e.g., establishes Jesus' sonship as "the only begotten of God" at birth, reinforces Jesus' humanness as the Second Adam via the genealogy and

---

[6] Adebola, "Christology" thinks that Luke distinctively stresses in his two-volume work Jesus' *manhood* (pp. 78–91) to show how Jesus appears as the man through whom God reveals his final saving plan in redemptive history (pp. 106–25, 165–69).

[7] Talbert, "Anti-Gnostic Tendency," pp. 259–71; Talbert, *Luke and the Gnostics*; followed with qual. by Radl, *Lukas*, p. 91. See also our discussion of Talbert's anti-gnostic purpose on pp. 49–51 below. For another polemical approach to Luke's christology, Martini, "Riflessioni sulla cristologia," pp. 525–34 proposes that Acts 1–10 indicates that Luke was combating a one-sided attitude coming out of Galilee that focused almost exclusively on Jesus as wonder-worker and on an intense apocalyptic expectation of his imminent return, at which time he would miraculously transform the world.

temptation narratives, and in the Nazareth story stresses what Jesus' work as God's servant will entail. Hence, Luke attempts to make clear in his version of the baptism story that (1) the Spirit's descent in bodily form means that the Spirit cannot be divorced from matter at Jesus' baptism; (2) Jesus' baptism is his anointing for service, not his being begotten as God's Son, which happened at birth; and (3) God's declaration of Jesus as his Son at the baptism means primarily that Jesus shares our full humanity.

Thus, for Talbert, Luke focuses on Jesus' baptism and ascension both to fend off a gnostic move to separate spirit and flesh in Jesus and to endorse the church's belief in the full humanity of Jesus.

Exemplar christology

G. W. H. Lampe sets out to discover whether Luke–Acts bears "a distinctive presentation of the person and work of Jesus," i.e., "a peculiarly Lucan portrait of Christ." He finds such a portrait in Luke's emphasis on *the imitation of Christ* – although he leaves it largely undeveloped.[8]

Lampe qualifies his discussion by observing that unlike Paul, Luke does not think in terms of a mystical or personal union of the exalted Jesus with his followers. No "body of Christ" concept is evident. But the concepts of the Holy Spirit and the name of Jesus establish a close bond between Jesus and his church. Luke's main christological interest is explicating this bond: "The experience of Jesus, his mighty works, wonders and signs, his sufferings and his mission of salvation, repentance and remission of sins to the end of the earth are exactly reproduced in his people, first in the Church's mission to Israel under Peter's leadership, then in the wider sphere of Paul's carrying of the gospel to Rome" (p. 175).

In developing this relation between Christ and his followers, Luke wrote his Gospel, according to Lampe, to illustrate through Jesus' life and teaching the sort of things that his followers could imitate. Luke pays considerable attention in his Gospel to Jesus' choice of his successors, their training and preparation, and to the contrast of Jesus and his followers to unbelieving Israel. As Acts then demonstrates, after Jesus' ascension, the church is to *follow* and *imitate* him in his life.

---

[8]   Lampe, "Lucan Portrait of Christ," pp. 160–75, esp. pp. 167, 172–75; also Voss, *Christologie*, p. 171 (with qual.); Edmonds, "Luke's Portrait of Christ," pp. 7–14; O'Toole, "Parallels," pp. 195–212; O'Toole, *Unity*.

Christologies emphasizing Jesus' subordinate relation to God

A more dominant christological position, which many scholars now take as axiomatic in Lukan studies, holds that Luke deliberately subordinates Jesus to God's plan of saving history, largely in hopes of injecting new life into a church shaken by the parousia's delay. Not all scholars who see a subordination christology in Luke accept the latter premise. But defense of this premise has moved this position into the limelight as Luke's chief christological concern.

Subordination christology

Scholars broadly support, to differing degrees and for various reasons, the idea that Luke consciously and uniformly stresses Jesus' subordination to God. The standard passage is Acts 2:36.

Herbert Braun, in a brief but influential essay,[9] argues that Luke further signals this stance with his unique preference for the term ἀνίστημι when describing God's act of raising Jesus from the dead (cf. Acts 2:24, 32; 13:33–34; 17:31). "Im gezielten Gebrauch der Verben," he contends, "liegt die subordinatianisch gefüllte Explikation der ἀνάστασις" ("Luke's deliberate use of the verb brings out the subordinationist idea implicit in ἀνάστασις") (p. 533).[10]

In more encompassing terms Hans Conzelmann, whose statement now represents a major school of thought in Lukan studies in this regard, believes that Jesus' thoroughgoing subordination to God is traditional and is entwined part and parcel with Luke's primary christological concern.[11] Luke's view of salvation history not only presupposes it but demands it. The divine plan of salvation belongs exclusively to God; Jesus appears only as God's instrument within it. On the basis of God's intervention in redemptive history through Christ, Luke assures the church in view of the parousia's delay that God is still at work carrying out his program of salvation history. The theological cornerstone of Luke–Acts is God, not Jesus. For this reason, whether in relation to God, the Spirit,

---

9 Braun, "Terminologie," pp. 533–36; taken up in more detail by Wilckens, *Missionsreden*, pp. 137–40; followed by, e.g., Conzelmann, *Theology of St. Luke*, p. 175; Kränkl, *Jesus der Knecht Gottes*, pp. 130, 162–63. See the fourth section of chapter 8 for more lit. supporting the subordination and adoption positions and our critique of them.

10 But see Marshall, "Resurrection in Acts," pp. 101–103.

11 Conzelmann, *Theology of St. Luke*, pp. 173–79, 184.

angels, the cosmos, or world history, God consistently appears in Luke–Acts as superior to Jesus.

Christology adapted to the parousia's delay

Hans Conzelmann popularized this position with the publication of his dissertation under the title *Die Mitte der Zeit* (1953; ET: *The Theology of St. Luke*).[12] Building on the radical critical methods of Dibelius and Bultmann, he sees the controlling factor lying behind Luke–Acts as the problem of the parousia's delay. Luke attempts to reassess positively the proper place of the post-apostolic church in God's plan of saving history since it does not look as if Jesus will be returning anytime soon. For this reason, he intentionally shifts Jesus' parousia to a distant point in the future and gives the existence and function of the church new meaning for the present.

According to Conzelmann, Luke's theological emphasis is God's saving plan in history. Therefore, Luke's christology must be seen "primarily from the standpoint of the sequence of redemptive history, as are all the central themes in Luke's thought" (p. 184). Luke portrays Jesus as *an instrument of God*, both in his earthly life and in the memory of him after his removal from the earth: His death is understood as martyrdom, his resurrection as symbolic of the believer's hope, and his life as symbolic of God's program of universal mission. But because of the parousia's delay, his imminent role as coming Judge is moved to the distant future and his earthly ministry is now perceived as irretrievably time-locked in past history. His continuing activity for the church comes via the Spirit and his position as Lord in heaven.

Conzelmann additionally asserts that Luke never considers Jesus as Lord of the universe or as God's equal; instead, Luke consistently classifies Jesus as *subordinate to God*, making no distinction between the status of the earthly and the exalted Jesus. In both cases, Jesus remains subordinate to God. He asserts, furthermore, that a titular study would not be particularly beneficial in establishing Luke's christology: It would merely reflect Luke's "preference for traditional terminology" rather than assist in pointing out

---

[12] Followed by, e.g., Schulz, *Stunde der Botschaft*, pp. 284–91; Wilckens, *Missionsreden*; Gräßer, *Problem der Parusieverzögerung*; Schneider, "Christologie der Apg.," pp. 331–35; Schneider, "Lukanische Christologie," pp. 95–98; see also Lohse's contemporaneous contribution in 1954 in "Heilsgeschichte," pp. 145–64, but with some qualification.

any special traits in his reformulation of salvation history for theological reasons (pp. 170–72).

Servant-mediator christology

In his book *Jesus der Knecht Gottes* (1972), Emmeram Kränkl similarly stresses Jesus' mediatorial role, but in terms of a servant christology. Although he defends Jesus' servanthood as Luke's main christological interest, in comparison to other theological themes in Luke–Acts, he readily admits that it plays a secondary part. Luke develops it to buttress his primary soteriological concerns.

Accepting much of Conzelmann's thesis on Luke–Acts, Kränkl attempts to discern Luke's christology through an evaluation of the speeches of Acts. The speeches, he believes, are not pure fiction; Luke fashions them according to some diverse pieces of early church tradition. Nonetheless, the speeches theologically reflect a later orientation to second- and third-generation Christianity, the leading idea being salvation history conditioned by a delayed-parousia consciousness.

The christological center of the speeches is Jesus' ascension/exaltation. The significance of this event, he believes, uniformly stands behind Luke's depiction of Jesus' earthly career and heavenly session. In particular, Luke presents Jesus as subordinate to God. God is exclusively the creator of the plan of salvation; Jesus functions only as its mediator. The "Servant of God" title, which Luke ascribes to Jesus, Kränkl thinks best describes how Luke understands Jesus' mediacy: "So ist in diesem Prädikat die heilsgeschichtliche Stellung, wie sie Lukas auch in seinem gesamten Werk dem irdischen Jesus und dem erhöhten Christus zuweist, kurz und treffend umrissen" ("Luke's salvation-history position is briefly but strikingly depicted in this title; it uniformly expresses the way he perceives in both volumes the earthly Jesus and the exalted Christ") (p. 127, also pp. 210–11). It designates Jesus as culminating the line of OT servants of God, i.e., Moses, David, the prophets, even Israel, but not Isaiah's suffering servant (pp. 125–26). Therefore, the exalted Lord now stands, according to God's plan of salvation history, as the continuum between Israel and the church.[13]

---

[13] Apart from these general observations, Kränkl does not think that Luke's christology reveals a controlling christological concern (*Jesus der Knecht Gottes,*

Christologies emphasizing Jesus' function as Savior

Lukan scholars also propose a number of christologies which directly counter Conzelmann's position. They assert that Jesus' function as Savior plays the leading christological role in Luke–Acts. Jesus as God's instrument or mediator does not spring in Luke–Acts from some refashioned model of salvation history for eschatological reasons. Rather this intercessory role stems from Jesus' own person and work as Savior of the world. As with the biblical portrayal of God as Savior in both testaments, Jesus appears in Luke–Acts as embodying the same salvific status and authority. Hence, Jesus' function as Savior does not mandate a subordination to God as Conzelmann and others think.

Savior christology

Conzelmann's unwillingness to consider the significance of Luke's overall allegiance to traditional material – as especially seen in the Gospel – leaves his evaluation of Luke's christology somewhat suspect. This critical flaw has caused many scholars to question, to varying degrees, the legitimacy of deriving Luke's christology from the strictures of Conzelmann's salvation-history model. Luke's main christological concern, many feel, is not so much salvation history as it is the fact of salvation in Jesus.[14] I. Howard Marshall writes, e.g., that Luke's intention "was not so much to express the faith in terms of what has been called 'salvation-history' as rather to bear witness to the salvation revealed in Jesus Christ and proclaimed by the early church."[15]

Luke certainly wrote within the framework of salvation history

p. 212). It appears, however, that Kränkl tacitly – if not expressly – suggests otherwise. Whereas he devotes only a short excursus to παῖς θεοῦ (pp. 125–29), he discusses at some length Jesus' exaltation (pp. 149–86) and seems inclined to view it, at least as the speeches of Acts present it, as the unifying element within Luke's christology.

[14] See, e.g., van Unnik, "Sauver," pp. 32–34; van Unnik, "Confirmation," pp. 26–59, esp. pp. 49–55, 59; Schnackenburg, "Christologie," pp. 299–301, 307; Fitzmyer, *Luke I–IX*, p. 192; Marshall, *Historian & Theologian*; Marshall, "Gospel," pp. 289–308; Martin, "Salvation and Discipleship," pp. 366–80; Wilcock, *Message of Luke*, p. 17; Giles, "Salvation (1–2)," pp. 10–16, 45–49; Schweizer, "Jesus Christus," *TRE* 16, pp. 703–704; Schweizer "Lukanischen Christologie," pp. 43–65; also Dömer, *Heil Gottes*; Dupont, *Salvation of the Gentiles*.

[15] Marshall, *Historian & Theologian*, p. 19, also pp. 85–86, 93, 102, 116–17, 125, 176–78.

common to the rest of the NT. But it is questionable whether a delayed-parousia consciousness influenced to any great extent, if at all, his particular presentation of it. His primary intent was with christology and soteriology, not with salvation history. This position maintains that Jesus as Savior plays the preeminent role in Luke–Acts and is not to be relegated to a minor part, subsumed under some special leading interest in salvation history as Conzelmann would understand it. Luke–Acts provides no textual basis for distinguishing between the periods of Jesus (Luke) and the church (Acts). In both books Jesus appears as "the bringer of salvation."[16]

Redeemer christology

Arland J. Hultgren critiques Conzelmann's view of the Lukan Jesus by what he calls a redemptive christology.[17] Luke–Acts, he argues, does not represent two self-contained epochs. In Acts the exalted Jesus, through the Spirit, continues to perform his saving work on earth and in the Gospel the whole course of Jesus' earthly career has a transcendent character. Luke himself appears to rule out the subordination theme as Conzelmann defines it. The central element here is the way Luke structures his christology along the OT lines of promise and fulfillment, and redemptive history. The centerpiece of Luke's christology, Hultgren asserts, is Jesus' confirmation of God's redemptive plan in his own person and work.

The slim attestation to the cross as saving in Luke–Acts leads Hultgren to conjecture that Luke has distinctively reinterpreted for his readers the redemptive significance of the cross. The cross no longer appears as the *decisive* atoning act through which God reconciles the world to himself. Rather, it now forms one necessary step in a series of events – i.e., Jesus' suffering, death, resurrection, and ascension – leading to Jesus' glorification and to the fulfillment of scripture. The goal of Jesus' life is not the cross but his glorification, i.e., his heavenly reign.

According to Hultgren, the saving benefits of Christ's redemptive work in Luke–Acts essentially consist in the risen Lord's authority

[16] See esp. Schnackenburg, "Christologie," p. 300; Martin, "Salvation and Discipleship," pp. 367–72; Giles, "Salvation (1–2)," p. 47; here Lohse, "Heilsgeschichte," pp. 159–64 also departs from Conzelmann.

[17] Hultgren, *Christ and His Benefits*, pp. 81–89; his statement, however, is more a characterization of Luke's soteriology than a discussion of Luke's christology *per se*.

to forgive sins and to grant his followers the authority to proclaim in his name this reality to others. The gospel message thus confirms God's redemptive plan in Jesus, becomes a divine pledge of the church's future redemption, and affirms Luke's readership as the recipients of the promises God made to Israel.

Suffering servant christology

In contrast to Kränkl, Joel B. Green holds that Luke emphasizes Jesus' mediatorial role in terms of Isaiah's Servant of Yahweh and the soteriological theme of reversal.[18] Although Green is not always clear as to whether his discussion applies mostly to Luke's treatment of Jesus' death or also fittingly describes Luke's christology generally, the latter seems intended. Luke's interest in Isaiah's portrait of the suffering servant appears to interpenetrate implicitly Luke's larger writing interests. Green even seems inclined to think that it may comprise, or at least strongly influence, the substructure of Luke's entire two-volume work. Luke's suffering servant christology, Green believes, embraces the whole of Jesus' ministry, but pertains especially to his death and exaltation. The principal supporting passage here is Isa. 53:11. The humiliation and vindication of the servant envisages for Luke the central meaning of Jesus' servanthood. In Luke–Acts, the servant idea holds in similar tension the importance of Jesus' crucifixion and exaltation.

Luke depicts Jesus in this way, Green contends, to show how Jesus as Isaiah's servant embodies the idea of "reversal" or "transposition" in his effort to clarify the nature of salvation and discipleship. Luke repeatedly illustrates this reversal of position through Jesus' teaching and work, but most prominently in the events of his death and exaltation. As the humble Servant of Yahweh, Jesus accomplishes God's plan by obediently giving up his life on the cross, after which he is exalted, makes available salvation to all people, and so provides the model of true discipleship for his followers. Acts then bears out these realities in the church's life and mission.

---

[18] Green, "God's Servant," pp. 18–28; also Green, "Jesus on the Mount of Olives," pp. 41–43. Franklin, *Christ the Lord*, p. 63 also believes that Luke works with a comprehensive Isaianic servant christology, although it is not Luke's primary christological interest. See also our discussion of Franklin's position on pp. 47–49.

Christology of the cross

In a vein somewhat related to Hultgren and Green, Frieder Schütz connects Luke's main christological concern to Jesus' passion suffering, but for substantially different reasons.[19] He believes that the attention Luke gives to passages on suffering in both books indicates that his own church was undergoing severe opposition and persecution, mainly at the hands of the Jews.[20] To a church then baffled and dismayed as to why this was happening, Luke wrote to show them how God was using their present situation to carry out his saving plan.

Luke attempts to accomplish this by showing how Jesus' suffering is analogous to, and thus relevant for, Luke's community: "Lukas sieht," Schütz argues, "das Leiden der Gemeinde in gewisser Analogie zur heilsgeschichtlichen Bedeutung des Leidens ihres erhöhten Herrn" ("Luke sees the community's suffering as clearly analogous to the salvation-historical significance of its suffering exalted Lord") (p. 105). Jesus' suffering was part of God's plan. Luke makes this plain to his readers by depicting a christology of the cross. It details the severity of Jesus' death and culminates the suffering he had experienced throughout his ministry. The cross forms an important stage leading to his exaltation. It defines, in part, what it means for Jesus to be "Savior." For Luke's church, their suffering both confirms their allegiance to Jesus and appears as a primary means by which God spreads the gospel to all nations.

Christologies emphasizing Jesus' authoritative status

Scholars also defend christologies centering on Jesus' authoritative status, a status otherwise belonging only to God, as Luke's controlling christology. Here the accent is upon Jesus' Lordship.

Christology of beneficence (hero christology)

Frederick W. Danker believes that Luke intentionally presented Jesus as a "superstar," "hero," or "benefactor," on the basis of

---

[19] Schütz, *Leidende Christus.* For a parallel to Schütz's discussion on Christ's suffering according to Peter's speeches in Acts and 1 Peter (pp. 97–102), see Smalley, "Christology of Acts Again," pp. 88–91.

[20] But Schütz, *Leidende Christus,* pp. 126–38 is careful to point out that Luke–Acts should not be understood as anti-Jewish polemic, but as an appeal calling Jews to repentance.

Greco-Roman models of deities or people of extraordinary endow-
ment or class and exceptional in merit, in an attempt to bridge the
Jewish and Gentile religious-cultural experience. Danker writes:
"In search of a model that would aid him in his projection of the
significance of Jesus outside a purely Jewish frame of reference,
Luke opted for the Greco-Roman ideal of superior excellence."[21]

For this reason Danker believes that Luke describes Jesus in
terms of benefaction common to Greco-Roman parlance. Some
such examples in Luke–Acts include depictions of Jesus as "fine
and good; savior; instrument of divine purpose; liberator; healer;
helpful; displaying good will; pious and upright; sparing no
personal expense; effective in word and deed; worthy of imitation;
enduring hazard for the sake of others; friend of humanity;
immortal; and conferrer of benefits." Luke then focuses on events,
sayings, and deeds from Jesus' life and heavenly reign which further
enhance this depiction. But Luke also carefully distinguishes
between Jesus and God. They are mutually related but not identical
in person or status; God is the Parent and Jesus is the Son. So as
not to confuse this relation, Danker describes Jesus as "the Great
Benefactor" and God as "the Supreme Benefactor." By such a
description, Danker also intends to distinguish Jesus as superior to
all other benefactors.

Prophet-like Moses christology

From an OT orientation, David Moessner formalizes a christological trend in Lukan studies which sees a typological parallel
between Jesus and the Deuteronomic view of Moses as presented in
Luke's travel narrative.[22] He believes that such a parallel stands at
the heart of the christology of the central section of Luke's Gospel
(9:51–19:44) and, although he never says this outright, he implies
that it stands at the heart of the christology of Luke–Acts as well.
In a series of questions at the outset of his lengthy discussion of the
central section (chs. 3–4), Moessner writes:

---

[21] Danker, *Jesus and the New Age*, pp. 2–10 (quot. p. 3); also Danker, "Imaged
     through Beneficence," pp. 57–67, 184–86; Danker, *Benefactor*; Danker, "Graeco-
     Roman Cultural Accommodation," pp. 391–414; Danker, *Luke*, pp. 28–46,
     60–81, 100–106; followed by Krodel, *Acts* (PC), pp. 3–5; see similarly Talbert,
     "Concept of Immortals," p. 435.
[22] Moessner, *Lord of the Banquet*; also Minear, *To Heal and To Reveal*, pp. 102–21;
     Feiler, "Jesus the Prophet"; Johnson, *Writings*, pp. 207–23; and earlier lit. cited
     in Moessner, p. 336, n. 131.

Suppose we succeed in showing that Luke has the Mosaic figure in mind. To what extent does this profile function to motivate and integrate the material within the Central Section itself as opposed to competing figures and plots? Further, how central to the larger story of Jesus and his witnesses in both volumes is the Mosaic prophet of Deuteronomy? In short, for both the shorter and the larger literary units of Luke, *is the Mosaic prophet at the heart of Luke's overall portrait of Jesus*, or is it only one of several equally or more significant figures?[23]

In ch. 5, he answers the second question in the strong affirmative, which also implies a similar response for the first part of the final question.

Luke, he argues, specifically designs Luke 9:1–19:44 to present Jesus as the prophet-like Moses (cf. Deut. 18:15–19), who leads Israel on "a New Exodus" journey to the promised salvation. Luke maps this journey out according to the Deuteronomistic view of Israel's history, i.e., (1) a rebellious people, (2) to whom God sends a prophet, (3) whom they reject, and (4) are punished by God because of their unbelief. The central section of the Gospel (9:51–19:44) depicts Jesus on his journey as the prophet whom Israel, the λαός of God, rejects.

Furthermore, according to Moessner, the transfiguration catena (Luke 9:1–50) previews the approaching journey and connects with Jesus a fourfold Moses–Deuteronomy typology. First, the prophet is called on the mountain to mediate the voice of God. Second, the reluctance and fear of the disciples (who represent Israel in Luke's transfiguration story) to listen to God's voice on the mountain foreshadows the rebellious nature of *all* Israel on the plain below. Third, the mountain experience confirms that the prophet must suffer and die. And fourth, the prophets' mediatorial work ultimately effects Israel's deliverance according to the promised salvation.

At the core of Luke's christology, Moessner believes, is the twofold Deuteronomic depiction of stubborn Israel, a people always resisting God, and of the mediating suffering and death of his chosen prophet, who accordingly redeems Israel from their sin. Therefore, as Deuteronomy depicts "Moses' death outside the land as a necessary punishment for the sin of all Israel" (p. 60), so too

[23] Moessner, *Lord of the Banquet*, p. 82 (my italic).

Luke depicts Jesus offering himself as "an atoning death on behalf of an intractably sinful nation, who stubbornly refuse to accept Jesus' preaching of the good news of the kingdom of God" (p. 323). Luke, moreover, uses many of the same Deuteronomic parallels between the prophet-like Moses and Jesus to describe the witnesses to Jesus in Acts, especially Stephen and Paul.

Messianic christology

According to E. Earle Ellis, "the main theme of the Gospel is the nature of Jesus' messiahship and mission."[24] Luke, however, does not develop this christological portrait to defend Jesus' messiahship but to show the nature of it. Luke accomplishes this by defining messiahship in terms of mission. Ellis believes that Luke structures his Gospel according to a series of episodes which make this christological theme apparent. Ellis groups the stories under the following headings: the messiahship and mission of Jesus (1:5–9:50), the teaching of the messiah (9:51–19:44), and the consummation of the messiah's mission (19:45–48).

Jesus appears in Luke–Acts as the instrument through which God brings salvation to Israel (via prophet-like Moses, Isaiah's suffering servant and new temple christologies) and to the whole world (via an Adam christology). His life, death, and glorification, moreover, become the "prototype" for Christians. For Luke, Jesus' mission as messiah, therefore, makes salvation universally available and provides the pattern for Christian living.

Kingship christology

Taking a somewhat similar line, A. R. C. Leaney defends Jesus' kingship as Luke's main literary and christological concern. Luke's main theme, he writes, "was the reign of Christ, how it is established, how it must be maintained."[25] Luke develops two lines of thought in this regard. First, he portrays Jesus as a royal personality and the series of events which led to his enthronement. Second, concerning the effect Jesus' kingship would have on those

---

[24] Ellis, *Luke*, pp. 9–12, 32–36 (quot. p. 10) briefly defends his claim from Acts as well, although he concentrates mainly on the Gospel material; Polhill, *Acts*, pp. 54–55 also argues for a "messianic christology" but restricts his comments to Acts. See also Richard, "Author and Thinker," p. 29.

[25] Leaney, *Luke*, pp. 34–37 (quot. p. 34); he draws equal support from Acts to defend his view.

who follow him, Luke emphasizes Jesus' kingly power to forgive sins, as experienced by his followers and proclaimed by them to others in his name.

The theme of Jesus' kingship, Leaney believes, is equivalent to or absorbs, as the case may be, all of the other christological designations in Luke–Acts. The theological keystone of Luke–Acts is Jesus' glorification. This event, rather than his return as Mark and Matthew have it, clearly depicts the glory that he already possesses as reigning king. His return will only be the final manifestation of that glory. Luke is primarily concerned about the present, a time when the church is to proclaim the gospel of the forgiveness of sins to the world.

Lordship (exaltation) christology

Perhaps the most common belief in regard to Luke's christology sees his writing interests as closely associated with strengthening the belief that Jesus is Lord. Eric Franklin[26] and Darrell L. Bock[27] offer two leading statements in this regard.[28]

Eric Franklin believes that Luke wrote "to strengthen and confirm, and if need be to reawaken, faith in Jesus as the present Lord, and it was to this end that his theological interpretation was directed."[29] Some crisis situation had knocked the readers' faith off balance, causing them to doubt the reliability and centrality of Jesus' Lordship. Luke's use of the title, κύριος, according to Franklin, reveals such a concern. Even in the Gospel, Luke expresses through the title, in narrative comment and direct address, christological beliefs which he shares with his readers. He writes of "past events in Jesus' life in hopes of rekindling a present realistic acknowledgment of that lordship" (p. 196, n. 4). The title,

---

[26] Franklin, "Ascension and Eschatology," pp. 191–200; Franklin, *Christ the Lord.*

[27] Bock, *Proclamation*, pp. 261–79; Bock, "Luke," *DJG*, pp. 503–504.

[28] See also, e.g., Reicke, "Risen Lord," pp. 157–69; O'Toole, *Christological Climax*; O'Toole, "Resurrection–Ascension–Exaltation," pp. 106–14; O'Toole, "Risen Jesus," pp. 471–98; Wilson, *Pastoral Epistles*, pp. 69–89; Donfried, "Understanding," pp. 112–22, esp. p. 114; Recker, "Lordship of Christ," pp. 177–86; Neyrey, *Christ is Community*, pp. 139–41. In the more general sense of a *divine christology*, see, in reference to Jesus' relation to the Spirit, Turner, "Spirit of Christ," pp. 168–90; Turner, "Divine Christology," pp. 413–36; also implicit in Turner, "Jesus and the Spirit," pp. 3–42; and in reference to Jesus' earthly and heavenly role as divine intercessor through prayer, see Crump, *Jesus the Intercessor*; Crump, "Scribal-Intercessor," pp. 51–65.

[29] Franklin, *Christ the Lord*, p. 48, also pp. 53, 56, 60, 66–67, 71–72.

κύριος, therefore, is preeminent among the christological titles of Luke–Acts and in both books is loaded with theological meaning.

Jesus' ascension also plays a key theological role in this regard. Its presence in Luke–Acts graphically reaffirms the reality of Jesus' exalted position in heaven at God's right hand. His earthly ministry forms a prelude to it. For Franklin, Jesus' messiahship, suffering, servanthood, and prophetic work are secondary themes. Their value appears mainly in the way Luke uses them to confirm the reality and nature of Jesus' present Lordship. In connection to soteriology, Luke deliberately downplays the past and emphasizes the present. The cross as a past event forms a prelude to the exaltation, but Luke does not consider it as saving. For Luke, the present reality of Jesus' Lordship is the means of salvation. Jesus as the exalted Lord now continually draws people to himself and makes salvation available to all people.

One other relevant factor here, Franklin maintains, is that Luke–Acts represents a theology of history. Franklin apparently attempts to reconcile a subordination christology, probably that of Conzelmann, with his Lordship christology. Luke wants to show how God's actions in Jesus form the climax of Israel's history. Jesus appears as the last and greatest in Israel through whom God redeems his people. The fact of Jesus' Lordship preserves the typological sense in which Jesus' life and ministry fulfill OT redemptive history. But the strong OT influence upon Luke's theology is also largely responsible for his thoroughgoing subordination of Jesus to the Father. Jesus is God's chosen instrument, none other than God's final redeeming act for Israel, and on account of his present Lordship, for all people.

Darrell Bock explicitly endorses Franklin's claim that Luke's desire to write of Jesus' Lordship is closely attached to his main writing concern.[30] He also affirms Franklin's belief that the OT is the key to understanding Luke's christology, although in contrast to Franklin, Bock claims that the OT conceptual background of Luke's christology is just as possible from the MT as it is from the LXX.[31] Bock, however, significantly departs from Franklin over what he feels Luke thinks the OT suggests concerning Jesus' Lordship and why Jesus' Lordship is important for Luke.

Bock argues that Luke's use of OT citations and allusions

---

[30] Bock, *Proclamation*, p. 380, n. 1.
[31] Rather than strictly from the LXX as Franklin suggests; cf. *Christ the Lord*, pp. 71–75.

indicates the christological train of thought he seeks to present in his two-volume work. The main christological categories here are essentially twofold, the first being subordinate to the second. First, from the outset of the Gospel up to Jesus' last days in Jerusalem, Luke stresses from OT ideas "the foundational declaration of Jesus as a regal Messiah-Servant." Second, from this point onward Luke shifts his focus to OT elements which suggest that Jesus is "a more than Messiah figure" to emphasize "the climactic declaration that Jesus is Lord" – Luke's "supreme christological concept" (p. 265).

According to Luke's use of the OT, Bock believes that Jesus as mediator or as God's instrument implies no subordination: the OT itself presents Jesus as God's incorruptible Son, which means, therefore, that he had to be raised from the dead (so Acts 2:33–36; 13:33) (pp. 185–86, 248–49). For Luke, the Lord Jesus is none other than God's equal. The goal, then, of Luke's christology is to present Jesus' Lordship in its fullest sense; he thinks that Luke has achieved this by Acts 13. From ch. 14 onward, OT christology ceases to appear in Acts. But this does not pose a problem for Bock. By this point in Acts, Luke has thoroughly established a christological foundation upon which the gospel can now be taken to all people. Acts 13 justifies such a mission on the basis of God's saving plan through Jesus the Lord.

Luke's OT christology, Bock maintains, is most adequately summarized as "proclamation from prophecy and pattern," rather than the more apologetic proposal of "proof from prophecy."[32] Luke primarily develops it according to his interest in proclaiming that God now offers salvation to all people, both Jew and Gentile, because Jesus as Savior is Lord of all.

C. F. D. Moule and Helmut Flender also support Jesus' Lordship as Luke's overriding christological concern, but with some notable qualifications and differences.

1. *Absentee and individualistic christology.* In comparing Lukan and Pauline christology, C. F. D. Moule argues that Luke presents in Acts a christology whereby the exalted Jesus is "temporarily absent" – i.e., "withdrawn to heaven" – from his church and the people on earth, and until his return is represented by the Spirit.[33] The frequent mention of the Spirit in both narrative and speech

---

[32] Cf., e.g., Schubert, "Structure and Significance," pp. 165–86.
[33] Moule, "Christology of Acts," pp. 165, 179–80; Moule, *Origin*, pp. 104–105 (with qual.); followed by, e.g., MacRae, "Christology," pp. 157–60 with qual. as well. For other lit. supporting Moule's view, see the first section of chapter 8.

material in Acts, Moule holds, supports this as Luke's prevailing view.

Furthermore, on the basis of the Spirit's role as a representative or substitute for the absent Christ, Moule postulates that the author of Acts also reveals an individualistic christology.[34] "Despite his royal exaltation and his undoubtedly divine status," Luke still views Jesus as "an exalted and divine individual."[35] Unlike Paul, who stresses the inclusive or corporate nature of the believer's union with Christ, Luke shows little or no inclination to present the Spirit as the mode of the exalted Jesus' presence among believers (however, traces of it may be found, Moule admits, in Acts 4:2; 9:4–5; 22:8; 26:15).

Although Moule feels that Acts does not suggest a uniform christology, by virtue of Jesus' absence and the pervasive presence of the Spirit in Acts, these christological perspectives would none-theless strongly influence one's interpretation of the book and indicate the importance of Jesus' Lordship for Luke.[36]

2. *Dialectical christology*. Concentrating largely on editorial differ-ences and building on Robert Morgenthaler's *das Zweiheitsgesetz* ('principle of doubling"), Helmut Flender detects in Luke–Acts a distinctive dialectical christology: "There is an early christological tradition both before and after Paul, which is based on Hellenistic thought and which postulates two modes of existence for Jesus Christ, one earthly, the other heavenly ... The Christology of Luke has to be understood along similar lines."[37]

The heavenly and earthly spheres of Jesus' existence, he argues, stand contemporaneously in climactic parallelism, thus preventing Jesus' earthly life from becoming mythological and simultaneously preserving the divine mystery of Jesus despite the Gospel presenta-tion of his earthly life. In Luke–Acts there is no "static" develop-ment of Jesus' two natures; instead, in line with Bultmann, Flender believes that Luke forces "the eschatological now" of Jesus upon his readers, an existential reality only perceived through "the eyes of faith."

Flender thinks that Luke developed a dialectical christology to show his readers how missionary preaching had penetrated secular

[34] Moule, "Christology of Acts," pp. 180–81; Moule, *Origin*, pp. 66–67.
[35] Moule, "Christology of Acts," p. 180.
[36] See also our discussion of Moule's "absentee christology" in the first section of chapter 8.
[37] Flender, *Redemptive History*, pp. 41–46, 56; followed by Ernst, "Jesusbild," p. 21; Ernst, "Christusbild," p. 110.

society. In addition, he believes, *contra* Conzelmann, that no unfolding pattern of salvation history is recognizable in Luke–Acts. Luke developed his view of redemptive history mainly for Christian self-definition: the church, as the true Israel, experiences God's salvation via the Holy Spirit and the exalted Christ. Jesus is not the center of history in any observable sense; but as Lord he is continually eschatologically (i.e., existentially) present in a timeless, non-observable way, as is God himself.

Son of God christology

Along more dogmatic lines, Gerhard Voss believes that at the heart of Luke's christology is the firm belief in Jesus' divine sonship.[38] No adoption is present. He supposes that Luke underscores Jesus' human sonship to avoid any docetic misunderstanding of Jesus. But alongside this teaching, "es gibt für Lukas," Voss insists, "keine Zeit, da Jesus nicht der Sohn gewesen wäre" ("There was, for Luke, never a time when Jesus was not God's Son").[39]

Via literary criticism, Malcolm Wren also thinks that "the concept of Jesus as son may well be *the* characteristic and *most* important aspect of Luke's writing."[40] Wren demonstrates this through a literary analysis of Luke 1–4. In these chapters Luke consciously creates a tension between the motifs of "continuity and fulfillment" and "discontinuity and novelty." In the birth narratives, e.g., Luke's use of Septuagintal style establishes its continuity with the Jewish past, but the surprising fact that Zechariah does not pass his name on to his son signals the unique role his son will come to play. Moreover, Mary's identification with Hannah's praise to God for lifting up the lowly (1 Sam. 2:7; Luke 1:52–53) links it with the past, but the unexpected manner of Jesus' conception anticipates a special new work of God to be realized in Jesus his Son.

The tension between the anticipated and the unexpected, Wren further argues, is heightened by the idea of unfolding epiphany within the continuous narrative itself. It is fundamental to Luke's understanding of Christ. Wren writes, e.g., that "by the very act of Jesus' conception, God has acted to save his people" (p. 306). Luke develops in the remainder of his work the spreading acknowl-

---

[38]   Voss, *Christologie*, pp. 173–75; Voss, "Herrn und Messias," pp. 237–46.
[39]   Voss, *Christologie*, p. 173.
[40]   Wren, "Sonship," pp. 301–11 (quot. p. 301, his italic).

edgment or rejection of this foundational truth, i.e., that Jesus is the Son of God.

Preexistence christology

The possibility of a preexistence christology in Luke–Acts strongly undergirds the notion of Jesus' divine sonship. In contrast to the subordination position and to the overwhelming consensus in Lukan studies that the author never mentions or even alludes to Jesus' preexistence, Jürgen Roloff leaves open the possibility that elements of a three-stage christology, reminiscent of Phil. 2:6–11 and Heb. 1:3–4, may be suggested in Luke–Acts.[41] The idea of preexistence was perhaps already associated with the title κύριος. Hellenistic Judaism may have already perceived wisdom, according to Prov. 8:22–31 and Sir. 24:33, as preexistent, thus facilitating the transfer of the idea to Jesus, which must have happened at a fairly early stage if the idea is present in Phil. 2:11 as Roloff supposes it is. In particular, Peter's identification of Jesus with Yahweh in Acts 2:21 (Joel 3:5a LXX) may reveal a preexistence christology. But Roloff further points out that if this meaning were implied in the text, it would clearly be anachronistic. Peter would almost certainly have spoken in Aramaic originally; but this interpretation of Joel 3:5 could have come only from the LXX version. Roloff does not press this interpretation as original to Peter. He recognizes that in Acts 2:36, at least, Luke properly represents and retains the older Palestinian two-stage christology.

The need for this study

In this survey we have considered eighteen proposals, variously emphasizing Jesus' manhood, his subordinate relation to God, his function as Savior, and his authoritative status, which scholars think represent, or at least strongly support, Luke's main christological concern. The broad spectrum of these proposals gives us valuable insight into the character and complexity of his recorded christology and into some of his personal christological convictions.

Certainly most of these characterizations represent genuine strands of Luke's christology. But the problem with this kind of

[41] Roloff, *Apg.*, pp. 54–55.

approach, as this survey shows, is that these different *Leitmotive* fail to provide us with a unified account of Luke's entire christological statement as collectively represented in most of these proposals. Furthermore, this approach fails to reconcile the apparent christological tension between the Lukan expressions of Jesus' Lordship and subordinate relation to God and the relation between his past earthly ministry and his present reign as Lord.[42]

Within Lukan studies, the need still exists to detect a Lukan writing concern which adequately explains the complex and diverse character of Luke's christology, one which synthesizes or draws together these various christological strands and tensions under some common rubric as originally intended by the author.

Method of approach

This work will first examine the character and purpose of Luke's christology in conjunction with his purpose in writing to assess, as much as is possible, in what ways his writing motives have determined or influenced what he says christologically. We shall next consider the possible influences of Luke's bed-fellows, Mark and Paul. Inherent in this kind of approach is the idea of synthesis as a method for assessing Luke's wealth of christological material. But before moving on, I should say more about some of these points and how I intend to use them in this study.

Synthesis as methodological prerequisite

Nowhere is the synthetic approach as a way of evaluating and describing Luke's christology clearly developed. Several scholars, however, have briefly mentioned or presupposed it in some relatively recent works, although mostly in reference to NT christology generally. Martin Hengel, e.g., supports a synthetic approach when he stresses that the main objective in describing any NT author's christology must involve "*an overall view* and not isolated consideration of the individual christological ciphers."[43] Although Hengel applies this warning specifically to the use of titular studies in the "isolated" sense, in reference to Luke–Acts, his caution could be broadened to include methods which focus solely on Q material of

---

[42] However, for one good attempt at this, see Bock, *Proclamation*, pp. 185–86, 248–49.

[43] Hengel, "Chronology," p. 38 (my italic).

the Gospel, redactional material unique to the Gospel, the speeches of Acts, or a single portrait of Jesus in either the Gospel or Acts or in the two combined to the exclusion or diminution of other christological portraits and material.[44]

In approaching the historical evidence regarding Jesus, I. Howard Marshall insists on a similar method when he describes the task of the interpreter: It is "to ask what is the correct interpretation of the evidence, the correct interpretation being the one which provides a coherent explanation of *all* the evidence."[45]

According to Joseph Fitzmyer, "it is the theology of the end product that has to be synthesized."[46] He explains that "a synthetic presentation of the theology of a NT writer will always remain a step removed from the writings themselves and will never replace them. A synthesis is produced by a modern interpreter who culls from the writings" (p. 144). This method "in the long run," he believes, "is more important than what can be ferreted out in the twentieth century as the theology of 'Q' or of the teaching of Jesus" (p. 144). In directing his comments toward Luke–Acts, he claims, "what is really needed is a synthetic approach to Lucan theology, not only as it appears in the Lucan redaction of traditional gospel material, but in the thrust of Lucan composition in both the Gospel and Acts" (p. 144).

Incidentally, in discussing Luke's christology, Fitzmyer fails to carry this out (cf. pp. 192–219). After briefly discussing the four phases of Christ's existence according to Luke–Acts – (1) from Jesus' virginal conception to his appearance in the desert to be baptized, (2) from his baptism by John to his ascension, (3) from his ascension to the parousia, and (4) the parousia itself (pp. 192–97) – he simply lists Luke's christological titles side by side and makes no real effort to relate them to each other and only loosely relates them to his four stated phases of Christ's existence (pp. 197–219). Nor does he discuss them in view of Luke's purpose in writing or consider other kinds of Lukan statements which may reflect his christological convictions (e.g., things which Jesus does and says, which are otherwise associated only with deity in scripture).

---

[44] See also, in reference to the study of NT christology generally, Hurtado, "Critique of Bousset's Influence," pp. 306–17; Hurtado, "Retrospect and Prospect," pp. 15–27; Osborne, "Hermeneutics," pp. 49–62; Keck, "Renewal," pp. 362–77.

[45] Marshall, *Historical Jesus*, p. 99 (my italic).

[46] Fitzmyer, *Luke I–IX*, p. 144.

We should also note that Lampe[47] and Talbert[48] take this procedure a step further. They think that Luke also intended his readers to understand his overall christological portrait synthetically. This is important. We must give this suggestion serious consideration. It raises the possibility that synthesis as a method validly operates on two levels: (1) for us as a way to reconcile/ understand Luke's complex christological expression, but also (2) for Luke as a possible literary device by which he intended to instruct his readers christologically.

Although we shall not explicitly focus our attention in this work on the idea of synthesis *per se*, our methodology presupposes it: for to determine most accurately the character and purpose of Luke's christology, we should consider *the whole of Luke–Acts* and attempt to detect whether an overall point of view unites *its christological features*.

Literary purpose as christological control

An important premise which we shall seek to demonstrate in the following chapters is that *Luke's recorded christology conforms to his writing concerns*. It seems that for most NT writers the reason(s) they wrote had significantly influenced what they chose to say about Christ. This tendency leaves open the possibility that each of them could have said considerably more. Regarding Luke–Acts, e.g., Donald Guthrie believes that "the amount of Christological material in Acts is severely limited by the author's purpose."[49] The author would have been able to say much more (e.g., about the sinlessness of Christ, which is part of Luke's christology in Guthrie's view), but in this instance at least, he deliberately chose not to, owing to his reasons for writing. Birger Gerhardsson believes that the same can be said of Luke's presentation of Jesus in his Gospel.[50]

To what extent, then, does this probable christological restraint on Luke's part also account for other aspects of NT christology which he has omitted or sharply curtailed in his writings? In particular, the lack of the typical Pauline phrases on atonement and union with Christ, the Markan ransom concept, and the Johannine

---

[47] Lampe, "Lucan Portrait of Christ," p. 160.
[48] Talbert, "Anti-Gnostic Tendency," p. 260.
[49] Guthrie, *Theology*, p. 231.
[50] Gerhardsson, *Gospel Tradition*, p. 54.

logos concept? Do any of these christological themes form "part of the iceberg that is under the surface and yet is an integral part" of the christology of Luke–Acts?[51]

Conversely, why did Luke emphasize what he did about Jesus and christology? E.g., in contrast to Mark (and Matthew, for the most part), why did he begin his story with Jesus' birth? Why did he give the Nazareth episode programmatic importance in Luke–Acts? Why did he add a sizeable amount of Jesus' teaching? Why did he develop the travel narrative? And why did he refer as he did to the cross, resurrection, ascension, and exaltation? Why, moreover, did he add an *Acts of the Apostles*? Why did he feature Peter, Stephen, Philip, and Paul in it? Why did he refer to Jesus as he did in the preaching of the early church? And why did he end his account with an expanded treatment of Paul's imprisonment and trial scenes?

Modern critics frequently assign Luke an inferior status as theologian. C. F. D. Moule represents such a tendency when he writes, "where Luke's own mentality can be discerned, it is different in certain respects from Paul's or that of the Johannine writings and is nearer, one may guess, to the 'average' Christian mentality than to that of these giants."[52] But is Moule's estimation fair to Luke? Was Luke merely "impersonating various outlooks, reflecting his sources" (p. 182), or was he acting himself as a responsible theologian, developing his christological constructs in such a way as to reinforce his own specific literary motives?

W. Ward Gasque considers the question of the purpose of Acts as perhaps the most important question that has been asked in the history of Acts critical studies.[53] The same could be said of Luke–Acts. The question of literary purpose is of crucial importance to our attempt to detect whether there is a coherence to Luke's christology. It may act as a type of literary control in that it places limits on what we can and cannot say about his explicit christological intentions. It would, e.g., characterize as improbable any proposed unifying christology which represents a few isolated texts but leaves more important and common christological material in the Gospel and Acts unaccounted for.

This work will probe the relation between Luke's christology and his literary purpose, keeping in view the possibility that his

---

[51]   Van Unnik, "Once More St. Luke's Prologue," p. 10.
[52]   Moule, "Christology of Acts," pp. 181–82.
[53]   Gasque, *Interpretation*, p. 50.

originality as a writer may, in fact, correspond to his originality as a theologian.

Two instrumental points of contact: Mark and Paul

Another element of our approach, as we have touched on already, is to compare the character and purpose of Luke's christology with Mark and Paul – NT writers with whom he implicitly professes contact through his use of Mark's Gospel and his alleged contact with Paul in the "we-sections" of Acts. These writers may supply us with "independent criteria" for determining why Luke said what he did christologically.[54]

Concerning Mark, as has often been noted, much can be learned of Luke's writing intentions, style, theology, and so on by observing how he interacts redactionally with Mark's Gospel. Mark's writing was doubtlessly suitable to its recipients. But it remains highly probable that while agreeing with its contents, Luke found it unsuitable in adequately expressing the concerns he wanted to put into writing for his readers. In this sense, Luke wrote to improve Mark. This implies that if certain christological objectives were central to Luke's primary writing concern, his handling of Mark's Gospel may assist us in discerning what they may have been.

Concerning Paul and the compatibility of his letters and Acts, Colin J. Hemer conjectures in his magisterial work *The Book of Acts in the Setting of Hellenistic History* (1989): "While paying due regard to factors like redaction, we are committed to an alternative approach, and experimental methods, with the possibility of a radically different base for the knowledge of Paul. If there is a prospect of fruitful interlocking of Acts and Epistles in the first-century context, this is crucial for determining the place of Paul in Christian origins" (p. 21). Hemer proceeds to make a strong case for the "interlocking of Acts and Paul's letters in the first-century." This also means that Paul's letters may be crucial for determining the place of Luke in Christian origins. This further raises the possibility that Paul's writings may contain "a roughly contemporaneous" christological parallel for understanding Luke. We shall not simply presuppose, however, that this is the case; we shall try to form our opinion on the basis of what the evidence most reasonably suggests for our study.

---

[54] See Hemer, *Hellenistic History*, pp. 27–28.

My intention here is not to prejudge Luke–Acts in light of Mark or Paul.[55] Rather, in reference to Mark, we shall attempt to assess whether Luke's interaction with the Second Gospel sheds light on his own writing concerns and christology. In reference to Paul, we shall examine whether any of his writings reveal a writing concern which appropriately parallels Luke's and the character and purpose of his christology.

Conclusion: the way forward

What I hope to achieve in the following pages is to push open a few doors in the study of Luke–Acts and NT christology which "critical orthodoxy" has often considered closed. I aim to do this by detecting *a most probable scenario* from the Lukan material which makes good sense of Luke's reason for writing, his literary affinities with the synoptic tradition and Paul, and the part his christology plays in this. More specifically, I should like to determine in what way christology is central to Luke's purpose and in what way his purpose in all probability governs what he has chosen to say christologically. We shall approach this study from four angles.

We shall begin our study in chs. 2–3 by examining what scholars have put forward as Luke's main reason for writing and by proposing a hypothesis regarding Luke's writing concern, which draws into focus his diverse christological material under a unifying overall theme. The remainder of the work will directly or indirectly expand on this discussion of Luke's christology and the purpose of Luke–Acts. In chs. 4–7, we shall look at three themes which illustrate something of Luke's purpose and christological intentions through his redactional handling of Mark's Gospel. In chs. 8–10, we shall see from his writings that the belief in the supreme Lordship of Jesus is Luke's pronounced personal conviction (and one shared with his readers) and contributes significantly to his writing interests. In ch. 11, we shall explore how Luke's emphasis upon Jesus' humiliation–exaltation coincides with his belief in Jesus' Lordship in light of a fitting Pauline parallel and how it parallels his writing intentions. In ch. 12, we shall close by briefly stating the significance of this study for Luke–Acts and NT christology.

---

[55] For further criticism of this tendency, see esp. Tiede, *Prophecy and History*, pp. 12–13; also Wilckens, "Interpreting," p. 77; Marshall, *Historian & Theologian*, pp. 88–94; Fitzmyer, *Luke I–IX*, pp. 28–29, 143.

In anticipating some of our concluding remarks, we have set for ourselves in the final chapter a way of cross-checking the validity of our christological conclusions against our study of the broader context of Luke–Acts itself. It may be helpful to mention these four criteria at the outset of the work in that they show the direction our study will take – they roughly constitute its four parts.

For a christology to represent adequately a unifying overall christological point of view in Luke–Acts, it should (1) coincide with Luke's purpose in writing, (2) plausibly explain his redactional motives and the unique literary features of Luke–Acts, (3) resolve the stated ostensible christological tension between the Lukan expressions of Jesus' Lordship and subordination, and, above all, (4) explain the character and purpose of his diverse christologies.

PART 1

Luke's christology and the purpose of Luke–Acts

2

AN EVALUATION OF LUKE'S PURPOSE

Introduction

As observed in the previous chapter, an NT author's writing aim probably determines to a great extent what he chooses to emphasize doctrinally. Luke is no exception. He most likely does not tell us everything he knows about Christ. He is selective with what he writes, drawing together various christological traditions best aligning with his reasons for writing. To examine Luke's christology apart from literary purpose hence runs the risk of forming theological conclusions about the two-volume work not intended by the author himself.

Therefore, in this and the next chapter we shall try to gain some understanding of why he wrote. In this chapter we shall discuss some criteria for analyzing purpose and use them to evaluate the principal theories proposed by Lukan scholars. In the next chapter, I shall introduce another hypothesis, paying considerable attention to the importance that christology holds for it.

Some criteria for analyzing purpose

Even though Luke explicitly introduces his purpose in Luke 1:4, the uncertainty surrounding the meaning of the verb κατηχέω partially obscures his writing intentions and exemplifies the kinds of difficulty the modern reader faces in trying to determine why Luke wrote. Cadbury exclaims: "How much he does not tell us that we should like to know!"[1] Although he says this mainly in reference to the kind of material Luke chose not to include – material on the first thirty years of Jesus' life, the later years of Peter's life, the outcome of Paul's trial and his death – it applies just as well to the

---

[1] Cadbury, *Making*, p. 320.

circumstances which induced him to write. Many questions remain
unanswered. Did Luke write to an individual or did he have a
larger audience in mind? Were Luke's recipients largely Jewish or
Gentile, believing or unbelieving, known or unknown to him? Did
he write at the close of the apostolic period, in the sub-apostolic
period, or well into the second century? Why did he write – to
record history, resolve church tensions, gain legal status for the
church, evangelize, or possibly some combination of these?

Because of this lack of information, before examining Luke's
purpose we should first establish some ground rules which may
help to delimit what the interpreter can reasonably say about it.[2]
Most of these criteria are deducible from common sense, but for
various reasons are sometimes ignored or not closely adhered to.

Readers

Any proposal for identifying Luke's purpose should bear in mind
that, whatever his literary aim and techniques, they had to be
comprehensible to his readers – even if Luke's intended audience
were not personally known to him.[3] Luke's intended audience
probably included a wide range of people: from the wealthy to the
poor, the learned to the unlearned, the Jew to the Gentile, the God-
fearer to the God-less, the Greek to the Roman, the free to the
enslaved, and perhaps from the believer to the unbeliever. Surely he
would have used writing techniques effective to them. This means
that we should exercise caution in superimposing modern thought
forms upon Luke–Acts. The rule of thumb here is that whatever we
think about Luke's method and purpose, we should have good
textual evidence to support our conclusions and that these conclusions could have been as apparent to first-century readers.[4]

---

2   Interest in laying down some ground rules is not new to Lukan studies.
     Schneider, "Zweck," p. 47; Marshall, "Gospel," pp. 290–91 list four points for
     consideration. Maddox, *Purpose*, pp. 19–20; Gasque, "Fruitful Field," pp. 119–
     29 evaluate Luke's purpose according to Schneider's four points. But cf. the
     skepticism of Dahl, "Purpose," pp. 97–98 and Talbert, "Shifting Sands,"
     pp. 381–95 toward current methods and assumptions in doing this.
3   E.g., Allison, "Lukan Community," pp. 63, 67 argues that Luke–Acts was not
     intended for any one group, but for Christians everywhere, or for unbelievers as
     an evangelistic appeal; so Lentz, *Portrait of Paul*, pp. 171–72.
4   E.g., Flender, *Redemptive History*, p. 8 proposes a thoroughgoing dialecticism
     for Luke–Acts on the basis of (although different from) R. Morgenthaler's idea
     of *das Zweiheitsgesetz* (cf. Morgenthaler, *Lukanische Geschichtsschreibung als
     Zeugnis*, pp. 13–15). According to Flender, Luke expresses this dialecticism in
     three ways: complementary parallelism (pp. 9–20), climactic parallelism

Concrete occasion

Proposals should also consider the kind of circumstances which may have prompted Luke to write. Was he altering a pronounced bias at a critical time in the church's life or was he writing in a normal everyday situation? Was he responding to some specific occasion within the church or were his interests more general and personal – e.g., to trace out the historical and theological beginnings of the church? Some Lukan scholars doubt whether we can adequately answer these questions for lack of evidence. The information is too sparse to verify the scope of Luke's motives.[5] This qualification is valid. We must be willing to admit that our conclusions are approximate at best. Our task is to identify a possible situation within Luke's church which would "call for the sort of book Luke wrote."[6]

Furthermore, although it is permissible to speak in terms of a primary or overall writing concern perhaps generated by some specific situation affecting the readers, Luke probably also took the writing occasion to respond to any number of other needs or issues as well.[7] These may variously appear in Luke–Acts as "secondary" or "sub-themes," closely related to his primary writing concern or somewhat unrelated to it.

Author's stated aim

In prefacing this point, when speaking of the author's stated aim, we mean "the conscious aim of the author," which leaves open the

---

(pp. 20–27), and antithetical comparison (pp. 27–35). But it seems improbable that this dialectical method, an alleged "characteristic feature of Lucan style" (p. 8), was apparent to Luke's readers, if even to Luke himself. For further criticism of Flender's methodology, see L. E. Keck, *JAAR* 36 (1968): 250–51; J. C. O'Neill, *JTS* ns 19 (1968): 269–70.

5 E.g., Martin, *Foundations*, vol. 1, pp. 248–49 thinks that Marshall's claim that Luke wrote to "compose this record as a means of evangelism" (Marshall, *Historian & Theologian*, p. 221) is too general; Martin wanted him to be more specific, to ground Luke's purpose in "a particular problem or situation in the church." Marshall accepts the criticism ("Gospel," p. 290) but questions whether, in this instance at least, anything more specific can be said, owing to the limitations of our information.

6 Barrett, *Recent Study*, p. 53.

7 Such a phenomenon finds ready parallels in early Hellenistic writing practices (see, e.g., Alexander, "Hellenistic Letter-Forms," esp. pp. 87–94) and may apply to Luke–Acts as well.

possibility that unconscious," "subconscious" or "imperfectly formed" motives may also have influenced his writing.[8]

In v. 4 of the Gospel preface, Luke specifically mentions his literary intention, ἵνα ἐπιγνῷς περὶ ὧν κατηχήθης λόγων τὴν ἀσφάλειαν. This verse, however, is not itself without translational difficulties. The problem arises from the uncertain meaning of the verb κατηχέω. Lexical studies have produced two possible readings: the general apologetic sense "to inform"[9] and the specific catechetical sense "to instruct."[10] The first reading sees Theophilus as an unbeliever, perhaps sympathetic to Christianity, to whom Luke for whatever reason writes an ἀπολογία of Christianity; the second reading sees Theophilus as a convert to Christianity, to whom Luke gives further κατήχησις about his Christian faith, either to correct "inadequate or defective instruction" or to add "to what was already said."[11]

Luke's usage of the word dampens preference for one or the other reading. Both receive passing treatment in Acts ("to inform" 21:21, 24; "to instruct" 18:25). The litmus test should be Luke–Acts as a whole. Which reading makes the most sense of the Gospel and Acts as the leading idea? Acts certainly contains an apologetic aspect, especially from ch. 21 onward. But much of Acts and most of the Gospel seem somewhat incidental to a defense of the Christian faith *per se*, especially one directed toward unbelievers. If Luke, however, writes to the church – not just on its behalf – the idea of Christian teaching may make better sense of his entire work and provide a more adequate basis to evaluate his overall purpose.[12]

---

8   Cf. Marshall, "Gospel," p. 290; Cadbury, *Making*, p. 303; Barrett, *Recent Study*, pp. 52–53 respectively.

9   E.g., Zahn, *Introduction*, vol. 3, pp. 42–44, 82; Cadbury, "Preface of Luke," pp. 508–509; Cadbury, "Purpose," pp. 431–41; Volger, "Lk. 1, 4," pp. 203–205; H. W. Beyer, "κατηχέω," *TDNT* 3, pp. 639–40; Nolland, *Luke 1–9:20*, pp. 10–11.

10 E.g., Meyer, *Ursprung und Anfänge*, vol. 1, pp. 5–11, esp. p. 7; Colson, "Notes," pp. 300–309; Devoldère, "Prologue," pp. 714–19; K. Wegenast, "κατηχέω," *NIDNTT* 3, pp. 771–72; Crehan, "Purpose," pp. 354–68, esp. pp. 358–60; Minear, "Kerygmatic Intention," pp. 132–35; Fitzmyer, *Luke I–IX*, p. 301; Evans, *Luke*, p. 19; Johnson, *Luke*, p. 28.

11 Maddox, *Purpose*, p. 13.

12 But it is doubtful whether Luke had one exclusive purpose in mind; cf. Gasque, *Interpretation*, p. 303. Marshall, "Gospel," p. 290 points out that Luke may well have had "one or more principal and secondary aims." Maddox, *Purpose*, p. 6 thinks that Luke perhaps had "one overall purpose with a variety of aspects." Maddox and Marshall have developed a principle of exclusion to distinguish ancillary themes from those capable of representing Luke's overall purpose. Maddox, *Purpose*, p. 20 assumes that Luke writes to believers and thus deletes any purpose "aimed outside this category"; Marshall, "Gospel," p. 296 assumes

Broad textual support

A proposal of Lukan purpose should also have broad textual support. It should account for the multiple themes of the work, the breadth of the work, the author's literary ingenuity, and his fidelity to tradition. The sheer size of Luke–Acts, if nothing else, demands it. Anything short of this greatly increases the risk of misreading Luke.[13] This means that we should begin with "an examination of Luke's own methods."[14] Paul S. Minear nicely echoes this point but with a warning attached: "In the end we will receive more help for our task from the editor of this two-volume work than from any other writer, ancient or modern, that is *unless we adopt objectives which are genuinely alien to his.*"[15]

A contentious point in this procedure is redaction criticism. Redaction not only reveals material the author has *modified* but also clarifies tradition the author *preserves.* To concentrate only on material unique to a writer – a practice common to Lukan scholars[16] – fails to appreciate the whole picture. A writer's retention of tradition indicates his adherence to it. The danger in focusing on just the differences, as Marshall reminds us, is that "if we confine our attention to what can clearly be identified as redaction, we stand in danger of over-emphasizing a few elements in the total picture and thereby producing a distorted presentation of Luke's theology."[17]

the unity of Luke–Acts and thus rejects any theme that does not "take both parts of the story into account."

[13] E.g., Conzelmann, *Theology of St. Luke* bases his three periods of salvation history and delayed parousia theory on three passages: (1) Luke 16:16 – the period of Israel, of which John the Baptist was a part, also Acts 10:37; 13:25 (pp. 16, 20–26); (2) Luke 4:21 – the period of Jesus, also Acts 10:38 (p. 36); and (3) Luke 22:35–37 – the period of the church, to which Jesus is alluding in this text (pp. 13, 36). But knowledge of the time period to which John belongs according to 16:16 and the reference point of ἀλλὰ νῦν in 22:36 is extremely difficult to determine; cf., e.g., Marshall, *Luke,* pp. 628–29, 824–25 and lit. cited therein. Conzelmann's proposal needs better textual grounds. See the reply to Conzelmann on pp. 45–47; ch. 10. Talbert, *Luke and the Gnostics,* pp. 65, 83–97 also admits that no textual evidence in Luke–Acts supports his proposal that Luke wrote to combat gnosticism; cf. also Barrett, *Essays,* p. 98; Barrett, *Recent Study,* p. 62. See the reply to Talbert on pp. 49–51.

[14] Marshall, *Historian & Theologian,* p. 57.

[15] Minear, "Birth Stories," p. 130 (my italic).

[16] E.g., Conzelmann, *Theology of St. Luke,* pp. 18–19, 22, 25–26, 95–97, 117, 128; Talbert, "Anti-Gnostic Tendency," p. 261; Esler, *Community and Gospel,* pp. 3–4.

[17] Marshall, *Historian & Theologian,* p. 218; also Cassidy, *Jesus, Politics and Society,* p. 3 and p. 132, n. 8; esp. Carson, "Redaction Criticism," pp. 119–42, 376–81 and lit. cited in Cassidy and Carson.

Luke also doubtlessly presupposes considerable knowledge among his readers.[18] Theological and historical gaps and narrative transpositions may not indicate that Luke substantially alters the traditional meaning of the material or makes it up. Rather, factors having to do with purpose, knowledge shared with readers, and genre may well account for many of these textual differences.

Although we may never know for certain why Luke wrote, the hypotheses which come closest are the ones which all the material supports – material unique to the author, modified by the author, and preserved by the author.

Unity of Luke–Acts

The foregoing point raises the issue of the literary relation between Luke's Gospel and Acts. Was Luke–Acts initially planned and written as two parts of a unified work?[19] Or was Acts an after-thought written as an extension of the Gospel story or the Gospel appearing as a later addition to Acts?[20] Questions still remain.[21] But recent consensus nearly unanimously favors the unity position on the basis of strong textual evidence.[22]

Moreover, although the genre of Luke's Gospel decidedly differs

[18] E.g., Martin, *Portrait of Jesus*, p. 12; Maddox, *Purpose*, p. 45; Gerhardsson, *Gospel Tradition*, pp. 53–56.

[19] Or it was perhaps even written by two separate authors; so Argyle, "Greek," pp. 441–45. But in defense of common authorship cf. Beck's reply to Argyle in "Common Authorship," pp. 346–52.

[20] Schweizer, *Luke*, p. 11 agrees that Luke–Acts was planned from the outset, but also that a "further development of Luke's style" reveals a time interval between the writing of the two books. Russell, "Written First," pp. 167–74 raises the possibility that Acts was written before the Gospel; see further lit. and criticisms in Talbert, "Redaction Critical Quest," pp. 203–213; Talbert, *Literary Patterns*, p. 30; Fitzmyer, *Luke I–IX*, p. 53; Hemer, *Hellenistic History*, p. 405.

[21] See, e.g., Marshall, "Gospel," p. 291.

[22] For some recent defenses of the unity position, see Maddox, *Purpose*, pp. 3–6; Hemer, *Hellenistic History*, pp. 30–33. Creed, *Luke*, p. xi similarly defends the unity of Luke–Acts, but thinks that Acts should be considered a "sequel" rather than a "continuation" of the Gospel – the Gospel should be understood as "a unity in itself"; see similarly van Unnik, "Confirmation," pp. 26–27, 59; Parsons and Pervo, *Rethinking Unity*, pp. 126–27. Bultmann, *History*, p. 366 also supports the unity of the two books, but believes that "the specific stimulus of his work lay in the second part (Acts) to which the Gospel was but an *indispensable preliminary*" (my italic). For lit. contending that Luke–Acts was originally written as one volume and subsequently split in two with Luke 24:50–Acts 1:5 as an interpolation, see Kümmel, *Introduction*, p. 157, n. 6; cf., however, Cadbury, *Acts in History*, pp. 138–40. On the possibility that Luke planned to write a third volume, see lit. cited in Guthrie, *Introduction*, p. 359, n. 4; Quinn, "Last Volume," pp. 62–75 believes that the Pastoral Epistles are Luke's third volume.

from Acts and both books can be read individually, this does not negate their unity, or demand separate authorial intention as Pervo and Parsons suppose.[23] As Hemer, e.g., points out, despite generic differences between the Gospel and Acts, Acts nonetheless resembles "a unity of method and continuity with its sequel."[24] Thus, we should be cautious in endorsing an overall proposal which accounts for certain parts of Luke–Acts but leaves other large blocks of material unexplained or makes sense of one book but not the other.

Theological interest

Lastly, Luke shows a definite theological interest in his writing. Maddox writes: "The main thrust of studies on the gospels over the last quarter-century has been to establish the fact that the gospels, all four of them, are deliberate works of theology, in which even quite small details of wording may often be seen to have theological significance."[25] Luke is not simply writing hagiography or a history of the beginnings of Christianity. Theological concerns intimately relate to his writing aims; they form the heart and soul of his two-volume work. But a theological interest need not overrule *ipso facto* the possible historical integrity of the written material. In fact, it may be the very thing which most enhances the theological points Luke is trying to make.[26] And as mentioned already, Luke seems to presuppose some theological training among his readers.

In summary, these six criteria concerning readership, occasion, stated aim, textual support, unity, and theological interest do not tell us why Luke wrote. But as ground rules they may help keep us closer to what his objectives, perceptions, and methods in writing actually were.

Some suggested proposals

In view of the voluminous literature in this area,[27] I shall not attempt to discuss all the suggested proposals, but only the principal ones.

---

[23] Pervo, "Genre," pp. 309–16; Pervo, *Profit with Delight*; Parsons and Pervo, *Rethinking Unity*.

[24] Hemer, *Hellenistic History*, p. 78.

[25] Maddox, *Purpose*, p. 1.

[26] See further Gerhardsson, *Gospel Tradition*; Hemer, *Hellenistic History*, pp. 43–49, 86–87.

[27] See esp. the surveys of O'Toole, "Why did Luke write Acts?," pp. 66–76;

An apologetic defense of Christianity

A longstanding tradition within Lukan studies understands Luke–Acts as an *apology* of Christianity either as a defense directed toward Rome[28] or as a defense of orthodoxy within the church.[29] Acts as political apology is admirably developed by Burton S. Easton. Luke writes Acts, Easton believes, in order to urge Rome, via Theophilus, to look favorably upon Christianity as a religion which "should be tolerated by the state."[30] Luke argues that Christianity is, in effect, "nothing more nor less than Judaism" and, therefore, should be entitled to the same legal status as a *religio licita*. Although Luke considers Christianity as "the only true way" (p. 46), he refrains from detailing in Acts the differences between Judaism and Christianity for fear of confusing Roman officials with seemingly insignificant detail, thus ruining his chances of winning official recognition from Rome; instead, through the speeches in Acts, he defends "the nature of Christianity as he ... wishes it to be understood" (p. 37). Paul, however, was so convincing in distinguishing Judaism from Christianity that neither Rome nor Luke's Christian peers accepted his written appeal, dooming

---

Maddox, *Purpose*, pp. 19–23; Gasque, *Interpretation*; Gasque, "Fruitful Field," pp. 118–20.

[28] E.g., Loisy, *Actes*, p. 107; Cadbury, "Purpose," pp. 431–41; Cadbury, *Making*, pp. 299–316, esp. pp. 308–16; Cadbury, "Acts of the Apostles," *IDB* 1, pp. 37–38 (although he eventually jumps ship on this: cf. Cadbury, "Some Foibles," pp. 215–16); Riddle, "Occasion," pp. 545–62; Manson, "Life of Jesus," pp. 396–98; Easton, *Early Christianity*; Caird, *Luke*, pp. 13–15; Walasky, *Political Perspective*. For some variations on the political theme, Leaney, *Luke*, p. 7 thinks that Luke wrote to correct Roman misunderstanding as to Jesus' kingship. R. R. Williams, *Acts*, p. 26 thinks that Luke desired to convince Rome that it was foolish to oppose Christianity, for "the unlimited power of God" empowers it. Mattill contends that Luke intended his work as a trial defense for Paul in Rome; so Mattill, "Schneckenburger," pp. 108–22; Mattill, "Weymouth," pp. 276–93; Mattill, "Halévy," pp. 359–76; Mattill, "Evans," pp. 15–46; Mattill, "Rackham," pp. 335–50. Danker, *Jesus and the New Age*, pp. 2–5, 10, 24–25 believes that Luke wrote to make Christianity understandable to a Greco-Roman audience.

[29] E.g., Schneckenburger, *Zweck*; Trocmé, *Actes*, pp. 50–70, esp. p. 67; Jervell, "Teacher of Israel," pp. 153–83; Schneider, "Zweck," pp. 58–61 (with qual.); see also lit. cited in Guthrie, *Introduction*, p. 352, n. 2. Perhaps also Barrett, *Essays*, pp. 98–99; Barrett, *Recent Study*, p. 63 where Luke is said to vindicate Paul's anti-gnostic orthodoxy.

[30] Easton, *Early Christianity*, p. 42. Walasky, *Political Perspective*, pp. ix–x takes the *religio licita* idea a step further by seeing Luke's political bias as an *apologia pro imperio*.

his claim "that Christianity was a *religio licita* because it was truly a Way in Judaism" to failure and eventual obscurity (pp. 114–15).

Dissatisfied with the political slant of Easton's approach, since Luke seemingly shows little actual interest in courting Rome's favor, Jacob Jervell sees religious apology as Luke's primary aim for Acts.[31] According to Jervell, Luke writes "to explain and defend" Paul's missionary endeavors before Jewish Christians feeling threatened by unbelieving Jews, who accuse Paul of teaching sedition against Israel, the Mosaic Law, and the temple (pp. 154, 167–68). By showing the credibility of Jewish orthodoxy within the church, Luke exonerates Paul of all such accusations in hopes of preserving the special status of the church as the "people of God" (pp. 173–74).

The strength of Luke–Acts as *apology*, both in its political and religious forms, is that it makes sense of the final section of Acts (chs. 21–28). Most other theories are often hard pressed to fit this otherwise somewhat enigmatic conclusion of Luke's work into an overall scheme. The basic weaknesses, however, of this proposal, particularly in its political form, are numerous. First, it fails by criterion 5, in that it does not adequately account for Luke–Acts as a literary unit. It makes little sense of the material preceding Acts 21, except perhaps for Luke's Gospel prologue, if one is inclined to translate κατηχέω in v. 4 as "to inform" rather than "to instruct." How would Luke's lengthy description of, especially, Jesus' life and ministry strengthen this theme? It seems a terribly long introduction to the trial passages, and hardly comprehensible or relevant to most Roman officials.[32]

Second, it is doubtful whether the expression *religio licita* (occurring only in Tertullian, *Apol.* 21:1) represents an official Roman policy toward religious groups, including Judaism. Thus, according to criterion 1, it is uncertain whether Luke's readers, whether Roman officials or Jewish believers, would have thought in such terms.[33] According to A. D. Nock, the Roman policy toward the Jews was born out of expediency to prevent disorder and reflected Rome's general religious tolerance rather than specific legal policy.[34] According to Maddox, Roman literature exhibits no

---

[31] Jervell, "Teacher of Israel," pp. 153–83, esp. pp. 156–58, 173 for his critique of the political-apology theory.

[32] Barrett, *Recent Studies*, p. 63 convincingly rebuts the idea of Luke–Acts as political apology.

[33] See esp. Conzelmann, *Acts*, p. xlvii.

[34] Nock, "Religious Developments," pp. 465–511, as cited in Maddox, *Purpose*, p. 92.

specific "doctrine of permission."[35] He suspects, moreover, that what Tertullian meant by the phrase within the *Apology* itself is not as clear as some make it out to be. Esler also points out that Luke would not have willingly committed the probable Gentile element of his church to "the temple tax liabilities" they legally would have been obligated to pay on the basis of a *religio licita* appeal that Christianity fell under "the Jewish umbrella."[36]

Third, Luke's presentation of Christianity does not naturally suggest a favorable disposition toward Rome. In view of criterion 4, Luke–Acts as a political apology lacks the broad textual support that one would expect from such a writing endeavor. Richard Cassidy, in fact, contends that Luke in his Gospel portrays Jesus as dangerous to Rome.[37] Jesus, he argues, "rejected the use of violence and criticized the Gentile kings for their practice of dominating over their subjects" and "refused to defer to or cooperate with the various political officials who were responsible for maintaining those patterns" (p. 78). Jervell asserts, moreover, that the trial passages themselves cast the Roman officials in "a somewhat unfortunate light," which is "a curious way of proceeding *vis à vis* the court whose understanding or protection is being sought."[38] He draws further attention to Acts 4:27, where Luke describes Pilate as a murderer (p. 157); to the greedy and maneuvering Roman governors, Felix and Festus (p. 157); and to Luke's belief in a sovereign God, making "it difficult to imagine that it is Luke's desire to petition the Romans for favorable conditions and the opportunity to practice religion for the church" (pp. 157–58).

One final comment is especially relevant here. Scholars have increasingly come to respect Luke as a theologian. But to treat Luke–Acts as primarily a political apology is largely to ignore this aspect of his writings. If most of the details of the Gospel and the first half of Acts would appear incidental to a Roman official, Luke's theological agenda would be virtually unrecognizable. It thus also fails by criterion 6. Luke–Acts as a religious apology, however, appears as a definite concern of the author – particularly in the latter sections of Acts – but probably should be understood as a secondary theme of Luke–Acts rather than as its overall purpose.

---

[35] Maddox, *Purpose*, pp. 91–93; also Winn, "Elusive Mystery," p. 146 and n. 7.
[36] Esler, *Community and Gospel*, pp. 211–14.
[37] Cassidy, *Jesus, Politics and Society*, pp. 54–62.
[38] Jervell, "Teacher of Israel," p. 157.

A theology adapted to the parousia's delay

Conzelmann was one of the first to defend the claim that Luke wrote because of the parousia's delay.[39] Toward the end of the first century, the church, he argues, was undergoing an identity crisis bordering on disenchantment. Despite the eschatological teaching of Jesus and the church on the parousia, many from the earliest days of the church – including most of the apostles – were dying and Jesus had still not returned. How, then, were Luke's readers to understand their Christian destiny when confronted by such confusing signals? Luke writes to resolve this dilemma by reshaping the early church's theology to account for the parousia's delay.

For Conzelmann, Luke–Acts is the result of Luke's theological reflection in rethinking the "relation between history and eschatology" (p. 132). Luke replaces early Christian teaching on the parousia with a model of saving history made up of three epochs: (1) the period of Israel, (2) the satan-free period of Jesus, and (3) the period of the church, which sees a resumption of satanic activity (pp. 13–17). The church becomes "a historical entity" in its own right, having its own particular function in God's plan of redemptive history (*Acts*, p. xlv). Its role is to proclaim God's saving message to the world. The parousia, on the other hand, becomes relatively inconsequential for the church; it recedes to some distant, indeterminable point in the future.

The strength of Conzelmann's thesis is that it places Luke–Acts in company with other NT books on the issue of Jesus' non-return. The way in which Paul's prison letters, the Pastorals, and the writings of Peter, John, and Jude all show a decided interest in giving instruction, warning, and encouragement to believers most likely reveals a common awareness that the parousia would not take place before their deaths (cf., e.g., 2 Tim. 4:1–22, esp. vv. 6–8, 18; 2 Pet. 1:12–15).

But the severest challenge to Conzelmann's thesis, according to criterion 2, is that it seems to lack a concrete occasion which would have prompted such a writing endeavor. The approaching reality of death caused none of these later NT writers to abandon or alter radically their belief in an imminent return. How far, then, can we

---

[39] Conzelmann, *Theology of St. Luke*; to a lesser extent in Conzelmann, *Acts*. Cf. also Lohse, "Heilsgeschichte," pp. 145–64; Bovon, "Heil," pp. 61–74; and lit. discussed in Rasco, *Teologia*, pp. 41–46.

rightly insist that Luke specifically wrote to do this very thing? Conzelmann has not proven that we can for several reasons.

First, his presentation particularly runs into trouble in his proclivity to read his *own* inclinations into the text with slim textual evidence to support his suppositions. This is most evident in the way he exegetically defends Luke's alleged three-stage salvation-history scheme. He bases it on three references taken from the Gospel (16:16; 4:21; 22:35–37), the first and last of which are especially dubious in meaning within the Gospel itself. If Luke were actually writing in the way Conzelmann describes for reasons so important,[40] one would expect him *to be more explicit* about his intentions in the Gospel. In fact, if Luke–Acts chiefly represents a theological response to the parousia's delay, should not one expect explicit discussion of it in Acts, since the time of the church is when it becomes a problem? But as Conzelmann even admits, in Acts his thesis "is not so much developed as it is presupposed" (*Acts*, p. xlv). Hence, it suffers, according to criterion 4, from a lack of broad textual support.

This weakness becomes more visible in his failure to discuss the birth narratives,[41] his negative understanding of John the Baptist,[42] his satan-free period of Jesus' ministry,[43] his separation of the periods of Jesus and the church,[44] and his antithetical assessment of "history and eschatology."[45]

Second, it is questionable how obvious Conzelmann's description

---

[40] Conzelmann stresses that Luke consciously recasts his sources and eliminates the early expectation of an imminent return: see esp. *Theology of St. Luke*, p. 96; but cf. his confusing assessment at the top of p. 98 in this regard.

[41] After briefly discussing Luke's Gospel prologue (*Theology of St. Luke*, pp. 11, 14–15), Conzelmann begins exegetically discussing Luke's salvation-history model at Luke ch. 3 (p. 18), passing over the birth narratives altogether. But as Minear, "Birth Stories," pp. 111–30 has shown, Luke 1–2 strongly contributes toward Luke's overall purpose. Cf. Oliver, "Lucan Birth Stories," pp. 202–26; Tatum, "Epoch of Israel," pp. 184–95, who attempt to integrate Luke 1–2 into Conzelmann's scheme.

[42] Conzelmann, *Theology of St. Luke*, pp. 18–27, 161. But cf., e.g., Marshall, *Luke*, pp. 148–49, 628–29.

[43] Conzelmann, *Theology of St. Luke*, pp. 16, 27–29, 80–82, 106, 156–57, 170, 180. But cf., e.g., Robinson, *Weg des Herrn*, pp. 21–30; Marshall, *Historian & Theologian*, p. 87, n. 4.

[44] Conzelmann, *Theology of St. Luke*, pp. 13–17, 150–51, 170, 209–13. But cf. lit. cited on pp. 12–13 above.

[45] Conzelmann, *Theology of St. Luke*, pp. 95–136. But cf., e.g., Ellis, *Eschatology*, pp. 17–18; Gasque, *Interpretation*, pp. 295–96; Marshall, *Historian & Theologian*, pp. 107–11; see also our discussion of Luke's view of salvation history and eschatology in chs. 7 and 10.

of salvation history would have been to Luke's readers themselves. This is not to question the legitimacy of salvation history as a Lukan theme, or as a common NT theme,[46] but to question the way in which Conzelmann thinks that from reading Luke–Acts, Luke's readers (and modern readers for that matter) would have been able to see "how the whole story of salvation, as well as the life of Jesus in particular, is now objectively set out and described according to its successive stages."[47] This seems highly improbable. Conzelmann's thesis, therefore, also fails by criterion 1, in that the reader is here said to see something that an ancient reader probably would not have seen.[48]

Finally, the most conspicuous weakness of Conzelmann's theory is his failure to account for Luke's continuing eschatological interest. Eric Franklin tries to resolve this tension without giving up the notion that Luke writes to strengthen believers struggling in their faith because of the parousia's delay.[49] Luke's intention, however, was not to reassign the parousia to the distant future, but to "reinstate" it as eschatologically relevant for his church. Luke accomplishes this by developing a model of salvation history in line with the rest of the NT, through which he stresses the central importance of Jesus' present Lordship (p. 5). "Salvation history in his two volumes, though present, is used in the service of his eschatology *rather than as a replacement of it*" (p. 6, my italic; also p. 43).

For Franklin the ascension becomes the leading eschatological idea rather than the parousia. Luke writes to replace future hope with present belief: "Now is the time of Jesus' glory. He is the present Lord; the object of his work has been achieved; men can now have faith in his immediate status to which the parousia, when it comes, can add nothing" (pp. 28–29). The ascension, thus,

---

[46] E.g., Cullmann, *Salvation in History*, pp. 46–47, 237–38 sees Luke drawing upon a theme already common to his predecessors and shared by the other NT writers, although Cullmann believes that Luke makes distinctive use of it.

[47] Conzelmann, *Theology of St. Luke*, p. 132.

[48] Munck, *Acts*, p. lxxxviii critiques Conzelmann's work as "an unexpected marriage between existentialism and neo-Hegelianism." Although Munck's negative assessment is overstated, there may be a sense in which Conzelmann has read into Luke–Acts his own concept of time, one decidedly influenced by Hegel's dialecticism, which has traditionally characterized much of German philosophy and theology.

[49] Franklin, *Christ the Lord*, pp. 10, 20. Cf. his later work, *Interpreter of Paul*, p. 135, where he defines Luke's purpose as "a presentation of the truths of the gospel as he understood it."

represents the moment of Jesus' glorification, the confirmation of his divinity and the fulfillment of Israel's expectations. As a result, Jesus' Lordship now becomes the challenge for believers to repent before the imminent "End" arrives.

One of the merits of Franklin's argument, over against Conzelmann, is that he gives credit to Luke's expressed interest in the parousia and underscores the importance of Christ's heavenly session in relation to Luke's continuing eschatological interest. But here again the question arises as to whether the delay motif appears as the controlling theme of Luke–Acts. The main problem is the minor part it plays, especially in Acts. According to criterion 4, his thesis also suffers from a lack of textual support. Although Franklin, like Conzelmann, admits that Luke undeniably shows less interest in the parousia in Acts than in the Gospel (p. 27),[50] he still insists that Luke–Acts is a theological response to it. Because of this, he somewhat strains the meaning of the resurrection and ascension, the role of the Spirit, and the witness motif in order to keep the delay theme as Luke's central writing purpose.

Certainly the ascension plays a key role in Luke–Acts: historically, it terminates Jesus' earthly ministry; theologically, it represents Jesus' enthronement; and literarily, it bridges the two volumes. But to give it preeminence over the resurrection (see pp. 30, 33–34) seems somewhat artificial. According to Acts 1:22b, the reason the apostles wanted to fill Judas' spot was because they wanted another *witness to Jesus' resurrection*; witnessing the ascension, however, made one only eligible for consideration (v. 22a). In Acts, the resurrection preeminently becomes the basis of proclamation (2:31; 4:33; 17:18; 26:23), the guarantee of the future general resurrection of the dead (4:2; 17:32) and the believer's hope (23:6,8; 24:15,21). Furthermore, Franklin's claim that Luke was not primarily interested in salvation or mission but in witness (pp. 43–44, 146) gives a somewhat confusing meaning to the Spirit's work and the witness motif in Acts (see esp. 1:8).[51] Luke's eschatology may

---

[50] For similar admissions, see Conzelmann, *Acts*, p. 9; Rasco, *Teologia*, p. 32; Maddox, *Purpose*, p. 129; Marshall, "Gospel," p. 301. This is not to say that Luke shows no eschatological interest in Acts – see, e.g., Ellis, *Eschatology*; Giles, "Present–Future Eschatology (1–2)," pp. 65–71, 11–18; Mattill, *Last Things* – but only that it does not stand as his central concern, so Maddox, *Purpose*, p. 115.

[51] Cf., e.g., Marshall, *Acts*, p. 60: "The disciples must accomplish their task of being *witnesses* to Jesus. The scope of their task is world wide" (his italic); Haenchen, *Acts*, p. 144: "As Acts presents it, the Christian church is a *missionary* Church" (his italic).

indicate some level of awareness of the problem of the delay. But the limited attention he gives it also implies that it should probably be considered a secondary theme, if it is a conscious one at all.[52]

A polemic against heresy

Charles Talbert takes the position that Luke wrote his two-volume work to counter the rising problem of gnosticism within late first-century Christianity.[53] In focusing on material which he believes shows Luke's distinctive editorial hand via redaction (p. 15),[54] Talbert isolates three motifs supposedly reflecting Luke's anti-gnostic purpose: (1) an authentic witness motif, meant to affirm Jesus' humanity and his physical passion, resurrection, and ascension; (2) a true exegesis of scripture motif, meant to preserve the church's belief that the OT confirms Jesus as the Christ, that the Christ must suffer and rise from the dead, and the general resurrection; and (3) a succession of tradition motif, meant to protect apostolic teaching from heresy in the sub-apostolic period (pp. 55–56). Luke also intended Jesus' martyrdom at the hands of the Jews to refute the gnostic denial of the legitimacy of Christian martyrdom (p. 82).

Believing Luke–Acts to have been written near the time of John's Apocalypse, Talbert sees a similarity between the Ephesian heretics of Rev. 2:2, 6 and those of Acts 20:29. He thinks the problem in both instances is gnosticism (p. 13). He believes that a similar anti-gnostic polemic runs through Luke–Acts, John's Gospel, 1 John, the Pastorals, and 2 Peter, all written toward the turn of the first century (p. 70). Talbert justifies the fact that Luke never mentions his anti-gnostic purpose by appealing to a maxim suggested by Tertullian, that "truth precedes copy" (*Prae. haer.* 29) (p. 89, n. 12). In the case of Luke–Acts, the author idealized the apostolic age as a period free from heresy to show that gnosticism ("the copy") has corrupted the original ("preceding") teachings of the early church ("the truth") (p. 89). He feels that this concept is an

---

[52] As Marshall, "Gospel," pp. 290–91 insists, if anything, it was "an unconscious factor stemming from Luke's theological environment."

[53] Talbert, *Luke and the Gnostics*; also Talbert, "Anti-Gnostic Tendency," pp. 259–71; and alluded to in Talbert, "Redaction Critical Quest," p. 213. For more lit. supporting Luke–Acts as an anti-gnostic correction, see also, e.g., Klein, *Zwölf Apostel*; Mußner, "Gemeinde," pp. 113–30; and lit. cited in Talbert, *Luke and the Gnostics*, p. 14.

[54] Also Talbert, "Anti-Gnostic Tendency," pp. 260–61.

anti-gnostic device evident in Tertullian, Hegesippus, 2 Peter, Jude, and 1 Clement, thus increasing the possibility that Luke may have been familiar with it (p. 93).

Talbert's thesis, although interesting, is improbable for a number of reasons. First, his method is problematic. To use, as he does, a critical approach which largely ignores a sizeable amount of tradition greatly increases the chance of misreading Luke's intentions. It misjudges the possibility that Luke retained this material in the Gospel because he in fact agreed with it. His method is particularly weak in Acts. Since there Luke so thoroughly blends his own material with that of his sources, it becomes virtually impossible to know which emphases are distinctively his.[55] Hence, according to criterion 3, Talbert's thesis, which ignores so much Lukan material, does not seem fully reconciled with the author's stated aim.

Second, Luke, in fact, never explicitly mentions any kind of gnostic or docetic problem. With no textual support, Talbert's theory fails by criterion 4. The three motifs of witness, OT interpretation, and succession of tradition are each arguably valid themes within Luke–Acts. But none of them explicitly addresses a gnostic problem as Talbert imagines. It is highly questionable, furthermore, that Luke intended Jesus' death by the Jews as a critique of the gnostic idea of Christian martyrdom. This comment seems a telling sign that Talbert reads the problem of gnosticism into Luke–Acts rather than from it.

Here too, Talbert's thesis breaks down according to criterion 1, in that it is hard to see how these alleged Lukan writing techniques would have facilitated communicating an anti-gnostic polemic to his readers. Talbert's thesis forces a high level of interpretive skill upon Luke's readers. Even if they knew that Luke was countering gnosticism, they still seem left on their own to make the appropriate connections.

Third, his appeal to secondary sources does not strengthen his lack of textual support. He employs Tertullian's idea that "truth precedes copy" to justify Luke's silence on gnosticism. Talbert claims that this idea was a common anti-gnostic device used by Tertullian, Hegesippus, 2 Peter, Jude, and 1 Clement. But even here his purpose fails him. In at least the cases of Hegesippus, 2 Peter, Jude, and 1 Clement, the authors mention the villainous parties and leave no doubt as to the problems they were facing. It was in

[55] Marshall, *Historian & Theologian*, pp. 67–68.

Hegesippus the seven sects opposing James the Just; in Jude, "godless men, who change the grace of our God into a license for immorality and deny Jesus Christ our only Sovereign and Lord" (v. 4); in 2 Peter, "false teachers" (2:1–3), "blasphemers" (2:10–12), "adulterers" (2:13–14) etc.; in 1 Clement, "rash and self-confident persons" (ch. 1). Luke, however, even fails to do that! It is highly unlikely that the "fierce wolves" of Acts 20:29 were Luke's antagonists. Why would Luke wait until so late in the narrative and give such cursory and imprecise treatment to the false teachers who, according to Talbert, were causing him so much trouble?

Finally, Talbert never defines specifically what he means by gnosticism, nor the type of gnosticism (docetism?) Luke may have been confronting. Therefore, the possibility that the purpose of Luke–Acts was to refute a gnostic heresy seems slim; even as a sub-theme it is highly questionable.

A redefinition of relations between Christianity and Judaism

Albert Winn describes the purpose of Acts as geared toward bringing about a theological shift in Christian self-understanding.[56] Jewish and Gentile believers are in a quandary: as heirs to the covenants and promises of the OT, they in a sense now share in the national life of Israel, but the Jewish nation has rejected the gospel, the very fulfillment of these promises. How, then, are believers to understand themselves?

Luke sets out to resolve the problem, Winn believes, by appealing to divine providence. Israel's rejection of the gospel and the Gentiles' acceptance of it were part of God's plan. The church, consequently, becomes the true Israel to which the OT covenants and promises now belong; national Israel has forfeited its position as "the people of God." Luke further justifies this shift by showing that it was foreseen by Jesus and the OT and confirmed by the Spirit's presence and work in the church.

Robert Maddox and Jack Sanders take up Winn's position that Christianity has superseded Judaism.[57] Maddox thinks that Luke's church is undergoing an identity crisis. Judaism, heir to the OT promises, has rejected the gospel and the church. What, then, is its status as the people of God? Maddox refutes the positions of Jacob

---

[56] Winn, "Elusive Mystery," pp. 144–56.
[57] Maddox, *Purpose*; Sanders, *Jews*; Sanders, "Jew and Gentile," pp. 434–55.

Jervell[58] and G. D. Kilpatrick,[59] who believe that, according to Luke, the church is the "renewed Israel" and must remain within the Law.[60] He argues just the opposite.

Luke–Acts, Maddox believes, has a strong "anti-Jewish orientation," which must be considered along with its "Jewish and Gentile orientation" if Luke's purpose is to be fully understood. Luke's "orientation against Judaism" appears throughout Luke–Acts – e.g., in the Gospel prologue (Luke 1:4), Simeon's song (2:34), Jesus' teaching at Nazareth (4:16–30), the travel and passion narratives, Stephen's speech (Acts 7), and in Paul's sermons in Pisidian Antioch (13:46) and Corinth (18:6) – and is most graphically illustrated in the conclusion of Acts (28:14–28). Here in contrast to Paul, who is portrayed as having brought the gospel "to the ends of the earth" (Acts 1:8), the Jewish nation stands in a state of rebellion, rejecting "the Word of the Lord" (Acts 28:25–27; Isa. 6:9–10). In writing Luke–Acts, Maddox concludes, Luke reassures the believers of his own day that they, not Judaism, stand directly in line with the promises of God: "The full stream of God's saving action in history has not passed them by, but has flowed straight into their community-life, in Jesus and the Holy Spirit" (p. 187).

Jack Sanders goes a step further. Luke wrote to show that Judaism was in error and superseded by Christianity, and that the same can be said of Jewish Christianity as well. In strong, uncompromising "anti-semitic" language, Luke writes to show that Gentile Christianity is the legitimate successor to Moses, the Prophets and "biblical Israel."

The basic problem is not that Christianity has rejected Judaism but that Judaism has rejected Christianity. Luke describes Christianity as "the true and authentic Judaism" (p. 97). Expressions like "the people of God" (ὁ λαὸς θεοῦ) and "people" (λαός) mean "the church." On the other hand, Luke collectively sees the Jewish people as incorrigible. Through the figures of Jesus, Peter, Stephen,

---

[58]   Jervell, *Luke and the People of God.*

[59]   Kilpatrick, "γραμματεύς and νομικός," pp. 56–60; Kilpatrick, "Gentile Mission," pp. 145–58; Kilpatrick, "Mark 13:9–10," pp. 81–86; Kilpatrick, "Λαοί," p. 127; Kilpatrick, "Strata," pp. 83–88.

[60]   Another variety of this position falling somewhere between the views of Jervell and Maddox is Esler's claim, *Community and Gospel,* pp. 17, 46–47, 60, 69–70, 220–23, that Luke wrote to "legitimize" Christianity, i.e., to help his church "cope with its sectarian status" stemming from Jewish and Roman pressures, with its allegiance to church and state, and with social problems arising from its mixture of people from all levels of society. See also the views of Karris, "Missionary Communities," pp. 90–91; Pervo, *Luke's Story of Paul,* pp. 13–14.

and Paul, Sanders argues that Luke clearly shows how the Jews have repeatedly, willfully, and without remorse rejected Jesus, the gospel, and the church. Furthermore, repentant and unrepentant Israel are ultimately no different; both still try "to justify themselves on the basis of their 'Moses'" (p. 317). Hence, "in Luke's opinion," according to Sanders, "the world will be much better off when 'the Jews' get what they deserve and the world is rid of them" (p. 317).

The merit of this "self-identity" position is that it points out the Lukan texts which do seem to suggest an "anti-Israel" or "anti-Judaism" theme. But in saying this, we must *severely* qualify Sanders' – not Luke's! – tone of voice. For Luke to charge Judaism with a certain level of complicity in putting Jesus to death and of animosity toward the gospel and the church is not deserving of the label "anti-semitic."[61] Rather than having a personal disdain for the Jews, Luke may actually have developed this negative, more critical stance, as we shall shortly see, along very Jewish lines for very Jewish reasons!

The major weakness of Winn, Maddox, and Sanders' position is that they fail to give enough consideration to the places where Luke assesses Judaism positively and to texts where he seems eager to lessen Jewish guilt for rejecting Jesus. In criticism of Maddox, J. L. Houlden has pointed out a number of substantial pro-Jewish elements in Luke–Acts:[62] the success of the Christian mission in Jerusalem (pp. 54–55), Luke's unparalleled depiction of the solid Jewish background to Jesus and the church (pp. 55–56), the bent of the apostles and Paul in the Jewish direction (p. 56), and statements of Luke modifying Jewish guilt (pp. 56–59). In light of these omissions, the position of Maddox *et al.* fails by criterion 4.

Howard Marshall further adds, in response to Maddox and pertinent to Sanders as well, that if Luke–Acts were written after AD 70, the destruction of Jerusalem would have amply confirmed that God's favor was no longer with Judaism, and that for an earlier date, Jewish opposition did not seem to cause a confidence problem elsewhere in the Christian church.[63]

Luke more likely developed the two opposing Jewish strands in Luke–Acts to depict the church's identity according to the OT idea of "divided Israel," where the OT prophets frequently described the

---

[61] Cf. esp. Weatherly's critique of Sanders in "Jews," pp. 107–17.
[62] Houlden, "Purpose," pp. 53–65.
[63] Marshall, "Gospel," p. 305.

nation in terms of "a faithful remnant" and "an unfaithful majority."[64] Luke identifies the church with the faithful remnant, i.e., "true Israel." But this does not mean, as Jervell and Kilpatrick suggest, that the whole church as "the renewed Israel" must now abide within the Jewish Law; rather, the designation characterizes, as it did for faithful OT Jews, the church as living in obedience to God's revealed plan of salvation.

To identify an anti-Jewish theme as Luke's purpose is tenuous and misrepresentative of his thinking. Luke–Acts displays a mixture of feelings toward Judaism ranging from condemnation to praise; this should be our clue in understanding Luke on the matter. Luke casts the church and those who reject God's offer of salvation in Jesus according to the OT divided-Israel concept. But, as with the religious apology proposal, this more conciliatory position was doubtfully Luke's main purpose, although it seems a strong candidate as a secondary aim.

An interest in evangelism

Many scholars assert that Luke's purpose is closely related to his soteriology.[65] W. C. van Unnik, e.g., speculates that Luke wrote Acts as a sequel to the Gospel to give his readers a fuller picture of God's saving work.[66] The whole of Luke–Acts should be understood as a record of the things that Jesus began to do and teach, in that his life was the "showing forth of His saving activity," an activity which his followers would proclaim to the world (p. 49). Thus Luke wrote to confirm Jesus as Savior to unbelievers and to reaffirm Jesus as Savior to believers who were possibly wavering in their faith – perhaps modeled after or reminiscent of Heb. 2:2–3 (pp. 47–48, 59).[67]

---

[64] See as variously defined in George, "Israël," pp. 523–24; Jervell, "Divided People of God," pp. 41–74; Lohfink, *Sammlung Israels*, pp. 85–93; Tiede, "Theo-Political Claims," pp. 46–48; Houlden, "Purpose," p. 63; Brawley, *Jews*; Stanton, "People of God."

[65] E.g., Trocmé, *Actes*, pp. 41–50; Stanley, "Salvation," pp. 231–54; Dupont, *Salvation*; van Unnik, "Confirmation," pp. 49–55; O'Neill, *Theology of Acts*, pp. 140–41,176–78; Green, *Meaning of Salvation*, pp. 125–31; Rigaux, *Témoignage de Luc*, pp. 383–407; Marshall, *Historian & Theologian*, pp. 19, 88–94; Marshall, *Acts*, pp. 20–21; Marshall, "Gospel," pp. 297–304, 308; Martin, "Salvation and Discipleship," pp. 366–78; George, "Vocabulaire de salut," pp. 308–20; Giles, "Salvation (1–2)," pp. 10–16, 45–49; Morris, *Luke*, pp. 38–40.

[66] Van Unnik, "Confirmation," pp. 26, 57, 59.

[67] For the notion that Acts was primarily intended to edify believers, see further Haenchen, *Acts*, p. 103; Pervo, *Profit with Delight*, pp. xi–xii, 2–3, 10–11, though

Jacques Dupont sees Acts as bridging the origins of Christianity with the present experience of the church.[68] Acts rounds out Jesus' mission by exhibiting its universal message and confirms the fulfillment of God's saving plan by showing the Spirit-directed expansion of the church. An analysis of the introductions and conclusions of the two books shows that Luke's overriding theological interest is the universality of salvation, an emphasis which would have been unmistakable to his readers and is reiterated throughout the main body of the double work. Dupont compares the introduction and conclusion of the whole work and then the conclusion of the Gospel with the introduction of Acts (p. 13). Regarding the first comparison he concludes, "by thus placing Isa. 40:5 at the beginning of his Gospel story, and also drawing the conclusion of Acts from words that remind us of this same text, Luke betrays his strong interest in the idea that the salvation of God is manifested to all men" (p. 16); in the second comparison he finds the same universal idea expressed in Luke 24:47, "to all nations," and in Acts 1:8, "to the ends of the earth" (p. 19).

On the basis of the significant use Luke makes of the salvation word group in the Gospel (and Acts), unparalleled by the other Gospel writers, Howard Marshall also feels certain that salvation is the central motif in Lukan theology.[69] Luke's purpose, he argues, is to "promote and confirm faith in Jesus Christ," a purpose having application to both unbeliever and believer (pp. 19, 84).[70] In clarifying this proposal, he adds that Luke writes to supply catechetical instruction concerning "the origins of Christianity."[71] In conjunction with this, Marshall asserts, in reply to Conzelmann, that in Luke's adoption of the NT concept of salvation history, his emphasis is not so much on history itself, but on the saving significance of it.[72]

In still stronger terms, J. C. O'Neill sees Luke's purpose, at least according to Acts, as primarily evangelistic.[73] Luke wants to win

their wholesale skepticism toward the historical accuracy of much of Acts is unnecessary; cf., e.g., Hemer, *Hellenistic History*.
[68] Dupont, "Theological Significance," pp. 11–33.
[69] Marshall, *Historian & Theologian*, pp. 92–94, 102, 116–17.
[70] Although he is less certain that Luke–Acts was primarily written as an evangelistic tool; cf. Marshall, "Gospel," p. 303, n. 31.
[71] Marshall, *Gospel*, pp. 302, 304; also Williams, "Church History," pp. 155–56.
[72] Marshall, *Historian & Theologian*, pp. 19, 86.
[73] O'Neill, *Theology of Acts*, pp. 176–78; also Kistemaker, *Acts*, p. 31; White, *Case for Christianity*, pp. 20–26; Lentz, *Portrait of Paul*, pp. 171–72; Larkin, *Acts* (forthcoming); in less certain terms, Bruce, *Acts* (NICNT), p. 13.

the educated Roman public to Christianity. Secondarily, Luke intended Acts as an apology aimed at refuting Judaism (pp. 75, 95, 98–99) to demonstrate the innocence of Christianity (pp. 146, 150, 179–80); but its "burning inner purpose was, nonetheless, to bring men to faith" (p. 176). Though O'Neill's proposed second-century date for Luke–Acts, *c.* AD 115–30, is not convincing, his suggested evangelistic concern clearly hits at a writing interest central to Luke.

The strength of this position is that it makes sense of the introductions and conclusions of Luke–Acts, and much of its content and structure. But it is questionable whether it can stand on its own as Luke's purpose. First, in line with criterion 5, Maddox is skeptical as to whether an interest in evangelism reflects Luke's primary writing concern, in that it fails to account for Acts 21–28 and thus does not fully consider the unity of Luke–Acts.[74] But more importantly, one would think that if Luke were as evangelistically motivated as O'Neill has especially argued, he would have made a better effort to detail the saving significance of Jesus' death and resurrection.

Most scholars who affirm an evangelistic interest believe that Luke was Paul's traveling companion (although cf. O'Neill) and that as a writer he conservatively handled the traditional material at his disposal. It is clear from Paul's writings that the vicarious nature of Jesus' death was a core element of his soteriology. It is also evident in Paul that this teaching did not originate with him, but that for him it was already traditional as well.[75] In Luke's Gospel, on the other hand, this important early church tradition and Pauline teaching appears only fleetingly in Luke 22:17–20. And it makes no real appearance in the proclamation of the early church as recorded by Luke in Acts, except in 20:28. Why, then, did Luke not say more about the atonement? In this light, as a kind of gospel tract or as Christian catechetical instruction, Luke's writings would appear deficient . . . to some, gravely so.

On the other hand, it is also entirely possible that Luke saw something else as the means of salvation. Joel Green, e.g., argues that on the basis of Acts 2:33; 5:30–31; 10:43 a case can be made that for Luke the exaltation stands as the means of salvation, a conclusion which, he believes, the whole of the work supports.[76]

[74] Maddox, *Purpose*, p. 20.
[75] So, e.g., Hengel, *Atonement*, pp. 65–75.
[76] Green, "God's Servant," pp. 7–11; similarly Hultgren, *Christ and His Benefits*, pp. 84–85.

Moreover, on the basis of Pauline parallels (Rom. 4:24–25; 10:9–13; 1 Cor. 15:3–5; Phil. 2:5–11), Marshall thinks that Luke reflects an early church belief that sees Jesus' resurrection as saving in its own right.[77] But whether for Luke the cross, resurrection, or exaltation stand as the means of salvation, as Green notes, "Luke–Acts contains remarkably little explicit reflection on this issue."[78] If evangelism were Luke's primary writing concern, would it not be fair, according to criterion 4, to expect a more thoroughgoing explication of this issue which is so central to it?

As the main candidate, then, for Luke's purpose, the evangelism position does not fully satisfy. But in conjunction with Luke's interest in salvation, it was most likely closely attached to whatever his purpose may have been.

Conclusion: the need for strong textual grounds

As we have seen in this chapter, problems stemming from methodological, textual, and historical grounds weaken each of the principal purposes for Luke–Acts. None of them sum up adequately Luke's primary writing concern. But the Jewish issue and most definitely the salvation theme were conscious factors playing into it.

Cadbury warns that "it is quite possible to overemphasize this factor [i.e., an author's conscious purpose] in composition, to assign to it the most fanciful and exaggerated rôle."[79]

We have taken precautions against this by establishing the six criteria of audience, occasion, stated aim, broad textual support, unity, and theological interest as guidelines which any proposal should, if at all possible, explain in order to avoid flights of fancy and to come as close as possible to what Luke's intentions actually were. From our discussion, we have seen that the most overwhelming deficiency affecting each of these proposals is the lack of strong textual grounds. In four of the cases, it was a matter of scanty textual evidence; but in the case of Maddox *et al.*, it was more an issue of being highly selective with the Lukan material, ignoring the numerous important passages which suggest a contrary position (a problem facing Conzelmann and Talbert's proposals as well).

---

[77] Marshall, "Resurrection in Acts," pp. 103–105; Marshall, *Historian & Theologian*, p. 174.

[78] Green, "God's Servant," p. 8.

[79] Cadbury, *Making*, p. 15.

Our task in ch. 3 will be to advance the discussion concerning Luke's purpose by developing a proposal which makes better sense of all the Lukan material and which, at the same time, encourages inclusion of some of these other themes (e.g., esp. religious apology, definition of Christian self-understanding and evangelism). Moreover, we shall begin there to explore the connection of Luke's recorded christology to his purpose in writing.

3

A PROPOSAL FOR LUKE'S PURPOSE

Introduction

Unlike NT epistolary writing, where an author's intentions are normally fairly clearly expressed, the underlying motives of Gospel writing can at best only be inferred from the material itself.[1] Luke states in his Gospel preface that he writes purposefully to a certain Theophilus. But, as we have seen from ch. 2, scholars differ considerably as to what that purpose actually was.

In this chapter, we shall attempt to detect a Lukan writing concern having strong textual grounds and necessitating the kind of christology Luke has given us. We shall introduce a probable literary occasion, taking into consideration (1) the area of concern, i.e., a probable scenario describing *why* Luke wrote, and (2) the written response, i.e., *how* Luke–Acts was a fitting response to it. The remainder of the book will in various ways develop this further.

We shall begin by examining the life situation of Luke's readers. This discussion will enable us to move more naturally into one on literary occasion. Our findings will be in terms of probability and plausibility. Our principal aim is to get as close as possible with the limited sources at hand to what the original circumstances and writing concerns were. The proposal's strength will ultimately be the extent to which it accounts for *all* the material.

---

[1] Luke 1:1–4 and John 20:30–31 are the clearest examples of motive among canonical Gospel writers. But even these instances do not provide much precise background information on occasion, audience, and specific authorial motive. In fact, Paul more explicitly states why he writes in his brief letter to Philemon than do the writers of the four Gospels and Acts put together! Von Campenhausen, *Formation*, pp. 122–23 points out that in essence the Gospel writers remain "silent concerning what it was that made them undertake their task, or the importance and function of their work." See also Cadbury, "Gospel Study," pp. 139–45.

The life situation of Luke's readers

Robert Karris has justifiably criticized Lukan scholars for failing all too frequently to link their proposals about why Luke wrote to the life situation of his readers.[2] These proposals, he laments, are often "too abstract and divorced from reality" (p. 219). Karris concludes: "For purposes, themes, or tendencies to have complete validity, it must be demonstrated that they arise from a concrete situation within Luke's community" (p. 219).

We shall examine the life situation of Luke's readers in two ways. First, we shall briefly define a time interval most suitably fitting the chronological implications of the text. Second, we shall describe the probable nature of Luke's church around the time he wrote.

The date of Luke–Acts

The question of date is vital to a study of the purpose of Luke–Acts. The kind of needs or problems the author sought to resolve and his methods for doing so would vary considerably depending on whether he wrote toward the end of the apostolic age or as late as the middle of the second century.

The *terminus a quo* for dating Luke–Acts is no earlier than Paul's second year under house arrest in Rome (see Acts 28:30), *c.* AD 62; the *terminus ad quem* is no later than the appearance of Irenaeus' *Against Heresies*, *c.* AD 170–80, which contains the first explicit reference to Luke–Acts in early Christian literature (*Haer.* 3.13.3). Within this time span scholarly opinion as to when Luke–Acts was written essentially groups itself into five time periods: (1) toward the end of Paul's second year under house arrest in Rome to the outbreak of the Neronian persecution in AD 64[3] or, more generally, sometime before the destruction of Jerusalem in AD 70;[4] (2) *c.*

---

2   Karris, "Sitz im Leben," pp. 219–33 (from which I cite); later republished with minor revisions (his initial section on methodology being omitted) as "Poor and Rich," pp. 112–25.

3   E.g., Harnack, AD 60, *Date of Acts*, pp. 90–135; Loisy, pre-AD 64, *Luc*, p. 12; Clark, pre-AD 64, *Acts*, p. 310; Harrison, AD 63, *Introduction*, pp. 192–93, 226–28; Parker, pre-AD 64, "Former Treatise," pp. 52–58; Goodenough, AD 60–64, "Perspective," p. 58; Robinson, AD 57–60, *Redating*, pp. 57–60; Reicke, AD 60–62, *Roots*, pp. 179–80; Riley, AD 60–64, *Making of Mark*, p. 249; Hemer, AD 62, *Hellenistic History*, pp. 403–404, 414; Wenham, AD 62, *Redating*, pp. 229–38.

4   E.g., Torrey, *Composition and Date*, pp. 69–70; Sahlin, *Messias und das Gottesvolk*, p. 46; C. S. C. Williams, "Date," pp. 283–84; C. S. C. Williams, *Acts*, pp. 13–15; Mattill, "Rackham," pp. 335–50; Tiede, *Prophecy and History*, pp. 68–70, 128; Moessner, *Lord of the Banquet*, pp. 314–15; Bock, "Luke," *DJG*, p. 500.

AD 70;[5] (3) from post-AD 70 to the end of the first century;[6] (4) the decade following publication of Josephus' *Jewish Antiquities* in AD 93;[7] and (5) in the second century before the appearance of Irenaeus' *Against Heresies, c.* AD 170–80.[8]

But several observations reduce this ambit of time considerably. First, because of a lack of textual support, Lukan scholars have not widely held position (5), that Luke–Acts was written in the second century for apologetic reasons.[9] Second, the content of Luke–Acts more naturally suggests a first-century date.[10] And third, Lukan scholars generally hold that those proposing position (4), that Luke used Josephus' *Jewish Antiquities* as a source,[11] greatly overstate the evidence.[12] Perhaps the most that can be said about the source

[5] E.g., Wikenhauser, *Apg.*, pp. 21–22; Manson, *Studies*, p. 67; Marshall, *Luke*, pp. 34–35; Ellis, *Luke*, pp. 55–60; Nolland, *Luke 1–9:20*, p. xxxix; see also lit. cited in Kümmel, *Introduction*, p. 186, n. 119.

[6] E.g., Plummer, AD 75–80, *Luke*, pp. xxix–xxxiii; Dibelius, AD 70–90, *Fresh Approach*, pp. 64–65; Dibelius, *Studies*, p. 72; Creed, AD 80–85, *Luke*, pp. xxii–xxiv; Dupont, AD 70–80, "Utilisation apologétique," p. 306, n. 2; Trocmé, AD 80–85, *Actes*, pp. 70–72; Conzelmann, AD 80–100, *Acts*, p. xxxiii; Conzelmann, "Development of Early Christianity," pp. 298–316; Haenchen, AD 70–100, *Acts*, pp. 112–16; Kümmel, AD 70–90, *Introduction*, pp. 150–51; Robinson, late first cen., *Weg des Herrn*, p. 45; Hengel, AD 80–90, *Acts*, pp. 62–65; Fitzmyer, AD 80–85, *Luke I–IX*, pp. 53–57; Maddox, AD 75–95, *Purpose*, pp. 7–9; Bruce, *c.* AD 80, *Acts* (NICNT), p. 12; Bovon, AD 80–90, *Lukas. 1, 1–9, 50*, p. 23; Polhill, AD 70–80, *Acts*, pp. 30–31.

[7] For early advocates of this position, see Harnack, *Date of Acts*, pp. 114–15; Hunkin, "Luke and Josephus," p. 94. Later advocates include the editors of *BC* 2, p. 359; with reservation, R. R. Williams, *Acts*, pp. 19–21, 64–65.

[8] E.g., Couchoud, AD 135–45, "Marcion's Gospel," pp. 265–77; Knox, AD 125, "Vocabulary," pp. 193–201; Knox, *Marcion*; Knox, "Pauline Letter Corpus," pp. 279–87; Enslin, AD 115–25, "Luke and Paul," pp. 81–91; Enslin, "Marcion," *IDB* 3, pp. 262–63; Enslin, "Once Again," pp. 253, 270–71; O'Neill, AD 115–30, *Theology of Acts*, pp. 21–22, 116–17, 138; Koester, AD 125–35, *Introduction*, vol. 2, p. 310; Townsend, AD 150, "Date," pp. 47–62; Mack, early second cen., *Lost Gospel*, p. 186; see also lit. cited in Fitzmyer, *Luke I–IX*, p. 57.

[9] E.g., in reply to Knox, who claims that a second-century compiler expurgated Marcion's corrupting influence upon some primitive Gospel (a kind of Proto-Luke) and refashioned it into canonical Luke; cf. Wilshire, "Canonical Luke," pp. 246–53 and the critical reviews cited on p. 246, n. 5. In reply to O'Neill, who argues that Acts was written *c.* AD 115–30 to defend the innocence of Christianity and to win converts, and was unknown to Justin Martyr, see esp. H. F. D. Sparks, *JTS* ns 14 (1963): 457–66; also C. K. Barrett, *LQHR* 31 (1962): 76–77; R. M. Wilson, *SJT* 15 (1962): 434–36; H. Conzelmann, *ThLZ* 96 (1971): 586–87; C. F. Evans, *JTS* ns 23 (1972): 203–10.

[10] See further Plummer, *Luke*, pp. xxx–xxxi; Harrison, "Resurrection," pp. 221–30; more extensively Hemer, *Hellenistic History*, pp. 159–220.

[11] For a comprehensive list of possible parallels, see Schreckenberg, "Flavius Josephus," pp. 179–209.

[12] E.g., Hunkin, "Luke and Josephus," pp. 89–108; Dibelius, *Studies*, pp. 186–87; Hemer, *Hellenistic History*, pp. 162–63; Polhill, *Acts*, pp. 171–73.

relation between Luke and Josephus is that they used a common source.[13] But even this is doubtful.[14]

Because of the insecure footing of positions (4) and (5), we can safely anchor the range of time to the period AD 62–90. The main chronological fixture on which the dating of Luke–Acts hinges is not Marcion's Gospel or Josephus' *Antiquities*, but the destruction of Jerusalem in AD 70.

Opinion is divided over whether Luke wrote with the destruction of Jerusalem in view. Those supporting a post-AD 70 date argue that Luke edited Mark's apocalyptic discourse *ex eventu* (Mark 13:1–2, 14–20; par. Luke 21:5–6, 20–24; non-Markan Lukan allusions may include 13:1–5[6–9], 35a; 19:41–44; 23:27–31). They suppose, e.g., that Luke describes in 21:20 (cf. Mark 13:14) a siege which has already taken place and for this reason specifies in Jesus' teaching that "desolation *will* come upon Jerusalem" (κυκλουμένην ὑπὸ στρατοπέδων Ἰερουσαλήμ). At 21:24, unique details are then supplied of the actual conflagration: the slaughter of many inhabitants, the captivity and transportation of prisoners to other nations, and the sack of the city by the Gentiles. Again in 19:42–44 (a non-Markan passage) Luke adds details to the passage in light of the events of the siege, the construction of earthworks, the slaughter of Jerusalem's inhabitants, and the city's fall. Furthermore, Alfred Plummer conjectures that in 21:20 Luke omits Mark's warning in 13:14, "let the reader understand" (ὁ ἀναγινώσκων νοείτω) because "these dangers were past," and no need for admonishment would be necessary;[15] others feel that Luke's omission of Mark 13:18, "Pray that this will not take place in winter," reflects historical understanding of the time of the actual siege.[16]

C. H. Dodd, however, is not convinced that Luke 19:42–44 and 21:20–24 necessarily reflect actual knowledge of Jerusalem's de-

---

[13] Ehrhardt, "Construction and Purpose," pp. 85–86.

[14] Cadbury, *Making*, p. 327 concludes that even if Luke knew of Josephus' works, he did not use them, for he would not have sensed the necessity to use such secondary works to verify his chronological allusions. Schreckenberg, "Flavius Josephus," p. 198 suggests that Luke possibly drew his material in Acts 5:36–37 from "a literary or oral source," but doubts whether Josephus used or knew of it. Moreover, Hemer, *Hellenistic History*, concludes: "The work of Luke is marked by carefulness but that of Josephus by carelessness" (p. 219, also pp. 94–99); where Luke is restrained with his data, Josephus is "prone to sensationalize and exaggerate" (p. 97).

[15] Plummer, *Luke*, p. xxxi.

[16] For a good summary defense of this position and more lit. on it, see Fitzmyer, *Luke I–IX*, pp. 53–62; Fitzmyer, *Luke X–XXIV*, pp. 1253–60, 1342–47.

struction in AD 70.[17] Although Dodd believes that Luke–Acts was written *c.* AD 90,[18] he thinks that "the more homogeneous form" of Luke 21:20–24 in contrast to "the somewhat disjointed arrangement" of Mark 13:14–20 may reflect older, pre-AD 70 and perhaps pre-Markan material.[19] Mark 13:14–20 and Luke 21:20–24 represent two different forms of the prophecy, with Luke copying Mark verbatim only twice – in v. 21a (Mark 13:14) and v. 23a (Mark 13:17). "There is here a special reason," Dodd summarizes, "for supposing that at least in xxi. 20–4 [Luke] is making use of older material: the Marcan language of 21a, 23a, stands out like a patch upon an otherwise homogeneous fabric, which must therefore have existed before our present Third Gospel was composed" (p. 79). The pre-canonical Lukan source was fashioned according to Hebrew poetic style and OT history, especially Nebuchadnezzar's razing of Jerusalem and the temple in 586 BC, and LXX language and thought forms. Dodd concludes: "There is no single trait of the [Lukan] forecast, which cannot be documented directly out of the OT" (p. 79).

G. H. P. Thompson also points out that (1) Luke may have clarified the meaning of Mark 13:14 for his readers' sake, (2) the predictions of Jerusalem's downfall may have come from Jesus himself, and (3) if Jerusalem had fallen, Luke would probably have mentioned it in the same way he parenthetically commented that the famine predicted by Agabus "happened during the reign of Claudius" in Acts 11:28.[20]

Acts indeed poses a conundrum for a post-AD 70 date. Instead of openly discussing the implications of the destruction for the church, Luke never mentions it. This seems odd. Reference to it would have suitably strengthened his emphases on the universality of the gospel (1:8), Stephen's negative assessment of the temple (7:44–50) and reiteration of Jesus' words concerning its destruction (6:14; cf. Mark 14:58), the Jerusalem Council and Judaizing problem (ch. 15, esp. vv. 1, 5), Paul's defense of Christianity before the Jews (chs. 22–23), Felix (ch. 24), Festus (25:1–22), and Agrippa (25:23–26:32), and his reaction in Rome to Judaism's general rejection of the gospel (28:17–28).

---

[17] Dodd, "Fall of Jerusalem," pp. 69–83; also Flückiger, "Zerstörung Jerusalems," pp. 385–80; Reicke, "Destruction of Jerusalem," pp. 121–23, 126–30. As precursors to Dodd, see Rackham, "Early Date," pp. 76–87; Torrey, *Composition and Date*, pp. 69–70; Martin, *Portrait of Jesus*, pp. 18–19.

[18] Dodd, *Apostolic Preaching*, p. 17.

[19] Dodd, "Fall of Jerusalem," p. 71.   [20] Thompson, *Luke*, p. 8.

Those who defend a pre-AD 70 date depend largely on arguments from silence. They assume that Luke's silence tacitly implies that the event has not yet taken place. Other factors as well allow for such a conclusion. E.g., while detailing the deaths of Stephen (7:54–8:1) and James (12:2), Luke records nothing of Peter and Paul's.[21] If, moreover, the Lukan and Pauline corpora overlap relatively little,[22] this may also indicate a date prior to the collection of Paul's writings, which would probably not have happened until sometime after his death. It is also possible that had Luke written after AD 70, he would have omitted reference to the Sadducees, who as a Jewish party at this time waned in political influence among the Jews and had little to do with the issue of Christian–Jewish relations.[23] Moreover, Luke records nothing of the Neronian persecution in AD 64, the Jewish revolt, and events leading up to Jerusalem's destruction in AD 70, or of the political instability surrounding the Roman emperorship in the late sixties and early seventies. In fact, Luke portrays the emperorship as a more normal, fixed office (see Acts 25:8–12, 21, 25; 26:32; 27:23–25; 28:19), nothing suggesting the tumultuous period beginning with the latter part of Nero's reign in AD 64–68, continuing through those of Galba (AD 68–69), Otho (AD 69), and Vitellius (AD 69) to the establishment and solidification of the Flavian dynasty under Vespasian in AD 69–79. The other possibility here is that Luke writes sometime after this period during the reigns of Vespasian or Titus (AD 79–81), but before the unstable reign of Domitian (AD 81–96).

A definitive first-century date for Luke–Acts, either before or after AD 70, is beyond reach with the limited historical data

---

[21] Some feel that Paul's martyrdom is presupposed in his farewell speech in Acts 20:18–35; e.g., Conzelmann, *Acts*, p. 228; Haenchen, *Acts*, pp. 731–32 *et al.* This evidence, however, is not conclusive; cf., e.g., Reicke, *Roots*, pp. 177–80; Hemer, *Hellenistic History*, pp. 406–408.

[22] But cf. Aejmelaeus, *Rezeption*, who argues that Luke had Paul's letters before him, including Eph., Col., 2 Thess., and the Pastorals, as he thinks is esp. evidenced in Paul's Miletus address (Acts 20:18–35). Although this is entirely possible, it is difficult to demonstrate conclusively a source relationship between them (even in the Miletus speech) as can be done with Mark and Q in Luke's Gospel. Aejmelaeus' own assessment that "dies war natürlicherweise nicht der *einzige* Abfassungszweck der Apg" (p. 72, his italic) ("this was naturally not the *only* writing purpose of Acts") may well account for this. For earlier lit. on Luke's dependency upon Paul's letters in Acts, see Fitzmyer, *Luke I–IX*, p. 49; more recently, Walker, "Pauline Corpus," pp. 3–23; Goulder, "Pauline Letters," pp. 97–112.

[23] Marshall, "Resurrection in Acts," pp. 97–98.

presently available. A strong case can be made for a pre-AD 70 date, though not an irrefutable one. More substantial material is needed to augment the existing evidence. If, however, the author of Luke–Acts did know Paul, this would help set time constraints on when he wrote. The sudden shift of address to the first person in Acts 16:10–17; 20:5–21:18; 27:1–28:16, and to a more intimate, detailed account in chs. 21–28 seems to imply some personal involvement at these points. The recipients of Luke–Acts may also have had some kind of contact with the apostle. If this is true, Cadbury believes that in dating the work "each year after 80 AD becomes increasingly improbable."[24] Thus the most probable date for Luke–Acts falls somewhere between AD 62 and 80, a period then within which Luke's writing occasion should be found.

Excursus: the "we-sections" of Acts

The most natural reading of the we-sections of Acts supports the supposition that the author was personally present on these occasions. The evidence for this is strong. A wide range of scholars have argued in some detail for it mainly on the merits of the text alone: e.g., from Germany, M. Schneckenburger, T. Zahn, A. Harnack, E. Meyer, A. Wikenhauser; from Britain, J. B. Lightfoot, R. B. Rackham, W. M. Ramsay, A. C. Headlam, J. M. Creed, A. N. Sherwin-White, C. H. Hemer, F. F. Bruce; from America, J. H. Ropes, A. D. Nock, H. J. Cadbury.

E.g., the Greco-Roman historian A. D. Nock stresses that outside Greek and Roman "literature which is palpably fictional," the "we" expression almost always signifies the author's participation in the events of the corresponding narrative.[25] The only possible exception to this, he notes, may be found in the fictitious *Life of Nikolaos of Sion*, where the occasional "we" is most likely the "we" of an eyewitness (p. 503, n. 2). For this reason he concludes that the we-sections of Acts "must be taken at their face value," meaning in this instance that Luke was a traveling companion of Paul (p. 503).

Furthermore, Cadbury argues that Luke's use of παρακολουθέω ("to investigate") in v. 3 of his Gospel preface necessarily implies that the author himself actively participated with Paul in the we-sections of Acts.[26] This is compelling. Ernst Haenchen's assertion

---

[24] Cadbury, *BC* 2, p. 358.
[25] Nock, *Gnomon* 25 (1953): 502–503.
[26] Cadbury, "Knowledge," pp. 401–20; Cadbury, "'We' and 'I' Passages," pp. 128–

that Luke 1:1–4 refers only to the Gospel and not Acts, and thus that the author cannot claim personal participation in the we-sections of Acts, [27] is inadequate, for while saying this he omits any consideration of the unity of Luke–Acts and the relation of the Gospel preface to the double work.[28]

Vernon K. Robbins' argument that the we-sections of Acts reflect a fictitious literary device patterned after the first-person plural of the so-called "genre of sea voyage narrative of Hellenistic literature" is unsustainable for a couple of reasons.[29] First, although he considers the we-sections and Gospel preface as important to Acts according to his reading of them, [30] he omits any reply to the earlier contrasting views of Nock, Cadbury, and Ropes on these very points.[31] And second, as Hemer and Barrett have pointed out, Robbins' so-called evidence from Hellenistic literature suggests nothing of the sort.[32]

Jürgen Wehnert's proposal that the we-sections represent a Jewish stylistic device whereby speaking in "the first person" gives the appearance of authority and authenticity to the account fails to account adequately for the "immediacy" of chs. 27–28.[33] As Hemer points out, the uncharacteristically high amount of *inconsequential detail* (for some examples, see p. 389) are *best* explained by the author's recent personal recollections of these experiences, whereas much of the rest of Acts is characterized by the author's "indirect-

---

32; also Ropes, "St. Luke's Preface," pp. 70–71; Hemer, *Hellenistic History*, pp. 327–28 but with caution.

[27] Haenchen, "Itinerar," pp. 362–66.

[28] See Fitzmyer's similar criticism of Haenchen in his review of Haenchen's *Acts* commentary in *TS* 33 (1972): 584. For a recent defense of the Gospel preface's relation to both volumes, see Riley, *Preface to Luke*, pp. 109–30. For more recent affirmation of the conclusions of Nock, Cadbury, and Ropes, see Fusco, "Sezioni-noi," pp. 73–86; Borse, "Wir-Stellen," pp. 63–92; Hemer, *Hellenistic History*, pp. 312–34; Thornton, *Zeuge*.

[29] Robbins, "We-Passages," pp. 5–18; and its revision, "By Land and by Sea," pp. 215–42, esp. pp. 216–17, 225, 229–30; also Plümacher, "Wirklichkeitserfahrung," pp. 2–22.

[30] Robbins, "By Land and by Sea," pp. 238–42.

[31] See also, e.g., Pervo, *Profit with Delight*, who contends that the author of Acts was grossly incompetent as a historian but brilliant as "a historical novelist" (pp. 3, 11, 138). But in doing so, he precariously assumes that the "we-sections" of Acts are fictitious, for he nowhere defends his position except to say in a footnote that it is "all but untenable" (p. 143, n. 3).

[32] See Hemer, "First Person Narrative," pp. 81–86; Hemer, *Hellenistic History*, pp. 317–19; Barrett, "Paul Shipwrecked," pp. 52–56. See also the detailed work of Smith, *Voyage and Shipwreck*, who traces firsthand Paul's voyage to Rome.

[33] Wehnert, *Wir-Passagen*; cf. Hemer, *Hellenistic History*, pp. 388–90, also p. 315, n. 20, and pp. 329–34.

ness" to the events, in that much of what he writes in the earlier sections of Acts was gleaned from sources or reminiscences of others.[34]

In summary, this means that for our study of Luke's christology we should also consider the ramifications of the author of Luke–Acts as Paul's traveling companion. We need to assess whether the christology of Luke–Acts allows for such a relationship and how his christology would be affected by such a relationship.

The nature of Luke's church

Luke wrote out of a concern for the church. But what was it like? He hints at its setting, and social and ethnic makeup, in several sub-themes traceable throughout his two-volume work. First, his pronounced interest in cities strongly suggests that his church was situated in an urban setting.[35] Second, his repeated references to the poor and warnings to the wealthy most likely delimit its social strata and no doubt shed some light on the kinds of problems they were facing.[36] Finally, concerning its ethnic makeup it seems wise to take Mary Moscato's position that Luke wrote for a mix of Jewish and Gentile believers rather than for primarily one or the other in view of his discernible interest in Jewish and Gentile Christianity.[37]

Stephen Wilson's belief that "the author of Luke–Acts also wrote the Pastoral Epistles"[38] indicates another possible angle from

---

[34] For more on this, see Rapske, *Paul in Roman Custody.*

[35] For a thoroughgoing treatment of the πόλις theme in Luke–Acts, see Conn, "Perspectives and the City," pp. 409–28; from only the Gospel, see Hultgren, "Interpreting," pp. 362–63.

[36] See, e.g., Johnson, *Literary Function*; Cassidy, *Jesus, Politics and Society*, pp. 20–49; Karris, "Poor and Rich," pp. 112–25; Beck, "Christian Character (II)," pp. 86–95; Nickelsburg, "Riches," pp. 324–44; Mealand, *Poverty and Expectation*, esp. pp. 103–104 for an annotated bib. on "Studies of the Lucan Attitude to Wealth"; Seccombe, *Possessions and the Poor*; Esler, "The Poor and the Rich," in *Community and Gospel*, pp. 164–200, esp. pp. 171–79, where he discusses the plight of the urban poor in antiquity; Dumais, "Évangélisation des pauvres," pp. 297–321; Schmidt, *Hostility to Wealth*, pp. 135–62; Green, "Jesus and the Poor," pp. 59–74; also lit. cited in Rese, "Lukas," p. 2324.

[37] Moscato, "Current Theories," p. 359; also Marshall, *Acts* (NTG), pp. 36–38. For recent studies on Luke as closely associated with Judaism, if not himself a Jew, and writing to predominantly Jewish readers, see Meierding, "Jews and Gentiles"; Sterling, *Historiography*, p. 330. For recent studies on Luke as a Gentile writing to predominantly Gentile readers, see esp. Fitzmyer, *Luke I–IX*, pp. 57–59; Stein, *Luke*, pp. 26–27; Riley, *Preface to Luke*, pp. 31–42.

[38] Wilson, *Pastoral Epistles*, p. 1; also Moule, "Problem of the Pastoral Epistles,"

which to discern the condition of Luke's church at the time of writing.[39] Although his view on the authorship of the Pastorals is debatable, it suggests that Luke–Acts shares some similarities in outlook with other later NT books – e.g., of the kind seen by Wilson between Luke–Acts and the Pastorals. J. L. Houlden remarks that "Luke–Acts and the Pastorals belong to the same milieu, both in the history of the early Christian Church and in the world of thought of their time."[40] Luke–Acts most likely generally arose within a similar kind of church situation.

The problems affecting later apostolic and sub-apostolic first-century Christianity and the way its church leaders sought to address them, according to the NT, move us closer to the nature of Luke's church around this same period of time. The problems ranged from persecution to apostasy and at times threatened the church's very lifelines.[41]

With the spread of Christianity and increased contact with pagan culture, the church encountered scattered and sometimes intense *opposition from unbelievers*. This often took the form of verbal abuse: believers were publicly maligned for their witness to Christ (2 Tim. 4:14–15; Heb. 10:32–33; Rev. 2:9) and for not participating in their former licentious lifestyle (1 Pet. 4:4). Other forms of oppression included confiscation of property (Heb. 10:34), suffering (2 Tim. 1:11–12), imprisonment (Eph. 3:1; 2 Tim. 2:8–9; Heb. 10:34), satanic opposition (1 Pet. 5:8–9), and even martyrdom (Rev. 6:9–11; 16:5–6; 17:6; 18:24; 19:1–2). John's Apocalypse records a time among the churches of Asia Minor when Roman (e.g., Rev. 12:3–13:1a; 13:1b–18; 17:3–18) and Jewish (e.g., Rev. 2:9; 3:9)

---

pp. 430–52; Moule, *Birth*, pp. 281–82; Harrison, *Introduction*, p. 342; Gilchrist, "Authorship and Date," pp. 265–68; Strobel, "Schreiben," pp. 191–210; de Lestapis, *Enigme des Pastorales*, pp. 129–30, 146–49; Feuillet, "Epîtres Pastorales," pp. 181–225; Quinn, "Last Volume," pp. 62–75; Quinn, *Titus*, p. 19.

[39] E.g., Kümmel, *Introduction*, p. 374 fully rejects Lukan authorship of the Pastorals "because of the large theological differences between the two groups of writing." Brox, "Verfasser," pp. 62–77 does so on philological, theological, historical, and exegetical grounds, though he is perhaps somewhat overly prejudiced against such a possibility. In a more sympathetic light, Fee, *1 and 2 Timothy, Titus*, labels this position "an attractive one" (p. xxxvii), but wonders "why Paul would have changed his compositional style at this point in his life" in allowing his amanuensis so much freedom to the point of becoming the writer (p. xl, n. 39). See also Guthrie, *Introduction*, pp. 621–22. But cf. Longenecker, "Ancient Amanuenses," pp. 281–97.

[40] Houlden, *Pastoral Epistles*, pp. 25–26.

[41] For more on some of the kinds of problems confronting the NT church, see *TAB*, pp. 699–710.

authorities intensely suppressed them for their unwillingness to participate in non-Christian practices.

The first-century church, which represented a wide cross-section of society and culture, also had to absorb and deal with many *sociological difficulties* inherited from its longstanding members and new converts. This phenomenon created sometimes severe relational complexities, and at times challenged its very unity. The relationship, e.g., between believers and non-believers in marriage (1 Pet. 3:1–6), slave and master (Eph. 6:5–9; 1 Pet. 2:18–21), and generally with secular authority (1 Pet. 2:13–15) needed special guidelines in rectifying certain abuses and clarifying Christian roles. Within the church, poverty (Rev. 2:9), conflicts of interest, and quarrelsomeness (Phil. 4:2; 2 Tim. 2:14) also demanded specific attention.

Furthermore, as Christianity developed, *a spiritual and religious malaise* grew alongside it, ever threatening its internal well-being. This problem took different guises. It appears, e.g., as a lack of spiritual growth stemming from spiritual ignorance (Heb. 5:2) or theological immaturity (Heb. 5:11–14) and as willful backsliding stemming from loss of spiritual fervency (Rev. 2:4–5; 3:2–3, 15–16) or lack of spiritual decisiveness (Rev. 2:14–15, 20) and discernment (Rev. 3:17). It also manifests itself in the neglect of doing right (Heb. 13:16), selfish ambition (Phil. 1:15–18; 1 Tim. 6:3–5, 10; 3 John 9–10), desertion (2 Tim. 1:15; 4:10, 16; Heb. 10:25), and apostasy (Heb. 3:12; 6:4–6). The main reason for this spiritual decline was the increase of heretical teaching within the church, introduced by false teachers (1 Tim. 1:6–7; 6:3–5; 2 Tim. 3:13; Titus 1:10–16; 2 Pet. 2:1–3, 10–22; Jude 4, 8–13, 16; Rev. 2:14–15, 20), antichrists (1 John 2:18; 4:3), and satanic opposition (1 Tim. 5:15).

A result of false teaching within the church was *the corruption of theology*. False teaching challenged the sound doctrine of faith (1 Tim. 6:20–21; 2 Tim. 4:3–4; 2 Pet. 2:1; 3:15–16). It threatened to replace it with forms of idolatry (1 John 5:21), ascetic tendencies (Col. 2:20–23; 1 Tim. 4:1–5, 8), useless arguments (1 Tim. 1:3–7), and doctrinal perversions. These perversions included the ideas that the resurrection of the dead had already occurred (2 Tim. 2:17–18), that circumcision was necessary for salvation (Phil. 3:2; Titus 1:10–11), and that Christ's incarnation was perhaps only imaginary (1 John 1:1–4; 4:1–3; 2 John 7).

These problems presented a formidable challenge to the late apostolic and sub-apostolic church. The perils of persecution, heresy, and disunity were daunting obstacles; they spurred on church leaders to inform and encourage their believing communities. The very existence of these canonical documents reveals one important way that this was done: church leaders *wrote* to preserve the doctrine, integrity, and unity of the church.

These writings underscore *the importance of instruction* for the first-century church: negatively in warning against false teaching (e.g., Col. 2:20–23; 1 Tim. 4:1–8; 6:20–21; 2 Tim. 2:14–26; 3:1–9; Titus 3:9–11; Heb. 6:4–12; 12:14–29; 13:9–14; 2 Pet. 2:1–3:18; 1 John 2:18–27; 3:7–10; 4:1–21; 2 John 7–11) and refuting its practitioners (e.g., Phil. 3:2–3; Col. 2:16–19; 1 Tim. 1:3–4, 6–11, 20; 6:20b-21; 2 Tim. 2:17–18; Titus 1:10–16; Jude 3–24; Rev. 2:2, 6, 9, 14–15, 20–25; 3:9), and positively in trying to relate theology to life. E.g., they exhort believers to emulate Christ (1 John 2:6, 28), become mature in Christ (Phil. 3:17; Heb. 6:1–3), be holy (1 Pet. 1:13–16, 22), imitate the lives of faithful believers (Heb. 6:11–12; 13:7), do good (Titus 3:14), support each other in Christian love (1 Tim. 1:5; 2 Tim. 2:24–26; Heb. 3:13; 13:1, 3; 1 Pet. 4:8; 1 John 3:11; 4:7, 21; Jude 20–23), live in harmony (Eph. 4:1–3; Heb. 12:14; 1 Pet. 2:11–12, 17; 3:8–9), teach sound doctrine (Titus 2:1), and persevere against evil (1 Tim. 4:14–16; Heb. 10:19–25, 32–39; 11:1–12:13; 1 Pet. 5:8–9; 1 John 2:28; 3:7; 4:1–3; 2 John 7–11; Jude 17–25).

Likewise, they prayed for each other (Eph. 3:14–21; Phil. 1:3–6, 9–11; Col. 1:9–12; 4:12; 1 Tim. 2:1, 8; Heb. 13:18–19) and created ministry positions to meet specific needs (1 Tim. 5:9–10). They at times viewed persecution as God's will (Phil. 1:29–30; 2 Tim. 3:12; 1 Pet. 4:12–16, 19), as divine discipline producing holiness (Heb. 12:7–11), and as the proving ground of genuine faith (1 Pet. 1:6–7). They understood Christ as their model in suffering (Col. 1:24; 1 Pet. 2:19–23). Believers were to consider suffering a blessing for doing right (1 Pet. 3:14–17), and not to be ashamed of living godly lives in the face of it (Eph. 3:13; 2 Tim. 1:7–8).[42]

These NT concerns of particularly later first-century Christianity point to a relatively new development within the early church: *the phenomenon of second-generation Christianity*. This phenomenon does not refer to a literal church membership made up of mostly second-generation Christians; rather it defines the perennial kind of situation facing most any established church, whether it primarily consisted of first-generation Christians or otherwise.

---

[42] For more on some of the corrective measures taken by the NT church, see *TAB*, pp. 710–18.

By the late apostolic and sub-apostolic periods, for more and more church situations, Christianity was no longer new. Christians were more liable to lapse into complacency and compromise. Added to this was the demise of the apostles and eyewitnesses, a problem which threatened to isolate the church from Jesus and Pentecost. These problems required church leaders to address theologically the changing situation. The importance of apostolic teaching then becomes paramount for clarifying doctrine, church organization, and Christian self-understanding.

One factor becomes increasingly important to an established church, whose members had probably never known the earthly Jesus: the need for its leaders to teach them how Jesus lived and, accordingly, for them to model their daily lives after his life. E.g., 1 John 2:5b–6 exhorts such a group of believers: "This is how we know we are in him [Christ]: whoever claims to live in him must walk as Jesus did." Believers were to conform to the servant-like attitudes and behavior characterizing Jesus' life, i.e., his obedience and submission to God's will, selfless love of others, and so on.

The *Sitz im Leben* of Luke's church most likely resembles this broader picture. Franz Prast plausibly argues at some length that the phenomenon of second-generation Christianity characterized Luke's church according to the kind of authorial motive underlying the inclusion of Paul's Miletus speech in Acts 20:17–38.[43] This probable condition of Luke's church partly then provides us with the context for and perhaps a clue to uncovering his specific reasons for writing.

The literary occasion of Luke–Acts

Certain problems, issues or circumstances most assuredly prompted Luke to write. The difficulty is that he does not clearly define for us what they were. We must therefore discern a most probable literary occasion according to the kind of emphases he records in the text.

---

[43] Prast, *Presbyter und Evangelium*, pp. 165–76, 345–52. He rightly insists, moreover, that this literary occasion does not imply an early catholicism on Luke's part (p. 173, n. 49, pp. 206–11), for Luke (*contra* Käsemann, "Paul and Early Catholicism," pp. 236–51 *et al.*), with the other NT authors, is not institutionalizing Christianity. See also, e.g., Conzelmann, *Theology of St. Luke*, p. 145, n. 5, p. 195, n. 1; Elliott, "Early Catholicism," pp. 220–30; Dumais, "Ministères," pp. 424–29; Maddox, *Purpose*, pp. 185–86; Giles, "Early Protestantism (1–2)," pp. 193–205, 3–20; Morris, "Early Catholicism," pp. 4–16; Barrett, *Church, Ministry and Sacraments*, pp. 77–101.

Some preliminary points on definition, however, need clarification before we begin. First, by literary occasion I mean a fitting written response to a specific situation demanding attention.[44] Within Luke–Acts, many often understand it as *a negative response* to a situation affecting the church stemming from some moral perversion, heretical teaching, or form of misrepresentation. But a fuller description should also include (1) the idea of *need* or *deficiency* where Luke supplements the reader's present Christian understanding of things[45] and (2) the idea of *reminding* where Luke reemphasizes certain kinds of Christian teaching already familiar to the readers in order to encourage them to persevere in their Christian walk. Second, Luke probably wrote under ordinary circumstances rather than in a crisis situation. He does not show a controlling desire to correct "a violent or pronounced bias" of his readers.[46] Finally, in our attempt to discern motive we must keep in mind Luke's "multiplicity of interests." "To discover the exact interests and uses of the material now in our gospels," Cadbury warns, "is a difficult and sometimes dangerous task. Those who have sought a single clue have mostly gone wrong. Above all things the multiplicity of interests must be emphasized."[47] This prevents the tendency to marshall all the material under one banner and so skew other valid Lukan emphases.

As we have argued, the phenomenon of second-generation Christianity in all probability characterized Luke's church when he wrote. The readers apparently knew the content of apostolic teaching and preaching well. Their knowledge most likely paralleled the Ephesian elders' in Acts 20. In Paul's farewell address, he summarily says to the Ephesian elders that he preached to them "the kingdom" (v. 25), "the whole will of God" (v. 27), and "the word of God's grace" (v. 32), which includes the highly unusual expression that God vicariously shed his own blood, i.e., through his son, for the church (v. 28). These expressions all variously describe "the gospel."

Clearly Paul has given the Ephesians much more information than what Luke recounts here. E.g., Paul's reference to the vicarious nature of Jesus' death and the language he uses to describe it

[44] See further Bitzer, "Rhetorical Situation," pp. 1–14.
[45] Luke exemplifies this sort of thing in Priscilla and Aquila's instruction of Apollos in Acts 18:24–26. For a similar definition, see Marshall, "Gospel," pp. 306, 308.
[46] Cadbury, *Making*, p. 299.
[47] Cadbury, *Making*, pp. 38–39.

graphically illustrate this. Luke–Acts nowhere develops this information, including the Acts passages which detail Paul's ministry to
the Ephesians (cf. 19:1–20:1, 16–38). Paul in the Miletus speech
assumes that his listeners were already well versed in these important theological, soteriological and christological matters.

Luke, therefore, assumes the same for his readers. He seems not
to fear that they would fail to know what Paul meant by these
summary statements. Surely they knew more Christian teaching
than what Luke–Acts records, or else the meaning of the expression
"God bought the church with his own blood" would be danger-
ously confusing – as it would nearly suggest a patripassianistic
point of view – on the basis of the contents of Luke–Acts alone.
Luke's readers were in all probability able to unpack this compressed theological statement in Acts 20:28.[48] On the basis of these
textual grounds, it is therefore arguable that Jesus' death as
vicarious represented not only Paul and Luke's thinking,[49] but the
thinking of Luke's readers as well.

Moreover, these undefined Pauline summary statements[50] may
well indicate that the readers understood their implied meaning in
part from firsthand contact with Paul. In view of Luke's probable
companionship with Paul, perhaps Paul founded the church to
which Luke writes or at least he, or his testimony and teaching,
were well known to some of them. The evidence is inconclusive, but
the possibility that Luke's readership had some kind of personal
contact or association with Paul is most probable.

For this reason, Maddox's assertion that Paul "is more important for what he represents [to Luke] than for his own sake" needs
some clarification.[51] It is true that it is doubtful whether Luke
wrote to benefit Paul personally (e.g., to defend Paul before Roman
or Jewish authorities). Luke may well have written sometime after
Paul's death. Nevertheless, it should not be left unstated that a
primary reason Paul so suitably appears as Luke's "hero" in Acts is
that Luke and his readers were in all probability personally
acquainted with him. This personal link is important. It makes Paul
a flesh and blood example of the kind of teaching Luke sought to

---

[48] So Roloff, *Apg.*, p. 306.
[49] Marshall, *Acts*, p. 334.
[50] Johnson, *Acts*, p. 367 summarizes concerning the Miletus speech: "It is important
to recognize that Luke accurately represents not only a number of distinctively
Pauline themes, but does so in language which is specifically and verifiably
Paul's."
[51] Maddox, *Purpose*, p. 70.

convey in writing to his readers. A role model who was well known to the readers would greatly enhance the persuasiveness of some of the leading literary aims in Luke–Acts. Paul more likely than not was such a model.

The circumstances which prompted Luke to write may well be closely tied to fears among his readers over the imminent threat of Paul's death or from its recent occurrence. Luke–Acts is perhaps a written summons to the readers to persevere in the faith, somewhat akin to Paul's charge to the Ephesian elders in Acts 20:29–31. Van Unnik's proposal that Heb. 2:1–3 closely parallels the literary occasion and aim of Luke–Acts – to secure firmly in Christian teaching the wavering faith of a group of believers[52] – is intriguing, but it is doubtful whether it reflects the spiritual condition of Luke's audience. The intended audience of Hebrews is apparently already adrift. But warnings associated with this kind of spiritual condition do not govern the content of Luke–Acts as they do Hebrews (cf., e.g., Heb. 5:11–6:8; 10:26–31).

A more accurate NT parallel, which may also have links to the historical circumstances surrounding Luke–Acts, is Paul's letter to the church at Philippi. In the letter Paul exhorts the readers to remain diligent in the faith despite whatever kinds of difficulties they may have to face. In developing this writing aim, he summons them to conform to the attitude of the Lord Jesus Christ as the ultimate model for Christian living (Phil. 2:5–11). The christology of Philippians is expressly directed toward this end. The letter contains no mention of the vicarious nature of Jesus' death; this soteriological factor is merely assumed. Rather the submissive and obedient attitude with which Jesus freely approached his humiliation and exaltation is supremely exemplary to the believer. As such it should characterize every believer.

Luke–Acts bears a remarkable likeness to this Pauline writing concern in its silence on the atoning significance of Jesus' death and its emphasis on the exemplary aspects of Jesus' life for the believer. In fact, Luke probably intentionally avoids much reference to the atoning nature of Jesus' death so as not to confuse believers in how they are to conform to Jesus' life. In the Gospel, Luke carefully documents how Jesus appeared as God's humble but divine servant-king, who faithfully carried out his divinely appointed mission consummating in his suffering, death and resurrection. The

---

[52] Van Unnik, "Confirmation," pp. 47–48, 59.

Gospel's opening chapters establish Jesus' divine nature (1:5–4:13); the Nazareth story, which Luke uses to inaugurate Jesus' public ministry on account of its thematic importance to him (4:16–30), establishes what Jesus' demeanor as the messiah would be, i.e., one of humble service. The lengthy travel narrative (9:51–19:27) furnishes in its entirety Jesus' teaching on discipleship. Acts, in turn, illustrates how the early church imaged Jesus in their own lives and ministries, especially as embodied in Paul's missionary career.

Conclusion

Much more, however, needs yet to be said in this regard to demonstrate the legitimacy of this proposal. We shall defend it in considerable detail in ch. 11. But it is necessary that we precede this discussion with two others which, in their own right, reveal the character and purpose of Luke's christology, but also give the proper Lukan christological perspectives undergirding his portrayal of Jesus as the standard for Christian living. In chs. 4–7 we shall examine how Luke's interaction with Mark is revealing of Luke's christology; in chs. 8–10 we shall examine Luke's thoroughgoing conviction concerning Jesus' supreme Lordship. It is then against the backdrop of this understood divine christology between Luke and his readers that we can properly assess christologically Luke's desire to portray Jesus as servant.

PART 2

Luke's christology and Mark's Gospel

4

MARK'S GOSPEL – A WINDOW TO LUKE'S CHRISTOLOGY

Introduction

This task now before us is to assess what we can learn about Luke's christology from his interaction with the synoptic tradition – in particular, the Gospel of Mark. Ernest Best remarks: "The questions relating to purpose, date, authorship, occasion in respect of any New Testament books are interconnected and a decision on one affects the decisions on others."[1] This is surely true in the case of the Synoptic Gospels, Mark and Luke.

Markan priority

Redaktionsgeschichte has been especially useful in isolating a couple of possible sources for Luke's Gospel: the Gospel of Mark and a collection of sayings material (the so-called Q). It becomes immediately evident, however, when comparing Q with Mark that Luke relied, possibly quite heavily, upon Mark for the content and format of his Gospel (and also, perhaps, for some of the content and format of Acts, as we shall observe in ch. 7).[2] Although the Markan material comprises only about one-third of Luke's Gospel, it nonetheless seems to have influenced considerably the way Luke composed, selected, and edited the material of the other sections.[3]

---

[1] Best, "Purpose," p. 19.
[2] Cadbury, *Making*, pp. 159–60 comments that Luke's handling of Mark models a principle of classical style, where single sources are usually followed consecutively, and when it is necessary to abandon one, another is followed in the same way; see further Aune, *Literary Environment*, p. 139; Downing, "Compositional Conventions," p. 71 and lit. cited on p. 71, n. 8. For Luke's preference in following Mark rather than Q in composing his Gospel, see Marshall, "Gospel," p. 293.
[3] See further Fitzmyer, "Priority of Mark," pp. 131–70; also Wood, "Priority of

Siegfried Schulz even goes as far as to say that the "central significance" of Mark "lies in the fact that he was the first and the only one to write a Gospel."[4] "There is no other theologian or author in the New Testament except Luke," Schulz adds, "who has even remotely taken up and perfected the impulses which led to Mark's gospel" (p. 166). Although he overstates the case a bit, he does underscore the probable importance of Mark's Gospel for Luke.

Luke's Gospel preface may also imply that Luke writes to "upgrade" Mark.[5] Something more was needed – to say this, however, in no way lessens the value of Mark's Gospel for his readers or its integrity and reliability as a traditional witness to Jesus' life and the beliefs of the early church.[6] V. 3 may intimate what this was. Here Luke uses the terms ἀκριβῶς ("carefully"), πᾶσιν ("everything"), ἄνωθεν ("from the beginning"), and καθεξῆς ("orderly") to describe the meticulous, comprehensive and systematic treatment he has given his Gospel account.[7] These writing concerns may indicate a level of incompleteness within "the former writings" (1:1) – Mark included – and the need for clarification to communicate more meaningfully the Gospel tradition to his own readers according to his own writing objectives.

The "inadequacy" of Mark's Gospel

The problem of discerning authorial motive has troubled Markan studies as well. In a recent survey of Markan purpose, Ernest Best asserts: "We may indeed not be able to answer any of the questions relating to Mark's occasion and purpose, or at least not with any certainty."[8] This problem becomes even more complex if one believes that Mark's Gospel was written first, for the redactional vantage point we have with Matthew, Luke, and John is then lost with Mark. As Theodore Weeden contends, too often our con-

---

Mark," pp. 17–19; Stonehouse, *Origins*, pp. 48–77, esp. p. 73. Even Streeter, *Four Gospels*, p. 160 admits that, while Luke retains only about 53 percent of the actual words of Mark, for much of the other 47 percent "he substitutes similar matter from another source."

4   Schulz, "Mark's Significance," pp. 158–66 (quot. p. 158). For more on the possibility of Luke's personal contact with Mark, see Guthrie, *Introduction*, p. 102.
5   Maddox, *Purpose*, p. 176.
6   See further Gerhardsson, *Gospel Tradition*, pp. 29–30, 54.
7   Fitzmyer, *Luke I–IX*, pp. 289, 296–300.
8   Best, "Purpose," pp. 19–35, esp. p. 20. For a good lit. survey of Markan purpose, see Johnson, *Writings*, pp. 169–71.

scious and subconscious awareness of the other Gospels color, if not distort, our reading of Mark; he feels that we must attempt to read it as did its first-century recipients, that is "without preconceived knowledge of its contents and without the prejudicial knowledge of the other Gospels."[9]

Because of these hermeneutical quandaries in Markan research, Luke Johnson thinks that "in some ways, this shortest of the gospels is also the strangest and most difficult to grasp."[10] He feels that the slim attestation to Mark in patristic literature bears this out (p. 174).[11] So too Martin Hengel labels Mark "a disputed Gospel." "No Gospel," Hengel writes, "has occupied scholars so intensively over the last decade as that of Mark, and nowhere has the discussion been more heated than in connection with it."[12] He concludes that its controversial nature stems from a *coincidentia oppositorum*, which simultaneously sees Mark as a creative theological treatise and as a work faithful to history and tradition (pp. 39–41).

By this somewhat negative assessment of Mark's Gospel, I do not intend to disparage it or to malign scholarly work on it, but to point out that *for outsiders* some inherent complexities are associated with it, complexities which may involve Mark's christology as well.

Several leading Markan christological assumptions

A chief difficulty in interpreting Mark's Gospel is that the author presupposes some foundational theological teaching among his readers. He occasionally gives outsiders only glimpses of some of this. Best theorizes that Mark's readers were already well acquainted with the information he gives them about Jesus.[13] For our purposes, three important christological points receive only scant attention in Mark: (1) the significance of the resurrection, (2) Jesus'

---

[9] Weeden, "Heresy," p. 148.

[10] Johnson, *Writings*, p. 147. Regarding some of the difficulties encountered in determining Mark's theology, see Reploh, "Unbekannte Evangelium," pp. 108–10.

[11] See also Martin, *Evangelist & Theologian*, pp. 80–83; Hengel, "Gospel of Mark," p. 2. For a favorable assessment of Mark during this period, see Kealy, *Mark's Gospel*; of Papias' comments specifically, Rigg, "Papias," pp. 161–83; Mullins, "Papias," pp. 216–24; Kürzinger, *Papias*.

[12] Hengel, "Historical Problems," p. 31.

[13] Best, "Purpose," p. 29.

relation to the Spirit, and (3) the salvation-historical implications of Jesus' passion work.

The significance of the resurrection

The central focus of Mark's Gospel is Jesus' passion: It forms the Gospel's literary climax and becomes the matrix where the historical and theological dimensions of the Christ event are most significantly worked out. Albert Outler remarks: "The time brackets in Mark's Gospel are the Baptism and the Empty Tomb. In between, the Passion dominates the narrative, overshadowing the public ministry and the parables ... Each of the Gospels is cruciform in its own way, but Mark's has a special preoccupation with the Cross and its significations."[14]

Mark develops several themes concurrently in building up to the passion: Jesus' pronouncements, the disciples' ignorance, and Jewish hostility. He records seven pronouncements foreshadowing Jesus' death and resurrection – five by Jesus (8:31–32; 9:9; 9:31; 10:33–34; 14:25, 28) and two by Jewish ridicule of what Jesus had evidently said (14:58; 15:29). Immediately following Peter's confession of Jesus as the Christ (8:27–30), Mark begins, in vv. 31–32, to disclose his *theologia crucis*, i.e., that the Son of Man according to divine plan must suffer, die, and be raised to life again.

This juncture marks a programmatic shift in the Gospel. After Peter's confession, Mark increasingly heightens the idea that Jesus as the messiah must suffer. Jesus warns Peter, James, and John to keep the transfiguration experience quiet until after the resurrection (9:9), makes suffering a part of his teaching to his disciples in Galilee (9:31) and again on the way to Jerusalem (10:33–34), and intimates it with the metaphors of bread and wine at the passover meal (14:22–25). Mark also alludes to the resurrection in the cryptic statement "but after I have risen, I will go ahead of you into Galilee" (14:28). The accusation that "he would destroy the temple and rebuild it in three days" hurled at him by Jewish leaders at his trial (14:58) and bystanders at the cross (15:29) probably also stems, in stilted form, from Jesus' passion teaching.

Mark intensifies the passion theme further by juxtaposing Jesus' awareness of his approaching suffering with the disciples' inability to comprehend it. Only they were told of it; yet they remained in

---

[14] Outler, "Canon Criticism," p. 239.

complete ignorance of it. As a prelude to this, Mark shows in the first part of the Gospel the trouble the disciples had in coming to terms with the "person" of Jesus. After Jesus' calming of the storms (4:35–39; 6:45–51) and feeding of the multitudes (5,000 in 6:31–44; 4,000 in 8:1–21), the disciples still appear as lacking faith (4:40), terrified (4:40–41; 6:50), amazed (6:52), hardened of heart (6:52; 8:17–21), and, in general, struggling to understand just who Jesus is (esp. 8:17–21!).

Following Peter's confession (8:27–30), the focal point of Mark's ignorance motif essentially shifts from "who Jesus is" to "what he has come to do." Peter's rebuke of Jesus for his prediction of suffering (8:32), prompting Jesus to castigate him for attempting to thwart God's plan (v. 33), suitably demonstrates this. Mark records similar displays of ignorance toward Jesus' passion and resurrection by Peter, James, and John after the transfiguration (9:10) and later by the disciples generally (9:32). The disciples' obliviousness to Jesus' struggles in Gethsemane (14:32–42), their desertion at his arrest (14:50), and Peter's denial during his trial (14:53–72) also illustrate that they were not thinking along the same lines as Jesus. This contrast of perspective between Jesus and his disciples is a christological feature of Mark, stressing that only Jesus was a fitting sacrifice to God. Best remarks: "It is perfectly natural that if Mark wishes to explain the true meaning of the cross he should present the disciples as those who misunderstand."[15]

Mark sharpens his passion theme further by counterbalancing the disciples' ignorance with the antagonism of the Jewish religious leaders. As early as ch. 2, after Jesus heals the paralytic in Capernaum (vv. 1–12), they mutter accusations of blasphemy against Jesus on account of his claim to forgive sins (vv. 6–7), and as early as ch. 3, they plot to kill him for violating the sabbath (vv. 1–6, esp. v. 6; and later for cleansing the temple, 11:12–19, esp. v. 18). Throughout his public ministry they pepper him with questions over fasting (2:18–22), sabbath observance (2:23–28), rules of cleanliness and uncleanliness (7:1–23), marriage (12:18–27), divorce (10:2–12), authority (11:27–33), and political allegiance (12:13–17), and think that his power of exorcism comes from satan himself (3:22–30, esp. vv. 22, 30). Jesus, in turn, warns his disciples of the hypocritical (8:15), self-righteous (12:38–40) influence of the Phar-

---

[15] Best, "Role," p. 388.

isees, and predicts his own death at their hands (8:31–32; also 12:1–12). Chs. 14–15 bear these prophecies out.

Mark most visibly accents the passion theme in the way he tersely and somewhat surprisingly ends his Gospel with Jesus' resurrection in 16:1–8.[16] His vivid portrayal of the empty tomb and of the flight of the terrified women dramatically climaxes his passion build-up and encapsulates his christological statement announced in his Gospel preface and prefigured in the rest of the Gospel – that Jesus is the Christ, the Son of God (Mark 1:1).

Although Mark's shorter ending seems a fitting conclusion to his Gospel, his meager treatment of the actual resurrection event and its implications for believers seems lacking. It may be true that for the author Mark 14:28 and 16:7 implicitly refer to the events that had transpired between the risen Jesus and his followers prior to the ascension and that he "intended his readers to interpret these insertions in the light of the tradition of the church."[17] This still, however, leaves much christological information, important to the Christian message, left unsaid.

Similarly, Mark leaves Jesus' comment about the resurrection in 9:9–10 hanging in apparent ambiguity. In v. 9, Jesus instructs Peter, James, and John not to speak to others about the transfiguration episode until after he has risen from the dead. But from the time of Jesus' trial before Pilate onward (15:1–16:8), the disciples do not appear again in Mark's account. V. 10, moreover, mentions that the disciples were not even sure what he meant by saying that "he would rise from the dead." How and when did they in fact pass from ignorance to illumination? And more generally, what is the significance of the resurrection – a doctrine so central to the Christian faith – for the church and the world? The reader is never told.

Jesus' relation to the Spirit

Mark begins his Gospel with John the Baptist, the forerunner of the messiah, preparing the way for "the Christ." In 1:8, John contrasts "the Coming One" with himself: whereas his baptism of

---

[16] Markan scholars have generally accepted 16:8 as Mark's intended ending. See further our discussion in the first section of chapter 6. But for a recent position still favoring the longer ending and lit. on the issue in general, see Farmer, *Last Twelve Verses.*

[17] So Stein, "Short Note," pp. 449–50.

repentance was with water, the messiah's will be with the Holy Spirit. Though this comparison avows the superiority of Jesus over John, and perhaps over prophets in general, and provides another foil for Mark's portrait of Jesus, it also strangely introduces a fundamental work of Jesus to which the writer never explicitly returns.

Mark in fact says very little about the Spirit in the Gospel.[18] Concerning the Spirit's work, he records that at Jesus' baptism the Spirit descended upon him in the form of a dove (1:10), led him into the wilderness to be tempted by satan (1:12), and, according to Jesus, inspired David's speech (12:36); furthermore, in teaching, Jesus warns against blaspheming the Spirit (3:29), and promises the Spirit's presence in witness (13:11). But Mark *nowhere* clearly details Jesus' relation to the Spirit and its christological (and pneumatological) significance for the church.

A reading of just Mark's Gospel leaves a number of important questions unanswered. Was Mark simply assuming that his readers were familiar with the events at Pentecost and that they would naturally understand the meaning of Mark 1:8 in light of it? Or is John's promise understood as fulfilled in some other sense in Mark? Furthermore, what is Jesus' relation to the Spirit? Why does he baptize with the Spirit? When will people be baptized with the Spirit? To whom does this happen? And what does this mean for them (and for us)?

Salvation-historical implications of Jesus' passion work

The concepts of salvation and proclamation and how they fit into redemptive history also play relatively minor roles in Mark's Gospel. Mark gives them little explicit treatment. He essentially expresses salvific language in two ways. First, it appears in human response to Jesus' person and work: prefigured in the preaching of John the Baptist (1:4–5), the miracles of Jesus (1:40–45, esp. v. 41; 2:1–12, esp. v. 5; 5:22–24, 35–43, esp. v. 36; 5:25–34, esp. v. 34; 7:24–30, esp. vv. 26–29; 7:31–37, esp. v. 32; 8:22–26, esp. v. 22; 9:14–29, esp. vv. 22–24; 10:46–52, esp. v. 52), Peter's confession of Jesus as the Christ (8:27–30), the answer of the teacher of the Law

---

[18] Similarly, he writes little about baptism. As a literal act it refers to the work of John to the people of Judea (Mark 1:4–5) and Jesus (1:9) and thus describes his message of repentance (1:4; 11:30); figuratively, it depicts Jesus' suffering and death (10:38–39).

Jesus as the Christ (8:27–30), the answer of the teacher of the Law (12:28–34, esp. v. 34), and the woman's anointing of Jesus (14:1–9).

Second, it forms part of Jesus' teaching (2:17; 4:3–9, 13–20, esp. vv. 8,20; 8:34–38; 9:23; 9:42–50; 10:14–15, esp. v. 15; 10:17–31; 11:22–26). Of these, the better examples include the healing of the paralytic (2:5), the bleeding woman (5:34), the boy with an evil spirit (9:22–24), blind Bartimaeus (10:52), Peter's confession (8:27–29), Jesus' mission to call sinners to repentance (2:17), the good seed in the parable of the sower (3:8, 20), and the faith of little children and entrance into the kingdom of God (10:15).

On the other hand, it notably does not appear in a number of Jesus' miracles (1:21–28; 1:29–31; 1:32–34; 3:1–6; 3:10–11; 5:1–20; 6:30–44; 6:56; 8:1–10). Mark seems more concerned in these instances to draw special attention to Jesus' nature and power than to make any overt connection between Jesus and the recipient on the matter of faith. Also, as we have already seen, neither Jesus' disciples nor the Jewish leaders provide positive examples of faith. Nor do Jesus' family (3:20–21), the people of his hometown (6:1–6), Herod (8:15), or Roman officials in general (10:33–34).

Mark's Gospel lacks clear, thoroughgoing exposition on the nature of salvation, its fulfillment in Christ, and its salvation-historical implications for Israel, the church, and the world. The proclamation of the gospel, the corollary to salvation, is even more problematic in Mark. It is discernible in John's preaching about the messiah (1:2–8), Jesus' itinerant preaching ministry (1:14–15; 1:38–39; 2:1–2; 2:17), the sending out of the twelve disciples (3:13–19; 6:6–13, 30), and the general spreading of news about Jesus because of his miraculous works (1:28; 1:45; 5:19–20). Mark's messianic secret motif perhaps also implies it in that a fully adequate proclamation of Christ necessitates the message of his death, burial, and resurrection.[19] This is possibly the reason Jesus commands Peter, James, and John to keep silent about his transfiguration until after the resurrection (9:9). But the problem with this latter passage is that Mark never does anything more with it! What exactly are they to proclaim?

Mark's reticence to do more with the proclamation theme is seen in other instances as well. In 1:17 Jesus says that he will make Peter and Andrew "fishers of men." We, however, last see them in the Gospel as having abandoned Jesus! What did Jesus specifically

[19] For a survey of the messianic secret motif from Wrede to the present, see Kingsbury, *Christology*, pp. 1–23.

mean by this? How and when did this come about? In 10:45 Jesus speaks of himself as "a ransom for many." Though the vicarious nature of Jesus' death certainly represents Mark's belief, he never illustrates its transforming effects in the lives of Jesus' followers. In 13:9 Jesus predicts that his followers will bear witness to him before religious and political authorities. When would this take place? Who would do it? And how would it be done? Finally, in 13:10 Mark records that the gospel must be preached to all nations, and in 14:9 that wherever the gospel is preached throughout the world, Jesus' anointing by the woman will also be told. What exactly is the gospel message that would be preached? How and when would the gospel move outside Palestine? And what is meant by "the nations/ world," Diaspora Judaism or Gentiles as well? Moreover, what becomes of the Jewish people? We last see the Jewish leaders in Mark shaking their fists at the crucified Jesus, so to speak, heaping abuse upon him (15:31–32). Do they and the Jewish people in time respond favorably to the resurrected Jesus? Or has God abandoned them because of their hardness of heart? And how do the nations fit into this almost entirely Jewish matrix of promise and fulfillment?

The paradox between Mark's allusions to the proclamation theme and his striking silence regarding its actual implementation after the resurrection and how it effects God's plan of saving history again leaves much unsaid.

Excursus: other fragmentary christological themes in Mark

We have only dealt here with the major fragmentary Markan christological themes. But there are several others as well.

1. *Deficiency of teaching.* A number of scholars have rightly noted that Mark makes a concerted effort to present Jesus as teacher.[20] Mark devotes about 30 percent of his Gospel to Jesus' teaching and often presents him as teacher, without mentioning the substance of his teaching. E.g., he depicts Jesus as teaching regularly in synagogues (1:21–22, 27; 6:2), by the lake (2:13; 4:1; 6:34), and in the Jerusalem temple courts (11:17–18; 12:35, 38; 14:49, "everyday'"); 10:1 records that Jesus customarily taught the crowds. In fact, the synagogue (3:1), lake (3:7; 4:35–41; 5:21; 6:45, 47–52), house (3:20,

---

[20] E.g., Schweizer, "Anmerkungen," pp. 37–38; Meye, *Jesus and the Twelve*, pp. 30–87; Martin, *Evangelist & Theologian*, pp. 111–17; Graudin, "Jesus as Teacher," pp. 32–35; Achtemeier, "Reflections," pp. 465–81; France, "Teaching of Jesus," pp. 101–36; Robbins, *Jesus the Teacher*.

31–35; 5:21–24, 35–43; 7:24–30; 9:28), and mountainside (3:13–15; 9:2–10) indicate in Mark places where Jesus instructs others, either publicly or privately, about himself and the things of God. Also, the disciples (4:38; 9:38; 10:35; 13:1), Jewish leaders (12:14, 19, 32), a father of a demon-afflicted son (9:17), and a rich man (10:17, 20) call Jesus διδάσκαλος; Jesus even uses it as a self-designation (14:14). Mark's presentation of Jesus as teacher and the substance of his teaching is christologically relevant to his Gospel. R. T. France points out that, for Mark, the fact that Jesus taught confirms his messianic role and the substance of his teaching gives dominical guidance to Mark's readers.[21]

Despite all of this, however, a lack of Jesus' actual teaching still persists (only about 212 verses altogether!). For this reason, Burton L. Mack believes that the other three Gospels reflect a conscious attempt on the part of the authors to expand the actual content of Jesus' teaching, which is strongly alluded to but slimly illustrated in Mark.[22] In stronger terms, Beda Rigaux thinks that Matthew and Luke intentionally improved on Mark's severe deficiency of not recording enough of Jesus' actual teaching.[23] Gerhardsson raises the possibility that Mark knew of a Q collection and respected it, but chose for whatever reason not to integrate it into his own Gospel.[24]

2. *Puzzling use of amazement language.* The idea of amazement regularly punctuates Mark's developing story-line (it occurs in all but two chapters), and more importantly may provide a hermeneutical key to unlocking Mark's sudden and somewhat enigmatic conclusion in 16:8. But Mark's reason for using it is still not all that clear. Even some in the first-century church may have had trouble understanding his Gospel because of the dubious meaning of this motif.[25]

3. *Lack of narrative order.* Mark omits in his Gospel the birth account and the early events of Jesus' life. His handling of the events of Jesus' ministry seems without chronological order as well. His career is portrayed more like a multi-media presentation, with episodes of Jesus' life phasing in and out and each progressively building toward the passion climax, than a consecutive biography.

---

[21] France, "Teaching of Jesus," pp. 101–36.
[22] Mack, *Myth of Innocence*, pp. 356–57.
[23] Rigaux, *Testimony of St. Mark*, p. 133.
[24] Gerhardsson, *Gospel Tradition*, pp. 54–55.
[25] But see Dwyer, *Motif of Wonder.*

Luke Johnson and others point out that even Papias, the second-century bishop of Hierapolis in Phrygia, sees it as necessary to defend Mark's lack of narrative order (as cited in Eusebius' *Eccl. Hist.* 3.39).[26]

Conclusion: Luke's revision of Mark as christologically revealing

We have discussed these fragmentary christological themes in Mark not to disparage it – Mark must be understood in light of the author's own motives[27] – but to evaluate the way Luke handles these important themes briefly treated in Mark. In ch. 3 we saw how Luke's church was in a transitional stage as it was losing contact with those who witnessed firsthand Jesus' life and ministry, and discussed the birth and growth of the early church. A much greater demand for written instruction was becoming necessary. Mark, on the other hand, was not primarily concerned to establish a continuity from Jesus' life through the early church to that of his own day. In this sense, there was room for such a work as Luke gives us. Therefore, in light of Markan priority and Luke's desire to add to the writings of his predecessors, the question arises: Does Luke reveal something of his christology in revising Mark according to his purposes in writing?

Our aim in the next three chapters will be to observe what Luke's revision of the fragmentary Markan christological themes on "Jesus and the Resurrection" (ch. 5), "Jesus and Spirit Baptism" (ch. 6), and "Jesus and Salvation History" (ch. 7) reveals to us about the purpose and character of his christology.

[26] Johnson, *Writings*, p. 147.

[27] Mark's motives are undoubtedly christological, as suggested in his Gospel preface (1:1). Hunter, *Introducing the NT*, p. 37 states that Mark's aim was "*to persuade* his readers in Rome that Jesus of Nazareth was the Christ, the Son of God" (my italics). And so Meye, *Jesus and the Twelve*, p. 30 comments: "The very first line of Mark's Gospel bids the reader to view every aspect of the Gospel from a christological perspective."

5

JESUS AND THE RESURRECTION

Introduction

The climax of Mark's Gospel, and of the Gospel tradition generally, is the suffering, death, and resurrection of Jesus the messiah. This means that, for Mark, the miracles of Jesus, all apocalyptic hopes, the messianic secret, the issue of discipleship, and the formation of the Gospel "would, by necessity, be misunderstood, if one were not aware of Jesus' road to the cross and even following him on the same road."[1] The passion appears as the key event in Mark to which all the other stories are expectantly drawn and, hence, inextricably bound.

But what is most interesting here is that none of the characters in Mark's Gospel, or even his readers, ever meet the resurrected Jesus. Reasons why Mark may have chosen to end his Gospel this way are not immediately clear to us from the canonical text as we know it. Some important questions affecting christology remain unanswered: When did the disciples meet the resurrected Jesus? How did Jesus appear to them? To whom did he appear? How did they know it was he? What did he say and do during this time? How did his followers respond? And what is the importance of the resurrection for the church and the world? Our aim in this chapter is to examine what Luke shows us of his christology in the way he interacts with Mark's presentation of Jesus' resurrection.

Mark's Gospel: Jesus' resurrection assumed

Mark leaves several significant statements unresolved in his account concerning Jesus' resurrection. They are Mark 16:1–8; 14:28/16:7; 9:9–10. These texts are problematic for us since we cannot simply fill in the unwritten details, although in all prob-

---

[1] Schweizer, "Christology of Mark," p. 39.

ability Mark's readers could and thus his presentation would have posed no real problems for them.

The textual problem

Mark's unexpected conclusion in 16:8[2] has raised unending comment among Markan scholars.[3] Did Mark originally end or intend to end his work with the abrupt ἐφοβοῦντο γάρ clause in 16:8? Or did he finish it with a longer ending, which has for whatever reason disappeared? C. E. B. Cranfield lists four possible solutions to the problem: (1) the Gospel was never finished, (2) the conclusion was lost or destroyed by some mischance, (3) the conclusion was deliberately suppressed, and (4) 16:8 was intended as the ending.[4] Few scholars support positions (1)[5] and (3).[6] Recent consensus favors position (4),[7] but the second position still has its advocates.[8]

[2] The longer versions of Mark's conclusion as contained in our versions of the Greek NT are nearly universally rejected by textual critics as not original to Mark; but in defense of 16:9–20 as authentic to Mark, see Farmer, *Last Twelve Verses*; Lubsczyk, "Kurios Jesus," pp. 133–74. At best, some Markan scholars see parts of these appended verses as contained in or suggestive of an unknown longer ending original to Mark's Gospel. See further pp. 93–94.

[3] See, e.g., Hurtado, "Recent Study," pp. 49–50 for a recent survey of the discussion, as well as earlier ones mentioned ibid., p. 50, n. 1; see also the massive lit. pertaining to the subject in Pesch, *Markus. 1, 1–8, 26*, p. 47.

[4] Cranfield, *Mark*, p. 470.

[5] But see Cranfield, *Mark*, p. 471; see also the earlier arguments of Zahn, *Introduction*, vol. 2, pp. 479–80; Rawlinson, *Mark*, p. 270. Another version of the theory is that Mark either intended to write a companion volume, similar to what Luke did in Acts, or actually did so, with Luke using it as a source for the early chs. of Acts; 16:8 would not therefore end Mark's work, but link the Gospel to his second volume. For advocates of this theory, see Guthrie, *Introduction*, pp. 78, 371.

[6] But see Graß, *Ostergeschehen und Osterberichte*, pp. 16–19; Trompf, "First Resurrection Appearance," pp. 325–26; see also lit. cited in Martin, *Foundations*, vol. 1, p. 219, n. 170; Schweizer, "Christology of Mark," p. 33, n. 27 also allows for the possibility.

[7] E.g., Moule, "St. Mark XVI.8 Once More," pp. 58–59; Weeden, *Traditions in Conflict*, pp. 45–50, 101–37; van der Horst, "Can a Book End with *GAR*?," pp. 121–24; Synge, "Mark 16:1–8," pp. 71–73; Graham, "Mystery and Ambiguity," p. 44; Pesch, *Markus.1, 1–8, 26*, pp. 46–47; Lindemann, "Osterbotschaft," pp. 298–317; Boomershine, "Apostolic Commission," pp. 225–39; Boomershine and Bartholomew, "Narrative Technique," pp. 213–23; esp. Magness, *Sense and Absence*; Lincoln, "Promise and Failure," pp. 283–300; Stock, *Mark*, pp. 25–30, 426–32; Dwyer, *Motif of Wonder* (forthcoming); Danove, *End of Mark's Story*, esp. pp. 203–30; see also earlier lit. cited in Kümmel, *Introduction*, p. 100, n. 72; Martin, *Foundations*, vol. 1, p. 219, n. 172. For a concise summary of the reasons why scholars believe 16:8 to be Mark's intended ending, see Osborne, *Resurrection Narratives*, pp. 55–58.

[8] E.g., Knox, "Ending," pp. 13–23; Taylor, *Mark*, pp. 609–10; Seidensticker, *Auferstehung Jesu*, pp. 85–86; Metzger, *Text of the NT*, pp. 226–28; Metzger,

Markan scholars are similarly divided on the meaning of Jesus' promise in 14:28: "but after I have risen, I will go ahead of you into Galilee." Does Mark imply Jesus' post-resurrection appearances here in token form so as not to lessen the dramatic impact of his Gospel conclusion? Or does he intimate a different thematic interest which along with 16:7 has no direct correlation to the resurrection appearances as such?[9] Scholars generally agree that it refers literally to Jesus' resurrection appearances.[10] A minority feel that it refers to the parousia,[11] the establishment of the kingdom of God,[12] a future eschatological encounter with the risen Christ,[13] a conversion experience,[14] a summons to follow Jesus' example, which leads from Galilee to the cross,[15] or to the Gentile mission.[16] The reason

Textual Commentary, p. 126, n. 7; Schweizer, Mark, pp. 366–67; Ladd, *Resurrection*, p. 83; Osborne, *Resurrection Narratives*, pp. 63–65.

[9] On the relevance of Galilee to the whole issue, see Stemberger, "Galilee," pp. 409–38.

[10] E.g., Best, *Temptation*, p. 176; Best, *Gospel as Story*, pp. 76–78; Schweizer, *Mark*, pp. 307–308, 365–66; Bode, *First Easter Morning*, pp. 37, 49; Kümmel, *Introduction*, p. 100; Pesch, *Markus. 8, 27–16, 20*, pp. 381–82, 534–35, 538–40; Stein, "Short Note," pp. 445–52; Lindemann, "Osterbotschaft," p. 313; Hooker, *Message of Mark*, p. 120; Osborne, *Resurrection Narratives*, p. 52; Pokorný, "Markus," p. 1986; Lincoln, "Promise and Failure," p. 295. Wilckens, *Resurrection*, pp. 33–34 explains the ending on the basis of a lack of information from the tradition handed down to him: like Paul in 1 Cor. 15:5, Mark only knew of the fact of the appearances, but not that Jesus had appeared to any of his disciples. Fuller, *Formation*, pp. 63–64, 67 believes that Mark wrote no more because he knew of no resurrection narrative that explained how Jesus' resurrection resolved the messianic secret (cf. Mark 9:9).

[11] E.g., Lohmeyer, *Galiläa und Jerusalem*, pp. 10–14; Michaelis, *Erscheinungen des Auferstandenen*, pp. 61–76; Bartsch, "*Wachet aber zu jeder Zeit!*," pp. 21–22; Hamilton, "Resurrection Tradition," pp. 415–21; Marxsen, *Mark the Evangelist*, pp. 83–92, 111–16; Marxsen, *Resurrection*, pp. 162–64; Weeden, *Traditions in Conflict*, pp. 111–16; Perrin, *Resurrection Narratives*, pp. 29–30, 33, 35–40.

[12] Weiss, *Primitive Christianity*, vol. 1, pp. 14–18 thinks that 14:28 voices a very old expectation of the disciples that following the resurrection Jesus would lead the disciples back to Galilee after joining them in Jerusalem, and there establish the kingdom of God; as it turned out, however, this was an unfulfilled fantasy, for Jesus never led them back to Galilee (p. 18). Nineham, *Mark*, p. 446 has some preference for this view as well. See also lit. cited in Marshall, "Resurrection in Luke," p. 57, n. 11.

[13] Léon-Dufour, *Resurrection*, pp. 136–37.

[14] Stock, *Mark*, pp. 29–30, 426–32.

[15] Miller and Miller, *Mark as Midrash*, pp. 380–81.

[16] E.g., Hoskyns, "Adversaria Exegetica," pp. 147–55; Boobyer, "Galilee and Galileans," pp. 334–48, esp. pp. 338, 348; Evans, "Galilee," pp. 3–18; Karnetzke "Galiläische Redaktion," pp. 249–57; Schreiber, *Theologie des Vertrauens*, pp. 178–79; Dschulnigg, *Sprache*, pp. 614–15. Or perhaps secondarily as the place from which the mission originated; so Fuller, *Resurrection Narratives*, p. 62; Osborne, *Resurrection Narratives*, p. 53. Rau, "Markus," pp. 2193–97 sees

for the ambivalence stems from Mark's terse handling of the resurrection event. This leaves the meaning of 16:7 unclear.

Mark's abbreviated treatment of the Easter experience also leaves Jesus' reference to the resurrection in 9:9–10 hanging in apparent ambiguity. It is surprising that Mark does not, for the benefit of his readers, devote at least one story to the resurrected Jesus appearing to Peter, James, and John in order to resolve their stated confusion about what Jesus meant when, after his transfiguration, he said to them that he would rise from the dead (cf. v. 10). After reading the Gospel, Mark leaves us wondering how and when they pass from ignorance to illumination. The reader simply never finds out. Ladd considers this a serious problem in Mark's Gospel as we know it.[17] Mark 9:9–10, he contends, suggests that the resurrection was "a watershed in the understanding of Jesus' person and mission" and because of this would need to be commented on in the Gospel conclusion; for this reason he believes the original ending to be lost (p. 84).

A Markan solution

After reaching its grand finale with the empty tomb, Mark's Gospel ironically never provides us with the kind of information we would most expect and perhaps would most want to have. How can we make sense of the problem without disparaging the Second Gospel? On the one hand, these textual problems do make credible the effort to put forward various theories such as a lost, suppressed, or unfinished ending. A conclusion resembling those of the other Synoptic Gospels would greatly diminish the tension caused by Mark's silence on Jesus' resurrection and post-resurrection appearances. For this reason, scholars have proposed a number of reconstructed endings, in part, from information contained in Matthew and Luke–Acts.[18]

Galilee as primarily signifying a mission extending to Diaspora Judaism; see also ibid., p. 2196, n. 392 for more lit. on the Gentile mission theory.

[17] Ladd, *Resurrection*, p. 83.

[18] E.g., Schweizer, *Mark*, p. 366 thinks that Mark's longer ending resembled Matt. 28:9–10, 16–20. Bartsch, "Schluss des Markus," pp. 241–54 believes that Mark was familiar with 1 Cor. 15:3–7 and would not have ended his Gospel with v. 8; the content and style of the supposed longer ending would have been similar to Matt. 28:2–5, 9–10. Farmer, *Last Twelve Verses*, esp. pp. 107–109, attempts to show that most of the longer ending (16:9–20) was the original ending, written by Mark sometime before he wrote the Gospel. Osborne, *Resurrection Narratives*, pp. 63–65 reconstructs a shorter ending on the basis of Matt. 28:9–10, as does

If, however, the ending were something different from the canonical text as we have it, one would expect to find more reliable manuscript evidence for it, or if incomplete, some comment about it in the Apostolic Fathers and patristic literature. If it were missing any earlier, the first-century church should have been able to reproduce it quite accurately from memory[19] (assuming that it was finished in the first place). But early church history offers no hint of any kind that the canonical ending was not the original one or the intended one.[20] The relative abundance of later manuscript evidence containing the longer endings may, in fact, suggest that the Gospel originally did end with 16:8 and that the later church was not satisfied with it and tried to amend it.[21] Matt. 28 and Luke 24 may be the earliest written attempts to do exactly that.

If this is true, we still need to show that Mark's peculiar handling of the resurrection would not have been particularly enigmatic to his readers. The solution is probably quite simple: the events surrounding Jesus' resurrection were well known to the readers. Robert Stein, e.g., does not think that Mark's minimal treatment of Jesus' post-resurrection appearances in 14:28 and 16:7 posed any special problem for his intended readers. Mark simply "intended his readers to interpret these insertions in the light of the tradition of the church."[22] To them it would have been the most natural interpretation (p. 450 and n. 5). Concerning the ending itself, Rudolf Pesch believes that on the basis of Mark's connection of the

Trompf, "First Resurrection Appearance," pp. 317–27 with the additional help of Markan ending-material implied in second-century Christian lit., esp. that of Ignatius and Justin. Haefner, "Bridge," pp. 67–71 speculates that Acts 1:13–14 smoothly links Mark 16:8 to Acts chs. 3–4 (the so-called Jerusalem A source) forming his complete ending, which Luke then used as a continuation of his Gospel. Still of interest is Moule's idea in "Mark XVI.8 Once More," pp. 58–59 of a brief unspoken but assumed ending of an exchange of greeting where the absence of it in narrative typifies an attitude of urgency, in this case for the women to report at once to the disciples what they had seen. For summaries of other reconstructed endings, see Bartsch, "Ursprüngliche Schluß der Leidensgeschichte," p. 412, n. 4.

19 So, e.g., Enslin, "Mark 16:8," p. 68.

20 So esp. Kümmel, *Introduction*, p. 100. For an extended discussion of the textual support of 16:8 as the original ending, see Aland, "Bemerkungen," pp. 157–80; Aland, "Schluß," pp. 437–41, 457.

21 For a discussion of the possible endings of Mark as shown from the known manuscripts, see Aland, "Schluß," pp. 436–48; Metzger, *Textual Commentary*, pp. 122–26.

22 Stein, "Short Note," p. 450. It was perhaps preserved and passed on in the Eucharist tradition; so variously Reicke, *Roots*, pp. 139–49, esp. pp. 147–48; Gerhardsson, *Gospel Tradition*, p. 55; also Dahl as cited in Schweizer, "Christology of Mark," p. 36 and n. 3.

women's fear to the substance of the angel's message, the readers would know how the Gospel story ended.[23]

If, in fact, Mark were writing to a church well acquainted with Peter's teaching, it is easy to imagine that they already knew many of the details of Jesus' post-resurrection appearances and how the disciples eventually understood the point of Jesus' teaching about the cross and resurrection.[24] The readers would have been able to fill in the gaps. In fact, prior knowledge of this is what would have made Mark's 16:8 ending most surprising and effective. The audience would have been expecting something more. Mark was undoubtedly well aware of how much his audience knew. Otherwise, his work would have seemed almost presumptuous and a reading of it potentially misleading to the believers he was presumably trying to encourage.

Mark possibly also intended his Gospel as a gospel tract of sorts to win unbelievers to Christ. But if this is the case, he expects even more of the reader, unless here again the Gospel supplemented or introduced other teaching and preaching on the matter.

To sum up, the textual evidence strongly supports that Mark intended the resurrection's jolting but brief treatment at the Gospel's end. But presumption of such knowledge perhaps limited the Gospel's potential usefulness to other church leaders. For this reason, it probably stimulated Matthew and Luke to write more about it in their Gospels.[25]

Luke–Acts: Jesus' resurrection demonstrated

In adapting Mark's Gospel to his own literary intentions, the task now before us is to determine to what extent Luke filled in some of the gaps and smoothed out some of the trouble spots in Mark's treatment of the resurrection and how this revision reveals his christology.

A preliminary comparison

From the standpoint of a synoptic comparison, Luke does not seem altogether satisfied with Mark's presentation of Jesus' resurrection – both in what Mark says and leaves unsaid in 9:9–10; 14:28/16:7;

---

[23] Pesch, *Markus. 1, 1–8, 26*, pp. 46–47.

[24] So, e.g., Campenhausen, "Events of Easter," p. 51, n. 41.

[25] As Weeden, *Traditions in Conflict*, pp. 102–103 briefly suggests.

16:1–8 – where Matthew seems less bothered by it. We shall see that whereas Luke consistently wants to modify the problematic parts of these Markan passages, if not to omit them altogether, Matthew seems less inclined to do so. We shall briefly look at each passage according to its sequential order in Mark.

Mark 9:9–10

In the transfiguration story Luke's conclusion differs considerably from Mark's account. Mark concludes the episode with Jesus' command in 9:9 that Peter, James, and John remain silent concerning all they had just seen on the mountain until after his resurrection, adding in v. 10 that they were puzzled about what Jesus meant in saying that he would rise from the dead. Luke, on the other hand, omits Jesus' command and reexpresses the disciples' silence as a statement of fact in 9:36b (αὐτοὶ ἐσίγησαν καὶ οὐδενὶ ἀπήγγειλαν). He drops Mark 9:10, as well as the story of the coming of Elijah in Mark 9:11–13.[26] Luke, however, does not completely drop the idea of the resurrection from the episode. It seems implicit in the adverbial expression "at that time/in those days" (ἐν ἐκείναις ταῖς ἡμέραις), which he attaches to the preceding statement of the disciples' silence. Joseph Fitzmyer thinks that this expression most likely refers to Jesus' earthly ministry.[27] The implication here, Howard Marshall believes, is that at some later point in time the three disciples did speak of the vision, at a time when "the significance of its meaning would become fully apparent."[28] As Heinz Schürmann observes, this most naturally refers to a time after the resurrection.[29]

In short, Luke smooths over the whole Markan section by using his rendering of Mark 9:9 to link the transfiguration story (Luke 9:28–36) to the episode of Jesus' healing of the boy with an evil spirit (9:37–43; Mark 9:14–29): the silence theme recaps the transfiguration and their descent from the mountain leads into the next story. Except for some mostly cosmetic changes, Luke only other-

---

[26] Perhaps Luke omits this story because of the possible confusion over the reference to Elijah. In Mark 9:4–5 (Luke 9:30–33; Matt. 17:3–4) Mark has the OT prophet in mind, but in vv. 11–13 he refers to John the Baptist (cf. Mal. 4:5–6), as Matthew seems compelled to make clear by his additional comment in 17:13.

[27] Fitzmyer, *Luke I–IX*, p. 804.

[28] Marshall, *Luke*, p. 389.

[29] Schürmann, *Lukas. 1, 1–9, 50*, p. 563.

wise expands Mark's account, esp. in 9:31–33a. Luke may have also decided to emphasize the disciples' ignorance of the resurrection in the more visible context of the third passion prediction, because there it involves all of the disciples rather than just Peter, James, and John.[30]

Matthew's handling of Mark 9:9–10 also shows an attempt to smooth out its awkward character. He retains Mark's rendering of Jesus' command in v. 9 almost in full (cf. Matt. 17:9), but like Luke he drops the comment about the disciples' ignorance in v. 10. Matthew retains Mark's subsequent story about Elijah (Matt. 17:10–12), but makes an effort to clarify the apparent Markan ambiguity in 17:13. But retaining reference to the resurrection does not pose a problem for Matthew as it does for Mark, since Matthew records a post-resurrection appearance of Jesus where he tells the disciples to make known all that he has commanded them (Matt. 28:18–20).

Mark 14:28/16:7

As we have already seen, these two brief allusions to Jesus appearing in Galilee following Easter morning are all that Mark gives us concerning a possible post-resurrection ministry. But for whatever reason, Luke does not retain them. He shows no parallel to Mark 14:28 in his version of Jesus' prediction of Peter's denial in Luke 22:31–34 and drops the prophetic thought of Mark 14:27–28 (that "all the disciples will fall away on account of him") from his Gospel. Nor does he follow Mark's order. After his account of Jesus' teaching on servanthood during the Last Supper in 22:24–30, he immediately follows with his version of Jesus' prediction of Peter's denial while still in the room where they had eaten the passover meal (as does John 13:36–38, which also lacks Jesus' saying in Mark 14:28).

Luke similarly lacks reference to Mark 16:7 in his resurrection account. He mentions Galilee only in 24:6 in recalling Jesus' Galilean passion predictions.[31] Otherwise he makes no further reference to it in Luke–Acts, except to identify his followers who

---

[30] Concerning how Mark 9:9 may fit positively into Mark's scheme of things, see Hooker, "Transfiguration," p. 59.

[31] Marshall, *Luke*, p. 886 further points out that the wording of Luke 24:7 is closely reminiscent of the Galilean predictions of Mark 8:31 (Luke 9:22) and 9:31 (Luke 9:44, though Luke significantly shortens Mark here), also Luke 24:20–21; ἀνθρώπων ἁμαρτωλῶν is perhaps a generalization that could include the Gentile

were from there (e.g., Luke 5:1–11; 23:49, 55; Acts 2:7). The resurrected Jesus does not appear to his disciples there, but in Jerusalem (Luke 24:33–49). Luke in all probability is not opposed to Mark's idea of a Galilean appearance,[32] but merely stresses for literary reasons parts of the tradition which concentrate on Jerusalem in preparation for its central – and perhaps symbolic – geographical location for the spread of the gospel in Acts.[33] As importantly, Luke fundamentally agrees with what Mark assumes knowledge of in 14:28/16:7, i.e., that Jesus has risen and that he has appeared to his disciples.

Matthew, in comparison, seems much less inclined to alter Mark 14:28/16:7. In fact, Nils Dahl suggests that Matthew and Mark may represent two versions of the same report.[34] The justification for such an assumption, as Alexander Sand observes, lies in the close agreement between the two versions of the angel's message (cf. Matt. 28:5–7; Mark 16:6–7).[35] Apart from beginning with the postpositive δέ instead of Mark's ἀλλά, he retains Mark 14:28 verbatim in Matt. 26:32, as he nearly does in his version of the whole episode (26:30–35; cf. Mark 14:26–31). He keeps to the Markan order as well. Likewise, he follows Mark 16:7 almost as completely in Matt. 28:7. His notable alteration is dropping Mark's specific reference to Peter; instead, the women are told to go and tell the disciples, of whom Peter would be one, that Jesus has risen from the dead. He, moreover, repeats Mark 16:7 again, this time in a saying of Jesus in Matt. 28:10.

A tendency we see emerging here is that Matthew closely follows Mark except when clarity demands otherwise, whereas Luke is more inclined to alter Mark. Matthew and Luke's response to these Markan passages seems to indicate that both were somewhat uncomfortable with Mark's assumptive handling of Jesus' resurrection appearances as implied in 14:28/16:7.

---

authorities as well (cf. Mark 10:33–34; Luke 18:32–33); σταυρόω is probably taken over from Mark 16:6 in light of the event.

32 E.g., Osborne, *Resurrection Narrative*, pp. 281–82 positively assesses the apparent dichotomy between the two; see also Tasker, *Matthew*, pp. 271–72; Marshall, "Resurrection in Luke," pp. 58–63; Ladd, *Resurrection*, pp. 86–90; Mounce, *Matthew*, p. 275.

33 So Fitzmyer, *Luke X–XXIV*, p. 1540.

34 Dahl, "Passionsgeschichte," p. 17.

35 Sand, *Matthäus*, p. 580.

Mark 16:1–8

Assuming at this point that 16:8 is Mark's intended ending, we cannot help but notice some major differences between Mark and Luke's Gospel conclusions.[36] In contrast to Mark, Luke recounts for his readers:

1. that although the women at the tomb were awestruck (24:5), they did tell the disciples about Jesus' resurrection (vv. 9–11, 22–23);
2. that Peter confirmed that the tomb was empty (vv. 12, 24);[37]
3. something about the experience of Jesus' followers between his death and post-resurrection appearances to them (vv. 9–33);
4. something about Jesus' earthly ministry (vv. 19–20);
5. something about what the disciples thought Jesus would do before his unexpected death (v. 21);
6. that the disciples did see the resurrected Jesus (vv. 15–31, 36–51);
7. that the disciples struggled with believing that Jesus was in fact alive (vv. 11, 22, 36–43);
8. that Jesus confirmed his bodily resurrection to them (vv. 36–43);
9. that the disciples came to understand for the first time who Jesus really was (vv. 26, 34, 45–49);
10. that divine providence was at work in the disciples' perception of Jesus (vv. 16, 31–32, 45);
11. that the resurrection fulfilled Jesus' life, teaching, work, and passion predictions (vv. 6–8);
12. that Jesus' life and passion fulfilled OT scripture (vv. 25–27, 44, 46);
13. how important the passion theme was for Luke's literary motives (vv. 6–8, 20–21, 25–26, 44, 46);

---

[36] See also pp. 113–14.

[37] Schubert's assumption ("Structure and Significance," p. 172, n. 18) that Luke 24:12 is a "doubtful reading" and "a clumsy and unnecessary attempt to fill out the statement of vs. 24a" is overly skeptical. Reasonable external and internal evidence supports its authenticity; so, e.g., Leaney, *Luke*, pp. 28–31; Metzger, *Textual Commentary*, pp. 184, 191–93; Hendricksen, *Luke*, p. 1058; esp. Osborne, *Resurrection Narratives*, pp. 113–15. Luke's inclusion of v. 12 may well reflect his personal interest in "double-witness" (a concept popularized by Morgenthaler) to substantiate that the tomb was indeed empty.

14.   that Jesus continued teaching his disciples (vv. 25–27,36–49);
15.   that Jesus ascended into heaven (v. 51);
16.   that after Jesus' ascension the disciples continued their association with the Jerusalem temple (v. 53);
17.   that the exalted Jesus would continue to work among his followers (v. 49);
18.   that his followers were to proclaim the significance of Jesus' resurrection to others (vv. 47–48);
19.   that Jesus will pour out God's Spirit upon them to empower their witness (v. 49).

Luke's conclusion is rich in detail, both as backward-looking to Jesus' earthly ministry and forward-looking to his exalted state.

Matthew's resurrection account (28:1–20), on the other hand, follows closely our observed pattern in the previous two Markan comparisons: he retains the gist of Mark's version, except where he clarifies what Mark assumes. He also adds some material to his account. This is most evident in his use of OT imagery to describe the young man (cf. Mark 16:5) as an angel of the Lord (Matt. 28:2–7)[38] and in his detailing of the guards' reaction to what has happened at the tomb (vv. 11–15).[39] He nonetheless adheres to the essential thrust of Mark 16:1–8.

We first see this in 28:2, where Matthew doubly resolves the women's concern in Mark 16:3 about moving the large stone from the mouth of the tomb: "[1] There was a violent earthquake, [2] for an angel of the Lord came down from heaven and ... rolled back the stone." In stating this, he also identifies the young man who appeared to the women in Mark 16:5 as an angel of the Lord. Second, Matthew shows Jesus himself (28:9–10) repeating the angel's injunction to the women (28:7; cf. Mark 16:7) that they should tell the disciples to go to Galilee, where they would meet him as he has already promised them (cf. Matt. 26:32; Mark 14:28). And in contrast to Mark, the reader finally meets the resurrected Jesus. Third, Matthew resolves the enigmatic promise of Mark

---

[38]   E.g., Allen, *Matthew*, p. 301; Bode, *First Easter Morning*, pp. 50–51, 58. Léon-Dufour, *Resurrection*, pp. 143–45 regards this episode as a possible theophany.

[39]   For a survey of how this episode reflects Matthew's writing concerns, see Osborne, *Resurrection Narratives*, pp. 83–84. In reference to his apologetic concerns, see Dahl, "Passionsgeschichte," p. 19; Campenhausen, "Events of Easter," pp. 62–64; Bode, *First Easter Morning*, pp. 52, 57; Kratz, *Auferweckung als Befreiung*, pp. 70–72; Sand, *Matthäus*, pp. 592–94; France, *Matthew*, pp. 405–406, 409–10; Broer, *Grab Jesu*, pp. 61–62.

16:7: the resurrected Jesus reiterates the promise to the women (28:9–10) and fulfills it by appearing to the disciples in Galilee (v. 16). It seems that the promise for both evangelists, therefore, refers primarily to Jesus' resurrection appearances. Fourth, Matthew clarifies Mark's awkward ending in 16:8. Like Mark, Matthew records in 28:8 that the women were afraid (μετὰ φόβου) and hastily left the tomb, but he adds that they were, nonetheless, "filled with joy and ran to tell his disciples."[40] Finally, Matthew records in 28:16 that the disciples did in fact meet Jesus in Galilee.

Matthew's resurrection narrative mostly supplements Mark's Gospel. We have seen this especially in 28:2, 8–10, 16, where he explicates knowledge implicit to Mark's ending.[41] Although he shows little interest in taking his account much further than this,[42] the close adherence may explain why commentators frequently tend to use Matthew's Gospel to reconstruct a possible lost ending for Mark.

Luke's resurrection narrative, in contrast, is much richer in information. In noting the details of Luke's resurrection account, one cannot help but sense his authorial motive coming through. These details confirm to the reader the significance of Jesus' resurrection in connection to his earthly life and present heavenly reign. There is no contest between Mark and Luke (or between Matthew and Luke for that matter) regarding the amount of information given. Even the existing longer endings for Mark fall decidedly short.

Hence, it is doubtful that Mark wrote or intended to write a longer ending to his Gospel. If Mark assumed knowledge among his readers, the three troublesome passages we have analyzed do not necessarily prove awkward for Mark, but only for Luke and Matthew. Mark's ending does not seem primarily aimed at providing information but at creating an impression on the basis of prior knowledge of apostolic teaching on the matter. And as we have seen, Mark accomplishes his aim rather well. On the other

---

[40] As Moule, "Mark XVI.8 Once More," pp. 58–59 has pointed out, this is the possible meaning, although implicit to Mark's Gospel ending.

[41] So, e.g., Aland, "Schluß," p. 465; Palmer, "Resurrection," pp. 215–16, 222; Goulder, "Parallels," p. 235. But to conclude with Perrin, *Resurrection Narratives*, p. 50 that Matthew was not particularly interested in an appearance story "since he gives only the baldest details" in 28:16 is unwarranted for it rules out the probability that Matthew also assumed some knowledge of the resurrection story among his readers.

[42] Pesch, *Markus. 1, 1–8, 26*, pp. 41,46.

hand, Luke and Matthew's tendency to clarify Mark suggests that even first-century readers had some difficulty with Mark's Gospel. If this is true, it leaves an implausibly short period of time for a longer ending to drop out of circulation. Thus Mark 16:8 was in all probability the original ending.

A comparison between Luke and Matthew's resurrection accounts sheds further light on Luke's literary intention with the resurrection theme. Matthew's ending, as we have seen, largely supplies the kind of information which would make Mark's ending less enigmatic. But, in contrast to Luke's ending, Matthew gives:

1. no description of what the disciples were doing or thinking between the time of Jesus' death and post-resurrection appearances;
2. no explicit confirmation that the tomb was in fact empty (although this is, perhaps, the intention of Matt. 28:11–15);
3. no graphic proof of Jesus' bodily resurrection;
4. no direct reaffirmation of Jesus' resurrection as the fulfillment of his earthly work and of the OT scriptures;
5. no reference to divine providence at work in any of this;
6. no explicit promise that the Spirit would be given for the empowering of future ministry;
7. no ascension account;
8. no suggestion as to how the exalted Jesus would continue to work among his followers.

Certainly the resurrection was of utmost importance to Matthew. But contrasting Matthew and Luke's respective narratives leaves little doubt that Luke had a more thorough revision of Mark in mind. The way Luke interacts with Mark's build-up to Jesus' resurrection in his Gospel and handles the theme in Acts further supports this. Luke emphatically shows Jesus as the focus of the resurrection and God as the power behind it. For understanding the character and purpose of Luke's christology, this emphasis is crucial.

A Lukan solution

We shall attempt to substantiate this conscious literary development and assess what it signifies for Luke's christology according to three successive stages suggested by Luke himself: the resurrection anticipated (Luke 1–23), realized (Luke 24–Acts 1:11), and proclaimed (Acts 1:12–28:31).

The resurrection anticipated (Luke 1–23)

In anticipating Jesus' death and resurrection, Luke largely follows the same pattern we observed in Mark's build-up to the event: (1) Jesus' announcement of it, (2) the disciples' ignorance of it, and (3) the mounting Jewish opposition that brought it about. We shall evaluate Luke's Gospel according to the same points.

1. *Jesus' announcement of it.* Luke's Gospel contains roughly thirteen references to Jesus' resurrection. The clearest of these appear in his passion predictions to the disciples (9:22, 44; 18:31–33; 22:37).[43] The others, though less explicitly so, either point toward it or presuppose it. Lukan material which may implicitly point toward it includes Jesus' raising the widow's son at Nain (7:11–15) and Jairus' daughter from the dead (8:40–42, 49–56; Mark 5:22–24, 35–43; Matt. 9:18–19, 23–26), Jesus' message to John that he raises people from the dead (7:22; Matt. 11:5), the parable of the rich man and Lazarus (16:19–31, esp. v. 31), the parable of the wicked tenants (20:9–16; Mark 12:1–9; Matt. 21:33–41) – a foreshadowing of Jesus' death at the hands of the Jews (cf. esp. 20:15; Mark 12:8; Matt. 21:39) – and Jesus' allusion to Ps. 118:22, where the rejected stone will become the cornerstone (20:17–19; Mark 12:10–12; Matt. 21:42–46) – a prefiguring of his resurrection/exaltation. Lukan material which may implicitly presuppose Jesus' resurrection includes his teaching on the general resurrection of the dead (20:27–40; Mark 12:18–27; Matt. 22:23–33) and his comment to the disciples that he will not partake of the passover again until the kingdom of God comes (22:15–18; Mark 14:25; Matt. 26:29).[44]

Moreover, in contrast to Matthew, Luke is more selective in the way he incorporates Mark's record of Jesus' passion announcements.[45] For reasons already discussed, of the twelve Markan passages prefiguring Jesus' death and resurrection, Luke omits the

---

[43] See further Bayer, *Predictions*, pp. 190–96.

[44] But Elliott's hypothesis ("Resurrection," pp. 87–89) that Jesus' passover visit to the Jerusalem temple in Luke 2:41–52 was meant to prefigure his future death and resurrection is not compelling.

[45] Matthew has taken over *all* of Mark's passion prefigurements of Jesus (Matt. 9:18–19, 23–26 – Mark 5:22–24, 35–43; Matt. 16:21 – Mark 8:31; Matt. 17:9 – Mark 9:9; Matt. 17:22b–23a – Mark 9:31; Matt. 20:18–19 – Mark 10:33–34; Matt. 21:33–46 – Mark 12:1–12; Matt. 22:23–33 – Mark 12:18–27; Matt. 26:12 – Mark 14:8; Matt. 26:29 – Mark 14:25; Matt. 26:31–32 – Mark 14:27–28; Matt. 26:61 – Mark 14:58; Matt. 27:40 – #Mark 15:29b), shares one saying in common with Luke (Matt. 11:5 – Luke 7:22), and uniquely adds only one other prediction of Jesus in 26:2.

awkward ones (9:9; 14:27–28; 14:58; 15:29). In addition, he omits Mark's story of the woman at Bethany who anoints Jesus' head with oil (14:3–9; Matt. 26:6–13), an act prefiguring the preparation of his body for burial (v. 8; Matt. 26:12). Luke may have done this to avoid confusing the reader with his somewhat similar story of the sinful woman's anointing of Jesus in 7:36–50. Apart from the seven passion passages that Luke has taken over from Mark (Luke 8:40–42, 49–56/Mark 5:22–24, 35–43; Luke 9:22/Mark 8:31; Luke 9:44/Mark 9:31; Luke 18:31–33/Mark 10:33–34; Luke 20:9–19/ Mark 12:1–12; Luke 20:27–40/Mark 12:18–27; Luke 22:15–18/ Mark 14:25), he shares one in common with Matthew (Luke 7:22/ Matt. 11:5) and has five unique to his own Gospel (Luke 7:11–15; 9:51; 14:14; 16:19–31, esp. v. 31; 22:37).

Like Mark, Luke first explicitly mentions the resurrection in connection with Peter's confession (Luke 9:22; Mark 8:31; cf. Matt. 16:21a) and again just prior to Jesus' triumphal entry (18:31–33; Mark 10:33–34; Matt. 20:18–19). But unlike Mark (10:1; Matt. 19:1–2), Luke gives Jesus' death and resurrection special literary status in his editorial comments in 9:51 (and 9:31).[46] He deliberately pictures the entire travel narrative (9:51–19:27) in the shadow of the cross and in the glory of the empty tomb. Luke explicitly heightens Mark's conviction that to see Jesus aright is to see him in light of his full passion work. In this sense, Conzelmann rightly insists that the divine plan fulfilled in Jesus' resurrection "casts light not only on ... Jesus' death, but also on his deeds and on his whole being."[47]

2. *The disciples' ignorance of it.* Luke adopts in the second strand of anticipation Mark's description of the disciples' ignorance toward Jesus, i.e., their inability to understand who he is and what he has come to do. Luke alone, however, expands Mark theologically to include the role of divine providence in the matter.

Like Mark, Luke writes that the disciples had trouble understanding who Jesus was. E.g., when Jesus calmed the storm, fear and amazement seized them toward this man who could command the raging elements to do his will (8:25; Mark 4:41; Matt. 8:27). Some deficiency in faith is also intimated in their inability to heal

---

[46] So, e.g., Schubert, "Structure and Significance," pp. 183–85; Lohfink, *Himmelfahrt*, pp. 212–17; Marshall, *Luke*, pp. 384–85; Fitzmyer, *Luke I–IX*, p. 800 and lit. cited therein; Schürmann, *Lukas. 1, 1–9, 50*, p. 552. But cf. Friedrich, "Entrückungschristologie," pp. 48–77; Tyson, *Death of Jesus*, pp. 98–99.

[47] Conzelmann, *Theology of St. Luke*, p. 154.

the boy with the unclean spirit (9:37–43, esp. v. 41) and in Jesus' teaching about entrance into the kingdom of God (18:15–17; Mark 10:13–16; Matt. 19:13–15). But Luke uniquely diminishes its forcefulness. He omits, e.g., the story of Jesus walking on the water (Mark 6:45–50; Matt. 14:22–27) and Mark's explanatory comment that they did not understand its significance because their hearts were hardened (6:51–52; however, cf. Matt. 14:28–33). Likewise, he drops the episode of Jesus' feeding of the 4,000 (Mark 8:1–10; Matt. 15:32–39) and his ensuing reprimand of them (Mark 8:14–21; Matt. 16:5–12).

This same pattern of *conforming to Mark but lessening its forcefulness* holds true of Luke's handling of the disciples' inability to grasp the nature of Jesus' mission. With Peter's confession, we observed in Mark's Gospel a change in focus in the ignorance motif. From this point onward Mark expressly describes the trouble the disciples had in figuring out *what* Jesus meant by his passion announcements rather than in understanding *who* he was. Luke follows this same pattern but softens the severity of Mark's description. E.g., in the episode following Peter's confession, Luke completely omits Peter's rebuke of Jesus and Jesus' response to him after citing Mark almost verbatim in the passion announcement itself (9:22; cf. Mark 8:31; Matt. 16:21). This removes from the context the tension caused by Peter's ignorance. He drops from the transfiguration story (9:28–36) Mark's comment in 9:10 that the disciples were unsure of what Jesus meant when he said that he would rise from the dead (so also Matt. 17:1–9). After Jesus' second passion announcement, Luke alone adds to Mark's statements on the disciples' ignorance and fear (9:32; Matt. 17:23b) that they were meant not to know yet – its meaning was to stay hidden a little longer (Luke 9:45). Luke appends a similar comment to Jesus' third passion announcement in 18:34 where Mark records nothing of the kind (Mark 10:33–34; Matt. 10:18–19).

This pattern is also evident in Luke's account of Jesus' betrayal. On the one hand, the disciples still do not realize what is imminent. E.g., during the last supper they argue over which of them would be the greatest (22:24); they struggle with sleep in Gethsemane (vv. 39–46); and they prepare to fight by Jesus' side if betrayed (vv. 49–50; cf. Jesus' comment in v. 51). On the other hand, Luke tones down the *extent* of the disciples' ignorance and failure. He notes, e.g., that they fell asleep in Gethsemane out of "exhaustion from sorrow" (λύπη, v. 45), implying that they may not have been as naïve about the coming trauma as Mark (14:37) and Matthew (26:40) apparently indicate. He also omits reference to their flight en masse after Jesus' arrest (cf. Mark 14:50–52; Matt. 26:56b).

Another special Lukan characteristic in this regard is his inclination to stress the cosmic nature of the struggle. Judas, for instance, is not just betraying Jesus for selfish reasons, but is shown as part of a larger drama involving the machinations of satan himself (22:3; see also John 13:27; cf. Mark 14:10; Matt. 26:14). Luke 22:31–32 pits Jesus and satan as adversaries fighting over the ownership of the disciples, especially Peter. The crucial element in this is Jesus' prayer for their ultimate perseverance.[48] The same is true in Gethsemane, where Luke focuses on Jesus' prayer rather than on the disciples' failure to stay awake (22:40–46).[49]

What we see emerging here is Luke's emphasis that divine providence is at work in all of this. Neither Mark nor Matthew presents us with such a picture. Mark writes twice that the disciples' hearts were hardened (6:52; 8:17), but it is doubtful that the expression αὐτῶν ἡ καρδία πεπωρωμένη refers as much to an act of God as to the tremendous difficulty the disciples had in comprehending Jesus. Matthew omits the Markan expression from both stories. Here again Matthew follows the basic thrust of Mark's Gospel both textually and chronologically, though he also softens Mark's negative tone toward the disciples. Matthew, e.g., replaces Mark's harsh conclusion to the story of Jesus walking on the water with an ascription of worship to Jesus (cf. Matt. 14:33 to Mark 6:51b–52); resolves the disciples' ignorance concerning Jesus' meaning of the leaven of the Pharisees (16:12) left unresolved in Mark (cf. 8:21); omits from his transfiguration narrative that the disciples were confused about what Jesus meant by rising from the dead (Matt. 17:9; cf. Mark 9:9–10); drops the emphatic adverb ἐκπερισσῶς from Peter's assurance that he would follow Jesus at all costs (cf. Matt. 26:35 to Mark 14:31); and drops the somewhat awkward Markan expression that the disciples did not know what to answer Jesus when he returned to them a second time in Gethsemane because they were sleeping (cf. Matt. 26:43 to Mark 14:40).[50] For Luke, however, the disciples' failure to grasp the meaning of Jesus'

---

[48] See further Crump, *Jesus the Intercessor*, pp. 154–57.

[49] So Marshall, *Luke*, p. 833. See further Kingsbury, *Conflict in Luke*, pp. 127–39 on the disciples' passage from ignorance to illumination.

[50] For more examples, see Allen, *Matthew*, pp. xxxiii–xxxiv; Barth, "Matthew's Understanding of the Law," pp. 105–24.

passion announcements was not only because they were unable to understand such things, but as importantly, if not more so, because *they were providentially not meant yet to understand.* Their time had not yet come.

Moreover, in contrast to Mark, Luke's coupling of the disciples' ignorance with divine providence accentuates Jesus' uniqueness still more: no one but Jesus knew what awaited him in Jerusalem and its significance for God's plan of salvation, and only he was able to carry it out.

3. *The mounting Jewish opposition.* Like Mark, Luke mentions Jewish complicity in the events leading up to Jesus' crucifixion. In the first passion announcement Luke records Jesus as saying that he would suffer and be rejected by the Jewish authorities (9:22). But in contrast to Mark (and Matthew), his presentation is more carefully orchestrated, showing subtleties of expression not found in either of the first two Gospels. Whereas Mark tends to lump the Jewish leaders into one group, Luke tends to portray the Pharisees, at least, in a better light.[51] Luke also makes it a special point to broaden those implicated in the crime to include the Roman authorities. Thus, whereas the Jewish rage against Jesus reaches a fortissimo level in Mark almost from the start, the hostility in Luke's Gospel is a gradually building crescendo peaking at Jesus' passion.

Jesus' first encounter with the Jewish leaders in Mark is a hostile one. They accuse him of blaspheming God for claiming to forgive the paralytic's sins (2:6–7). By ch. 3, after Jesus healed the man's shriveled hand in the synagogue on the sabbath, the Pharisees and Herodians appear as devising ways to kill him (v. 6; as they do again in 11:18). This antagonism never abates. It only ferments, bubbling over periodically into more confrontation with Jesus, whether in attempts to find fault with his actual teaching, his sabbath observance, or his authority to exorcize demons.[52] Further-more, Jesus' condemnatory words toward the Pharisees only heighten the conflict: e.g., concerning their hypocrisy (8:15) and self-righteousness (12:38–40). Jesus also twice specifically predicts his coming suffering at their hands (8:31; 10:33) and, through parable, his death (12:1–12).

Luke, on the other hand, ameliorates considerably Jesus' contact with the Jewish authorities. E.g., we do not see them plotting to kill

---

[51] So, e.g., Ziesler, "Pharisees," pp. 146–57.
[52] For more Markan examples of this, see pp. 83–84 above.

him until after his triumphal entry (19:47–48; Mark 11:18–19). In
6:11, Luke replaces ἀπόλλυμι ("to ruin, destroy, kill someone,"
Mark 3:6; Matt. 12:14) with τί ἂν ποιήσαιεν τῷ 'Ιησοῦ ("what they
might do to Jesus"), thus modifying the hostility of the Pharisees
and Herodians toward Jesus.[53] In the Beelzebub controversy, Luke
softens the tension by omitting any specific reference to the source
of the accusation; it was simply uttered by "some in the crowd"
(11:15; cf. "the Jerusalem scribes" in Mark 3:22; "the Pharisees" in
Matt. 12:24). He similarly modifies the story of those seeking a sign
from heaven. In 11:16, unspecified members of the crowd request
the sign; whereas it is the Pharisees in Mark 8:11–13 and the
Pharisees and Sadducees in Matt. 16:1–4 (also "the scribes and
Pharisees" in Matt. 12:38–39). Furthermore, on three different
occasions Luke uniquely records that Jesus dined as a guest in the
house of a Pharisee (7:36; 11:37; 14:1). Another kind of Lukan
softening can be seen in the remark that "some" (τινες) of the
Pharisees wanted Jesus to rebuke his disciples for praising God on
his behalf during his triumphal entry (19:39). Luke lessens the
criticism by implying that this opinion was not necessarily that of
the whole group, but only of a certain element within it. Luke most
likely expresses in these examples his own attitude toward the
Jews.[54]

Despite this Lukan perspective, we must also note that in the first
two-thirds of the Gospel, where he mollifies the harshness of the
Jewish authorities toward Jesus in Mark, the hostility is still nonetheless there and growing. Jesus' rejection in Nazareth (Luke 4:16–
30) may well foreshadow his eventual rejection by the Jewish
leaders in Jerusalem. In chs. 5–6, we encounter Jewish opposition
to Jesus in a series of episodes contrasting Jesus' teaching and
authority with that of the Pharisees – Jesus' healing of the paralytic
(5:17–26), dining at Levi's house with tax collectors (5:29–32),
healing of the man's withered hand in the synagogue on the
sabbath (6:6–11); and the Pharisees' questioning him about fasting
(5:33–39) and plucking grain on the sabbath (6:1–5). Only Luke
comments that the Pharisees, by refusing John's baptism, had in
effect rejected God's plan of salvation for themselves (7:30). He
records in 9:22 Jesus' first announcement of his future suffering at
the hands of the Jews. On a somewhat stronger note, after Jesus'

---

[53] Fitzmyer, *Luke I–IX*, p. 611.
[54] For more on Luke's perspective toward the Jews, see Weatherly, *Jewish Responsibility*.

castigation of the hypocrisy of the Pharisees and experts in the Law, Luke stresses that they strongly opposed Jesus and besieged him with questions in hopes of entrapping him (11:53–54). He portrays the increasing animosity toward Jesus in a number of other passages unique to his Gospel as well: Jesus humiliates his adversaries (13:17), which undoubtedly includes part of the Pharisaic group mentioned in ch. 11; the Pharisees closely watch Jesus on the sabbath to see if he will break it, which he does (14:1–6); the Pharisees sneer at Jesus because of his comment about their love of money (16:14); and Jesus criticizes the self-righteousness of some in the crowd, doubtlessly in reference to certain Pharisees among them (18:9–14).

Following Jesus' entrance into Jerusalem, Jewish hostility toward Jesus escalates into a determined, unified effort to kill him (19:47–48; Mark 11:18–19). The summary comment of Jesus' parable of the wicked tenants accentuates this (Luke 20:19; Mark 12:12; Matt. 21:45–46). Luke also follows virtually word-for-word Mark's account of Jesus' scathing harangue against the scribes and Pharisees in Mark 12:37b–40 (cf. Luke 20:45–47). Luke stresses, moreover, the complicity of the Jewish authorities in Jesus' arrest: in Mark they send a group to arrest Jesus (14:43, 48; Matt. 26:47–48,55); in Luke "the chief priests, the officers of the temple guard and the elders" specifically form part of that group (22:52).

In the trial scenes, Luke boldly highlights the Jewish leaders' unwavering push for Jesus' death. Luke uniquely records that they level a threefold political accusation implicating Jesus as a threat to Roman hegemony in Palestine (23:2), adding further the charge that he stirs up the populace (v. 5) – perhaps implying a threat of insurrection.[55] That the Jewish Sanhedrin (cf. 22:66; 23:1) would stoop to such duplicity in light of their disdain for their Roman overlords only magnifies their personal animosity toward Jesus (for their insufficient grounds to convict Jesus, see further Acts 13:28b). This is heightened further as Pilate finds Jesus not guilty of sedition (23:4). In the next episode, where Jesus stands trial before Herod

---

[55] Perhaps the accusations in Luke 23:2, 5 are an explication of the unnamed κατηγοροῦσιν of Mark 15:3–4 (cf. also Matt. 27:12–14). The political complexion of the charges is a deliberate Jewish ploy to turn Jesus over to the Roman court, which has the authority to put to death any insurgent against Caesar; so Manson, *Luke*, pp. 254–55. The overtone of a possible political charge trumped up by the Jewish leaders against Jesus is most likely foreshadowed in Luke's version of the episode of paying tribute to Caesar (20:20b; cf. Mark 12:13; Matt. 22:15–16); so Fitzmyer, *Luke X–XXIV*, p. 1295.

(Luke 23:6–12), Luke describes the chief priests and scribes as "vehemently accusing him" (v. 10). But even Herod finds him innocent.[56] In a summary statement (23:13–16), Luke adds that Pilate chidingly informs the Jewish leaders that neither he (v. 14) nor Herod (v. 15a) found Jesus guilty of seditious behavior. This episode is a Lukan declaration of Jesus' innocence. Harold Hoehner argues that Pilate sent Jesus to Herod knowing that Herod would come to the same conclusion about Jesus' innocence as he did. Otherwise he would not have sent him. The Roman governor wanted to ingratiate himself with Herod and the Jews to ameliorate some previous indecorous decisions on his part which Herod possibly found particularly offensive. Had Herod disagreed with Pilate's verdict on Jesus, this would only have stiffened Jewish resentment toward Pilate.[57] In the final trial scene, where either Jesus or Barabbas would be released, Luke streamlines his account, possibly to accentuate the Jewish motive to have Jesus put to death (23:18–23; cf. Mark 15:6–14; Matt. 27:15–23). We can see this in three ways.

First, *the Jewish response.* Following Pilate's verdict that Jesus be released in 23:16, we suddenly – and unexpectedly – hear the instantaneous, unprompted, and unanimous shout of the Jewish accusers for Barabbas to be released and Jesus to be killed (v. 18). Who is Barabbas? Unlike Mark (and Matthew), Luke tells us only parenthetically *after* the event in v. 19 rather than before it (cf. Mark 15:6–11; Matt. 27:15–17, 20). Luke 23:17 is probably a gloss based on Mark 15:6 and Matt. 27:15, perhaps to smooth over Luke's unexpected introduction of Barabbas in v. 19.[58] Luke, moreover, never shows the Jewish authorities inciting the crowds against Jesus (cf. Mark 15:11; Matt. 27:20); instead their outcry is collective, spontaneous, and decisive. In 23:18, Luke stresses the unanimity of the Jewish group against Jesus with the adverb παμπληθεί ("altogether/with one voice"). The composition of the group (see v. 13) appears representative, composed of the chief priests (τοὺς ἀρχιερεῖς), the rulers (τοὺς ἄρχοντας), and the people (τὸν λαόν). In response to their third shout for Jesus' crucifixion, Luke punctuates their hostile attitude with marks of

---

56 But as Neyrey, *Passion*, p. 80 points out, this is not to say that Herod was at all partial to Jesus, as is esp. evident in the way he treated Jesus' followers in Acts (cf. 4:27; 12:1–5).

57 Hoehner, "Antipas," pp. 88–90.

58 Metzger, *Textual Commentary*, pp. 179–80.

urgency, insistence, and persuasiveness (v. 23; cf. Mark's less descriptive account in 15:14b, also Matt. 27:23b; however, note Matthew's similar expansion in 27:24–25). At the end of the episode, Luke writes that Pilate, with resignation, turned Jesus over to the desire of their will (v. 25), i.e., that he be crucified (vv. 18, 21, 23).

Second, *Pilate's statement of Jesus' innocence*. Building on Pilate's two previous defenses of Jesus (23:4,13–16), Luke records a third time that the Roman governor spoke to the Jews yet "again" (πάλιν, v. 20; cf. Mark 15:12; Matt. 27:22), presumably in hopes of finally convincing them of Jesus' innocence (see also Acts 3:13b). Luke amplifies the contrast of wills here: it is not Pilate's will (θέλων, v. 20) to release Jesus that ultimately wins out, but the Jewish will (τῷ θελήματι αὐτῶν, v. 25) to have him crucified. The impassioned Jewish desire for Jesus' death in the end supersedes the Roman court of law.

Third, *the irony of Barabbas' release*. Luke twice notes that Barabbas had been thrown into prison for insurrection and murder (vv. 19, 25). Although referring to it somewhat parenthetically in the first instance, he gives it special force in the second. Jesus is to die on false charges of insurrection; the real insurrectionist is to be set free. The one whom Roman law held innocent is condemned to suffer the fate that the other truly deserved. According to Luke, Jewish guilt in Jesus' death is indubitable.

Before leaving this point, we need to observe yet two other distinguishing Lukan traits regarding culpability for Jesus' death: Luke stresses Gentile complicity and the role of divine providence in it. He specially foreshadows this reality in his version of Jesus' third passion prediction. In the first part of the prediction he replaces Mark's reference to Jewish involvement with the idea that everything that has been written in the OT about Jesus' sufferings will be fulfilled (Luke 18:31; cf. Mark 10:33; Matt. 20:18). But in the second part of the prediction he closely adheres to Mark's statement of Gentile involvement in the passion (Luke 18:32–33; cf. Mark 10:34; Matt. 20:19). Even though Luke seems to cast Pilate and Herod in a more positive light during the actual trial scene in contrast to the malicious behavior of the Jewish leaders, his negative assessment of both the Jews and Gentiles in Acts 4:25–28 seems reminiscent of this passion prediction. Certainly his harangue against Pilate, Herod, and the Gentiles in Acts 4:27a bears Jesus' prophecy out. But the connection of the nations, peoples, kings, and rulers of Ps. 2:1–2 to the Gentile and Jewish authorities in 4:27 also suggests that their mutual conspiracy in Jesus' death fulfilled God's providential plan (Acts 4:28; see also "lawless men" [ἀνόμων] in Acts 2:23, which is usually associated with the Gentiles) and was predicted in scripture (Luke 18:31; Luke's use of "prophets" in this verse may generically refer to the whole of OT prophecy).

The notions of divine providence and scriptural fulfillment is fundamental to understanding Luke's assessment of Jewish and Gentile guilt in Jesus' death. He repeats the combination often (e.g., Luke 9:31; 18:31; 22:37; 24:25–26, 44, 46; Acts 2:23; 3:18; 4:25–28; 13:27–29; also Acts 4:10; 17:3; 26:22–23), adding, moreover, that both the Jewish people and their leaders acted in ignorance (Acts 3:17; 13:27). This implies that they could also be forgiven (cf. Luke 23:34).[59] The forgiveness extended to Israel is not unlike the way Peter himself could be forgiven his ignorance and denial of Jesus (cf. Luke 22:31–34).

But in emphasizing divine providence, Luke does not intend to soften the fact that the Jews crucified Jesus, as is reinforced by his repeated reference to their collusion in Acts (e.g., 2:23, 36; 3:13–15; 4:10, 27; 5:30; 7:52; 10:39; 13:27–29). Rather, in line with the concept of "divided Israel," he seems to be saying that unrepentant Israel has not been permanently separated from God's favor because of their disobedience. God's plan of fulfilling all that the OT has said about Jesus has one further stage to it. This one is of illumination and salvation. The basis for it is the resurrection. Because of it, the Jews, as well as the Gentiles, now stand ready to perceive Jesus as Lord and Christ and to respond to him as such – a phenomenon which perhaps Luke 23:48 foreshadows and Acts repeatedly exhibits (e.g., ch. 2). Though Luke agrees with Mark (and Matthew) that Jewish antagonism was the chief factor leading to Jesus' death, he revises Mark's rather uniformly negative treatment of the theme by ultimately focusing on its positive outcome in Jesus' resurrection and the salvation in which, according to divine plan, even his antagonists can now share because of it.

In summary, Luke in his Gospel distinctively anticipates Jesus' resurrection in the special prominence he gives to the passion announcements, in his lessening of Mark's forcefulness regarding the disciples' ignorance of Jesus' person and approaching passion

[59] Marshall, *Acts*, p. 92.

work coupled with the role of divine providence in this, and in his handling of the Jewish complicity in the events leading up to Jesus' crucifixion. This is not to say that Jesus' resurrection is any less central to Mark (or Matthew), but only to emphasize Luke's handling of it.

The resurrection realized (Luke 24–Acts 1:11)

My intent at this juncture is not to give a source and tradition-critical analysis of the resurrection passages – although I believe that the textual evidence suggests that they stem from oral and written tradition and not imaginative reconstruction[60] – but to supplement briefly our previous discussion of the significance of Jesus' resurrection for Luke's readers as recorded in these passages.

Luke provides a wealth of information to his readers in these two accounts of Jesus' resurrection:

1. Literarily, he fills out Mark's resurrection account (esp. in ch. 24), ties together his Gospel and Acts accounts, suggests the basic outline of Acts, and connects the Baptist's prediction to the inauguration of the church. The more prominent parallels between the Gospel and Acts include Jesus' appearances to his disciples (Luke 24:13–43; Acts 1:3a), some of Jesus' teaching to his disciples (Luke 24:32, 45; Acts 1:1b–2,3b), the promise of the Holy Spirit (Luke 24:49; Acts 1:4–5, 8), a record of Jesus' ascension (Luke 24:50–51; Acts 1:9), a special literary interest in Jerusalem (Luke 24:47; Acts 1:8), and Jesus' command to proclaim the gospel to all nations (Luke 24:46–48; Acts 1:8).

2. He gives a short biographical recounting of Jesus' life and suffering, and tells his readers something about the disciples' whereabouts, thoughts, and actions between the time of Jesus' death and his appearances to them and immediately following his ascension (Luke 24:52–53; also Acts 1:12–2:1).

3. He shows, for apologetic reasons, that the tomb was empty and that Jesus did appear bodily to his followers.

4. Pedagogically, he summarizes some of Jesus' instructions to his followers as to their mission and source of empower-

---

[60] *Contra*, e.g., Pokorný, *Genesis of Christology*, pp. 109–56.

ment in the coming days, points out the general topic of Jesus' instruction, i.e., the kingdom of God, and mentions that the disciples had begun to understand how Jesus fulfilled scripture.

5. He mentions God's work in all of this and Jesus' coming work alongside the Father's in heaven, including his giving of the Spirit.

6. He reminds his readers of the promise that Jesus will return.

7. Confessionally, he shows that at this time the disciples were already thinking of Jesus as Lord and worshiping him as such (as does Luke himself in 24:3).

8. He highlights thematically the universal, redemptive importance of Jesus' resurrection and the divine mandate to proclaim it to the world.

9. He reveals his authorial interest in reaffirming to his readers the reliability of the resurrection as a historical event and matter of faith.[61]

Luke assuredly records here the kind of information his readers needed to hear. In the NT, Luke's resurrection narratives describe most clearly the historical transition from Jesus' earthly career to the church's founding (cf. Matt. 28; Mark 16; John 20–21; 1 Cor. 15:3–7).[62] Jesus' resurrection is the moving force behind the church's growth and work; it also guarantees the hope of his promised return (esp. Acts 1:11; also 3:21).[63]

The resurrection proclaimed (Acts 1:12–28:31)

Consonant with our study thus far, it should not be of great surprise to learn that Luke shows special thematic interest in the resurrection in Acts. It often appears explicitly in discourse and implicitly in the numerous narrative references to the gospel preached. Concerning the latter, even though in these instances Jesus' resurrection is not specifically mentioned, it certainly is to be understood in light of Jesus' words in Luke 24:46 concerning the

---

[61] Schubert, "Structure and Significance," p. 171 rightly comments in view of Luke 1:1–4 that in the Gospel and Acts resurrection narratives Luke was not telling his readers essentially anything new.

[62] So Evans, *Resurrection*, p. 96.

[63] See, e.g., Hoffmann's discussion entitled, "Die 'historische' Begründung der Auferstehungshoffnung durch den Erweis der Tatsächlichkeit der Auferstehung Jesu bei Lukas," in "Auferstehung I/3," *TRE* 4, pp. 461–62.

substance of the gospel message preached: "that the Christ will suffer and rise from the dead on the third day." This appears in Acts as either in descriptive terms for the gospel (e.g., the good news, 5:42; 13:32, the gospel, 8:25,40; 16:10, the kingdom of God, 19:8; 28:23, 31, the message of salvation, 13:26, the way of the Lord, 18:25, the will of God, 20:27, the word of God, 8:14; 11:1; 12:24; 13:5, 7, 46; 17:13; 18:11) or in the act of communicating it (e.g., through preaching, 2:14–39; 5:29–32; 10:34–43; 13:16–41; 17:16–31, testifying, 4:33; 8:25; 9:22; 10:24; 26:22–23, speaking, 4:31; 9:28; 14:3; 16:13,32, defending, 9:29; 18:28, teaching, 2:42; 4:2, 18; 5:21, 25, 28, 42; 13:12; 18:11, and observing it in the Lord's Supper, 2:42, 46; 20:7,11). Coupled with the explicit occurrences, the theme appears, often repeatedly, in all but two chapters in Acts (chs. 21, 27).[64]

Turning to the passages where the resurrection is explicitly mentioned, we see that Luke has made a deliberate attempt both to defend it apologetically and to draw out its soteriological implications for his readers. Luke apologetically stresses that Jesus' resurrection can be verified historically, scripturally, and theologically. The *historical verification* comes by way of by Jesus himself, the testimony of eyewitnesses, and the presence of the Holy Spirit. According to Acts 1:3, Jesus demonstrated ἐν πολλοῖς τεκμηρίοις ("by many convincing proofs") to his apostles (cf. v. 2) that he was in fact alive, arisen bodily. This was not a once-and-for-all appearance, but repeated over an extended period of time (cf. δι' ἡμερῶν τεσσεράκοντα, 1:3; ἐπὶ ἡμέρας πλείους, 13:31). Accordingly, in Acts 1:21–22, the requirement for filling the vacant spot left by Judas among the twelve was to have been with Jesus from his baptism by John to his ascension; most importantly, the candidate must have seen the resurrected Jesus (see also 13:31).

The importance of eyewitness testimony plays a decisive role in the speeches of Acts (e.g., 2:32; 3:15; 4:18–20; 5:32; 10:39–42; 13:31). It authenticates the profession that Jesus is Lord and Christ and demands that the listener believe in Jesus as such.[65] Paul's personal encounter with the resurrected Jesus as Lord on the way to Damascus (9:1–6; also 22:6–15; 26:12–18) and Stephen's vision

---

[64] That Stephen sees Jesus standing at God's right hand (7:55–56, 59–60) in some sense attests to Jesus' resurrection in light of his mentioned death in v. 52; so Ladd, "Christology," pp. 38–39.

[65] For more on reasons why Luke may have restricted the eyewitness accounts in Acts to that of the apostles, see Menoud, "During Forty Days," pp. 168–70; Marshall, *Historian & Theologian*, p. 43.

of the exalted Jesus (7:55–56, 59–60) may also figure apologetically for Luke as two more examples of firsthand testimony to the resurrected Jesus.

Another form of verification is the Spirit's presence in the church (5:32). Standing trial before the Sanhedrin for teaching in Jesus' name (v. 28), Peter tells them that the apostles' loyalty ultimately lies with God, who has given his Spirit to those who obey him (vv. 29, 32). Peter in effect says to the Jewish authorities that the Spirit's presence demonstrates that God has raised Jesus from the dead (v. 30) and exalted him to his own right hand (v. 31). Thus to reject Jesus is to reject God, his work, and his Spirit.

Luke also defends Jesus' resurrection *scripturally* in the Jewish contexts of Peter's Pentecost speech and Paul's synagogue sermon in Pisidian Antioch. In the first instance, Peter appeals to Ps. 16:8–11 (Acts 2:25–28) as foreshadowing Jesus' resurrection[66] and to Ps. 110:1 (Acts 2:34) as shedding more light on Jesus' Lordship (see Bock, pp. 181–86). Paul, in the second instance, cites Ps. 2:7 (Acts 13:33), Isa. 55:3 (Acts 13:34), and Ps. 16:10 (Acts 13:35) in substantiating Jesus' resurrection (see Bock, pp. 245–57). Luke possibly reflects in these two episodes the manner in which the early church taught and defended Jesus' resurrection from the OT scriptures to a Jewish audience (cf. Acts 9:29; 17:2–3, 17; 18:4, 19, 28), and Jesus' own teaching on the matter (cf. Luke 24:27, 45).

Lastly, Luke stresses *theologically* that Jesus' resurrection was divinely accomplished. In Acts, Luke consistently reiterates that it was God who raised Jesus from the dead (2:24, 27, 32; 3:15, 26[?]; 4:10; 5:30; 10:40; 13:30, 32–33, 34, 37; 17:31). Its validity is reinforced in almost every instance by some form of empirical verification: by eyewitnesses (2:32; 3:15; 5:32; 13:31), the Spirit (5:32), or the crippled man healed (4:10)! Luke stresses that God deliberately "caused the resurrected Jesus to be seen" (ἔδωκεν αὐτὸν ἐμφανῆ γενέσθαι, 10:40) for this very reason (v. 41)!

Luke specifically highlights in Acts the saving significance of the resurrection. Jesus' resurrection becomes God's proof that he will save and judge the world through him (17:30b–31). God's purpose in this is salvific, to turn both Jew and Gentile to him (3:26). It forms the basis of the good news (17:18; also 25:19), the grounds for faith in Jesus (2:36–41; 3:1–10, 15–16; 4:8–22), and through

---

[66] For a detailed discussion of the resurrection and Ps. 16:8–11, and a survey of the relevant lit., see Bock, *Proclamation*, pp. 170–81.

implication, the believers' ultimate guarantee of the future general resurrection of the dead (23:6; 24:10–21). In fact, the resurrection itself appears as saving.[67]

What is noteworthy in Luke's handling of the resurrection in Acts is that virtually every explicit reference he makes to it occurs in discourse material (except Acts 1:3; 17:18). But this does not mean that he was writing *extempore*. First, Marshall has adequately shown that Luke's resurrection presentation is well grounded in the broader tradition of the early church.[68] This suggests a type of control on the personal liberties he may have taken in writing the work. The fact that Luke's presentation of the resurrection lines up with NT teaching may imply that what he is saying here largely mirrors the teaching he received from his Christian predecessors.

Second, Hermann Strathmann points out that Luke casts Jesus' resurrection "as no less an objective fact than the passion."[69] In Acts, "the witness to facts and the witness to truth," he argues, "are one and the same – the unavoidable result of the fact that the Gospel presents a historical revelation" (p. 492). Facts are not "doctrines, myths, or speculations," but "facts which took place in the clear light of history at a specific time and place, facts which can be established and on which one can rely" (p. 492). Thus Strathmann rightly concludes: "The concept of the witness to the content of the gospel is grounded in his marked concern to expound clearly the historical foundations of the evangelical message" (ibid.). Whether the resurrection had actually occurred in this way is moot. But Luke gives the impression in Acts that he believed that it did. Luke presents the resurrection, according to C. F. D. Moule, as an absolute reality, one that forms the "Christological watershed dividing the Gospel from the Acts."[70] It seems that someone writing only one generation removed from the alleged event would not attempt to stress its historicity with such calculated objectivity unless he had been taught that this was how it had indeed happened. W. C. van Unnik plausibly argues that the whole of Acts "is meant as *a witness to the truth*," i.e., confirming "the actuality of the resurrection by those who saw it."[71]

---

[67] See further Marshall, *Historian & Theologian*, p. 174.

[68] Marshall, "Resurrection in Acts," pp. 92–107.

[69] Strathmann, "μάρτυς," *TDNT* 4, pp. 492–93 (quot. p. 492). Concerning the disciples' witness of Jesus' appearances in Acts 1:3, see Bauernfeind, *Apg.*, p. 20.

[70] Moule, "Christology of Acts," pp. 160–65 (quot. p. 165).

[71] Van Unnik, "Confirmation," pp. 53–56 (quots. p. 56, my italics, p. 54 respectively). *Contra* Talbert, *Luke and the Gnostics*, pp. 17, 22–32, who suggests

Third, this fits well with Luke's motive of reassuring his audience about the beginnings of Christianity.[72] In contrast to Mark, Luke does not seem inclined to surprise his readers with an unexpected handling of a familiar theme such as Jesus' resurrection. Further- more, he seems compelled to reaffirm rather than reinterpret the theological message of the source-traditional material.[73] It seems, then that his readers would have found his treatment of the resurrection in the Acts discourses logical and a substantiation of what they had already known.

Conclusion: the resurrection and divine providence

I have attempted to show in this chapter that in the process of writing a Gospel Luke's handling of the resurrection theme reveals a conscious improvement of Mark's somewhat enigmatic and confusing presentation and that his revision of Mark reveals some- thing of the character and purpose of his own christology.

The most peculiar aspect of Mark's Gospel is his resurrection account. Mark specifically builds up to it through Jesus' passion predictions, the disciples' ignorance, and Jewish opposition. Jesus additionally explicitly refers to it in 9:9–10 and 14:28. But despite this, the resurrected Jesus never appears to any of his followers or to the reader. As we have seen, this ambiguity has created all kinds of speculation as to what Mark may have meant by these terse sayings, especially 14:28/16:7, and as to the possibility of a longer ending. For Mark, however, the stunned silence of the frightened women at the tomb in 16:8 most likely appears as an *implicit* but powerful way of illustrating just who Jesus is, a belief based ultimately on the fact of his resurrection and apostolic witness.

For Luke, however, the resurrection *explicitly* appears as the *fundamentum in re*.[74] Luke's redactional handling of Mark 9:9–10; 14:28/16:7; 16:1–8 demonstrates this. Although Matthew seems less concerned in these instances to deviate from Mark's handling of the resurrection, he also attempts to clarify these awkward passages. But unique to Luke's revision of Mark is his emphasis upon the

that the author created the witness motif as "an anti-Gnostic device" (p. 32) in his attempt to portray an "idealization of the apostolic age as a period free from heresy" (p. 92); see also Talbert, "Anti-Gnostic Tendency," pp. 261–66.
[72] Van Unnik, "Confirmation," pp. 56, 58–59.
[73] Cadbury, *Making*, p. 97; Marshall, *Historian & Theologian*, pp. 19–20, 92–93.
[74] Hoffmann, "Auferstehung II/1," *TRE* 4, p. 504.

role of divine providence in the tensions which led to Jesus' death and resurrection, and their providential resolution in Acts.

This discussion intimates a most interesting question that I have not yet formally raised. It concerns the relationship between "the Resurrected One" and "the One who raises him from the dead." Within the Gospel, Luke uniquely emphasizes that Jesus' passion work is according to divine plan; God, moreover, appears especially in Acts as the power behind the resurrection. What kind of relationship between the two does Luke imply here? An adoption or subordination christology? Or a divine status equal to God the Father? Searching out Luke's christological convictions on these matters will become the focus of our study in ch. 8.

6

JESUS AND SPIRIT BAPTISM

Introduction

A most descriptive Gospel expression of God's work for the present age is that "the Coming One will baptize with the Holy Spirit" (Mark 1:8; pars. Matt. 3:11; Luke 3:16; also John 1:33). This prophecy sums up the goal of Jesus' work – in him a new people are now called the church of God.[1] The reception of the Spirit embraces the whole of Christianity; his presence marks the church as God's church.[2]

But the reader of Mark's Gospel is hard pressed to find much information on this promised reality. "As the Gospel stands, there is no obvious further reference to this prophecy" after Mark 1:8.[3] In fact, the Holy Spirit, as Ernest Best observes, "hardly features in the Gospel" at all.[4] In the words of Holt H. Graham: The Spirit "is incidental to his account of the gospel of and ... about Jesus Christ."[5] "In contrast," Best adds, "to John who allows for a continual contemporarization of Jesus with his doctrine of a Spirit who leads the church into truth Mark hardly speaks at all of the contemporary work of the Spirit in the church."[6]

Mark leaves several important questions concerning Spirit

---

[1] Denney, "Holy Spirit," *DCG* 1, p. 731; also Rayan, *Breath of Fire*, p. 31.
[2] Denney, "Holy Spirit," *DCG* 1, pp. 731, 738. According to Bruce, "Holy Spirit," p. 177, for Luke and Paul, the ministry of the Spirit was "the great new fact of their time." So Barclay, *Promise of the Spirit*, p. 46 entitles Acts "The Acts of the Holy Spirit," for the Spirit "is the principal actor in the drama of the expanding church." Stählin, "πνεῦμα Ἰησοῦ," p. 234 entitles it "Die Zeit der Herrschaft Jesu Christi durch das Pneuma" ("The Age of the Lordship of Jesus Christ through the Spirit"); see also ibid., p. 234, n. 19 for similar ascriptions. Léon-Dufour, *Evangelien*, p. 228 refers to Luke as "The Gospel of the Holy Spirit."
[3] Motyer, "Rending of the Veil," p. 156.
[4] Best, *Gospel as Story*, p. 77.
[5] Graham, "Mystery and Ambiguity," p. 43.
[6] Best, *Gospel as Story*, p. 134.

baptism unanswered: Who is the Coming One who will baptize with the Spirit? When will this take place? And to whom will the Spirit be given? We shall examine in this chapter what Luke reveals to us about his christology in the way he enlarges upon Mark's handling of the Baptist's promise that "the Coming One will bestow the Spirit."

Mark's Gospel: Spirit baptism assumed

The paucity of material on the Spirit in Mark's Gospel characterizes the tendency of the broader synoptic tradition.[7] In this sense, Matthew and Luke are not all that dissimilar to Mark. The synoptic tradition's slim attestation to the Spirit is a fact which C. K. Barrett insists must be accounted for.[8]

The Spirit in the synoptic tradition

Scholars have put numerous hypotheses forward to explain the relative silence on the Spirit in the Synoptic Gospels. E. F. Scott, e.g., believes that unlike the intermittent coming of the Spirit upon the OT prophets, the Spirit permanently rested upon Jesus – though he was unconscious of the Spirit's presence – because he was the messiah.[9] Hans Windisch thinks that the Gospel tradition suppressed "pneumatic" language in order to emphasize a more developed christology.[10] Vincent Taylor feels that the Spirit's presence was undisputed among the early Christian communities; thus they felt no need to appeal to Jesus' teaching to substantiate it.[11] R. N. Flew suggests that because of the disciples' limited insight, Jesus refrained from saying much about his "richer and

---

[7] E.g., Barrett, *Holy Spirit*, p. 115 writes: "The fact plainly is that the Evangelists were not particularly interested in general references to the Spirit, either to emphasize them or to suppress them," p. 115. About Mark and Matthew, Schweizer, "πνεῦμα," *TDNT* 6, p. 402 notes that "there are surprisingly few statements about the Spirit." As to the Synoptic Gospels generally, Barclay, *Promise of the Spirit*, p. 21 remarks: "The first thing that strikes us is the meagreness of the material ... the references to the Spirit are few and far between." Hengel, *Charismatic Leader*, p. 63 remarks that in relation to Jesus' activities in the synoptic tradition the Spirit's role is mostly secondary. Even Beasley-Murray, "Spirit," p. 463 admits that there is "a general lack of emphasis on the Holy Spirit in the Gospels."

[8] Barrett, *Holy Spirit*, p. 115.

[9] Scott, *Spirit*, pp. 67, 69, 71, 80.

[10] Windisch, "Jesus und der Geist," pp. 231–34.

[11] Taylor, "Spirit," pp. 42, 53–60, esp. pp. 53–55.

profounder" understanding of the Spirit; instead he chose to live out his reinterpretation of the Spirit's work in his own ministry.[12] Gerhard A. Krodel speculates that Jesus concentrated on speaking about the kingdom of God, rather than on the means (i.e., the Spirit) by which it would be brought about.[13] Jacques Guillet holds that Jesus did not say much about the Spirit until the eve of his departure, for he had to disappear first before his followers would properly understand that the Spirit was "capable . . . of making his presence and his person live in their hearts."[14] C. K. Barrett maintains that like the OT prophets, Jesus rarely spoke of the Spirit because he was reluctant to claim personal inspiration for his words and deeds and because he desired to keep his messiahship secret.[15] J. H. E. Hull holds that the humility of Jesus, his servant-like character, kept him from teaching more about the Spirit.[16] Martin Hengel asserts that Jesus' unique claim to authority on the basis of "the immediacy of His relation to God" made it unnecessary for him to have to resort to the Spirit as an intermediary.[17]

Most of these theories probably reflect to differing degrees the thinking of the synoptic and Johannine traditions.[18] But more can still be said. Robert M. Mansfield argues that Mark's Gospel "presupposes and evidences a developed pneumatology,"[19] which is both explicit and implicit, and prevails throughout the Gospel (pp. 5–6, 133). The concept of "Gospel," he contends, is not fully intelligible apart from what he somewhat ambiguously terms the past and present "inspiration" of the Spirit (p. 5, also p. 13, n. 49). By this he means that the Spirit for Mark was "the divine authority

---

[12] Flew, *Jesus and His Church*, pp. 65–72, esp. pp. 70–71. Schweizer, *Holy Spirit*, p. 50 suggests a similar idea: "The best way to teach about the Holy Spirit is simply to count on him, and without saying too much about him simply let the Spirit permeate one's life." See also Wainwright, *Trinity*, pp. 207, 214–15.

[13] Krodel, "Functions of the Spirit," p. 22.

[14] Guillet, "Holy Spirit," pp. 31–32, 36–38.

[15] Barrett, *Holy Spirit*, pp. 117–20, 140–62 comments that "to have claimed a preeminent measure of the Spirit would have been to make an open confession of Messiahship, if, as seems to have been the case, there was a general belief that the Messiah would be a bearer of God's Spirit" (p. 158). See also Robinson, *Holy Spirit*, p. 130.

[16] Hull, *Holy Spirit*, pp. 34–36, esp. p. 36.

[17] Hengel, *Charismatic Leader*, pp. 63–64, 67–71, for "the reason why the Spirit had to give place was ... because [Jesus] appeared with a 'charismatic authority' which wholly transcended that of contemporary apocalyptic prophets" (pp. 63–64).

[18] On the compatibility of Jesus' teaching on the Spirit between the Synoptics and John, see Turner, "Holy Spirit," *DJG*, pp. 350–51.

[19] Mansfield, *Spirit and Gospel*, p. 6.

who empowered the preaching (word and act) of the historical Jesus," and continues as "guarantor of [Mark's] written Gospel" to the church (p. 5).

Few would contest that Mark actually felt this way. But how much of this so-called "developed pneumatology" is discernible within the Gospel itself? Mansfield rightly reminds us that the Spirit permanently remained upon Jesus throughout his earthly ministry; but Mansfield's inclination to tag Spirit-terminology onto nearly everything Jesus says and does in Mark seems excessive and unwarranted for Mark himself does not do this.

Mansfield's thesis exaggerates Beasley-Murray's claim that one should not only consider the number of times the Spirit theme occurs but should also "weigh their significance" for the literary context in question.[20] Mansfield even admits that explicit attestation to the Spirit in Mark's Gospel is slim.[21] His thesis does not adequately explain Mark's (or the wider synoptic tradition's) silence toward the Spirit.

Why, then, does the synoptic tradition not devote considerably more attention to the Spirit's presence and activity during Jesus' earthly ministry? From a historical-critical point of view, Guillet and Hengel's theories probably come closest. But Hengel's theory especially can be developed further. The reason the evangelists do not say more, assuming their silence reflects Jesus' own relative silence,[22] may also have to do with the fact that Jesus is physically present. It is not only his "authority based on the immediacy of his relation to God" that is involved here, but the immediacy of himself to people. Jesus as the Son of God is an immediate and direct revelation of God to others; the Spirit's intermediary role of revealing God to people becomes secondary. Whether Jesus was conscious of the Spirit's presence (as I believe he was) or not (so E. F. Scott) is somewhat immaterial. The center of attention is Jesus – from the evangelists' point of view and from Jesus' own perspective. The Spirit, nonetheless, permanently remains on him.[23] But once Jesus ascends to heaven, as Acts attests, the Spirit is given either to represent Jesus or to mediate his presence to the church. In support of this, most of Jesus' teaching about the Spirit has to do

---

[20] Beasley-Murray, "Spirit," p. 466.
[21] Mansfield, *Spirit and Gospel*, pp. 6, 133.
[22] So Moule, *Phenomenon*, pp. 43–81,100–14; Moule, "Christology of Acts," pp. 160–66; Lemcio, "Intention of Mark," p. 187.
[23] So Scott, *Spirit*, pp. 67, 69, 71, 80; George, "Esprit saint," p. 532 *et al.*

with the Spirit's role during this interval of time, i.e., between his ascension and parousia, when he will be physically absent from his people.

In addition, we can see from a redactional standpoint that the silence of the Synoptic Gospels is uneven. For Mark and Matthew, the Spirit theme is minor. But Luke's Gospel shows an increased interest in the Spirit theme. In his Gospel Luke prepares the reader for its thematic importance in Acts, a book replete with material on the Spirit.

Luke's increased pneumatological interest, therefore, may indicate that in the process of writing his Gospel he needed to expand Mark's sparse treatment of the Spirit theme – in particular, Mark's apparent decision not to go beyond assuming the fulfillment of the Baptist's prophecy in 1:8 as common knowledge to his church. This further implies that, christologically, Mark's depiction of the "earthly" Jesus alone was likewise not enough, for an account of Jesus' exaltation seems prerequisite to a fuller record of his giving of the Spirit. Thus a pneumatological heightening of Mark's Gospel in this regard would require a corresponding christological heightening and would be revealing of Luke's own christology. But before assessing Luke on this, we need to understand how Mark most probably understood the Baptist's prediction.

Mark's Gospel and the Baptist's prediction

NT scholars have given considerable attention to the somewhat surprising fact that Mark never explicitly records anything more about the Baptist's prediction after 1:8.[24] Markan scholars essentially take one of two views.

Some see 1:8 fulfilled, at least partly according to Mark, in Jesus'

---

[24] As Hurtado, "Mark," *DPCM*, p. 580 points out: "Mark does not elucidate what he understood the metaphor of Spirit baptism to represent." Hooker, *Message of Mark*, p. 10 states: "the promise remains an unfulfilled prediction"; see also Graham, "Mystery and Ambiguity," p. 45; Donahue, "Parable of God," p. 384; Lemcio, *Past of Jesus*, p. 39. Barrett, *Holy Spirit*, p. 125 writes: "Mark gives no indication that this event took place before the resurrection, and he must therefore have understood it to have belonged to the subsequent period." Similarly, Green, *Holy Spirit*, p. 41 comments: "Mark emphasises it by only allowing one reference in his Gospel to Christians having the Holy Spirit, and that in a prophecy about what would be their lot in the days after the passion (13:11)." And so Petersen, *Literary Criticism*, p. 71 writes: "13:11 is the only indication in Mark that the prediction of 1:8 might have come to pass"; see also Brown, "Water-Baptism," p. 138; but cf. Best, *Gospel as Story*, p. 120.

earthly ministry. Johannes Schreiber, e.g., sees Jesus' baptism with the Spirit as literally fulfilled in the Spirit's descent upon him in the form of a dove at his baptism by John, although, he argues, it was not the same as John's water baptism.[25] Others see the prediction as fulfilled along some metaphorical line in Mark. Herschel H. Hobbs believes that Jesus' baptism with the Spirit refers redemptively to the vital inner work he would perform in the hearts of people.[26] J. E. Yates holds that from Mark 1:14 onward the Baptist's prediction is fulfilled within Jesus' ministry toward Israel as a twofold act of divine judgment upon the wicked and purification of the righteous.[27] John Bowman believes that it represented some form of infusion of divine power that the earthly Jesus had given his disciples for preaching.[28] Wolfgang Feneberg thinks that it acted as a Markan literary marker coupling Jesus' baptism with the Spirit in 1:8 with the baptism he must undergo in 10:38–40 to demarcate the period of Jesus' ministry outside Jerusalem. This twofold meaning of βαπτίζειν, he believes, is the key to understanding Mark.[29] Dale and Patricia Miller believe that Mark understood it as a midrashic interpretation of Elijah to represent an act of internal spiritual cleansing which Jesus would perform in his followers.[30] Ched Myers thinks that it symbolizes a future confrontation of Jesus and his followers with political powers.[31] Stephen Motyer speculates that "the rending of the veil" in 15:38 stands as a Markan Pentecost. It proleptically represents a "bestowal of the Spirit analogous to the proleptic destruction of the Temple."[32]

It is unquestionably true that, according to Mark, Jesus did preach a divine message of judgment and salvation to Israel and did empower his disciples for ministry. In a limited sense Mark may have understood the Baptist's prediction to have taken place during Jesus' earthly ministry. But its fullest expression seems predicated upon Jesus' resurrection and exaltation. "It is the concerted teaching of the whole New Testament," E. M. B. Green asserts,

---

[25] Schreiber, *Theologie des Vertrauens*, p. 175.
[26] Hobbs, *Mark*, p. 20.
[27] Yates, "Form of Mark 1.8b," p. 337; Yates, *Spirit and the Kingdom*, pp. 14, 32–37.
[28] Bowman, *Mark*, p. 106; see also his discussion of Mark 6:7 on pp. 106, 152.
[29] Feneberg, *Markusprolog*, p. 170.
[30] Miller and Miller, *Mark as Midrash*, p. 54.
[31] Myers, *Binding the Strong Man*, pp. 127, 278.
[32] Motyer, "Rending of the Veil," p. 156.

"that the Christian experience of the Holy Spirit is possible only *after* the death and resurrection of Jesus."[33]

Markan scholars more commonly suppose that Mark primarily had Pentecost (Acts 2) in view.[34] This seems a viable alternative since the fulfillment of 1:8 in all probability takes place after the point at which Mark chooses to end his Gospel.[35] Mansfield raises the possibility that Mark may have had no knowledge of Pentecost and thus understood the fulfillment of 1:8 to have taken place in Galilee by Jesus upon his disciples sometime after his resurrection. But this interpretation is extremely tenuous for a couple of reasons: (1) if the second evangelist were John Mark and a companion of Peter and Paul as Mansfield believes (pp. 9–10), it seems hard to imagine that the second evangelist would be completely unaware of Pentecost; and (2) to read the fulfillment of 1:8 into the already troublesome passages of 14:28 and 16:7 strains belief![36] Moreover, the possibility that Mark did not originally end his Gospel with ἐφοβοῦντο γάρ in 16:8 but concluded with a longer ending, which contained a fulfillment of the prophecy, is thus far unsubstantiated.[37] No manuscript evidence of Markan endings suggests any such fulfillment.[38]

Furthermore, even if Mark's alleged original lost ending should turn up, it is quite possible, in light of the ending of Matthew's Gospel, that the original still would not contain any reference to the fulfillment of 1:8. Matthew records the Baptist's prediction in 3:11, but mentions in his own post-resurrection account in ch. 28 nothing of Jesus' conferral of the Spirit upon believers – whether in

---

[33] Green, *Holy Spirit*, p. 41 (my italic).

[34] E.g., Barrett, *Holy Spirit*, pp. 125–26; Farrer, *Mark*, pp. 62–63; Lampe, *Seal of the Spirit*, p. 41; Cranfield, *Mark*, p. 49; Schweizer, "πνεῦμα," *TDNT* 6, p. 398; Burkill, *New Light*, p. 145; Moule, *Mark*; Moule, *Origin*, p. 30; Ramsey, *Holy Spirit*, p. 22; Dunn and Brown, "Spirit," *NIDNTT* 3, p. 697; Krodel, "Functions of the Spirit," p. 62 (implicitly); Schmithals, *Markus. 1–9, 1*, pp. 79–81; Guthrie, *Theology*, pp. 515–16; Turner, "Luke and the Spirit," p. 50; Chevallier, "Esprit saint," p. 4 (implicitly); Best, *Gospel as Story*, pp. 73, 120; Lemcio, *Past of Jesus*, p. 39; Menzies, *Early Christian Pneumatology*, p. 141; see also lit. cited in Ladd, *Theology*, p. 36, n. 5.

[35] So esp. Hooker, *Message of Mark*, p. 10; Stock, *Mark*, p. 50.

[36] Mansfield, *Spirit and Gospel*, pp. 25–26, 133. Equally unconvincing is Taylor's suggestion in *Mark*, p. 157 that this promise may refer to the Christian rite of water baptism.

[37] E.g., Bacon, *Beginnings of Gospel Story* (as cited in Yates, *Spirit and Kingdom*, p. 10, n. 1) takes this position. But Bacon also asserts in *Mark*, pp. 190–91 that no record of it is left since Mark's original ending was so constantly revised that it "was really 'improved' out of existence."

[38] See, e.g., Metzger, *Textual Commentary*, pp. 122–26.

citing a further promise of it or in detailing its fulfillment; instead, he refers only to Christian baptism done in the name of the Father, Son, and Holy Spirit (28:19). In comparison to Mark and Matthew, Luke's Gospel conclusion (cf. 24:49) is unique in this regard. Therefore, it should be kept in mind, as C. K. Barrett cautions, that although a lost ending for Mark is an attractive conjecture, it is no more than that.[39]

The claim that Mark 1:8 envisages Jesus' outpouring of the Spirit upon the church following the resurrection and presumes knowledge of this experience among his readers seems wholly justified in light of his christological intentions for the Gospel. He did *not* write to account for the Spirit's presence in the church. He was concerned foremost with Jesus. His intended recipients probably knew full well how the Baptist's prediction came to fulfillment.[40] Morna Hooker comments: "Possibly Christian experience of the Spirit was so much a present experience for Mark and his readers that an account of its origin seemed unnecessary."[41] To provide such an account would perhaps have distracted the readers from his primary writing concern. Mark probably briefly mentioned it for christological reasons. The Baptist's prediction points out (1) Jesus' unique christological status as the Coming One who will confer the Holy Spirit and (2) the coming reality of Jesus' Lordship. In addition, with its occurrence at the Gospel's outset, Mark powerfully introduces the reader to the uniqueness of Jesus' person and work before the reader ever meets him.

On the other hand, potential first-century readers of Mark's Gospel unfamiliar with the teaching of Mark's church might not have been able to make these same christological connections. Or others would possibly need reassurance about the very teaching Mark was assuming. Whatever the reason, in using Mark as a primary source for his own Gospel, Luke considerably expands the Spirit theme in his writings – in particular, the Baptist's prediction that "the Coming One will baptize with the Spirit." In doing this, he also reveals something of his own christology.

---

[39] Barrett, *Holy Spirit*, p. 125; similarly Metzger, *Textual Commentary*, p. 126 and n. 7.

[40] So, e.g., Stock, *Mark*, p. 50.

[41] Hooker, *Message of Mark*, p. 10.

Luke–Acts: Spirit baptism demonstrated

Lukan scholars have not given much consideration to the possibility that Mark's assumptive handling of John's prediction may have contributed to Luke's desire to write a Gospel of his own. Burton Mack perhaps comes closest when he suggests that "Luke used the notion of the Spirit of God to bridge between the times and accentuate a constructive and compassionate ministry for Jesus."[42] For one wanting to clarify the continuity between Jesus and the church via the Spirit, Mark's Gospel would be inadequate. Presumably no such literature making this connection had yet been written. And if Luke had not written, our understanding of Spirit baptism and its impact within early Christianity would indeed be severely limited.

The Spirit and Luke's Gospel

All would agree that the Spirit theme dominates Luke–Acts.[43] R. E. O. White comments: "Luke sees the whole Christian movement, from its earliest beginning in John and from the conception of Jesus in the womb, to the ascension and afterwards, as inspired, governed, and empowered by the Holy Spirit."[44] "If St. Luke's 'former treatise,'" H. B. Swete adds, "gave prominence to the work of the Holy Spirit ... its sequel, the Acts, is wholly occupied with the work of the Spirit in the life of the Church."[45] E. F. Scott even goes as far as to say that "the two books of his history may almost be said to have their central motive in this view of Christianity as the outcome of the work of the Spirit."[46]

In comparison to Mark, Luke refers to the Holy Spirit almost five times as often in his Gospel (about twenty-two times to Mark's five times; and twice as often as Matthew). He retains each of Mark's references to the Spirit – the Baptist's prophecy that Jesus will baptize with the Spirit (3:16 – Mark 1:8; Matt. 3:11), the Spirit's descent upon Jesus in the form of a dove at his baptism by John (3:22 – Mark 1:10; Matt. 3:16), his leading of Jesus into the

---

[42]   Mack, *Myth of Innocence*, p. 357.
[43]   For a number of short but thorough studies analyzing Luke's usage of πνεῦμα, see Schweizer, "πνεῦμα," *TDNT* 6, pp. 404–15; Hill, *Greek Words*, pp. 253–65; Hull, *Holy Spirit*, pp. 187–93; George, "Esprit saint," pp. 501–505.
[44]   White, *Spirit*, pp. 34–35.
[45]   Swete, *Holy Spirit*, p. 64.
[46]   Scott, *Spirit*, p. 64.

wilderness where he was tempted by satan (4:1b – Mark 1:12; Matt. 4:1), Jesus' promise of the Spirit for witness (12:12 – Mark 13:11; Matt. 10:20), and his warning against blaspheming the Spirit (12:10 – Mark 3:29; Matt. 12:31–32) – except Mark 12:36 (Matt. 22:43), where Luke omits mentioning the Spirit as inspiring David's words (but cf. Acts 1:16; 4:25).

In addition to Mark, Luke emphasizes in his Gospel the Spirit's role in the coming of John and the messiah (1:15; 1:35 [twice]; 1:41; 1:67; 2:25–27 [three times]; 3:2) and his empowering presence in Jesus' ministry (4:1a; 4:14; 4:18 – Isa. 61:1–2; 10:21; 11:20), further supplements Jesus' teaching about the Spirit (4:18; 11:13), and adds Jesus' promise of the Spirit in a post-resurrection appearance (24:49). He, moreover, uniquely describes the Spirit as "the power of the Most High" (1:35), "the power of the Lord" (5:17), "the finger of God" (11:20), "what the Father has promised" (24:49a), "the power from on high" (24:49b),[47] and perhaps as wisdom (21:15, cf. Acts 6:10)[48] – however, that all of these designations refer to the Spirit is debated.[49]

Matthew, on the other hand, develops the Spirit theme less than Luke. He mentions, in a more diminished sense, the Spirit's agency in Jesus' conception (1:18, 20), draws attention to the Spirit's association with Jesus (12:18 – Isa. 42:1) and the ensuing conflict with the Jewish leaders over authority (12:28, 31–32), and includes the Spirit in the trinitarian formula of Christian baptism (28:19). In the last instance, Matthew shows a specific usage of the Spirit theme not found in Mark or Luke.

To grasp the importance of the Spirit theme for Luke in comparison to Mark, we should view the subject in light of Luke's unified work. Where Mark refers to the Spirit about five times, Luke does so around eighty-two times (Gospel – twenty-two times; Acts – sixty times). One reason for the Spirit's prominence in Acts is that here is where the Baptist's prediction is fully realized. The whole of Acts essentially illustrates its meaning and significance. What this ultimately discloses to Luke's readers, as we shall see, is

---

[47] For more on δύναμις and τέρατα καὶ σημεῖα as connoting the Spirit's healing ministry in Luke, see von Baer, "Heilige Geist," pp. 1–2; Turner, "Jesus and the Spirit," pp. 15–18; but cf. Schweizer's reservations in *Holy Spirit*, p. 59 in blending the two in reference to Jesus' healing miracles.

[48] See further Hengel, "Messianischer Lehrer der Weisheit," pp. 166–77.

[49] See Menzies, *Early Christian Pneumatology*, pp. 114–204. For more on Luke's distinctive treatment of the Spirit theme in his Gospel in comparison to Mark and Matthew, see George, "Esprit saint," pp. 533–34.

that the Spirit's presence in the church establishes a continuum between the earthly ministry of Jesus and Jesus' present reign as exalted Lord.

Luke–Acts and the Baptist's prediction

We can see Luke's intent to highlight the Baptist's prediction in Luke–Acts in his repeated allusions to it and in the way he heightens the element of promise inherent in it.

Luke's use of Mark 1:8

Luke's version of the Baptist's prediction in Luke 3:16–17 closely parallels Matthew (3:11–12) against Mark. This agreement reflects a common source between Luke and Matthew, a possible Q source which Mark did not use or abbreviated for whatever reason. Luke differs from Mark in four ways: Luke (1) reverses Mark's order ("I baptize you with water" ... "But one more powerful than I ... "), (2) omits Mark's postpositive δέ in 1:8, (3) adds καὶ πυρί in 3:16, and (4) follows the prediction with John's saying concerning the winnowing fork. But it is peculiar that Luke only refers in this instance to the prediction in its longer and perhaps more original form.[50] On two other occasions when he cites the Baptist's prediction (cf. Acts 1:5; 11:16) he follows Mark's rendering. It would appear, however, that the two versions are nearly synonymous. The Spirit and fire are equivalent terms explicating the OT ideas of purification and judgment.[51] This fits in well with Luke's apparent use of the divided Israel concept to explain the Jewish–Christian relation. This is especially visible in Acts 5:32, where the Spirit is given to those who obey God, but simultaneously testifies against those who reject God's plan of salvation in Jesus.[52]

Luke next refers to the prediction at the Gospel's conclusion. In Luke 24:49 Jesus tells his followers that *he* will send them "what his Father has promised," but they are to wait in Jerusalem ἕως οὗ ἐνδύσησθε ἐξ ὕψους δύναμιν. For Luke, ἐξ ὕψους δύναμιν and the Holy Spirit "are indissolubly related," if not identical expressions.[53]

---

[50] On the Q form as the more original form, see Marshall, *Luke*, p. 144; Menzies, *Early Christian Pneumatology*, pp. 135–36; Stein, *Luke*, p. 132.

[51] So, e.g., Dunn, *Baptism in the Holy Spirit*, pp. 11–13.

[52] See further Menzies, *Early Christian Pneumatology*, pp. 141–45.

[53] Grundmann, "δύναμις," *TDNT* 2, pp. 300–301.

This close relation perhaps reflects an OT blending of the two ideas.[54] Luke makes this same connection in the parallel construction πνεῦμα ἅγιον … δύναμις ὑψίστου in 1:35 of his birth narrative.[55] Thus in contrast to Mark and Matthew, Luke shows in his Gospel *who* "the Coming One" of the Baptist's prediction is. Just prior to his ascension, Jesus identifies himself as "the Coming One." In effect, Jesus promises his followers that, as exalted Lord, he will baptize with the Spirit.

Acts 1:4–5 makes this association still more clearly. Here Luke reiterates Jesus' promise in Luke 24:49 in terms reminiscent of Mark 1:8.[56] In v. 5, he specifically mentions John's contrast between his water baptism and the coming Spirit baptism, which in v. 4 Jesus refers to as "that which was promised by the Father." Luke clearly indicates from the context of Acts 2 (esp. v. 33) that the Spirit's coming at Pentecost fulfills the Baptist and the Father's promise.[57] He thus demonstrates for the first time in the life of the early church the knowledge that Mark assumes!

At another important juncture in Acts Luke again recalls John's prophecy. Luke describes in Acts 10 how the Holy Spirit came upon Cornelius, a God-fearer, and those who were with him. In response to some "circumcised believers" in Jerusalem critical of Peter's contact with these Gentiles (11:2–3), Peter defends what happened in Caesarea on the basis of the indubitable coming of the Spirit upon Cornelius and those with him (11:15–17). He clinches his defense by stating that the Spirit came upon the Gentiles in fulfillment of Jesus' promise that he would give the Spirit to his

---

[54] So Windisch, "Jesus und der Geist," pp. 225–30. Menzies, *Early Christian Pneumatology*, pp. 122–28, 204 argues, however, that "δύναμις is mediated by the Spirit but not equivalent to it" (p. 204); Menzies, "Spirit and Power," pp. 11–20. But cf. Turner, "Power of Jesus' Miracles," pp. 124–52.

[55] In a dual sense Luke describes the Spirit of God as the principal agent in the birth of the church as he was in that of the Messiah; so Lincoln, "Theology and History," p. 204. But Minear, "Birth Stories" rightly cautions that while both have "an analogous thematic role" for their respective books (p. 129), nowhere in Luke–Acts is there "an explicit reference to … 'the virgin birth' of the church" (p. 130); and thus "the first two chapters of the Gospel 'set the stage' for all subsequent speeches and actions" (p. 130).

[56] For lit. specifically on the Luke 24:49 – Acts 1:4–5 parallel, see, e.g., Dupont, "Theological Significance," pp. 16–19; Kasting, *Anfänge*, pp. 41–42; Talbert, *Literary Patterns*, pp. 59–61; Wilckens, *Missionsreden*, pp. 56–57, 94–95; Tannehill, *Luke*, pp. 293–98; Menzies, *Early Christian Pneumatology*, pp. 198–204.

[57] So, e.g., Wainwright, *Trinity*, p. 215; Wilson, *Gentile Mission*, p. 124; Dunn, *Jesus and the Spirit*, p. 194; Marshall, "Pentecost," p. 351; Brown, "Water Baptism," pp. 135, 141; Schweizer, *Holy Spirit*, p. 62; Barrett, *Holy Spirit*, p. 141, n. 4; Manson, *Sayings of Jesus*, pp. 40–41.

followers (vv. 16–17). Peter's recalling of the Baptist's prophecy as τοῦ ῥήματος τοῦ κυρίου refers back to Jesus' post-resurrection utterance in Acts 1:5. Peter undeniably understood the occasion as "a Pentecost to the Gentiles." The episode is unique and climactic. Through the Gentiles' manifest reception of the Spirit God has revealed to the Jewish church his intended plan to extend salvation to the Gentiles as well.

In two other contexts, Luke may yet again implicitly refer to the Baptist's prediction, contexts which may also illustrate his stated writing aim (cf. Luke 1:4). In Acts 18:24–28, Luke tells the story of Apollos, a Jew from Alexandria, who had a masterful knowledge of the scriptures and of Jesus (vv. 24–25a), but who only knew of John's baptism (v. 25b). While in Ephesus, Priscilla and Aquila noticed this deficiency and took him aside to instruct him in "the way of God [i.e., God's whole plan of salvation[58]] more adequately" (v. 26b). Luke unfortunately does not detail the content of their instruction or Apollos' specific deficiency. It would seem that Apollos had received the Spirit (cf. the expression ζέων τῷ πνεύματι; par. Rom. 12:11), but in some way his thinking was still incomplete or in need of some correction.[59] Luke's qualifying comment regarding John's baptism in v. 25b suggests that it may have had something to with receiving Christian water baptism and understanding the nature of Jesus' Spirit baptism.[60] For according to Luke–Acts, not to know about Jesus' conferral of the Spirit misses out on a fundamental sign that Jesus is Lord and still present among his people.

Luke never mentions the coming of the Spirit upon Apollos but does stress that subsequent to his instruction by Priscilla and Aquila he greatly encouraged believers and staunchly defended Jesus as the messiah before the Jews (vv. 27–28). With this story Luke clarifies the importance of understanding Spirit baptism for Christian teaching, edification, and defense of the faith, a kind of clarification quite similar to his stated aim to Theophilus himself.

In the contiguous episode (Acts 19:1–7), Luke recounts a similar story where Paul in Ephesus encounters a small group of men, whom Luke designates as μαθητάς (v. 1). I take μαθητής here to mean "Christian disciple" as it does everywhere else in Acts;

---

[58] Michaelis, "ὁδός," *TDNT* 5, p. 90.
[59] For a survey of the various views, see Polhill, *Acts*, pp. 396–97.
[60] See further Menzies, *Early Christian Pneumatology*, p. 270 and the extensive lit. cited on p. 270, n. 5.

whether the twelve were Christians in the post-resurrection sense of the word, or followers of God more in the OT sense does not lessen the importance of the fulfillment of the Baptist's promise for the story.[61] They had only participated in John's baptism. They were unaware that the Spirit had been given (vv. 2–3).[62] Paul subsequently rectified this deficiency (v. 4), baptized them in the name of Jesus (v. 5), and transmitted the Spirit to them (v. 6). The point here is not whether they were believers or not, though they had apparently responded favorably to John's message, but that the "Lord" Jesus had fulfilled John's prophecy and that their spiritual understanding and experience had to be adjusted in light of it. The verbal similarity between Paul's phrase τὸν ἐρχόμενον μετ' αὐτόν in Acts 19:4 and the Baptist's ἔρχεται δὲ ὁ ἰσχυρότερός μου in Luke 3:16 textually supports that Luke has Jesus' fulfillment of the Baptist's prophecy in mind in Acts 19:1–7.

They probably knew that John was the forerunner to the Christ and that the intended end of John's ministry was to prepare a people for the coming messiah. But apparently these disciples did not know that Jesus was the messiah. Therefore, to make their knowledge complete, they needed to know the message of Jesus' death and resurrection and that he now reigns as the exalted "Lord" in heaven and from there has poured out the Spirit upon his followers.[63] Jesus is "the Coming One" announced by John. Their speaking in tongues and prophesying (v. 6) conclusively shows the eradication of their ignorance of Jesus' Spirit baptism. This passage illustrates yet again Luke's desire to explicate the meaning of John's prophecy for his readers.

The prediction as promise to believers

Fundamental to the Baptist's prediction in the synoptic tradition is the belief that the messiah will baptize with the Spirit those who are repentant of heart. In contrast to Mark and Matthew, however, who limit the promise of the Spirit to the saying of John (Mark 1:8;

---

[61] So, e.g., Rengstorf, "μαθητής," *TDNT* 4, pp. 455–59; Norris, "Christians Only," pp. 100–102.

[62] Jeremias, *Proclamation*, pp. 81–82; Michaelis, "Johannes-Jünger," pp. 717–36; Johnson, *Acts*, p. 337; Polhill, *Acts*, p. 399. Some even speculate that the disciples were unaware of Jesus' coming; so, e.g., Parratt, "Rebaptism," pp. 182–83; Giblet, "Baptism," p. 169.

[63] So Polhill, *Acts*, p. 399.

Matt. 3:11), Luke corroborates the saying from other sources of authority and discloses the identity of its recipients.

1. *The corroboration of the prediction.* As with Mark (and Matthew), Luke first mentions the promise in John's preaching about the Messiah (Luke 3:16). But Luke uniquely supplements it with Jesus' teaching. In Luke 24:49 and Acts 1:4, Jesus tells his disciples that he will give them what the Father has promised – i.e., the fulfillment of the Baptist's prediction (so Acts 1:5).[64] Luke 11:13 may allude to the promise as well. Here Jesus parallels a father's giving of good gifts to his son with God's gift of the Holy Spirit to those who obey him.[65]

Furthermore, in the Pentecost sermon, Peter appeals to the OT (Joel 2:28–32; Acts 2:17–21) to substantiate God's promise that he would pour out his Spirit in the age to come – Acts 5:32; 11:17; 15:8 may also allude to this divine promise. Luke also uses apostolic preaching to corroborate the Baptist's promise. The best example of this is found again in Peter's Pentecost address in Acts 2 (but perhaps also in 5:29–32; 19:1–7). Here Peter declares that the Spirit's visible reality in the church proves that Jesus is truly exalted and the messiah (Acts 2:33), and so promises, in appeal, the gift of the Spirit to those who will believe the gospel of Jesus Christ (v. 38). "The *kerygma* in Acts," Dodd concludes, "lays emphasis upon the Holy Spirit in the church as the sign that the new age of fulfilment has begun."[66] Thus, in comparison to Mark (and Matthew), Luke uniquely reinforces the Baptist's promise of the Spirit and its fulfillment in Jesus through the Father's promise, Jesus' instruction, the OT and apostolic preaching.

2. *The disclosure of its recipients.* According to the synoptic tradition (Luke 3:1–18; Mark 1:2–8; Matt. 3:1–12), the Baptist's promise of the Spirit appears strictly intended for the Jewish people. The designation τοῦ λαοῦ in Luke 3:15 (and τὸν λαόν, v. 18) most likely collectively refers to the Jewish people, of which the

---

[64] Although Jesus' teaching on Spirit baptism in Acts 1:4–5 appears traceable to Luke 24:49, in light of their parallel structure both texts appear as general "recapitulations" of Jesus' earlier teaching on the matter, e.g., Matt. 10:20 (Luke 12:12); John 14–16; so Marshall, *Acts*, p. 58, or in terms of summary "Erinnerungen" as is common elsewhere in Luke–Acts, e.g., Luke 24:6–8, 44; Acts 11:26; 20:35; so Pesch, *Apg. 1–12*, pp. 66–67.

[65] Of the five textual variants – πνεῦμα ἀγαθόν, ἀγαθὸν δόμα, δόματα ἀγαθά, ἀγαθὸν δόμα πνεύματος ἁγίου, and ἀγαθά – the attestation for πνεῦμα ἅγιον in Luke 11:13 is impressive and most likely the original; so Metzger, *Textual Commentary*, p. 158.

[66] Dodd, *Apostolic Preaching*, p. 26.

ὄχλοι (vv. 7,10), τελῶναι (v. 12), and στρατευόμενοι (v. 14) were a part.[67] Unlike Mark and Matthew, however, Luke distinctly combines John's promise of the Spirit with the universal nature of the gospel message. According to Luke 24:47–49, Acts 1:4–5 (coupled with v. 8) and perhaps the "all" of Acts 2:17 (Joel 2:28),[68] the recipients of the promised Spirit widens to include Gentiles as well. Although Jesus' command to preach the gospel εἰς πάντα τὰ ἔθνη (Luke 24:47) and ἕως ἐσχάτου τῆς γῆς (Acts 1:8) does not clearly express this and was probably not readily apparent at first to the early Jewish church in Jerusalem, as Acts illustrates, this was God's every intention.

Initially, as Acts 1–7 makes clear, Christianity was solely a Jewish phenomenon. The Pentecost event in Acts 2 was resoundingly a Jewish experience. Luke describes the crowd as God-fearing Jews (v. 5, Ἰουδαῖοι, ἄνδρες εὐλαβεῖς), Jews and proselytes (v. 11, Ἰουδαῖοί τε καὶ προσήλυτοι), fellow Jews (v. 14, ἄνδρες Ἰουδαῖοι), men of Israel (v. 22, ἄνδρες Ἰσραηλῖται) and more categorically, the whole house of Israel (v. 36, πᾶς οἶκος Ἰσραήλ); identifies Peter, the other apostles, and the gathered throng as brothers (vv. 29, 37), although ἄνδρες ἀδελφοί should be understood in the ethnic sense, for not everyone responded to Peter's preaching, as the participial clause in v. 41 (οἱ μὲν οὖν ἀποδεξά-μενοι τὸν λόγον αὐτοῦ) suggests; and mentions that the believers continued their association with the temple (v. 46). The location of Acts 3–7 is also in and around Jerusalem and the recorded episodes are strictly Jewish in complexion. It is not until the Jewish persecution of the church in 8:1–3 that we read of believers, or anyone else for that matter, leaving the city. Up to this point, Luke describes the young church as nestled in the Judean hills of Palestine, growing within the confines of Judaism.

But with the outbreak of persecution against the church in connection with Stephen's death, Luke shows believers for the first time leaving Jerusalem for other parts of Judea and Samaria, and

---

[67] So Fitzmyer, *Luke I–IX*, pp. 467–71; Sanders, *Jews*, pp. 162–64.

[68] Tentatively, Marshall, *Acts*, p. 73 and n. 3. The problem is the referent of πᾶσαν σάρκα and those of the following four personal pronouns (ὑμῶν). Do they refer strictly to Peter's immediate Jewish audience or do they embody a wider audience, including Gentiles? As the story-line of Acts unfolds, we see that the Gentiles were divinely meant to be included, but it is doubtful whether the early Jewish church in Jerusalem had anticipated this expansion (cf., e.g., Acts 10:1–11:17, esp. 10:34; 11:17). For a summary of the manuscript tendencies concerning the Joel citation in Acts, see Metzger, *Textual Commentary*, pp. 296–97; Epp, *Theological Tendency*, pp. 66–72.

preaching the gospel message wherever they went (8:4). In particular, Luke focuses on Philip, who won converts among the
Samaritans (8:5–8, 12), a group despised by the Jews (e.g., Luke
9:51–54). Peter and John's conferral of the Spirit upon the Samaritans by laying on of hands revealed to the apostles that God had
accepted the Samaritans into the church (8:14–17). This scenario is
exceptional and of special importance for Luke, for again in the
case of the Gentiles (e.g., Cornelius and his household, 10:19, 44–
45, 47; 11:12, 15–18; 15:8–9) the Spirit's manifest coming incon-
trovertibly reveals to the Jewish believers that God is at work in the
church in a way far exceeding their own expectations.

That God freely bestows the Spirit on those who repent and
believe the gospel regardless of cultural, ethnic, or geographical
barriers may also partially explain Luke's metaphorical use of the
term "gift" to describe the reception of the Holy Spirit (Acts 1:4;
2:38; 8:20; 10:45; 11:17).[69] Therefore, according to Luke, both the
Giver and the Gift become the subject-complement of the gospel
message preached and received, a gospel message knowing no
boundaries.

Conclusion: Spirit baptism and the exalted Jesus

In this chapter, I have attempted to show that in the process of
writing a Gospel Luke's handling of the Spirit baptism theme
reveals a conscious expansion of Mark's treatment of John the
Baptist's prophecy that "the Coming One will baptize with the
Spirit" and in so doing reveals something of his own christology.

We have seen that after John's prophecy in Mark 1:8, Mark
never returns to it in his Gospel (at least not explicitly so!). Mark
most probably assumes that his readers would have understood
Pentecost as its fulfillment on account of Peter's probable previous
teaching about it in Mark's church. For Mark, John's utterance in
1:8 in conjunction with his statement about his unworthiness in v. 7
seems intended to illustrate Jesus' uniqueness and superiority over
John (and through implication to the crowds, the disciples, the
natural and demonic realms, his antagonists, and ultimately death

---

[69] Whether Luke derived the idea of "gift" from Q as reflected in Luke 11:13 (par.
Matt. 7:11) or from Ps. 68:18 is uncertain. For lit. defending Ps. 68:18, see, e.g.,
Dupont, "Ascension du Christ," pp. 219–28; Turner, "Spirit of Christ,"
pp. 176–79. Bock, *Proclamation*, pp. 181–83, however, doubts whether any
allusion is being made to the Psalm, for Acts 2 makes no reference to Moses or
the Law.

both physical and spiritual). It coincides with the way Mark develops his christological portrait elsewhere in his Gospel.[70]

Luke, however, for reasons connected to his own writing purposes, expands Mark on this very point. Luke's repeated allusions to the Baptist's prophecy, his corroboration of it from the Father's promise, Jesus' teaching, OT scripture and apostolic preaching, and his attempt to illustrate its reality within the church's mission in accordance with the universal nature of the gospel message supports this. Luke's reversion to the Markan rendering in Acts 1:5 and 11:17, especially after recording the longer Q form in Luke 3:16 (possibly because of its being the more original), may suggest a conscious link with Mark's Gospel.

Furthermore, for Luke to develop the Spirit baptism theme as he did requires, in contrast to Mark, additional christological development as well. As Mark apparently assumes, according to church tradition, it was the exalted Jesus who poured out the Spirit in fulfillment of the Baptist's prediction. This reality then requires that Luke recount for his readers something about Jesus' exaltation, i.e., his enthronement in heaven, in order to depict the outpouring of the Spirit at the feast of Pentecost in Acts 2 (so esp. v. 33!).

The christological ramifications of the Baptist's prediction need further study as it may throw additional light on the character and purpose of Luke's christology. Alongside Luke's development of the Spirit baptism theme in Luke–Acts, a peculiar theological concern surfaces, one not made explicit in Mark (or Matthew). This involves the relation between the Gift and the Giver. In the OT, conferring the Spirit as Jesus did was a work reserved for Yahweh alone. Why then, according to Luke, was Jesus also able to give the Spirit? Discovering Luke's christological conviction on this issue will become the focus of our study in ch. 9.

[70] See further, e.g., Hooker, *Message of Mark.*

7

JESUS AND SALVATION HISTORY

Introduction

Mark's Gospel is the proclamation of Jesus Christ, the Son of God
(1:1).[1] It "is fundamentally the Easter message."[2] Although Jesus'
words in 1:15 – μετανοεῖτε καὶ πιστεύετε ἐν τῷ εὐαγγελίῳ – may
well be original to him as they echo a familiar plea of the OT
prophets[3] and may, in fact, preserve a distinction, in the language
used, between Jesus' preaching and that of the church,[4] one cannot
help but hear the post-Easter message resounding in them even at
this point.[5] It seems fair to conclude that for Mark, "Jesus was not
only the herald of good tidings; he was also himself the content of
the good tidings he announced."[6] For this reason, some have suggested that Mark develops his work according to the early church's
preaching,[7] and that his entire Gospel could be understood as a
saving proclamation based on Jesus' earthly ministry and passion.[8]

But despite his interest in proclamation, Mark devotes little
space in his Gospel explicitly to salvation-history themes. A
number of important questions go unanswered. When and how did
Jesus' death and resurrection become a means of belief? What was
to become of Judaism? How was the gospel to spread throughout

---

[1]   But this is not to deny the historical reliability of the account itself. The Gospel
is, for Mark, the historical report authenticating the Easter message. See further
Martin's critique, in *Evangelist & Theologian*, pp. 73–75, of Marxsen, *Mark the
Evangelist*; more recently, the same criticism would hold true of Mack, *Myth of
Innocence*.

[2]   Pokorný, "Markusevangelium," p. 1987; also Best, "Purpose," p. 30; Oberlinner,
"Botschaft vom Kreuz," p. 62.

[3]   So Lane, *Mark*, pp. 49–50 and n. 37, p. 65 and n. 94 and lit. cited therein.

[4]   Lemcio, "Intention of Mark," p. 189.

[5]   Pokorný, "Markusevangelium," p. 1988; Martin, *Evangelist & Theologian*, p. 27.

[6]   Cranfield, *Mark*, p. 36; also, Pesch, *Markus. 1, 1–8, 26*, pp. 106–107; Gnilka,
Markus. 1, 1–8, 26, p. 68.

[7]   Moule, *Phenomenon*, pp. 104–105, 114.

[8]   Martin, *Evangelist & Theologian*, pp. 161–62.

the world? What was the significance of Jesus' coming in God's saving plan? How does a reader of Mark fit into it? And what does this indicate about Jesus' future return?

In this chapter we shall examine what Luke reveals to us about his christology in the way he interacts with Mark's minimal handling of these salvation-history themes, particularly the universal importance of Jesus as Savior within God's saving plan.

Mark's Gospel: salvation history assumed

In comparison to Luke and Matthew, Mark's use of the σώζω word group seems thin.[9] Martin Hengel reaffirms this conclusion. But he quickly points out that although Mark mentions the atoning significance of Jesus' death only twice (10:45; 14:24) and once that Jesus forgives sins (2:5–12), these theological reflections are, nevertheless, deliberately placed at important junctures within the narrative to give them more extended meaning within the Gospel itself.[10] In addition, scholars commonly accept that the confessions of the centurion at the cross (15:39) and the divine messenger at the tomb (16:6) encapsulate the basic message of the preaching of the early church. Thus, despite its minimal use of salvation language, Mark's Gospel illustrates the Christian belief that Jesus' "death and resurrection are indissolubly connected" and "epitomize the whole of Christian proclamation."[11]

Donald Senior further laments that critics too often do not consider enough Mark's interest in salvation history.[12] Although the theme is indeed less pronounced here than in Matthew or Luke–Acts, numerous characteristic Markan features can be "coherently linked together under this overriding principle" (p. 78). Foremost here is worldwide missions. The key text is Mark 13:9–11. Mark shows that according to Jesus' teaching and work, the Israel-first principle (7:27) gives way to the eschatological principle (13:10), i.e., that the gospel should be preached to all nations. Mark's persistent effort to chart the Jewish leaders' rejec-

---

[9] See further Green, *Meaning of Salvation*, pp. 119–22; Delorme, "Salut," p. 80; Lemcio, "Intention of Mark," p. 191.

[10] Hengel, "Problems in Mark," pp. 37–38; also, Taylor, *Mark*, pp. 124–25; Delorme, "Salut," pp. 79–108. Schweizer, "Jesus Christus," *TRE* 16, p. 703 believes that the ransom saying in 10:45 refers to Jesus' whole earthly career.

[11] Oberlinner, "Botschaft vom Kreuz," pp. 61–65 (quot. p. 62).

[12] Senior, "Struggle to be Universal," pp. 78–80. Cf. Conzelmann's qualifying comments in "Present and Future," pp. 38–41.

tion of Jesus paves the way for "the God-intended transfer from Israel to a worldwide community" (p. 80). Thus, "the goal of Mark's salvation-history reflection is to validate and encourage the church's worldwide mission" (p. 80).

Hence, one may justifiably conclude that the underlying saving importance of Jesus' death and its implications for proclamation in Mark's Gospel weigh heavily upon the author's intention. But Moule still insists that Mark does not go to great pains in detailing the connection between salvation and Jesus' life, death, resurrection, the post-Easter ministry of the disciples and its ramifications for believers.[13] Following Moule's lead, Lemcio plausibly suggests that Mark does this out of a desire to preserve the pre-Easter reality of Jesus' non-developed teaching in this area. Mark writes to believers who use Jesus' sayings. But he nonetheless seeks to maintain "the distinction between their own post-Easter beliefs and those of Jesus."[14]

The textual problem

A number of texts within Mark's Gospel signal a salvation-historical awareness but are largely left undefined or unsubstantiated. The main passages in question are 1:17; 9:9–10a; 10:45; 13:9–10; 14:9. In 1:17 Jesus summons Simon (Peter) and Andrew to leave their nets and follow him, for he will make them ἁλιεῖς ἀνθρώπων. Within Mark, Peter and the disciples do preach the good news to others (6:7–13), but the part they would personally play "in the international mission of the church" is nowhere illustrated.[15] The prophecy remains for the most part unfulfilled.[16] In fact, at the Gospel's end the disciples have not yet seen the resurrected Jesus and remain in ignorance. When, then, did they understand and begin to proclaim the gospel to others, drawing people into the church as "fishers of men" as Jesus had foretold?

In 9:9–10a Jesus orders Peter, James, and John not to tell anyone about the transfiguration until he rises from the dead. The reason for this temporary call to silence is that knowledge of the resurrection will give them the proper perspective for understanding the event. To know precisely who Jesus was and what he had come to do demands knowledge of the resurrection. But Mark's Gospel

---

[13] Moule, *Phenomenon*, p. 107.   [14] Lemcio, "Intention of Mark," p. 188.
[15] Hurtado, *Mark*, p. 11.   [16] Cf. Lane, *Mark*, pp. 67–69.

leaves unfulfilled the reader's expectation that the disciples eventually did in fact make the christological adjustment in their thinking.

In the ransom passage (10:45), Jesus tells the disciples that "the Son of Man has come not to be served but to serve and to give his life as a ransom for many." But does Mark adequately illustrate in his Gospel that Jesus has given his life as a ransom for *anyone*? Whereas he effectively shows on what basis Jesus has become a ransom through his death and resurrection, he does not document how this is borne out in the lives of his followers. Mark leaves the redemptive and christological significance of the designation unsubstantiated: Who are "the many"? How does this message get to them? And how do they variously respond?

Further, Mark leaves the kerygmatic content and significance of 13:9–10 imprecisely stated. What will compel some of the Jewish leaders to resist and persecute Jesus' followers "on account of him" (ἕνεκεν ἐμοῦ) as v. 9 intimates? And what gospel (τὸ εὐαγγέλιον, v. 10) is to be preached to all nations? The answer to both these questions lies in Mark's connection between the conclusion and the opening verse of the Gospel: the full gospel of Jesus Christ ends with the empty tomb.[17] Its reality is what becomes the offense to the Jews and the substance of the message Jesus' followers preach. But Mark's Gospel does not substantially describe how the fulfillment of 13:9–10 had started to take place, although 14:28/16:7 may allude to this, and how it reached universal proportions, although the very existence of the Gospel itself may reveal the fact of it and, in part, the means by which it is being accomplished.[18]

Lastly, in 14:9 Jesus says that wherever the gospel is preached throughout the world, the woman's anointing will also be remembered. But the Gospel itself does not make clear that this verse illustrates "the missionary vocabulary of the Gentile-Christian Church in a traditional saying of Jesus."[19] Mark does not explicitly tell the reader what εἰς ὅλον τὸν κόσμον refers to. His readers would, of course, know in what way they fit into it. But other readers would not necessarily be able to make this connection. Does the phrase primarily refer to Diaspora Judaism or does it include Gentiles as well? And in either case, when and how did the gospel move out of Palestine into this worldwide setting?

---

[17] So esp. Pokorný, "Markusevangelium," pp. 1985–88.
[18] So esp. Zmijewski, *Eschatologiereden*, p. 144; Pesch, *Markus. 8, 27–16, 20*, p. 285.
[19] Taylor, *Mark*, p. 534.

A Markan solution

These passages elucidate Mark's perspective – and probably his readers' as well. Mark puts together an account of Jesus' life in full knowledge of its outcome and its meaning to him. The way he closely combines "Jesus as the proclaimer of the kingdom of God" with "Jesus as the object of belief" evidences this. But to proclaim the latter idea in its fullest sense requires knowledge of his crucifixion, death, and resurrection.

Mark could not help but write his Gospel in this way. The climax of Jesus' earthly ministry provided the very rationale for the church's faith and witness. Jesus was to some degree the object of the disciples' faith during his earthly career, although Mark shows considerable restraint in reading back post-Easter christological perspectives onto Jesus' life;[20] the Easter experience, however, renewed and deepened their belief in him with a fullness hitherto unknown to them.[21] Mark writes with this added reality in mind.

Thus, as we have done in the previous two chapters, it seems fair to conclude once again that Mark presupposes some knowledge among his readers. In these instances, he apparently assumes that they too could fill in the gaps regarding the salvation and proclamation themes, and to discern his hand in the way he expresses them. Mark seems not to fear a misreading of these verses, or else he would have added more qualifying material to lessen that possibility.

This kind of reader insight allows Mark to concentrate more specifically on his topic of interest: Jesus and not the disciples' response to him. The church's principal message was Jesus and that salvation was found in him alone. The person and work of the disciples, though important, was subordinate. They had no "soteriological dignity" of their own. Thus they "could not but fall into the background, for the community wished to be informed not about the 'words and deeds' of the first disciples but purely and solely about the activities of their Lord."[22] For this reason, Taylor believes that in Mark "a faith-union is implied, but this idea is not expressed in any Markan saying."[23]

For some, however, needing for whatever reason a more compre-

---

[20] So Moule, *Phenomenon*, pp. 106–14; Lemcio, "Intention of Mark," pp. 187–206.
[21] So van Bavel, "Auferstehung," pp. 9–23.
[22] Hengel, *Charismatic Leader*, p. 79.
[23] Taylor, *Mark*, p. 125; also Moule, *Phenomenon*, p. 107.

hensive account of the beginnings of Christianity, would Mark's presentation of salvation history have been sufficient? Questions like the following would still need answering: How and when did Jesus' followers come to trust in him after his resurrection? How and when did the cross of Jesus become a means of belief? What is the message that would be preached? How did the gospel move out of Palestine? How are Gentile believers to understand themselves as members of a church whose origins were primarily Jewish? Has God rejected Israel? Was a Gentile–Jewish church part of God's intended plan? What continuing role does the exalted Jesus play in the furtherance of the gospel? And what may the spread of the gospel indicate concerning the time of Jesus' return?

We now need to assess whether Luke supplies detailed information on the kinds of omissions and questions just described. In interacting with Mark along these lines, Luke may again disclose to us something of his own christology.

Luke–Acts: salvation history demonstrated

Although it is true (1) that Luke knew and used Mark's Gospel and in a sense rewrote it; (2) that anybody who chose to work in this way would be consciously improving Mark; and (3) that some of the changes in the Gospel represent conscious attempts to supplement or to say something different than Mark, we can take the discussion a step further. If the content of Luke's Gospel represents a literaturization of Mark within the limits imposed by a Gospel, may not the idea of writing a second volume and some of the contents and shaping of that second volume also be influenced by the Markan source? Has Luke applied to Acts material or concepts taken over from his Markan source as he did in his Gospel? And if so, in what sense is this revealing of his christology?

A preliminary comparison

We shall begin by observing Luke's handling of the Markan passages as outlined above (1:17; 9:9–10a; 10:45; 13:10; 14:9).

Mark 1:17

In contrast to Mark's version of Jesus' calling of his disciples in 1:16–20, Luke records no similar episode at this juncture in his

Gospel; instead, he expresses the idea somewhat later in 5:1–11 between the narrative sequence of Mark 1:39/Luke 4:44 and Mark 1:40–45/Luke 5:12–16. Certainly Luke was familiar with Mark – as the linguistic parallels show, esp. Luke 5:1–3, 10–11.[24] But to delay reference to Jesus' call until after the summary statement of his preaching in Judea (Luke 4:44, Ἰουδαίας refers to the whole of Palestine; so also Luke 23:5; Acts 10:37) gives the entire episode "more psychological plausibility." Luke depicts Peter, James, and John responding intelligently to someone they already know.[25]

More importantly, Luke changes the emphasis of the episode itself. Mark places the accent upon Jesus: δεῦτε ὀπίσω μου, καὶ ποιήσω ὑμᾶς γενέσθαι ἁλιεῖς ἀνθρώπων (1:17). Jesus' words form an appeal with a resulting benefit attached, a kind of condition with ἁλιεῖς ἀνθρώπων forming a part of the apodosis. Becoming "fishers of men" is contingent upon following Jesus. In both parts, Mark places the spotlight on Jesus: Jesus makes the appeal, is the one to be followed, and is the one who will enable them to win others. That they eventually did proclaim Jesus as promised is secondary to Mark.

Luke, on the other hand, places the accent on Peter, ἀπὸ τοῦ νῦν ἀνθρώπους ἔσῃ ζωγρῶν (5:10), and more broadly James and John (cf. their similar responses in v. 11). All three figured prominently in such a role in the early church and fit this description in Acts, James being mentioned as the first martyr (Acts 12:2), presumably on account of his leading role in propagating the gospel, evident in Herod's attempt to appease the Jews by arresting some of the central figures of Christianity, i.e., James and Peter (vv. 3–4).[26] Luke presents the call as a statement of fact. It reflects a turning point in Peter's commitment to follow Jesus. His coming work in "catching others alive" is now the logical outcome of his resolution

[24] See further Marshall, *Luke*, pp. 199–201 and lit. cited therein.
[25] Fitzmyer, *Luke I–IX*, pp. 71, 560, although Luke's story is perhaps more than a transposition; it may have a historical parallel of its own. Luke quite possibly has another occasion in mind; so, e.g., Morris, *Luke*, p. 112; Marshall, *Luke*, pp. 199–201, 206. Mark's Gospel esp. reminds us that Jesus repeatedly appeared preaching along the shores of Galilee (1:16–20; 2:13; 3:7–12; 4:1–2). Even John records that the disciples returned there to fish following Jesus' crucifixion (21:1–11). Luke's account may record more specifically the last in a series of calls that Jesus issued to the fishermen, as the more decisive ἀπὸ τοῦ νῦν clause allows in comparison to Mark's more neutral and indefinite καὶ ποιήσω ὑμᾶς γενέσθαι (1:17).
[26] Cf. Fitzmyer, *Luke I–IX*, p. 569; Feldmeier, "Portrayal of Peter," p. 62 *et al.*, who argue that Luke has only Peter in mind.

to follow Jesus.[27] The whole episode takes on a missions orientation,[28] with ἀνθρώπους ἔσῃ ζωγρῶν now forming its "punch
line."[29]

Matthew's presentation in 4:18–22, however, neither digresses
from Mark's narrative sequence preceding the story, nor significantly alters its wording. Except for omitting γενέσθαι, the force of
which is retained in ποιήσω, he follows Mark 1:17 (cf. Matt. 4:19)
word for word. Thus unlike Luke, who intentionally develops the
soteriological emphases behind Mark's "fishers of men," Matthew
seems more inclined to follow Mark.

Mark 9:9–10a

We have already seen that Luke summarizes Mark 9:9–10 in Luke
9:36b to remove Mark's awkward reference to the resurrection
from the episode. But Luke additionally makes the point in 9:36b
that the disciples eventually did tell others what they had seen at
Jesus' transfiguration. The time expression ἐν ἐκείναις ταῖς
ἡμέραις indicates this. The phrase suggests a Lukan viewpoint.
For a period of time the three were silent about it; but that period
is now past. Presumably "in these days" (cf. τὰς ἡμέρας ταύτας,
Acts 3:24), of which Luke would also be a part, they speak openly
about it.

The point of demarcation was undoubtedly the resurrection – for
even after the transfiguration, the disciples did not understand that
Jesus must suffer and die, and be raised again (cf. Luke 18:31–34).
To preach Jesus without knowledge of the passion would have
given rise to "a superficial preconception of what messiahship and
sonship signifies."[30] They would probably have perceived him as
some sort of revolutionary and not as the final revelation of God's
salvation to humanity.[31]

In this passage Luke makes a special effort to clarify Mark
soteriologically. Mark gives the impression that the disciples

---

[27] For more on the philological distinction between the Markan and Lukan phrases
and the soteriological implications for Luke, see Wuellner, *Fishers of Men*,
pp. 232–38, esp. p. 238.

[28] So, e.g., Hengel, *Charismatic Leader*, p. 78; Schürmann, *Lukas. 1, 1–9, 50*,
pp. 271–72; Hendricksen, *Luke*, p. 285; Marshall, *Luke*, pp. 199, 206; Fitzmyer,
Luke I–IX, p. 563; Schneider, *Lukas. 1–10*, pp. 123, 126; Nolland, *Luke 1–9:20*,
p. 221.

[29] Fitzmyer, *Luke I–IX*, p. 562; also, Marshall, *Luke*, p. 206.

[30] Lane, *Mark*, p. 323.   [31] Summers, *Luke*, p. 117.

obeyed Jesus' command to silence, but he does not indicate whether they did eventually proclaim its significance after the resurrection. Luke, on the other hand, treats as a matter of fact the disciples' silence by referring to it as a time in the past, implying that they now openly talk about it. The perfect tense of ὁράω in v. 36 (ὧν ἑώρακαν; cf. ἃ εἶδον, Mark 9:9; τὸ ὅραμα, Matt. 17:9) additionally suggests that they did not forget what they had seen, and since the resurrection were proclaiming it accurately.[32]

Matthew omits Mark 9:10a ("they kept the matter to themselves"), but, as with Mark, closely preserves Jesus' command to silence in 17:9 (Mark 9:9).

Mark 10:45

A puzzling phenomenon of Luke's soteriology is his omission of Mark's ransom passage (10:45) in his record of Jesus' teaching on service during the Last Supper (Luke 22:24–27, cf. esp. v. 27b). Luke reflects two possible strands of Gospel tradition at this point: Mark's account of Jesus' teaching on true service instigated by the request of James and John for privileged position shortly preceding Jesus' triumphal entry into Jerusalem (Mark 10:35–45; cf. esp. Luke 22:24–26 to Mark 10:41–44); and John's account of Jesus' teaching on the same theme as prompted by his washing of the disciples' feet in preparation for the Passover Feast (John 13:12–17; cf. esp. Luke 22:27 to John 13:15–16). How strongly either of these strands influenced Luke 22 remains uncertain. It is doubtful whether the source question can be adequately answered.[33]

What is certain, however, is that Luke knew of the Markan saying but chose not to use it.[34] He retains the service idea but leaves out the ransom saying. He alludes to it in the bread and cup formulae in 22:19–20 (if this is accepted as genuine) and in Paul's Miletus address in Acts 20:28b. Luke's writings do not lack the idea of Jesus' death as a ransom, but only clear reference to it.[35] But why did he drop Mark 10:45?

Scholars propose numerous reasons. The answer possibly lies (1) in Luke's preference of sources, which may have lacked the

---

[32] Marshall, *Luke*, p. 389.
[33] For a good summary of the debate, see Fitzmyer, *Luke X–XXIV*, pp. 1412–14; for a plausible resolution, see Marshall, *Luke*, p. 811.
[34] Marshall, *Historian & Theologian*, p. 170; Goppelt, *Apostolic Witness*, p. 283.
[35] Fitzmyer, *Luke X–XXIV*, pp. 1212–13; Goppelt, *Apostolic Witness*, pp. 282–83.

saying;[36] (2) in his theological interests, which may have put less stress on a theology of the cross; (3) in his literary motives, which may have attempted to smooth over some of the unwritten assumptions connected with Mark's ransom saying; or (4) in some combination of these.

In developing the third point further, Luke may not have been satisfied with the seeming ambiguity of the qualifying phrase ἀντὶ πολλῶν (cf. also Mark 14:24, ὑπὲρ πολλῶν; Matt. 26:28, περὶ πολλῶν to Luke 22:20, ὑπὲρ ὑμῶν). Numerous commentators understand the Markan phrase in a restrictive sense.[37] They think that the designation parallels the rabbinic and Qumran interpretation of αὐτὸς ἁμαρτίας πολλῶν ἀνήνεγκεν in Isa. 53:12 (LXX), where the expression refers in the limited sense to the people of God, the eschatological covenant community. Others assert that ἀντὶ πολλῶν includes all of humanity,[38] on the basis that the Qumran writings[39] and the Hebrew equivalent *rabbim*[40] allow for the inclusive sense. At 1 Tim. 2:6 the inclusive sense may also be suggested, that Jesus has given himself as a ransom ὑπὲρ πάντων. If this passage derives from Mark 10:45, as is commonly thought, or both were independently translated from the same source,[41] πάντες may represent the Greek equivalent to the more ambiguous Hebrew *rabbim* or Aramaic *saggiin*, terms which literally translate as πολλοί in Greek. Hebrew and Aramaic have no word for "all."[42]

Luke possibly takes for granted the vicarious meaning of Jesus' death,[43] as the token references in Luke 22:19–20 and Acts 20:28 may suggest. Luke's primary soteriological interest is the *universal* scope of the gospel message. Although Mark 10:45 may well mean that Jesus died for all, it is, nevertheless, an awkward expression[44]

---

[36] So Page, "Authenticity," pp. 148–53.

[37] E.g., France, *Jesus and the OT*, pp. 120–21, 123; Barrett, "Mark 10.45," p. 24, who feels that the phrase refers to Israel as a whole with emphasis upon those who are neglected; Brown, "λύτρον," *NIDNTT* 3, pp. 197–98; Lane, *Mark*, pp. 384–85 and lit. cited in n. 93; Mann, *Mark*, pp. 416–20.

[38] E.g., Schmid, *Markus*, pp. 202–203; Graber, "πολλοί," *NIDNTT* 1, pp. 96–97; Popkes, *Christus Traditus*, p. 174; Hengel, *Atonement*, pp. 42, 50.

[39] Gnilka, *Markus. 8, 27–16, 20*, p. 104; Stuhlmacher, "Existenz," pp. 424–25.

[40] Moulder, "OT Background," p. 121, following Jeremias, *Eucharistic Words*, pp. 179–82, esp. pp. 181–82.

[41] So Lindars, "Mark 10.45," p. 294.

[42] Jeremias, *Eucharist Words*, p. 179; see also his discussion of *kol* (Heb.) and *kolla* (Aram.) on p. 179, n. 4.

[43] Cadbury, *Making*, p. 281; Hengel, *Atonement*, p. 71.

[44] So Moule, *Origin*, pp. 119–20; also Marshall, *Work of Christ*, pp. 41–42.

and perhaps liable to confuse Luke's point regarding the universal appeal of Jesus' death and resurrection. Choosing not to alter the saying, Luke may have preferred to leave it out, emphasizing instead the ransom and service themes separately in 22:19–20 and 22:24–27.[45]

In contrast, Matthew seems little concerned with this distinction. He closely follows the Markan wording of the episode in 20:20–28 and almost precisely that of Mark 10:45 in 20:28. He follows Mark's order, placing it between Jesus' passion prediction (Mark 10:32–34; Matt. 20:17–19; Luke 18:31–34) and the healing of Bartimaeus (Mark 10:46–52; Matt. 20:29–34; Luke 18:35–43). And like Mark, he makes no reference to it in his version of the Last Supper.

Mark 13:10

Another striking feature of Luke's soteriology is his omission of Mark 13:10 in his version of the Olivet discourse. Although the source discussion underlying Luke 21:5–38 remains speculative, Luke most probably had Mark before him.[46] Fitzmyer, e.g., observes that Luke's version parallels Mark 13 in narrative sequence, basic content, and much of its wording, although it is "clearly not a slavish reproduction" (p. 1324). This means, then, that whatever the source(s) he may have used, Luke knew of Mark 13:10 but deliberately chose not to use it. This omission is extraordinary in view of his pervasive interest in the mission theme.

Theories concerning why Luke may have dropped Mark 13:10 from his version of the Olivet discourse are many. Erich Gräßer, e.g., believes that Luke omitted the saying because the Markan version he used did not contain it. A later hand added it to Mark.[47] Günther Harder supposes that Luke dropped it because the universal mission had not yet begun by the time he had written his Gospel.[48] Hans Conzelmann, on the other hand, argues that it had already occurred by the time Luke wrote. For this reason he

---

[45] *Contra* Wilson, *Gentile Mission*, p. 50, that Luke's alteration of ὑπὲρ πολλῶν (Mark 14:24) to ὑπὲρ ὑμῶν (Luke 22:19–20) removes Mark's universal reference. To emphasize the Christian use of the ransom idea in the context of believers celebrating the Lord's Supper, as Luke may well be doing, does not preclude the idea that Jesus died for all; it only removes the ambiguity of the qualifying prepositional phrase within the given liturgical context.

[46] For thorough summaries of the source discussion, see Marshall, *Luke*, pp. 755–58; Fitzmyer, *Luke X–XXIV*, pp. 1326–30.

[47] Gräßer, *Problem der Parusieverzögerung*, p. 160.

[48] Harder, "Eschatologische Geschichtsbild," pp. 78–79.

wanted to sever the period of mission from that of the end. The latter follows the former but does not influence it.[49] Richard Hiers,[50] and more recently J. Bradley Chance,[51] argue that Luke removed the saying from the traditional material to avoid giving the impression that Jesus had erred since the universal mission had already been accomplished, but the parousia had not taken place. Robert Maddox thinks that Luke left it out because persecution had already set in well before the gospel had been preached to all nations.[52] David Tiede believes that Luke dropped it because he had no interest in the Gentiles themselves in ch. 21, but in God's vengeance-vindication response toward Israel.[53] Martin Hengel speculates that Luke had a possible aversion to the use of the substantive τὸ εὐαγγέλιον for fear of some misuse of the term and for this reason left it out.[54] Stephen Wilson,[55] Jacques Dupont,[56] and more recently Michael Dömer[57] assert that Luke reexpressed the idea in 24:46–47, giving it more visibility in line with his literary intentions. Lars Aejmelaeus[58] and F. F. Bruce[59] feel that Luke reserved the subject for Acts, where it would become more appropriate to the theme of that book.

The most probable theories are those of Wilson/Dupont/Dömer and Aejmelaeus/Bruce. A consensus among Markan scholars sees Mark 13:10 as inserted parenthetically between vv. 9 and 11.[60] Although Luke omits Mark 13:10 from his apocalyptic discourse, he does record a similar saying in his Gospel conclusion: the gospel – i.e., that in Christ's passion work, repentance and forgiveness of sins can be found – will be preached εἰς πάντα τὰ ἔθνη (24:46–47).

---

[49] Conzelmann, *Theology of St. Luke*, p. 128, and p. 214, n.1; see further lit. cited in Schneider, *Lukas. 11–24*, pp. 420–21. Zmijewski, *Eschatologiereden*, pp. 156–57 additionally suggests that ἀπαγομένους in Luke 21:12b *in nuce* amply expresses the idea of Mark 13:10. Conzelmann, "Geschichte und Eschaton," pp. 210–21 later adds that Mark 13:10 clearly presupposes the parousia's delay on the basis that the passage is not a traditional saying (p. 219). His argument is not convincing, however, mainly because the saying has good support as being traditional, as our discussion will show.

[50] Hiers, "Delay of the Parousia," p. 147.   [51] Chance, *Jerusalem*, pp. 95–97.

[52] Maddox, *Purpose*, p. 116.   [53] Tiede, *Prophecy and History*, p. 93.

[54] Hengel, "Titles," p. 169, n. 51; see also Conzelmann, *Theology of St. Luke*, p. 221 and lit. cited in Conzelmann, *Mitte der Zeit*, p. 119, n. 1, and p. 206, n. 2; Fitzmyer, *Luke X–XXIV*, p. 1340.

[55] Wilson, *Gentile Mission*, pp. 47–48.

[56] Dupont, "Portée christologique," pp. 131–34; Dupont, "Epreuves des chrétiens," p. 1124.

[57] Dömer, *Heil Gottes*, pp. 104–105.

[58] Aejmelaeus, *Miletrede*, p. 142.   [59] Bruce, "Eschatology," p. 63.

[60] For a summary of the reasons why, see Taylor, *Mark*, pp. 507–508.

This passage, in contrast to Mark, grounds unequivocally the gospel of Jesus in his death and resurrection. Howard Marshall plausibly suggests that Luke's account of Jesus' command to mission most likely reflects material congenial to earlier church tradition.[61] In other words, Luke does not create a scenario to make better logical sense of Mark 13:10, but in all likelihood reflects the kind of things his predecessors believed Jesus to have said at that time.[62]

Such a missiological inclusion in Mark's Gospel ending, on the other hand, would perhaps not have served Mark's purposes as well. It may have lessened the forcefulness of his christological intent. Mark apparently chose to emphasize in token form Jesus' call to world missions at other relevant points conducive to his narrative setting: 13:10 and 14:9. Luke may have known that Mark inserted 13:10 at this point and thus felt justified in omitting it from his parallel account (Luke 21:12–19; cf. Mark 13:9–13). In keeping with his conservative use of sources, the record of Jesus' call to world missions in ch. 24 would conform to the belief of the early church and, for him, provide the starting point and paradigmatic theme for his subsequent book.

Even Matthew appears to modify Mark significantly at this point. He omits εἰς πάντα τὰ ἔθνη in his parallel to Mark 13:10 (cf. Matt. 10:18). But the idea does appear in the apocalyptic discourse (Matt. 24:14), Jesus' comments about the woman's anointing (26:13), and his post-resurrection instruction (28:19).

Mark 14:9

In his Gospel, Luke drops the episode of the woman's anointing of Jesus in Bethany (Mark 14:3–9) and Jesus' saying that the woman's deed will be remembered wherever the gospel is preached throughout the world (v. 9). He probably does this so as not to confuse it with his story of Jesus' anointing by a sinful woman (7:36–50). The thrust of the two stories is different. Whereas Mark's story focuses on Jesus' impending death, with v. 9 as parenthetical, Luke's entire story explicates the soteriological significance of Jesus. The pericope stands as "a proclamation of the

61 Marshall, *Luke*, pp. 903–904.
62 So also Mahoney, "Editorial Rewriting," p. 223; Taylor, *Mark*, p. 508; Cranfield, *Mark*, p. 400; Lane, *Mark*, pp. 461–63; Beasley-Murray, *Kingdom of God*, p. 290; and lit. cited in Pesch, *Naherwartungen*, p. 129, n. 388.

grace of God to sinners"[63] and establishes "faith as fundamental to salvation (through the forgiveness of sins)."[64]

Luke perhaps preferred the story of the sinful woman because it explicated some of the soteriological knowledge Mark assumed. This seems the case with Mark 14:9. Although the worldwide proclamation of the gospel is crucial to the church's self-understanding and most likely reflects Jesus' teaching,[65] the saying in Mark appears more as an appendix to the main idea of the episode and presupposes a degree of Christian teaching as well. In comparison, Luke's entire story vividly portrays the redemptive themes of repentance, forgiveness of sins, and salvation.[66] In addition, Luke retains the specific allusion to the universal mission of the church in the words of the resurrected Jesus in Luke 24:46–47 (cf. Mark 13:10). Matthew, on the other hand, follows closely in 26:6–13 the Markan narrative sequence and the episode's wording – v. 13 practically follows Mark 14:9 verbatim.

In summary, this brief preliminary synoptic comparison reveals that Luke consciously clarifies Mark's handling of salvation-history themes. Matthew's apparently deliberate but more conservative revision of Mark on these texts also indirectly shows this as a Lukan writing concern.

A Lukan solution – Acts as exposition of Mark 13:9–11

Luke gives the distinct impression in v. 1 of his Gospel preface that his work will involve an interplay between history (περὶ τῶν ... πραγμάτων) and theology (πεπληροφορημένων ἐν ἡμῖν), an intention he reaffirms in the opening verse of Acts as well. He intends the reader to understand his writings as a historical account that is theologically motivated – "historical" in the way he ordered his work as a history of the life of Jesus and of the beginnings of the early church.[67]

---

[63] Nolland, *Luke 1–9:20*, p. 352.   [64] Schneider, *Lukas. 1–10*, p. 177.
[65] *Contra* Wilson, *Gentile Mission.*   [66] Fitzmyer, *Luke I–IX*, p. 686.
[67] A fuller definition of "historical" should also include the question of historicity. Is Luke also telling us how it actually happened? The author gives us *no* adequate grounds on the basis of his preface for dismissing straightaway the possibility that his reporting was not also historically verifiable. It is perhaps these very grounds which premise his theological statements, granting the latter their veritability. *People-in-the-know would otherwise be able to denounce the Lukan material as misleading or spurious.* For more thorough discussions positively assessing the historicity of Luke–Acts, see Hengel, *Acts*; Hengel, *Between Jesus and Paul*; Sherwin-White, *Roman Law*; Bruce, "Historical Record," pp.

David Aune observes, moreover, that a synoptic comparison of Luke and Matthew to Mark reveals a process of "literaturization" whereby they appear to revise "Mark in the direction of an increasing literary sophistication and respectability."[68] Our preliminary comparison shows that in the process of writing Luke has improved on Mark's handling of salvation-history themes.

But Aune also conjectures that Mark's Gospel may indirectly give Luke a literary model of sorts for Acts as it did for his Gospel.[69] Though this cannot be proved conclusively, it seems quite probable. We shall seek to show, in particular, that the leading ideas of Mark 13:9–11 strongly parallel and perhaps influenced the structure and contents of Acts and how they are to be understood.[70] Mark 13:10 suggests the coherence of eschatology with the command to preach the gospel to the nations. Mark 13:9 supplies the kind of witness motif Luke uses in Acts to substantiate that the mission is in fact being accomplished. Mark 13:11 introduces the element of divine inspiration that will empower the disciples' testimony and becomes the trademark of apostolic witness in Acts. In this study, we shall see that Luke's eschatology closely parallels his Markan source.

Mark 13:10 (Luke 24:47; Acts 1:8)

As we have already seen in this chapter, most suggestions as to why Luke omitted Mark's mission saying have to do with the issues of universal mission and delay of the parousia. Although I have allowed for the possibility that Mark may have inserted the saying parenthetically between 13:9 and 11, I have argued, on the basis of Luke's use of the concept in Luke 24:46–47, that the saying was in all probability traditional. But the question remains whether Luke

2569–603; Bruce, "Chronological Questions," pp. 273–95; Marshall, "Gospel," pp. 289–308; Marshall, *Historian & Theologian*; Gasque, "Acts in History," pp. 54–72; Gasque, *Interpretation*; Hemer, "Luke the Historian," pp. 28–51; Hemer, *Hellenistic History*; Gempf, "Mission Speeches"; Lüdemann, *Early Christianity* (with qual.); Gooding, *Fresh Approach*, pp. 425–34; McRay, "Archaeology," pp. 69–82; Palmer, "Historical Monograph," pp. 1–29; see also lit. cited in Marshall, *Historian & Theologian*, p. 69, n. 4.

68 Aune, "Genre of the Gospels," pp. 17, 45.

69 Aune, *Literary Environment*, p. 139.

70 This use of Mark substantiates the general supposition of Trites, *Witness*, p. 133 that Luke had reformulated "the original notion of bearing witness before a court of law" as the substance of the whole of Acts in providing evidence to support the Christian position. See similarly Zmijewski, *Eschatologiereden*, p. 314.

preserves the eschatological meaning Mark attaches to it or whether he omits reference to it owing to a revised eschatological outlook.

The most relevant text for this discussion is Acts 1:8, a passage to which its Gospel antecedent points (Luke 24:47). Lars Aejmelaeus asserts that Mark 13:10 forms its background.[71] F. F. Bruce goes a step further. He suggests that Luke refrained from mentioning the Markan text in his Gospel to give it more appropriate literary value in Acts, where it would serve as the book's controlling theme.[72] Jesus' prophetic teaching regarding world evangelism would give Luke a recognized framework for structuring an account of the origin and expansion of the church. Its eschatological overtones, moreover, would be telling. Luke's use of time expressions and the mandate itself validate this proposal.

1. *Some time expressions.* Mark's apocalypse uses two time expressions relevant to our discussion.[73] They set out somewhat vaguely the order of events leading up to the end, i.e., the parousia. First, deception, wars, and rumors of war will form the ἀρχὴ ὠδίνων (13:8), but in and of themselves they do not form the τέλος, for the end is still future (cf. v. 7); and second, the gospel must πρῶτον be preached to all nations (v. 10). Vv. 32–37 qualify these expressions and the whole discourse with the warning that no one knows when the Son of Man will come ... so "Keep watch!"

Luke, in contrast, clarifies these two time expressions and gives them better orderly arrangement. Regarding the first block of material in Luke 21:8–11 – loosely paralleling Mark 13:5–8 – he states in v. 9 that "these things must happen first, but the end will not come right away." His wording does not alter the meaning of Mark's reading[74] as much as it clarifies the meaning of the potentially confusing descriptions of the last days as the τέλος and the ἀρχή. In other words, Luke intends to make clear that these events are just the *beginning*; there will be more to follow before the *end* of the last days actually arrives.

Concerning the second expression, Luke qualifies his parallel to Mark 13:9–11 (Luke 21:12–15) with the adverbial phrase πρὸ δὲ τούτων πάντων (v. 12a), which in effect is to say that preceding

---

[71] Aejmelaeus, *Miletrede*, p. 142.
[72] Bruce, "Eschatology," p. 63; also Maddox, *Purpose*, p. 55. *Contra* Schneider, "Zweck," pp. 52–53 and n. 40.
[73] For more on the succession of eschatological events for the whole of Mark 13, see Kümmel, *Promise and Fulfillment*, pp. 97–98.
[74] *Contra* Fitzmyer, *Luke X–XXIV*, p. 1327 *et al.* Cf. Marshall, *Luke*, p. 764.

the events just described, believers will be persecuted for bearing witness to Jesus. In comparison to Mark, Luke links up more coherently the unity of the witness, persecution, and divine inspiration themes according to their fulfillment in the eschatological timetable.[75] But he does not alter Mark's meaning.[76] Luke explains more precisely when the period designated by πρῶτον in 13:10 would occur.[77] His documentation of this is the book of Acts.

Here Luke also clarifies the chronological relationship of Mark 13:9, 11 to v. 10. Though Mark may give the impression that the missions command of v. 10 precedes the witness theme of verses 9 and 11, Luke affirms in Acts that the two themes were understood as taking place simultaneously. πρῶτον does not mean "first until," signifying that its completion must occur before the eschaton;[78] rather it designates the earliest stage of the period of the last days itself. Its fulfillment anticipates world history's final consummation in the Son of Man's return. This is the meaning of Matt. 24:14. According to the narrative flow of the Matthean discourse, τὸ τέλος in v. 14 most likely refers to the final consummation of the last days rather than to the coming of the eschatological period. The preaching of the kingdom of God to the whole world precedes the final end, i.e., the parousia.

Luke seems to write the introduction of Acts with the synoptic eschatological discourses in mind. Reference to the kingdom of God, the uncertainty of its time of restoration, the promise of the Spirit, the witness and nations motifs, and the promise of Jesus' return give rise to an eschatological expectation for the book. Howard Marshall remarks that the wording of Mark 13:10 "points forward to the experiences of the church recorded in Acts."[79] We should understand these experiences within the eschatological framework forecasted in Mark/Luke and demon-

---

[75] But in doing this Luke does not reveal a propensity for "date-fixing" of eschatological events and speculating on the time of Jesus' return. If anything, he may have been refuting a "radikale apokalyptische Tendenz" ("radical apocalyptic tendency"); so Kühschelm, *Jüngerverfolgung und Geschick Jesu*, p. 287.

[76] *Contra* Conzelmann, *Theology of St. Luke*, p. 128, who claims that, in light of Luke's preoccupation with the delayed parousia theme, the πρῶτον of Mark 13:10 becomes superfluous.

[77] Danker, *Jesus and the New Age*, pp. 331–32 makes this connection as well; but Luke doubtfully transferred the meaning of πρῶτον to 21:24. As Marshall, *Luke*, p. 774 observes, the salvation of the Gentiles began well in advance of the fall of Jerusalem.

[78] Cf. Kümmel, *Promise and Fulfillment*, p. 84.

[79] Marshall, *Luke*, p. 766.

strated in Acts.[80] The content of Acts is more closely related to Jesus' prophetic teaching about the kingdom of God and the hope of his imminent return than some scholars are willing to admit.[81]

According to Acts 1:3, for a period of forty days the resurrected Jesus taught the disciples about the kingdom of God. In response to their query regarding when the kingdom would be restored (v. 6), Jesus says that it is not for them to know when the Father will bring it to pass (v. 7). V. 7 is strongly reminiscent of Mark 13:32. In the Markan passage Jesus says that no one knows when the Son of Man will come except the Father. This is not to say, however, that the disciples will be without a clue. From the parable of the fig tree, the budding of leaves signifies that summer is not far away (Mark 13:28; Luke 21:29–30). So too when the eschatological events previously described begin to take place, this will indicate that the arrival of the kingdom of God is near (esp. Luke 21:31; also Mark 13:29).[82] Acts 1:8 as reminiscent of Mark 13:10 is eschatologically suggestive. The sending of the Spirit for a world-wide witness becomes the sprout suggesting that summer is near.

Conzelmann's claim that the adversative ἀλλά opening Acts 1:8 suggests that "the Spirit is no longer the power of the end time but its substitute" is not convincing.[83] Here the adversative contrasts Jesus' negative response in v. 7 with his positive one in v. 8, i.e., that despite the disciples' complete ignorance of the time and date of the kingdom's restoration (v. 7), they are not without any indication of its approaching fulfillment (v. 8). Eric Franklin rightly claims that the giving of the Spirit is "the pledge of its coming rather than its substitute."[84]

Nor is the assertion that Luke suggests no imminent expectation

---

[80] Hence, *contra* Schneider, *Lukas. 11–24*, p. 420, the πρῶτον of Mark 13:10 *is* understood in Acts 1:8. The mission command coincides with the eschatological period suggested in Luke 21:12.

[81] E.g., Merk, "Reich Gottes," p. 218; Gräßer, "Parusieerwartung," pp. 105–107; Maddox, *Purpose*, pp. 106–107; they detach preaching about the kingdom of God in Acts from the expectation of the parousia.

[82] *Contra* Zmijewski, *Eschatologiereden*, pp. 268, 285, who somewhat artificially removes from the parable the sense of the imminent expectation of the coming kingdom. This seems to be the point of the parable within the context of the discourse; so, e.g., Marshall, *Luke*, p. 778. Luke 21:31 does not primarily address the present in-breaking of the kingdom, but its final consummation. Luke 21:34–36, moreover, strongly retains the Markan "call to watchfulness" (cf. 13:33–37) in its striking conformity to the similar eschatological intent of 1 Thess. 5:1–11. See further Aejmelaeus, *Wachen vor dem Ende*.

[83] Conzelmann, *Acts*, p. 7.   [84] Franklin, *Christ the Lord*, p. 28.

in Acts 1:6–11 convincing.[85] A. J. Mattill concludes that the context better suggests, "the beginning of the end has come but the end of the end is yet to come."[86] The events in Luke 19:41–42 and 21:20–24 should be understood in similar fashion.[87] If the fall of Jerusalem had indeed taken place by the time Luke wrote his Gospel, the fact that some of these events had already transpired would strongly stand as yet another sign reinforcing the expectation of the end. The phrase οὗ ... καιροὶ ἐθνῶν (21:24) need not necessarily suggest an indefinite delay, but may designate another series or kind of event(s) characterizing the last days consecutive to, contemporaneous with, or overlapping those preceding (vv. 12–15) and following it (vv. 25–28).

2.   *The mandate to preach to all nations.*   A second indicator of the leading role that Mark 13:10 plays in Luke–Acts is its stress that εἰς πάντα τὰ ἔθνη [πρῶτον] δεῖ κηρυχθῆναι τὸ εὐαγγέλιον. Luke first picks up the theme in Luke 24:47, where he strikingly reiterates the wording and sense of the Markan passage. In v. 46, Luke defines precisely what the gospel message should be, adding accordingly in v. 47a that repentance and forgiveness of sins can be had in Jesus' name. Paralleling Mark, the message then is κηρυχθῆναι ... εἰς πάντα τὰ ἔθνη. The mission's starting point is Jerusalem. The force of the imperatival infinitive (in Mark, + δεῖ) is implicit to the context; Luke 24:46–49 comprises Jesus' command to his disciples (vv. 46–47 as an explication of v. 44 possibly assumes as well the imperatival force of δεῖ πληρωθῆναι of v. 44).

Luke elaborates on the meaning of εἰς πάντα τὰ ἔθνη in the parallel passage, Acts 1:8. The gospel will be preached in Jerusalem, in all Samaria and Judea, and to the corners of the earth.[88] In rough measure, this verse illustrates how Luke portrays the gospel in Acts as expanding in concentric circles to the city of Rome itself. The verse suggests both the geographical boundaries and the ethnic ones that will be crossed, i.e., from the heart of pious Judaism to the center of Godless paganism[89] – in short, to

---

[85]   E.g., Kaestli, *Eschatologie*, pp. 60–62; Wilson, *Gentile Mission*, pp. 84, 86; Schneider, *Lukas. 11–24*, p. 429.

[86]   Mattill, "Weymouth," p. 293.

[87]   *Contra*, e.g., Wilson, *Gentile Mission*, pp. 70–72; Zmijewski, *Eschatologiereden*, p. 313.

[88]   Trites, *Witness*, p. 140 compellingly argues that Acts 9:15 provides a further delineation of the missions program once it moves outside Palestine.

[89]   Reicke, "Risen Lord," pp. 166–67.

the entire civilized world.[90] The "Jerusalem to Rome" motif epitomizes Luke's conception of Jesus' command to preach the gospel to the nations.

But it is doubtful whether Luke thought that Paul's preaching at Rome fulfilled the missions command.[91] Luke probably gives us merely a glimpse of what actually happened during this time. His writings imply this. E.g., in Luke 24 Jesus appears to the eleven and their companions, proves to them that he is the Christ, and commands them to take this message to the nations. But of the disciples, we hear in Acts only briefly of a few specific missionary exploits of Peter and John, and after 15:7 Peter disappears altogether. What did the others do? Did they stay in Palestine? Did Luke know nothing about them? Or did they simply not feature in his work?[92] And what of the 120 Spirit-filled believers who proclaimed the gospel at Pentecost? They too drop out of the story completely.[93] With the table of nations in Acts 2:7–11, Luke indicates that the early Jerusalem church won converts from among all the nations represented. Whether these Jews were pilgrims who made the journey for the festival period or were residents of Jerusalem, did any of them take the gospel back to their homeland sometime after Pentecost or after the persecutions stemming from Stephen's martyrdom (cf. 8:2, 4; 11:19–20)? According to Acts 8 the Ethiopian eunuch also becomes a carrier of the gospel. He too simply disappears from the story.[94] Certainly, Luke is also aware that the gospel preceded Paul to Rome. But who took it there? And when? Luke probably never intended to document the missionary activities of these other believers in Acts, even if he could have done so.

But what is important is the eschatological significance Luke most likely understood as inherent in the mission's command.[95] To take the gospel to the ends of the earth eschatologically anticipates Jesus' return. And from the inception of Christianity, the church has been in the process of fulfilling it. The church is not just

---

[90] Baarlink, *Eschatologie*, p. 178.

[91] So van Unnik, "Apg. 1:8," pp. 386–401; Mattill, "Weymouth," p. 291; Marshall, *Acts*, p. 61; Goppelt, *Apostolic Witness*, p. 276; Grumm, "Another Look at Acts," p. 336; Pesch, *Apg. 1–12*, p. 70. *Contra* Hiers, "Delay of the Parousia," p. 155 and n. 1.

[92] See further Brawley, *Jews*, p. 39.   [93] See further Taylor, *Formation*, pp. 42–43.

[94] But Thornton's assertion, in "End of the Earth," pp. 374–75, that the Ethiopian eunuch's conversion fulfilled the last stage of Acts 1:8 lacks textual support.

[95] With qual., Hiers, "Delay of the Parousia," p. 154 and Mattill, *Last Things*, p. 152.

"between the times of Jesus' ascension and parousia" but "in the last days," as the Joel citation suggests.[96] To disassociate this period from the end times is mistaken (*contra* Conzelmann *et al.*). With the equipping of the Spirit for the proclamation of the gospel, the church has effectively entered into the early stages of the eschatological timetable. That the gospel reaches Rome means, for Luke, that the church is presently in the process of fulfilling Jesus' command "to preach the gospels to all nations." This reality in itself implicitly reinforces for Luke the hope of Jesus' imminent return.

Mark 13:9 (Luke 21:12–13)

The kind of confrontation the propagation of the gospel message would elicit within society sheds additional light on the eschatological stance of Luke's writings. The way Luke elucidates the thinking of Mark 13:9 in the life of the early church supports his adherence to the traditional eschatology of the early church. Although one could say that Luke "historicizes" Jesus' saying here, we should not mean by this that he expurgates all eschatological ideas associated with it. In fact, in line with his paradigmatic development of Mark 13:10 in Acts, the opposite conclusion would seem the more reasonable one.

In Mark 13:9, Jesus tells the disciples that because of him they will be turned over to "local Jewish councils" (συνέδρια), beaten in "synagogues" (συναγωγάς), and made to stand trial before "governors" (ἡγεμόνων) and "kings" (βασιλέων) in order to testify before them. As v. 11 indicates, the Spirit will assist their witness in this juridical setting. This pronouncement implies that God will divinely confirm the Christian message through persecution before both Jewish and Gentile authorities. God will authenticate his revealed plan of salvation in Jesus through Jesus' followers.[97]

The parallel passage in Luke 21:12–13 closely resembles Mark 13:9. Luke, however, specifically heightens the passage in five ways. First, in the opening words of v. 12, he juxtaposes the time sequence of the foregoing section (vv. 8–11) and that of the following material (vv. 12–19) with the phrase πρὸ δὲ τούτων πάντων. As I have already shown in this chapter, he did this to emphasize the

---

[96] See further Rasco, "Historia Salutis," p. 315. *Contra*, e.g., Schille, *Apg.*, p. 72.
[97] See Trites, *Witness*, pp. 130–31 for the similarity of witness while standing trial between Jesus and his followers in Luke–Acts.

place of the ensuing events within the eschatological timetable. Second, he emphatically restates the comment in Mark that Jewish and presumably Gentile authorities (also Luke 11:49) will harass the disciples because of their faith in Jesus. Third, he replaces συνέδρια with φυλακάς. The technical difference between συνέδρια and συναγωγάς was perhaps too subtle a distinction for his readers.[98] The terms may also form a hendiadys, and Luke considered them redundant.[99] φυλακάς, moreover, better complements the official action which the religious and civil authorities will take against the Christians. Luke apparently reserves τὸ συνέδριον to anticipate the encounters of the early church with the Jerusalem Sanhedrin in Acts (Mark uses it with Jesus' trial in 14:55; 15:1; Luke, in his Gospel, only in 22:66). In Acts the noun always occurs in the singular. Fourth, he expands Mark's ἕνεκεν ἐμοῦ to ἕνεκεν τοῦ ὀνόματός μου. His reason for doing so is in all probability connected with the special christological meaning he attaches to ὄνομα in Acts. Lastly, in v. 13 Luke clarifies the meaning of Mark's εἰς μαρτύριον αὐτοῖς with ἀποβήσεται ὑμῖν. This signifies, as commonly argued, the opportunity which the disciples will have in presenting the evidence of the Christian message about Jesus when standing trial.

On the basis of his handling of Mark's witness motif in 13:9 (and v. 11, as we shall discuss in the next section), Luke reveals the subject matter of nearly all of Acts. A corollary to the mandate to preach the gospel to the nations is the confrontation of Christian witness within society – within the confines of Judaism and more broadly the Roman empire.[100] Proof of this lies in the linguistic connections between the synoptic passages and Acts and the narrative structure of the book.

1. *Some linguistic parallels in Acts.* Linguistically, Luke 21:12–13 and Mark 13:9 have many parallels in Acts. This is true of terms and phrases specifically bearing out Jesus' prophetic teaching common to the two synoptic versions and of those unique to Luke and to Mark. Terms common to the two synoptic passages include παραδίδωμι (Acts 8:3; 12:4; 21:11; 28:17), συναγωγή (Acts 6:9; 9:2, 20[23]; 13:14, 42[45, 50]; 14:1[2, 5]; 17:1[5, 13]; 18:4[6, 12–13];

[98] Lohse, "συνέδριον," *TDNT* 7, p. 867, n. 47 and lit. cited therein; Zmijewski, *Eschatologiereden*, p. 131.
[99] Zmijewski, *Eschatologiereden*, p. 131 and lit. cited in n. 18.
[100] Concerning Luke's use of legal language in Acts, see Trites, "Legal Scenes," pp. 278–84.

19:8[9]; 22:19–20; 26:11; also Luke 12:11 – the bracketed passages detail the resulting Jewish harassment when not cited in the verse in which the term συναγωγή itself is used), ἡγεμών (Acts 23:24, 26, 33; 24:1, 10; 26:30), and βασιλεύς (25:13, 14, 24, 26; 26:2, 7, 13, 19, 26, 27, 30; also 9:15). Terms and phrases unique to Luke include διώκω (Acts 22:4; 26:11; also 9:4–5; 22:7–8; 26:14–15), ἐπιβάλλω τὰς χεῖρας (Acts 4:3; 5:18; 12:1; 21:27), and φυλακή (Acts 5:19, 22, 25; 8:3; 12:4–6, 10, 17; 16:23–24, 27, 37, 40; 22:4; 26:10).

Terms unique to Mark include δέρω (Acts 5:40; 16:37; 22:19), ἵστημι (Acts 4:7, 14; 5:27; 22:30; 24:20–21; 25:10; 26:6, 22) and συνέδρια (Acts 4:15; 5:21, 27, 34, 41; 6:12, 15; 22:30; 23:1, 6, 15, 20, 28; 24:20, although used here in the singular and always referring to the Jerusalem Sanhedrin).

Luke uses the language of his Gospel revision of Mark 13:9 in Acts; but he also clearly incorporates in Acts some of the Markan terminology omitted in his Gospel revision. This suggests that Luke's writing of Acts is to some degree positively influenced by his Gospel sources. He illustrates in the life of the early church what his Gospel and his Gospel sources anticipate. As such, Acts exposits the two synoptic passages. The story-line of Acts further supports this conclusion.

2. *The narrative structure of Acts.*   A challenge perennially facing Lukan scholars is the conclusion of Acts.[101] How does one reconcile Acts 21–28 with an overall purpose that takes into account the whole of the double work? What is the significance of Paul's imprisonment for Luke? And how does this section lend itself to the overall flow of the Acts narrative? Luke's sudden interest in detail and intimation of personal involvement in the events he narrates here suggest that in some way the context forms a climax toward which Acts – and perhaps even the whole of his writings – is moving. How Luke develops the themes of Mark 13:9 in Acts support this.

First, as clarified in Luke 21:13, Mark 13:9 suggests that Christians will have opportunity to present evidence for the Christian faith before Jewish and Gentile authorities. On the basis of the evidence they will give, even the highest courts of the day will have no other valid choice but to affirm the authenticity of the Christian message. Within the synoptic tradition, Luke is the only one who defines exactly what it means for Jesus' followers to be a

---

[101] See, e.g., Schneider, "Zweck," pp. 59–61; Maddox, *Purpose,* pp. 42–43; Jervell, "Teacher of Israel," p. 153; Roloff, *Apg.,* p. 288.

witness: to testify to others about Jesus' resurrection.[102] For Luke, in partial fulfillment of Mark 13:9, the act of giving proof is the *raison d'être* of Acts. It pervades virtually every story in Acts. E.g., according to Haenchen's division of Acts into sixty-eight individual units,[103] Luke spotlights the witness theme in all but eight stories (1:9–12; 1:13–14; 11:27–30; 20:7–12; 20:13–16; 21:1–14; 21:15–26; 27:1–44). And most of these preface ones that do. E.g., the stories of Paul's journey to Jerusalem (21:1–14) and his arrival there (21:15–26) anticipate his arrest, trials, and public witness (but even here, cf. vv. 11, 19; also 27:1–44, esp. v. 24).

Second, a corollary to the witness theme as suggested in Mark 13:9 and expanded in Luke 21:12 is that Jesus' disciples will be harassed and abused because of their testimony. Here again, Acts accentuates this point. Clear examples permeate the entire book, occurring in every chapter but chs. 1, 3, 10, 15.[104] The kinds of hostility leveled against the church ranged from verbal abuse to expulsion from local municipalities, beatings, imprisonment, court appearances, and even death. The antagonists included Jew and Gentile, men and women, civil and religious officials, common folk, and hooligan-like characters. Furthermore, as implied in the two synoptic parallels, persecution was part of the divine plan – but this is not to minimize the difficulties and suffering of the early church – in that it continuously impelled the carriers of the gospel to cross new geographical and ethnic boundaries. It impelled the gospel to the ends of the earth.[105]

Last, and perhaps the most outstanding feature indicating the influence of Mark 13:9 in Acts, is Luke's concern to show how the evidence for the gospel held up in the highest courts of the land: e.g., among the Jews, the Jerusalem Sanhedrin; among the Greeks, the Athenian Areopagus; and among the Romans, Caesar's court. Also included in the list should be the incident in Ephesus surrounding the Artemis cult (Acts 19:23–41); although not the verdict of an official hearing, the innocence of Christianity was explicitly described. Similarly, the instance in Corinth where Gallio, the proconsul of Achaia, threw the Jewish charge and the antagonists out of court before even hearing Paul's defense (18:12–17)

---

[102] Mahoney, "Editorial Rewriting," p. 225.

[103] Haenchen, *Acts*, pp. xi–xiii.

[104] So, e.g., Acts 2:13; 4:1–3, 5–21, 29; 5:17–18, 21b–26, 41; 6:11–14; 7:57–8:1; 8:1–3; 9:1–2, 13–14, 21, 23–25, 29b–30; 11:19; 12:1–19; 13:45, 50; 14:2, 4–6, 19; 16:19–24; 17:5–9, 13, 18, 32; 18:6, 12–17; 19:23–41; 20:3, 19; chs. 21–28.

[105] Marshall, *Historian & Theologian*, p. 211; also House, "Suffering," pp. 317–30.

may perhaps signify, for Luke, according to Colin Hemer, "a precedent to legitimize Christian teaching under the umbrella of the tolerance extended to Judaism."[106]

Regarding *the Jewish courts*, Luke explicitly recounts four separate occasions when Christians were made to stand trial before the Sanhedrin in Jerusalem. The accused variously include Peter and John (4:5–22), all the apostles (5:27–41), Stephen (6:12–7:57), and Paul (22:30–23:10; perhaps also 22:3–21). James' arrest perhaps also occasioned an opportunity to testify about the gospel before the Jewish authorities in a court setting. It is doubtful whether Herod would have had James killed without giving him the chance to present his case publicly (12:1–3), especially in view of Herod's intended trial of Peter (v. 6). The Sanhedrin possibly had a part in this as well (cf. v. 11). In connection to their testimony about Jesus, each episode contains some telling piece of evidence confirming their message as irrefutable before their accusers. In the first instance, it was the healed man standing in their midst (4:14–16).

In the second instance, it was the visible presence and possession of the Holy Spirit among those who believed (5:29–32). For the reader, another piece of evidence here is Gamaliel's warning to the Sanhedrin not to act impetuously against the apostles. For if the apostles' work was of divine origin, the Jewish leaders would not prevail against them and would, in effect, find themselves fighting against God. As Acts goes on to show, this was indeed the case on both counts. In Acts the Spirit stands as "the continuing evidence of the corollary of the resurrection" – its impeccable witness.[107]

In the third instance, it was Stephen's heavenly vision (7:55–56). In it he saw heaven opened, God's glory, and the Son of Man standing at God's right hand. The vision authenticated Stephen's testimony before his accusers, i.e., that Jesus as the messiah now stands before God as Stephen's intercessor but as judge of his unbelieving counterparts.[108]

In the final instance, it was the possibility that a divine being had spoken to Paul (23:9), presumably on the basis of Paul's description

---

[106] Hemer, *Hellenistic History*, p. 378.

[107] Maddox, *Purpose*, p. 41.

[108] Pesch, *Apg. 1–12*, pp. 263–64. For the view that this incident may suggest a transition from Jew to Gentile mission, see (with qual.) Pesch, "Vision des Stephanus," pp. 92–107, 170–83.

of his Damascus road experience as retold in 22:6–11 or less likely of his vision in the temple (22:17–21). Although this evidence does not in itself provide as much incontrovertible proof as was given in the other three instances, the admission forced the Sanhedrin to leave open the possibility that Paul had been commissioned by "divine directives."[109] It also associates, for Luke's readers, Paul's innocence in ways comparable to Pilate's acquittal of Jesus (Luke 23:4, 14, 22) and the innocence of the Christian witness in other court settings (Acts 5:34–39; 18:14; 19:37; 25:18; 26:31).[110] The fact of Paul's innocence established before his accusers the authenticity of his testimony: that the resurrected Jesus did appear to him as he had said.

Paul's speech in Athens (17:16–34) details the offering of evidence for the gospel in *a Greek court setting*. Although in decline, first-century Athens still retained a portion of its classical renown as a prestigious religious and cultural hub of the Mediterranean world – as is also perhaps intimated in Luke's sarcastic comment in 17:21. Paul's stay here was apparently brief, unlike those in Ephesus (two years, 19:10) and Corinth (18 months, 18:11). But the visibility Luke gives to the speech in Acts is probably because it succeeded in reaping some fruit among the intellectual elite of Greek society. Paul was asked to speak because of his teaching on Jesus' resurrection. That Luke mentions Dionysius, ὁ Ἀρεοπαγίτης (17:34), supports the idea that Paul stood before a formal meeting of the assembly rather than before an on-the-spot gathering of some of its members.[111] His teaching was new to the philosophers and contradicted their materialistic world view. In the speech, Paul builds his case on Stoic and Epicurean premises to establish "a common ground" with his listeners and simultaneously to critique the idolatrous, superstitious religion of the Athenian populace.[112] On this basis, Paul claims that in Jesus, God has defeated death and will one day, through him, judge all people. Because Jesus indeed arose from the dead, no one – members of the Areopagus or the Athenian populace – now stands before God's judgment seat without excuse. For Paul's audience, the resurrection of the dead is the sticking point. It opposed their "materialist resignation to the finality of

---

[109] Tajra, *Trial*, p. 97.   [110] Radl, *Paulus und Jesus*, p. 183.

[111] So Marshall, *Acts*, p. 285. That this trial was legal, however, remains a moot point; cf., e.g., Haenchen, *Acts*, p. 519, n. 1; Hemer, "Paul at Athens," pp. 349–50.

[112] Barrett, "Paul's Speech on the Areopagus," pp. 71–75.

death."[113] Dionysius' conversion and perhaps the assembly's desire to hear more from Paul on another occasion reflect the truth and power of Paul's message. The phrase οἱ δὲ εἶπαν of 17:32 is probably meant to contrast the conflicting opinions of the two groups.[114]

Luke indicates that the case of Christianity also prevailed within some of the highest levels of *Roman society and courts of law.* Where its presentation led to salvation is most clearly seen in the conversion of Cornelius, the Roman centurion, and his household (chs. 10–11). Divinely summoned to appear before Cornelius, Peter presented the gospel to him. The Spirit's manifest coming evidenced to all present that their belief was genuine and of God (10:44–46; 11:15–17). Another example is the conversion of the proconsul Sergius Paulus (13:6–12).[115] The Roman official apparently converted to Christianity because of its unparalleled authority. Elymas' blindness confirmed to him the distinctiveness and superiority of the Christian faith over the practitioners of magic commonly found attached to the nobility of the Greco-Roman world.[116]

Luke also records ten instances where the defense of the gospel came directly or indirectly into contact with the Roman court of law. Those occurring outside a formal trial setting include the Philippian magistrates' illegal mistreatment of Paul and Silas (16:22–23, 35–39);[117] the city clerk's warning to the mob in Ephesus that if they wanted to press charges against Paul, they were to do so in a legal assembly (19:35–41); and perhaps also Claudius Lysias' attempt to find out what the Sanhedrin's charges against Paul were (22:30–23:35). Those occurring within a formal court of law where

---

[113] De Vries, "Philosophy," *BEB* 2, pp. 1686–87 (quot. p. 1687).

[114] So Barrett, "Paul's Speech on the Areopagus," pp. 70–71.

[115] *Contra* Haenchen, *Acts*, p. 403 *et al.*, to deny the credibility of Sergius Paulus' conversion on the grounds that Luke fails to mention any ensuing baptism by Spirit or water and the founding of a house-church, which a person of his stature and means would certainly have undertaken, is not convincing. Luke is similarly silent on other occasions: e.g., with Dionysius, Damaris, and other unnamed converts at Athens (17:34), the converts at Thessalonica (17:1–9) and Berea (17:10–15). Luke's comment, on the other hand, that Barnabas and Mark returned to Cyprus to "visit the brothers in all the towns where we preached the word of the Lord and to see how they are doing" (15:36, 39) would suggest that local churches had, in fact, taken root and that some kind of follow-up was underway.

[116] So Nock, "Paul and the Magus," pp. 324–26, 330. For a detailed study of the prevalence of oracular activity during the Greco-Roman period, see Aune, *Prophecy*, pp. 23–48, esp. in reference to magic, pp. 44–47.

[117] See further Tajra, *Trial*, p. 29.

nothing is recorded of the defendant having had opportunity to present his case include presumably Herod's trial of James, whose verdict resulted in the accused's death; Gallio's acquittal of Paul before his Jewish accusers in Corinth (18:12–17); and in a possibly non-Roman juridical context, the appearance of Jason and a number of other believers before the civic magistrates of Thessalonica (17:6–9).[118]

But the best examples are Paul's court appearances in Caesarea before the governors Felix (ch. 24) and Festus (ch. 25), climaxing with his defense before King Agrippa (ch. 26). Despite Festus' interest in appeasing the Jewish leaders (25:9; cf. his predecessor Felix, 24:27) and Agrippa's knowledge of Jewish affairs, they could come up with no charge against him. Paul offers evidence drawn entirely from his own experience – he *never* appeals to Jesus' life or the experiences of the apostles and other members of the church to buttress his case. E.g., in the third account of Paul's Damascus road experience, the exalted Lord specifically tells him, "I have appeared to you to appoint you as a servant and as *a witness of what you have seen of me and what I will show you.* I will rescue you from your own people and from the Gentiles" (26:16b–17a). Such witness accurately describes the content of Paul's testimony in the trial settings before Jewish and Gentile authorities (22:1–21; 23:1–6; 24:10–21; 25:8, 10–11; 26:1–23, 24–27, 29). The center of his testimony is the reality of Jesus' resurrection (24:21; 25:19; 26:23, cf. v. 24!). Each of them was, however, already well acquainted with the Christian movement (24:22; 25:10; 26:26), about which even Agrippa himself would have been able to give evidence concerning its truth and reasonableness (26:23–25) in light of its publicity (v. 26a)[119] and his knowledge of the OT prophetic promises (v. 27).[120] Chs. 27–28 heighten this theme still further in expectation of Paul's defense before Caesar himself (27:24; also 23:11).

Paul Schubert rightly points out that with Paul's testimony

---

[118] For a plausible resolution, supporting the integrity of the Acts account, regarding the apparent contradiction between the seriousness of the charges brought against Paul and Silas and the magistrates' *laissez-faire* response toward apprehending them, see Judge, "Decrees," pp. 1–7.

[119] See further Malherbe, "Early Christian Apologetic," pp. 201–207.

[120] So, e.g., Haenchen, *Acts*, pp. 688–89; Marshall, *Acts*, p. 399; Weiser, *Apg. 13–28*, pp. 654–55. Tajra's negative interpretation of the scene (*Trial*, p. 169) is not convincing. He fully omits discussion of the two forms of evidence that Paul thought Agrippa himself would be able to supply (26:26b–27).

before King Agrippa he effectively fulfilled the words which had been spoken to Ananias at the time of the Damascus vision.[121] It was foretold that Paul would suffer because of Jesus' name but would also have opportunity to testify about him "before the Gentiles and their kings and before the people of Israel." These words of the Lord to Paul in Acts 9:15–16 are strongly reminiscent of Jesus' to his disciples in Mark 13:9/Luke 21:12–13 (also Matt. 10:17–18). Within Paul's own ministry, he in a sense fulfills Jesus' command in the synoptic parallels. Paul's witness epitomizes Luke's intention for Acts.

Thus Acts seems to comprise from cover to cover evidence of Jesus as Savior in terms of Mark 13:9/Luke 21:12–13. The trial settings in Acts most clearly justify this claim.[122] The disciples' official court appearances especially confirm the truth of the gospel before Jewish and Gentile authorities, as well as its superiority, distinctiveness, and innocence. Moreover, in line with the eschatological setting of the synoptic passages, Acts as *testimonium* accords well with Luke's view of the last days. The last days are not to be relegated to some remote time in the distant future, for even now Jesus' words are reaching their eschatological fulfillment as Luke himself ostensibly bears witness in Acts.

Mark 13:11 (Luke 12:11–12)

Having detailed some of the difficulties the disciples will face and the legal proceedings that their accusers will bring against them because of their witness, Jesus reassures them that when brought to trial they will not be without divine help. In Mark 13:11, Jesus promises them that the Holy Spirit will inspire their testimony. For this reason they need not worry about what they will say. Their accusers will be unable to make them look foolish before the authorities.

Although the Spirit is not explicitly mentioned as the source of divine help in Luke's Gospel parallel (21:14–15), Luke 12:11–12 fairly closely resembles Mark's account.[123] It occurs in a sequence of dominical sayings exhorting the disciples to persevere in the faith.[124]

---

[121] Schubert, "Final Cycle of Speeches," p. 7.
[122] Beasley-Murray, *Kingdom of God*, p. 327.
[123] For a discussion of the source question, see Marshall, *Luke*, p. 519.
[124] See Fitzmyer's comment, in *Luke X–XXIV*, pp. 962, 965, on "catchword bonding" in reference to 12:10–12.

Its broader context (12:1–59) is interlaced with an eschatological caution exhorting the reader to live rightly in view of the uncertainty of when the Son of Man will return. Following two logia against denying the faith (vv. 8–9, 10), the second of which refers to the unforgivable sin of blaspheming the Holy Spirit, Jesus promises the disciples in vv. 11–12 that the Spirit will divinely inspire their witness and help them to stand firm in the faith before their accusers.

Luke 12:11–12 adheres to the eschatological meaning of Mark 13:11. It essentially clarifies it in three ways. First, since the passage is separate from the eschatological context of Mark 13:11 (specifically, Mark 13:9/Luke 21:12), Luke 12:11a most likely explains the phrase καὶ ὅταν ... ὑμᾶς παραδιδόντες in Mark 13:11 to mean "ὅταν δὲ εἰσφέρωσιν ὑμᾶς before synagogues, rulers, and authorities." The "rulers and authorities" probably refer to Gentile authorities and signify that official Jewish and Gentile proceedings will be taken against the disciples. Second, v. 11b supplements Mark's version of not worrying about "what the disciples should say when standing trial" with not to worry about "how they should defend (ἀπολογήσησθε) themselves." The verb ἀπολογέομαι accentuates the apologetic nature of their speech. Third, v. 12 probably represents a succinct rewording of the meaning of its Markan parallel. Luke indicates that the Spirit will teach them how they should reply at that time. Gerhard Schneider rightly remarks that the Spirit appears here more as legal advocate than as teacher.[125] As their legal advocate before the authorities, the Spirit will provide the disciples with legal counsel to redress their opponents' accusations as they stand trial.

In Acts, Luke unquestionably portrays apostolic preaching as the primary means through which the Spirit speaks. Jesus' promise of the Spirit for witness (Luke 24:49/Acts 1:4–5; 1:8) therefore presumes his active involvement, implicitly at least, in most every instance of witness cited in Acts. But in numerous trial scenes in the earlier parts of Acts, Luke explicitly points out the Spirit's presence among the accused and his empowering of their defense of the gospel message (e.g., in 4:8–22, v. 8; 5:29–32, v. 32; 6:8–15, v. 10; 7:51–56, v. 55). In doing so, Luke shows the veracity of Jesus' promise in the mission of the early church.

---

[125] Schneider, *Lukas. 11–24*, p. 280.

In summary, Acts exposits the sense of Mark 13:9–11. In accordance with the witness theme, the concepts of Mark 13:9–11 apparently provide Luke with *a principle of selectivity* for choosing the kinds of material to include in Acts. It also suggests *the structure* by which the material was loosely and sequentially ordered, and indicates *an important theological framework* within which the book should be understood.

As we have seen, Luke shows no overriding predilection to alter the eschatological stance of his sources, particularly his Markan source. In fact, he seems more inclined to heighten Mark's meaning, as is evidenced in the way he clarifies and develops it in Luke–Acts. Conversely, the apparent "historicization" of the synoptic themes in Acts reveals no special attempt to "de-eschato-logize" the apocalyptic discourses on Luke's part; instead, Acts more accurately discloses his continued interest in promise and fulfillment themes. As Jesus' life, passion, and exaltation fulfilled OT prophecy and inaugurated the last days, so is the church's witness, in part, bringing to fulfillment some of Jesus' prophetic teaching regarding the last days. This reality only heightens rather than diminishes the expectation of the consummation of the last days in Jesus' return.

Proposals that Luke set out to rewrite Mark according to some non-eschatological view of salvation history are inadequate. For as Earle Ellis concludes: "The relationship of present and future eschatology forms the framework for Luke's 'history of salvation' theology."[126] The church, according to Luke, has one eye on the present and the other on the future.

Conclusion: Jesus as the center of saving history

Luke–Acts is a well-orchestrated production, featuring Jesus the Savior as the capstone of saving history. Any attempt at interpreting Luke–Acts must consider this thread carefully and deliberately woven throughout the two books. "It is hard to overestimate," E. M. B. Green sums up, "the importance of

---

[126] Ellis, "Present and Future Eschatology," pp. 27–41 (quot. p. 41); also Rasco, "Historia Salutis," pp. 311–12, 314; Michel, "Heilsgegenwart und Zukunft," pp. 101–15; Giles, "Present–Future Eschatology (1–2)," pp. 65–71, 11–18; Kühschelm, *Jüngerverfolgung und Geschick*, pp. 292–93. In fact, the "now and not yet" aspects of eschatology most likely originated in Jesus' teaching; see further Marshall, *Historical Jesus*, pp. 225–27.

salvation in the writings of Luke."[127] Luke is completely engrossed with salvation themes. As for the most part implied in Mark and unanimously affirmed in NT teaching, the belief that in Jesus the OT longing for the appearance of God as Savior to humanity has been fulfilled is a primary focus of Luke's. Luke seems convinced that the saving significance of Jesus transcends – but does not exclude – the region of Palestine and the ethnic borders of Judaism. It extends to the earth's limits, even to the "Godless" reaches of Rome itself. This factor, moreover, bears eschatological impor-tance, as Luke's exposition of Mark 13:9–11 in Acts reveals.

This analysis of Luke's interaction with Mark and what it reveals about his own christology indicates that he was not dissatisfied with what Mark assumed concerning salvation history, but only that he did not say more. In the process of writing, Luke does just that. He clarifies, underscores, and fills out the saving significance of Jesus as briefly suggested in or logically stemming from Mark according to his own writing interests. Luke coordinates this message of the early church under the banner of salvation history. As Howard Marshall rightly insists, it was Luke's view of theology that led him to write history.[128] This emphasis conforms to NT teaching on the matter, suggesting that the theme did not originate with him but was traditional. His originality is the written, paradig-matic visibility he gives it. Alongside Romans and Hebrews, Luke gives us one of the best-unified pictures in the NT of Jesus as Savior and the center of God's saving plan.

But in stressing that God culminates his saving plan in Jesus, particularly in his death and resurrection, what then, according to Luke, is Jesus' relation to saving history and its consummation in his return? This will become our focus of study in ch. 10.

In part 2 (chs. 4–7), it has been argued that Luke's interaction with Mark as a source is revealing of his christology, as demonstrated in the instances of the resurrection (ch. 5), Spirit baptism (ch. 6), and salvation history (ch. 7). This study leads us to another important angle from which to evaluate Luke's christology. Implicit in each of these themes is a key relational dimension. We have touched on them at the close of each chapter: in ch. 5, the relation of "the Resurrected One" to "the One who raises him from the dead"; in ch. 6, the relation of "the Giver" to "that which is Given"; and in

---

[127] Green, *Meaning of Salvation*, p. 125.
[128] Marshall, *Historian & Theologian*, p. 52.

ch. 7, the relation of "the Savior" to "salvation history and its consummation in his return." In part 3, we shall examine each one respectively – Jesus' relation to God the Father (ch. 8), the Spirit (ch. 9), and to the end of history (ch. 10) in our attempt to assess the character and purpose of Luke's christology.

What we see emerging here is the issue of Jesus' Lordship. What is Luke's attitude toward it? Does he view it in a restricted sense, as Conzelmann and others would argue, where Jesus appears as subordinate to God, reigning as Lord over the church but not as such over the world? Or does he view it in the unrestricted sense, where Jesus appears as the Father's co-equal, reigning supremely over the whole world as does the Father? The conclusions of this investigation will, moreover, assist our study in ch. 11 concerning how Luke views Jesus' humiliation and exaltation.

PART 3

Luke's christology and Jesus' Lordship

8

JESUS AND GOD THE FATHER

Introduction

We saw in ch. 5 that Luke makes a special effort to show that God providentially directed Jesus' passion and resurrection. This emphasis raises some interesting christological questions for Luke. How does the ascription of Jesus' Lordship in Acts 2:21 balance with the stress that Jesus depended upon God for his resurrection? Is there an implicit subordination christology here? How are we to understand this apparent tension?

R. P. C. Hanson believes that Luke "has little or nothing to say about Christ as a divine being in his own right and makes no attempt to work out philosophically his relation to God." [1] Lampe feels that Luke does not indicate much about the unity between Jesus and God: "despite the language of Christ's thanksgiving in Luke x. 22, the union between him and the Father is, as it were, an external bond." [2] They insist that one must turn to Paul or John for such christological descriptions. But does the textual evidence support this position?

In this chapter we shall study Luke's perspective on Jesus' relation to God the Father. We shall use C. F. D. Moule's view that Luke presents us with "an absentee Christology" in Acts to define the issue before us as we examine what Luke's portrayal of Jesus' heavenly reign indicates concerning his understanding of Jesus' relation to the Father.

An absentee christology?

Peter declares to the Jews in the Jerusalem temple courts that now

---

[1] Hanson, *Acts*, p. 39.
[2] Lampe, "Lucan Portrait of Christ," p. 172.

is the time for repentance and that Jesus "must remain in heaven until the time comes for God to restore everything" (Acts 3:19–21, v. 21 cited). This passage implies (but also 2:33a, 34; 5:31; 7:55–56) that for an undisclosed period of time Jesus will not appear to his followers in the same way he did during his earthly career. He resides temporarily in heaven. What, then, does the *sessio Christi* suggest, for Luke, concerning the nature of Jesus' present heavenly reign and the work he does from there?

In his contribution to *Studies in Luke–Acts* (1966), Moule describes this phenomenon as "a Lukan absentee christology."[3] He writes:

> More consistently than in any other New Testament writing, Acts presents Jesus as exalted and, as it were, *temporarily "absent,"* but "represented" on earth in the meantime by the Spirit ... That this is Luke's own attitude seems to follow from the fact that his narrative and his handling of whatever sources he may be using convey it, as well as explicit "preaching" on the lips of the apostles. (pp. 179–80, my italic)

> Jesus is shown in Acts as raised from death, exalted to heaven, destined ultimately to return, and meanwhile represented in the church's activities and expansion by the Holy Spirit, whose advent is the result of Christ's *"withdrawal."* (p. 165, my italic)

In his later work, *Origin of Christology* (1977), Moule modifies his position somewhat to include a more active presence and work of

---

[3]   See also Bousset, *Kyrios Christos*, p. 52; Fuller, *Foundations*, p. 159; Lampe, "Lucan Portrait of Christ," pp. 174–75; Lampe, "Holy Spirit," *IDB* 2, p. 633; Robinson, "Primitive Christology," p. 188, but primarily in reference to Acts 3; Franklin, "Ascension and Eschatology," p. 197; but later with qual. in Franklin, *Christ the Lord*, p. 55; MacRae, "Christology," pp. 158–59, but with substantial qual. of Moule's perspective on pp. 159–65; Ziesler, "Name of Jesus," pp. 28, 37–38; also Bruce, *Acts* (NICNT), p. 112. Reicke, "Risen Lord," p. 162 leaves room for the possibility. See further the lit. cited in O'Toole, "Risen Jesus," p. 472, n. 3. Cf. Schweizer, *Lordship and Discipleship*, p. 57; Schweizer, "Lukanischen Christologie," pp. 58–62, 64; Wikenhauser, *Apg.*, pp. 128–29; Ladd, "Christology," p. 39 briefly responds to Moule; Marshall, *Work of Christ*, pp. 46, 57; Marshall, *Acts*, pp. 93–94; Marshall, *Historian & Theologian*, pp. 179–80; Thüsing, *Erhöhungsvorstellung*, pp. 50–82; Thüsing, *Rückfrage nach Jesus*, p. 120; Stählin, "πνεῦμα Ἰησοῦ," p. 235; Perlewitz, "Modes of Presence"; Wilson, *Pastoral Epistles*, p. 77, n. 38; O'Toole, "Risen Jesus," pp. 471–98 responds to Moule, reprinted with slight expansion but without critical notes in O'Toole, *Unity*, pp. 38–61; Turner, "Spirit of Christ," p. 183; Giles, "Salvation (2)," p. 47; Neyrey, *Christ is Community*, pp. 139–41; Chance, *Jerusalem*, p. 97.

Christ through the Holy Spirit: "the Spirit communicates and extends the presence of Christ" (p. 104) in the sense that "the Spirit is christified" and "Christ is spiritualized" (p. 105). But he does not entirely relinquish the idea of absence: "The presence of the Spirit [in Acts] in a sense compensates for the absence (at least from sight) of the ascended Christ; and ... continues the work of Christ" (p. 104).

Moule rightly observes that Luke designs Acts to show that the Spirit represents the ascended Jesus to his church. Furthermore, in contrast to Jesus' visible involvement with his followers during his earthly career, one may speak of the exalted Christ as absent in the strictly *physical* sense. But this view does not fully describe Luke's christological perspective.

To begin with, if Luke intended to reassure his readers about what they had been taught, would he reaffirm to them a christological perspective rarely found elsewhere in the NT? Moule admits that in Paul, e.g., such an idea appears only in 1 Thess. 1:10.[4] He does not explain why Luke would have done this other than to say that this was his view. This leaves much unsaid, especially since Moule often comments on Luke's strong adherence to church tradition elsewhere.

Furthermore, to define Jesus' heavenly ministry in Acts as "an absentee Christology" diminishes the significance of his present heavenly session alongside the Father. It gives the impression that Jesus is now personally inactive in the church and its mission. But this position risks missing Luke's christological perspective and lessening the importance Luke attaches to Jesus' being where he is and doing the kind of things he does from there. Any discussion of Christ as absent must consider what it means to be absent. Certainly Luke does not picture God as removed from his creation or without a plan he is actively bringing to pass concerning it. Therefore, we should determine whether Luke–Acts reveals a correlation between the work of God and Jesus from heaven. Moule omits such a discussion. But before assessing what Jesus' temporary heavenly abode signifies for Luke, we should first look at how the OT writers portrayed Yahweh as immanently involved with his people.

---

[4] Moule, "Christology of Acts," p. 180

Yahweh as immanent deity

A notable feature of OT theology is the balance its authors draw between Yahweh's transcendence and immanence: God is incomprehensible, yet knowable; fully removed and distinct from creation, yet supremely concerned about it and providentially leading it to its restoration. How, then, does God reveal himself to people? And what are the theological implications for transcendent deity?

Some OT examples of Yahweh's self-revelation

The OT contains a wealth of examples concerning Yahweh's self-revelation through nature, actions in history, visionary communication, religious instruction, chance selection, and self-manifestation. We shall briefly look at the first five and go into more detail on the sixth.

General means of divine revelation

1. *Nature.* The created world is said to unveil God's glory and majesty, from the powerful forces of nature (Job 36:24–37:13; Ps. 29:1–11) to the splendor of the heavens (Ps. 8:1–4; 19:1–6).

2. *Actions in history.* Israel's exodus from Egypt (Exod. 20:1–2; 2 Kings 17:36; Mic. 6:4), their preservation in transit to Palestine (Ps. 78:1–4, 13–16, 23–29; Mic. 6:5), and their acquisition of Canaan proved to them the truthfulness of God's promise to Abraham and reassured them of his continuing presence (Ps. 105:1–45).

3. *Visionary communication.* God speaks directly to his people through visions (Num. 12:6; 1 Sam. 3:1; Isa. 30:10; Lam. 2:9; Ezek. 1:1; 12:22–28; Hos. 12:10), dreams (Gen. 20:3–7; 28:10–17; 31:24; Num. 12:6; 1 Sam. 28:6; 1 Kings 3:5–15; Dan. 1:17), and deep sleep (Gen. 15:12–16; Job 33:15–17; Dan. 8:18–19; 10:9–11).

4. *Religious instruction.* God reveals himself in religious instruction to people through prophetic revelation (Exod. 4:15–16; Deut. 18:18; 1 Sam. 3:19–21; 2 Kings 21:10; Amos 3:7–8) and the Law (Ps. 19:7–11; ch. 119; Isa. 30:8; Dan. 9:2).

5. *"Chance" selection.* God circumstantially reveals his will through the Urim and Thummim (Exod. 28:30; Num. 27:21; 1 Sam. 28:6) and the lot (1 Sam. 14:41–42; Prov. 16:33; Jon. 1:7).

Divine self-manifestation

Moreover, in addition to the many passages where Yahweh communicates his presence to people through this Spirit,[5] the OT also records numerous ways in which the transcendent God appears personally and directly to people. The primary modes of self-manifestation are the angel of the Lord (*malak yhwh*), the face (*panim*) of God, the glory (*kabod*) of God and the name (*shem*) of God.[6]

1. *The angel of the Lord (malak yhwh).* In the OT, the phrase mostly occurs in books recounting Israel's early pre-monarchical history (Gen. 16:7–14; 21:17–18; 22:11–14, 15–18; 31:11–13; Exod. 3:2–6; 23:20–21; Josh. 5:13–15; Judg. 2:1–5; 6:11–24; 13:2–23). These passages so closely link Yahweh to the angel of Yahweh that "the line between a representative and an actual appearance of God cannot be sharply drawn." [7] The epiphanic being speaks in the first person as God himself (Gen. 16:10; 21:18; 22:12, 16–18; Judg. 2:1–3; 6:16, 18), specifically designates himself as God (Gen. 31:13; Exod. 3:6; perhaps also Josh. 5:15; Judg. 6:23; 13:18), receives worship as God (Gen. 16:13; 22:14; Exod. 3:6; Judg. 6:22, 24; 13:22), and guarantees his continued divine presence in the form of an angel (Exod. 23:20–21; cf. Deut 4:37; Isa. 63:9). The angel of the Lord becomes "a sign of the presence of God" [8] and a form of divine manifestation.[9] Therefore, "one who sees the angel can say he has seen God." [10] Zechariah writes: "On that day the Lord will shield those who live in Jerusalem, so that the feeblest among them will be like David, and the house of David will be *like God, like the Angel of the Lord going before them*" (12:8).

2. *The face (panim) of God.* Though no mortal could possibly see God's *panim* in the fullness of its infinite glory and holiness and live (Exod. 33:20–23), the OT nevertheless repeatedly describes Yahweh's personal presence among his people metaphorically in

---

5 See further Baumgärtel, "πνεῦμα," *TDNT* 6, pp. 362–67; Lampe, "Holy Spirit," *IDB* 2, pp. 626–29.

6 See, e.g., Eichrodt, *Theology*, vol. 2, pp. 23–45; Jacob, *Theology*, pp. 75–85; Barr, "Theophany and Anthropomorphism," pp. 31–38; von Rad, *Theology*, vol. 1, pp. 179–89, 239–40, 285–89; Anderson, "God, OT View of," *IDB* 2, pp. 421–22; Vriezen, *Theology*, pp. 182–88, 207–210; Kaiser, *Theology*, pp. 106–107, 120–21, 133–34, 237–38; Zimmerli, *Theology*, pp. 70–81; Dyrness, *Themes*, pp. 41–45.

7 Dyrness, *Themes*, p. 42.

8 Eichrodt, *Theology*, vol. 2, p. 24.

9 Von Rad, *Theology*, vol. 1, p. 287.

10 Jacob, *Theology*, p. 76.

terms of "revealing his face to them." E.g., having seen the angel of the Lord, Jacob (Gen. 32:30–31; Hos. 12:3–5) and Gideon (Judg. 6:22) both claim to have seen God face to face (perhaps also Manoah, Judg. 13:20–23). The same is also said of Moses, because of his regular contact with God (Exod. 33:11; Num. 12:8; 14:14); in like manner God will deal with rebellious Israel (Ezek. 20:35). The phrase can also variously refer to entering the sanctuary, providential leading, omnipresence, inward communion with God, seeking divine help, favor, penitence and restoration, or receiving blessing from on high.[11] In short, the prevalent OT expression gives us yet another form of God's self-manifestation whereby his presence is made tolerable to people and guaranteed to them[12] without reservation[13] or restriction.[14]

3. *The glory (kabod) of God.* Another form of Yahweh's appearing in the OT is through his *kabod*. The *kabod yhwh* becomes "an important *terminus technicus* in describing theophanies."[15] Moses, in veiled form, saw God's glory pass before him (Exod. 33:18–23). Israel witnessed it in the cloud on Mount Sinai (Exod. 24:15–17; Deut. 5:24) and at the Tent of Meeting (Exod. 16:7, 10; Lev. 9:4b, 6, 23–24; Num. 14:10; 16:19; 20:6). His glorious presence filled the tabernacle (Exod. 40:34–35) and the temple (1 Kings 8:11; 2 Chron. 7:1; Ps. 63:2). Isaiah (6:1–4) and Ezekiel (1:25–28; 3:23; 8:4; 9:3; 10:4, 18–19; 11:22–23; 43:1–5) saw God's glory in their respective visions; and according to the prophets, the world will see God through his glory at a future point in time (Isa. 66:18; Hab. 2:14; Hag. 2:7; Zech. 2:5). In the OT the divine *kabod* acts as "an independent manifestation of God." [16] It reflects "the splendour of the transcendent God"[17] and becomes "a veritable theologoumenon of the divine presence." [18]

4. *The name (shem) of God.* In the OT, a name often parallels the nature of what it names.[19] When applied to Yahweh, his name is interchangeable with his person[20] and becomes a designation for

[11] Eichrodt, *Theology*, vol. 2, pp. 36–38; Jacob, *Theology*, pp. 77–79.
[12] Eichrodt, *Theology*, vol. 2, p. 38.
[13] Jacob, *Theology*, p. 78.
[14] Dyrness, *Themes*, p. 42.
[15] Von Rad, *Theology*, vol. 1, p. 240.
[16] Vriezen, *Theology*, p. 208.
[17] Eichrodt, *Theology*, vol. 2, p. 32.
[18] Jacob, *Theology*, p. 80.
[19] Zimmerli, *Theology*, p. 78.
[20] For more on the significance of God's "name," see Anderson, "God, Names of," *IDB* 2, p. 408.

God himself (Exod. 3:15; Deut. 28:58; Job 1:21; Ps. 8:1–9; 20:1; 103:1; Isa. 30:27; 48:9; 56:6; Jer. 44:26; Ezek. 20:44; 43:8; Amos 2:7; Zech. 14:9; Mal. 2:2). It reveals God's character (Gen. 21:33; Exod. 3:14–16; 33:19; 34:14; 1 Chron. 29:16; Ps. 124:8; Prov. 18:10; Isa. 63:16; Amos 4:13), represents his power and authority (Deut. 18:19; Ps. 118:10, 26; 124:8; Prov. 18:10; Jer. 29:9; Ezek. 39:7, 25; 43:8; Dan. 9:6), and signifies his presence among his people (Exod. 20:24; 23:21; Deut. 12:5, 11; 14:23; 16:6; 2 Sam. 7:13; 1 Kings 9:3; 11:36; 2 Kings 21:4, 7; 2 Chron. 6:20; 20:8; Neh. 1:9; Ps. 75:1; Isa. 18:7; 30:27–28; Jer. 7:12). The divine name guarantees God's presence to people in its totality,[21] without compromising God's sovereign transcendence.[22] It becomes, in effect, "the side of Yahweh presented to man."[23]

Theological implications for transcendent deity

The theological thrust of this discussion is that transcendent deity personally appears to people and communicates with them. The OT *never* presents the one to the negation of the other. Both qualities are present in God's character and work. The concept of divine providence illustrates this: transcendent deity who personally attends to the welfare of his creation. God has made himself known to people:

> He who forms the mountains,
>> creates the wind,
>> *and reveals his thoughts to man,*
> he who turns dawn to darkness
>> and treads the high places of the earth –
>> *the Lord God Almighty is his name.*   (Amos 4:13)

According to scripture, no one has seen God – not even Moses (cf. Deut. 4:12; 5:4); but God has impressed upon people something of his person and character through means varying from natural phenomena – e.g., thunder, cloud, fire, and so on – to theophanies, although never in the sense that he is limited or can be made identifiable with creation pantheistically or animistically.

The parallelism of passages like Ps. 106:32–33 and Isa. 63:10–14 indicates, furthermore, that Yahweh and his Spirit are closely

---

[21] Jacob, *Theology*, p. 85.
[22] Eichrodt, *Theology*, vol. 2, pp. 41–42.
[23] Bietenhard, "ὄνομα," *TDNT* 5, p. 257.

related in being, attribute, and activity (also Job 33:4; Ps. 104:29–30; 139:1–10; Ezek. 11:22–25). The OT teaches that without the Spirit, communion between God and people would be impossible.[24] The Spirit of God is expressive of divine immanence. But this is not the entire picture. As we have seen, the OT authors take the matter further by recording numerous self-manifestations of Yahweh where *he directly appears to people apart from the Spirit*. This phenomenon brings into sharper focus the biblical teaching that God is directly involved with his creation. For this reason the OT writers can correctly say without contradiction that God is unapproachable yet knowable by his own initiative (see esp. Exod. 29:45; Deut. 4:7, 39; Job 34:14; Ps. 33:13–15; Isa. 57:15; Jer. 23:23; Mic. 1:3).

The continuing presence of the exalted Jesus

In turning to Luke–Acts, how does the nature and work of the exalted Jesus compare to the OT depiction of Yahweh? Luke says much in this regard; not, however, in altering the OT depiction of God – according to Luke, God, e.g., continues to reveal himself via nature (Acts 14:15–17; 16:24–26; 17:27–28), history (Acts 7:2–53; 13:16–41), angels (Luke 1:11–20; Acts 27:23–24), visions (Acts 10:9–20; 11:5), personal testimony (Acts 2:36–37), miracles (Acts 2:22), his Spirit (Luke 2:26), his glory (Luke 2:9; Acts 7:55), and his name (Luke 13:35; Acts 15:14) – but in showing that the exalted Jesus behaves in like fashion.

Jesus and his Spirit

If the Spirit's presence describes Yahweh's immanence, in light of Acts 2:33, where Jesus is said to give the Spirit at Pentecost, the Spirit's presence would be a way of talking about Jesus' immanence as well.[25] Certainly Acts 2:33 and 16:7 indicate for Luke that the Spirit represents, if not mediates, the exalted Jesus' continued presence and activity. But Luke has more to say on the matter.

Adrian Hastings observes that where Luke begins both his Gospel and Acts with a powerful expression of the Holy Spirit, he slackens off somewhat in explicitly referring to the Spirit's presence

---

[24] Jacob, *Theology*, p. 127; Vriezen, *Theology*, pp. 212–13; Dyrness, *Themes*, p. 208.
[25] Turner, "Spirit of Christ," p. 183 and n. 69. See further ch. 9.

and activity in the remaining portions of both books.[26] Concerning the Gospel, this is not too surprising in light of the general reticence of the synoptic tradition in recording much about the Spirit's role in Jesus' ministry. But concerning Acts, it is unexpected. Joseph Fitzmyer specifically points out that the Spirit appears approximately fifty times in Acts 1–16, but only twelve times in chs. 17–28.[27] (His chapter division could be refined more precisely to 16:8 onward.) Even more striking is Paul's trial scenes in 21:17–26:32. They lack any reference to the Spirit. In view of the earlier parts of Acts (e.g., Peter and John before Jewish authorities, 4:8–22, esp. v. 8; Stephen before the Synagogue of Freedmen, 6:8–15, esp. v. 10), the synoptic tradition (cf. Luke 12:11–12; Mark 13:9–11), and Paul's filling with the Spirit (Acts 9:17), one would expect to find the Spirit mentioned as the divine source behind Paul's witness. But this is not the case. Instead, *Jesus appears as the empowering agent.*

A most intriguing passage that perhaps reflects *in nuce* Luke's theological perspective and literary interest in this regard is Acts 16:7. Here Luke writes that the divine Spirit directing the mission of the church is "the Spirit of Jesus," a title patterned after the well-known "Spirit of God" designation in pre-NT Jewish literature. This description invokes the idea of divine immanence. The connection of the Spirit to transcendent deity implies the deity's divine presence (Fitzmyer, pp. 33–34). This means that one can legitimately speak of Jesus here as the agent of the divine communiqué. Further, the notion of immanence suggested in this passage *also allows for the possibility* that as with Yahweh, Jesus could appear elsewhere in various forms of self-manifestation apart from the Spirit. The notable decline in references to the Spirit from 16:8 onwards may intimate a deliberate Lukan move in this direction. Luke's aim in using such a title at this juncture in the narrative may not only signal the intimate relation between Jesus and *his* Spirit, but anticipate in fuller measure a conscious heightening of *Jesus' direct involvement* in the church's mission in the remainder of Acts. This may have something to do with Luke's desire to show how Paul images Jesus in his life and ministry.[28]

Thus in 16:7 Luke may be directing the reader's attention away from the Spirit's presence in witness (cf. Luke 12:11–12) to Jesus'

---

[26] Hastings, *Prophet and Witness*, pp. 77–78.
[27] Fitzmyer, "Jesus in the Early Church," p. 33.
[28] See further our discussion on pp. 265–71 below.

(cf. Luke 21:12–15). At this point in Acts the latter prediction remains largely unfulfilled as it refers to Jesus. Whereas Luke records considerably less about the Spirit's presence in witness after ch. 16, Jesus' involvement becomes an explicit theological point of interest: 18:9–10; 22:7–10, 17–21; 23:11; 26:14–18, 23 (but also 7:55–56; 9:4–5, 10–17). Luke pictures Jesus (esp. in chs. 21–28) as providentially directing Paul's witness before the Jewish authorities in Jerusalem and the Gentile courts under Felix, Festus, and King Agrippa. This accords well with what Jesus had foretold to Paul via Ananias (cf. variously 9:15; 22:14–15; 26:16–18). In 23:11 Jesus reassures Paul of the eventual success of his missionary work and in 26:23 appears in essence as the one carrying it out!

We can, therefore, claim with some certainty that Luke thought of the work of Jesus and the Spirit as a coherent unity, paralleling that of Yahweh and his Spirit in the OT. The Spirit's ministry behind the church's witness stands as one way of speaking about Jesus' continuing presence and activity. But that Jesus appears gives us yet another.

The self-manifestations of the risen Lord

Through a number of self-manifestations, Luke portrays the exalted Jesus as transcendent but not personally removed from his people. E.g., in Acts Jesus periodically appears, visually and audibly, to some within the church. These christophanies do not represent all that Luke has to say about how Jesus communicates his presence during the period demarcated by the exaltation and parousia, but they do form a necessary part of the overall statement he develops. The opinion that Jesus' visionary appearances in Acts are only secondarily relevant to Luke's christology is inadequate.[29] We shall discuss what they signify concerning Jesus' Lordship in the next section.

Another particularly expressive and prevalent way Luke highlights Jesus' self-manifestation in Luke–Acts, commonly accepted by most Lukan scholars,[30] is through his *name*. Luke's use of the

[29] See, e.g., Lampe, *God as Spirit*, p. 72; MacRae, "Christology," pp. 159–60. In reply to Lampe, see the second section of chapter 9.

[30] E.g., Thüsing, *Erhöhungsvorstellung*, pp. 50–51; Marshall, *Historian & Theologian*, pp. 179–80, 196–97; Stählin, "πνεῦμα Ἰησοῦ," pp. 240–41; Perlewitz, "Modes of Presence," pp. 150–228; O'Toole, "Risen Jesus," pp. 487–91 and lit. cited on p. 487, n. 46. *Contra* Ziesler, "Name of Jesus," pp. 28–41, esp. the comments of O'Toole, p. 487, n. 46.

term resembles the OT's use of it for Yahweh.[31] This is especially true in the sense that ὄνομα stands for the person named, theologically implying the personal, active presence of transcendent deity among his people. The last verse of the Joel citation in Acts 2:21 (Joel 2:32) supports this. Here Peter associates salvation in "the name of the Lord" with the exalted Jesus.[32] In Joel, the designation *beshem yhwh* (MT), τὸ ὄνομα κυρίου (LXX), clearly refers to Yahweh (so esp. v. 26, *shem yhwh elohekem*). Hans Bietenhard observes that at times in the NT "the name, person and work of God are ... inseparably linked with the name, person and work of Jesus Christ." [33] In this instance, the link is so close that the two are virtually indistinguishable.

Luke's use of ὄνομα elsewhere in Luke–Acts strongly supports this identification of Jesus with "the Lord" of Joel 2:32. Luke prepares his readers in Luke 21:12b–13; 24:47 for this christological usage of ὄνομα in Acts. In 21:12b-13, he deliberately expands Mark's rendering of Jesus' apocalyptic discourse that Jesus' followers "will bear testimony before Jewish and Gentile authorities *for my sake* (ἕνεκεν ἐμοῦ)" (Mark 13:9b; Matt. 10:18b) to read "*on account of my name* (ἕνεκεν τοῦ ὀνόματός μου)" in v. 12b. In 24:47, Jesus instructs his disciples that "repentance and forgiveness of sins will be preached *in his name* (ἐπὶ τῷ ὀνόματι αὐτοῦ) to all nations." The interrelationship between the witness motif and the ὄνομα of Jesus in these two passages anticipates the christological significance of Acts 2:21, a passage which defines what the object of Christian witness will be – i.e., the Lord Jesus Christ – and the controlling meaning of ὄνομα in Acts.

Acts 2:21 represents the first of thirty-two times Luke uses ὄνομα with reference to Jesus' deity. Only in 15:14 (and in its accompanying OT citation, Amos 9:12, recorded in 15:17) does ὄνομα refer to God – here he is said to have called a people to himself. Otherwise, salvation is always offered in Jesus' name (2:21; 2:38; 3:16 [twice]; 4:7–18 [five times]; 8:12), which is said to fulfill all that the prophets have testified about him (10:43) – most likely an allusion back to 2:21. Moreover, believers in Acts heal (3:6; 4:30), teach (5:28,40), baptize (8:16; 10:48; 19:5), exorcize demons (16:18; 19:13), preach

---

[31] So Thüsing, *Erhöhungsvorstellung*, p. 51. For OT parallels in reference to Acts, see Abba, "Name," *IDB* 3, pp. 506–507.

[32] See further Bock, *Proclamation*, pp. 181–86. *Contra* Ziesler, "Name of Jesus," p. 36, who sees the ὄνομα phrase here as a reference to God.

[33] Bietenhard, "ὄνομα," *TDNT* 5, p. 272.

(9:27–28), witness (9:15), and serve in Jesus' name (15:26), as well as call upon (9:14, 21; 22:16), suffer for (9:16; 21:13; 26:9), and honor it (19:17). It is even used as a designation for believers, who have suffered "for the Name (ὑπὲρ τοῦ ὀνόματος)" (5:41). As applied to Jesus in Luke–Acts, "the name is ... indicative of the living power of Jesus at work in the church," [34] "since ... Jesus' name and Jesus himself are identical." [35] What believers do in Jesus' name is in effect being done by Jesus himself. It personifies the exalted Jesus, i.e., making immanent the transcendent Lord.

From another angle, Wilhelm Thüsing plausibly argues that Q also suggests "a ministry of the resurrected Jesus."[36] Although the actual sayings most likely have a pre-Easter origin traceable to Jesus,[37] the collection of the sayings followed his exaltation and giving of the Spirit. Therefore, the *kinds* of sayings preserved by the early church probably reflect the belief that the authority character- izing Jesus' earthly ministry also describes his current heavenly one. The tenor of Luke's Gospel but especially of Acts sustains this point of view.

In addition to the Spirit of Jesus, christophany, the name of Jesus, and the christological understanding of Q, the themes of witness, discipleship, the Eucharist, salvation, the lot, the present reality of history, and the transmission of Jesus' words and deeds perhaps also communicate Jesus' presence in Luke–Acts.[38] *Collec- tively* these forms of self-manifestations in Luke–Acts show that the exalted Jesus is not inactive until the parousia. He continues to work among his people. Thus, in response to Moule, it is better not to assert an absentee christology for Acts since the exalted Jesus like Yahweh is *not* absent.

Jesus as Yahweh's co-equal

Edmond Jacob in his *Theology of the Old Testament* (1958) lists three essential features describing the nature of Yahweh's divine presence: (1) he is *invisible*, thus essentially spiritual, i.e., transcen- dent; (2) he is *present*, dwelling in the midst of his people; and (3) he

---

[34] Marshall, *Historian & Theologian*, p. 179.
[35] Schweizer, "Jesus Christus," *TRE* 16, p. 704.
[36] Thüsing, *Erhöhungsvorstellung*, pp. 55–82, esp. p. 57 (quot. p. 41).
[37] So, e.g., Schürmann, "Vorösterlichen Anfänge," pp. 39–69.
[38] See, e.g., Conzelmann, *Theology of St. Luke*, pp. 186–87; MacRae, "Chris- tology," pp. 160–65; Perlewitz, "Modes of Presence"; Fitzmyer, *Luke I–IX*, p. 194; O'Toole, "Risen Lord," pp. 471–98.

is *unique*, of whom there is no other (p. 74). This description succinctly summarizes Luke's presentation of the exalted Jesus in Acts.

Concerning point (1), as Acts 3:21 (and 1:11) makes clear, Jesus is for the moment in heaven and presently *invisible* to people. Concerning point (3), Jesus' *uniqueness* most vividly appears in Peter's emphatic summation: "salvation is found *in no one else* [ἐν ἄλλῳ οὐδενί], *for there is no other name* [οὐδὲ γὰρ ὄνομά ἐστιν ἕτερον] under heaven given to men by which we *must* [δεῖ] be saved" (4:12); and Paul's: "for *he* [God] has set a day when he will judge *the world* [τὴν οἰκουμένην, i.e., humanity; cf. Ps. 9:8] with justice by *the man* [Jesus] he has appointed. He has given proof of this *to all men* [πᾶσιν] by raising him from the dead" (17:31; also 10:42). Concerning point (2), I have shown that as with the Father, Jesus, though transcendent, is still *personally present and active* among his people. When God is spoken of in Acts, for Luke, both Jesus and the Father fit the billing.

The use of κύριος for Jesus in Acts supports this theological viewpoint as Luke's personal conviction. The title appears in Acts in single and compound forms – the Lord (ὁ κύριος), the Lord Jesus (ὁ κύριος Ἰησοῦς), the Lord Jesus Christ (ὁ κύριος Ἰησοῦς Χριστός), and (the) Lord of all (πάντων κύριος)[39] – and always takes the article except where used vocatively and in 2:36; 10:36. By way of definition, the OT supplies the meaning of κύριος in Luke–Acts: Peter's understanding of the title to refer to Jesus in Acts 2:21 (Joel 2:32) instead of to Yahweh, as in its OT context, substantiates this.[40] Thus, Acts 2:21 may reflect Luke's personal belief about Jesus' relation to God the Father; it may indicate the intended conceptual background for all the uses of κύριος associated with Jesus in Luke–Acts (except, perhaps for some of the vocative ones).[41] Even if Luke uses the title at times more as a proper name for Jesus, its commonness would not automatically rule out the theological meaning it presupposes; such usage would merely

---

[39] For a listing of occurrences of each title in Acts, see Schneider, "Gott und Christus," p. 166, plus additional ambiguous ones mentioned on pp. 167–71.

[40] See, e.g., Rese, *Alttestamentliche Motive*, pp. 126–27; Bock, *Proclamation*, pp. 165–69.

[41] *Contra* MacRae, "Christology," p. 155, who fails to consider Acts 2:21 in his discussion. Conzelmann, *Theology of St. Luke*, pp. 171, 178 also insists that Luke never portrays Jesus' Lordship in the cosmological sense as ruler over the whole world; he, however, fails to consider Luke's substitution of Jesus for Yahweh in Acts 2:21.

connote a christological viewpoint "all Christians have come to acknowledge."[42] Werner Foerster further remarks that session by the right hand of God (Acts 2:36 etc.) means joint rule, thus implying a shared divine dignity between Jesus and the Father.[43]

A related phenomenon in Acts supporting these considerations is the ambiguity of κύριος as a designation for God or Jesus.[44] At times in Acts it is nearly impossible to distinguish exactly to whom Luke is referring. O'Neill postulates that either Luke's readers were able to make clear what was meant or it was not necessary to distinguish between the two – to speak of one was to speak of the other.[45] Luke was possibly intentionally vague in his descriptions at times because for him it was not theologically incorrect in these instances to consider either God or Jesus as the divine referent.[46] In light of Luke's use of titles in Acts for God ("the Lord God" [twice], "the Sovereign Lord" [once]) and for Jesus ("the Lord Jesus" [fourteen times], "the Lord Jesus Christ" [three times]), he certainly could have been clearer in the more ambiguous instances had he wanted to.

Luke perhaps also consciously bears witness to the nature and reality of Jesus' present Lordship, as suggested by Moule, in the way he presents Jesus as prophet, Son of God, Savior, Son of Man, giver of the Holy Spirit, and Lord in his Gospel and Acts.[47] Luke treats these designations with reserve before the resurrection; he

---

[42] Fitzmyer, "Jesus in the Early Church," p. 33.

[43] Foerster, "κύριος," *TDNT* 3, p. 1089.

[44] So, e.g., O'Neill, "Use of *KYRIOS*," p. 159; Moule, "Christology of Acts," p. 161; Franklin, *Christ the Lord*, p. 54; Marshall, *Historian & Theologian*, p. 166; O'Toole, "Risen Lord," p. 478; de Jonge, *Christology in Context*, p. 107. Cf. Schneider, "Gott und Christus," p. 163, n. 11; detailed on pp. 167–71; he lists fourteen instances in Acts where there could be confusion as to the referent of κύριος, but believes there is no "blending" of the two; see also those cited in O'Neill, "Use of *KYRIOS*," p. 159. Although Schneider's explanations seem plausible, they do not rule out alternate conclusions. Cf., e.g., his comments on Acts 14:3 (p. 170) with those of O'Toole, "Risen Lord," pp. 477–78. Cf. also his later comment in "Christologie der Apg.," p. 333: "Nicht überall ist einwandfrei zu entscheiden, ob Gott oder Jesus Christus gemeint ist." ("It is not possible in every instance to decide without question whether God or Jesus Christ is meant.")

[45] O'Neill, "Use of *KYRIOS*," p. 166.

[46] For a possible Gospel anticipation of this, cf. Luke 1:43, "the mother of my Lord," and Luke 2:11, "a Savior, who is Christ the Lord," with Luke 2:26, "the anointed of the Lord/the Lord's Christ" ; so Stonehouse, *Witness*, pp. 169–70.

[47] Moule, "Christology of Acts," pp. 160–66; Moule, *Phenomenon*, pp. 56–61. Franklin, *Christ the Lord*, pp. 49–52 qualifies but does not convincingly rebut Moule's idea of Luke's reserved use of Lord in the Gospel; he does not consider enough the feasibility of Moule's argument on the basis of whether the other

waits until after the resurrection to present them as the great christological titles of early church preaching. His reluctance to describe the pre-Easter Jesus anachronistically stands in sharp contrast to what he records Jesus' followers as saying about Jesus after the resurrection. The similar restraint of the synoptic tradition[48] may imply that Luke's presentation of Jesus' Lordship in Acts is already common knowledge to his readers, and represents a pervasive christological belief passed down to them and to Luke rather than one somewhat original to him.

In view of what I have said thus far, how then does Luke intend the reader to understand Jesus as related to God? As subordinate? As adopted? Or as co-equal to the Father? Interestingly, Luke expounds little on the status of the exalted Jesus.[49] For Luke, Jesus is simply where he said he would be and doing the kinds of things suitable to that position. But to conclude that Luke does not think of a personal union between Christ and the Father is inadequate.[50] To put the matter in proper perspective, Luke does not reflect to any great extent on God's nature either.[51] He simply assumes it. Perhaps the reason, as Hans Conzelmann suggests, is that "there is no theological necessity for it." [52] Furthermore, Luke does not always give us clear exposition on what some of the titles and metaphors used of Jesus in Luke–Acts mean.[53] A good case in point is Jesus as "the Son of God." Perhaps he takes for granted that his audience can fill in the details. That possibility should caution us as to the kinds of conclusions we draw. If Luke did not write to expound the deity of Christ, to what extent do his writings reflect it?

Earlier in this chapter, we looked in some detail at the ways transcendent Yahweh personally involved himself with his people in the OT and at how the continuing work of the exalted Jesus in Acts often closely resembles this depiction. Why would Luke do this unless he believed Jesus to be God's co-equal? His writings certainly reveal a more than adequate knowledge of the OT. It is hard to imagine that he was not equally familiar with its teaching

---

titles point to a similar conclusion. O'Toole, "Risen Lord," p. 474 fails to interact with Moule altogether.

[48] See further Lemcio, "Intention of Mark," pp. 187–206.

[49] So, e.g., Hanson, *Acts*, p. 39; Ladd, "Christology," p. 39.

[50] Cf., e.g., Lampe, "Lucan Portrait of Christ," pp. 172, 174; Hanson, *Acts*, p. 39.

[51] Schweizer, *Challenge*, p. 91.

[52] Conzelmann, *Theology of St. Luke*, p. 149.

[53] MacRae, "Christology," p. 155; Schweizer, *Challenge*, p. 91.

on the incomparability of God and its thoroughgoing monotheism. To present Jesus as the Giver of the Spirit would suggest either that Jesus usurped divine prerogative or that he was considered as Yahweh's co-equal. On the basis of Acts 2:33, Max Turner plausibly argues that "to speak of Jesus directing God's Spirit (understood in this sense) would surely be tantamount to calling him God." [54] Similarly, to substitute Jesus for Yahweh, as implied in the phrase τὸ ὄνομα κυρίου in Acts 2:21, would denigrate the uniqueness of God unless Jesus were considered his equal. This would also hold true for the OT designation "the Spirit of God" and Luke's "the Spirit of Jesus" (Acts 16:7). As Stählin rightly observes, Acts 16:7 implies that "der Geist steht zu dem erhöhten Christus im selben Verhältnis wie im Judentum zu Gott" ("the Spirit stands in relation to the exalted Christ in the same sense as in Judaism to God").[55] In addition, along with the rest of the NT, Luke never loosely speaks of the Spirit in connection to any human source, i.e., the Spirit of Peter, of Paul, of John, and so on, but strictly of the Spirit's divine correlation. He parallels both God the Father ("the Spirit of the Lord," Acts 5:9) and Jesus ("the Spirit of Jesus," 16:7) in combination with the Spirit. This can only mean that he assumes their co-equal status; otherwise, God's uniqueness would be considerably diminished. Acts "pictures the exalted Jesus as filling the role of God himself to the church" [56] in that "for Luke Jesus acts as does the Father, and Jesus can do what the Father does."[57] Thus, with good reason we propose that Luke believed Jesus' Lordship to represent "a status equal to Yahweh."[58] Jesus appears as "co-regent" in Acts.[59]

In contrast, by definition, subordinationism is the "doctrine that assigns *an inferiority of being, status, or role* to the Son or Holy Spirit within the Trinity." [60] Some consider that Luke's emphasis

---

[54] Turner, "Spirit of Christ," pp. 183–84 (quot. p. 183).
[55] Stählin, "πνεῦμα 'Ιησοῦ," p. 247 and lit. cited in n. 68.
[56] Ladd, "Christology," p. 39.
[57] O'Toole, "Risen Lord," p. 487; also de Jonge, *Christology in Context*, p. 107.
[58] Fitzmyer, "Jesus in the Early Church," p. 33.
[59] Bock, *Proclamation*, p. 264. Wilson, *Pastoral Epistles*, p. 73 believes that Jesus' Lordship for Luke does not mean equal status with the Father; but he offers no support for his position. Jesus as God's co-equal would also make it extremely doubtful that Luke derived or adapted Jesus' Lordship from Philo's *logos* concept; see Kleinknecht's summary of Philo's *logos* concept in *TDNT* 4, pp. 88–90. This would have been completely unacceptable to Philo. For Philo the *logos* was the form or personification of God, but was never his co-equal. See further, e.g., Sanders, "Word," *IDB* 4, p. 870; Walls, "Logos," *EDT*, pp. 645–46.
[60] Kroeger and Kroeger, "Subordinationism," *EDT*, p. 1058 (my italic).

on God sending Jesus, raising him from the dead, exalting him, making him Lord, and granting him authority to bestow the Spirit suggests a subordination christology.[61] Adoptionism, moreover, theorizes "that Jesus was in nature a man who *became* God by adoption." [62] Some think that God's making Jesus his son (e.g., Luke 3:22; Acts 13:33) and Lord and Christ (Acts 2:36) indicates adoptionistic tendencies in Luke's christology.[63]

The weakness of the adoptionist view is that Lukan christology lends relatively little support to such a conclusion.[64] Rather Acts presents a messianic unveiling[65] of what was announced of Jesus in Luke's Gospel right from the start.[66] Bauernfeind raises the possibility that Luke, in editing Peter's Pentecost sermon, unintentionally gave the impression of adoptionism in 2:36, a christological conclusion he would not have thought of or supported.[67]

Similarly, belief in a subordinationist christology has not held full sway among Lukan scholars for numerous reasons.[68] Howard Marshall, e.g., demonstrates (*contra* Braun, Wilckens *et al.*) that no

---

[61] Stählin, "πνεῦμα 'Ιησοῦ," pp. 241–42 believes that it holds true only in a restricted sense – at Jesus' exaltation his subordination to the Father comes to an end. For a more thoroughgoing defense of the subordination position according to Braun, Conzelmann, Wilckens, and Kränkl, see pp. 9–11 above. See also, e.g., Jones, "Missionary Speeches," pp. 169–72; Hahn, *Titles*, pp. 311–12; Haenchen, *Acts*, p. 92; Moule, "Christology of Acts," p. 183, n. 18; Hanson, *Acts*, p. 39; Franklin, *Christ the Lord*, p. 54; Wilson, *Pastoral Epistles*, pp. 73–74, 77–79; Schneider, "Christologie der Apg.," pp. 334–35; Krodel, *Acts* (ACNT), p. 89.

[62] Vos, "Adoptionism," *EDT*, p. 13 (my italic).

[63] E.g., Bousset, *Kyrios Christos*, pp. 338–39; Wikenhauser, *Apg.*, pp. 47–48, 155–56; Hahn, *Titles*, p. 107; Flender, *Redemptive History*, pp. 38, n. 2, 51, 136 (but cf. p. 137); Vielhauer, "Paulinism of Acts," p. 44; Schweizer, *Lordship and Discipleship*, pp. 37, 59 (with qual.); Hayes, "Resurrection as Enthronement," pp. 333–45, esp. p. 336; Conzelmann, *Acts*, p. 21; MacRae, "Christology," p. 156; Hengel, *Acts*, p. 104 (with qual.); Dunn, *Christology in the Making*, pp. 35–36, 51; and lit. cited in Jones, "Missionary Speeches," p. 170, n. 1; Wilckens, *Missionsreden*, p. 170, n. 2.

[64] So Hanson, *Acts*, p. 69. With respect to Jesus' baptism and his sonship, see Voss, *Christologie*, pp. 173–75; Schneider, "Christologie der Apg.," pp. 334–35; Dennison, "Son of God," pp. 6–25. With respect to christology in Acts, see Taylor, *Person of Christ*, p. 31; Smalley, "Christology of Acts," p. 362. With respect to Acts 2:36, see Ladd, "Christology," p. 35; Rese, *Alttestamentliche Motive*, pp. 134–35; Neil, *Acts*, p. 78; Wilckens, *Missionsreden*, pp. 170–75. See also Roloff, *Apg.*, p. 60 and Mußner *Apg.*, p. 25, who think that Acts 2:36 reflects a "Zwei-Stufen-Christologie," where the servant Jesus becomes Lord (cf. Acts 3:13, 26; 4:27, 30) and has relatively little to do with an adoptionistic christology.

[65] Smalley, "Christology of Acts," p. 362.

[66] Jones, "Missionary Speeches," pp. 169–72; Neil, *Acts*, p. 78.

[67] Bauernfeind, *Apg.*, pp. 51–52.

[68] But to conclude, as does Ernst, "Jesusbild," pp. 19–20, that Luke's christology parallels Chalcedon is perhaps to overstate the issue as well.

subordination theory can be developed from Luke's use of ἐγείρω and ἀνίστημι.[69] Ned Stonehouse points out that the reciprocity of the Father and Son's respective sovereign revelational activity, as suggested in Luke 10:22, would also preclude assigning an inferior quality to Jesus.[70] Alfons Weiser cautions against reading later dogmatic ideas of subordinationism into Luke. He believes, e.g., that the Father had to give the Spirit to Jesus because of who Jesus was.[71] According to Howard Marshall, Jesus' exaltation publicly affirmed his preexisting status.[72] Jürgen Roloff even allows for the possibility that Luke's use of Joel 2:32 in Acts 2:21 suggests Jesus' preexistence on the basis of a three-stage christology comparable to Phil. 2:6–11; Heb. 1:3–4.[73]

In contrast to Conzelmann, Kränkl, and others, who insist that Jesus only mediates God's saving plan, in Acts Jesus makes known his own plan, appoints, sends, and protects those whom he chooses to carry it out, and leads his plan to completion. Jesus announces to Paul his saving plan to take the gospel to the Jews and Gentiles and leads it to completion through Paul (see esp. 9:15–16; 26:16–18; cf. Ezek. 2:1, 3; Jer. 1:7–8).[74] Paul is the instrument, not Jesus. In Acts 26:18, Jesus specifically mentions that he himself is the object of this saving faith!

Moreover, the OT may likewise have influenced the traditional NT expression that God will raise Jesus from the dead (Luke 1:68–75; 10:24; 16:16, 29–31; 18:31–33; 20:37–38; 24:25–27, 44, 46; Acts 2:22–33, 34–35; 13:33, 34, 35). Rather than indicating that Jesus was in any way inferior to God, it simply, but clearly, confirms that Jesus is, in fact, Lord and Christ because of Yahweh's participation in the resurrection event. Darrell Bock argues on the basis of the OT that Jesus as mediator or as God's instrument implies no subordination; the OT itself presents Jesus as God's incorruptible Son, which means therefore that he had to be raised from the dead (so 2:33–36; 13:33).[75]

---

[69]   Marshall, "Resurrection in Acts," pp. 101–103; also, Fitzmyer, *Luke I–IX*, p. 195.

[70]   Stonehouse, *Witness*, p. 167; also Marshall, *Luke*, pp. 437–38. Cf. Lampe, "Lucan Portrait of Christ," p. 172.

[71]   Weiser, *Apg. 1–12*, p. 94.

[72]   Marshall, *Acts* (NTG), pp. 60–61.

[73]   Roloff, *Apg.*, pp. 54–55; also de Boor, *Apg.*, p. 64.

[74]   OT references are taken from Marshall, *Acts*, p. 396.

[75]   Bock, *Proclamation*, pp. 185–86, 248–49; also Marshall, *Historian & Theologian*, pp. 162–63. Burger, *Jesus als Davidssohn*, pp. 137–41 creates too great a disjunction between the earthly Jesus in Luke and the enthroned Christ in Acts.

W. Carter Johnson observes that Peter's unqualified statement in Acts 4:12, "salvation is found in no one else, for there is no other name under heaven given to men by which we must be saved," rivals the otherwise unparalleled claim concerning Yahweh in Isa. 43:11, "I, even I, am Yahweh, and apart from me there is no savior." Luke considers Yahweh and Jesus as functionally, if not essentially, equivalent in work and nature.[76] Furthermore, Jesus himself anticipates his own divine work, according to Luke at least, during his earthly career in telling his disciples that he (Luke 21:12–15; cf. Exod. 4:12 and Yahweh) along with the Spirit (12:11–12) will assist their witness in days to come. Those days, for Luke, were clearly post-resurrection, as the exalted Jesus' continuing involvement in the church's witness in Acts shows.

Lastly, Charles Cosgrove points out that Luke leaves no doubt that Jesus was in control of his own destiny. Jesus knows that the divine plan will lead him to the cross, but he also seems fully aware that exaltation lies beyond it. For Luke, Jesus' voluntary submission and obedience to the Father's will characterizes his ministry.[77] Thus, Jesus' conscious response to the divine plan may suggest that Luke was presenting his christology according to a kind of humiliation–exaltation christology as expressed in Phil. 2:6–11. Here too the emphasis is not on Jesus' inferior status in rank or dignity but on his voluntary humble obedience in carrying out the Father's will – an obedience ultimately leading to death on a cross. If this parallel holds, it too draws into question the viability of speaking in terms of a Lukan subordination christology. We shall take this issue up in more detail in ch. 11.

Conclusion: Jesus' divine status as traditional

Lukan scholars make much of the fact that Luke says relatively little about Jesus' divine status. But as I have tried to show in this chapter, Luke portrays the exalted Jesus in terms strikingly similar to those describing Yahweh in the OT. The heart of the matter is Jesus' Lordship. What entitles Jesus to bestow the Spirit is that he is Lord of the Spirit. What entitles Jesus to initiate and carry out his saving plan for the church is that he is Lord of the church. And what will entitle Jesus to judge the world is that he is Lord of all.

In view of this Jesus–Yahweh parallel, it is questionable whether

---

[76] Johnson, "Deity of Christ," p. 77.
[77] Cosgrove, "Divine δεῖ," pp. 168–90.

Luke would have seen himself as categorically separating function from essence when commenting on Jesus' Lordship. According to the OT, what distinguished Yahweh from everything else was what he had done and said as seen in his decrees, creation, preservation, and providence; the divine qualities were often attributed to him accordingly. Luke describes Jesus in a similar way. He appears on an equal footing with God by virtue of what he does and says in working alongside the Father in decreeing, preserving, and leading the church.

That Luke was less specific concerning Jesus' divine status in all probability suggests that such knowledge was already common to his readers. Luke's genius is not to be found in the power of his christological "reflection" (as in the *logos* christology of Johannine literature) or "inventiveness" (as some would have it). When it comes to christology, Luke–Acts seems ostensibly traditional. Luke and his readers had most likely already firmly believed that Jesus was by nature as much God as God the Father was. Otherwise, Luke's elevation of Jesus to a divine status comparable to Yahweh's in the OT would have been strong grounds for dismissal of his writing effort, particularly if some of his intended readers were Jewish. Luke's genius is more likely to be found in the way he demonstrates that the exalted Jesus' heavenly work in the early church matches in many ways Yahweh's within OT Israel.

9

JESUS AND THE SPIRIT

Introduction

We saw in ch. 6 that the Spirit plays a major part in Luke–Acts, especially, as concerns Jesus, in connection to John the Baptist's promise that "the Coming One will baptize with the Spirit." Luke explicitly tells us in contrast to Mark (and Matthew) that "the Coming One" is Jesus and describes for us the fulfillment of that promise. In ch. 8, moreover, we have seen that, for Luke, the exalted Jesus' giving of the Spirit supports the idea that he is God the Father's co-equal, since in the OT only Yahweh gives the Spirit. But the issue now before us concerns Luke's understanding of Jesus' relation to the Spirit.

Vincent Taylor believes that within Acts "there is no marked emphasis upon the relation of the Spirit to Jesus Himself."[1] Thus, "for a further development of the relation of the Spirit to Jesus," he concludes, "we have to turn to the great New Testament writers" (p. 26). But is Taylor right? The only passages he discusses in this regard involve believers receiving the gift of the Spirit in Jesus' name (Acts 2:38; 9:17) and Jesus' anointing with the Spirit (10:38).

The OT clearly indicates that the Spirit of God is exclusively given by God.[2] In fact, pre-Christian Jewish literature nowhere explicitly anticipates that the messiah would bestow the Spirit of God. Probably the clearest allusions to the messiah bestowing the Spirit occur in Isa. 59:21; Test. Levi 18:11 (this passage, however, may reflect a later Christian interpolation). In Joel 2:28–32 it is Yahweh who gives the Spirit. What, then, does Luke believe concerning the relation of "the Giver to that which is Given" and

---

[1]   Taylor, *Person of Christ*, p. 25.
[2]   See, e.g., Baumgärtel, "πνεῦμα," *TDNT* 6, pp. 362–64; Lafferty, "Christology," p. 248.

to what extent do his beliefs parallel the OT's depiction of Yahweh's relation to the Spirit?

Jesus as Lord of the Spirit

Luke brings to his work the christological assumption that Jesus is *Lord* and that the Spirit's coming confirmed this to the early church. After initially explaining the charismatic experience of the 120 by appealing to Joel 2:28–32 (3:1–5 MT/LXX) in Acts 2:17–21, Peter devotes the main portion of his sermon (vv. 21–36) to the present christological reality and saving significance of Jesus, the man from Nazareth. Peter declares that this Jesus is both Lord and Christ (v. 36)! The proof lies in the Spirit's unmistakable presence as manifestly "seen" (ὤφθησαν, v. 3) and "heard" (ἦχος, v. 2) by the 120 in the sound of the rushing wind and the appearance of tongues of fire (2:2–3), and by the assembled Jews (2:33, ἐξέχεεν τοῦτο ὅ ὑμεῖς καὶ βλέπετε καὶ ἀκούετε) at Pentecost in the glossolalia of the 120 (cf. 2:5–13).

The Jewish onlookers, according to Luke, unknowingly bear witness to the truthfulness of Peter's claim in their admission that they have seen and heard something quite unusual. But they have no idea what has just transpired. Peter informs them that the reason for this incredible phenomenon is God's outpouring of the Spirit upon the 120 through Jesus his messiah. Literarily, Luke anticipates this declaration by twice recording Jesus' promise of the Spirit prior to the ascension (Luke 24:49; Acts 1:4–5). The events of Acts 2 fulfill this promise. The Spirit's coming thus confirmed to Jesus' followers that as Lord Jesus did give the Spirit and reaffirmed to them that all that he had said about himself during his earthly career was true. This, in effect, guarantees to them that his other promises will likewise come to pass.[3] Acts 2, therefore, shows us something of Luke's beliefs about Jesus' relation to the Spirit.[4] Gustav Stählin asserts that the very act of conferring the

---

[3]   Dodd, *Apostolic Preaching*, p. 26 parallels Luke's use of the Spirit in the apostolic preaching in Acts to the Pauline one of an "'earnest,' or first instalment, of the consummated life of the Age to Come (2 Cor. i. 22, v. 5; Eph. i. 13–14)." Moule, *Holy Spirit*, pp. 35–36 views the Spirit's role in Acts and elsewhere as a "pledge," guaranteeing "that God is at work through Jesus Christ ... until the final consummation" (p. 36). Moreover, Doohan, "Images of God," p. 31 comments that as a pledge, the Spirit "is not a substitute for Jesus, but rather the assurance that Jesus is still alive and active in his Church."

[4]   So Turner, "Jesus and the Spirit," p. 36.

divine Spirit signifies for Luke that Jesus is Lord of the Spirit (cf. vv. 20–21).[5] Luke's use of the Baptist's prediction and the Joel citation justifies this claim.

Luke uses the Baptist's prediction to prepare the reader for the pneumatological and christological significance of its fulfillment in and for the church. He follows Mark in introducing the promise via the Baptist (3:16; Mark 1:8), although he further sharpens the distinction between John and Jesus by depicting John's prophecy as a response to the Jewish crowds who were thinking that John was perhaps the messiah (Luke 3:15). The essential difference between Jesus and John rests in the nature and authority of their baptisms. Where John baptizes with water symbolic of repentance, the messiah baptizes with the very Spirit of God because he divinely possesses the authority to forgive sins.

Luke heightens the coming messiah's superiority by *identifying* his giving of the Spirit with Yahweh's giving of the Spirit in the OT. (Some OT examples of God as Giver of the Spirit include Gen. 6:3; Num. 11:29; Ps. 104:30; 139:7; 143:10; Isa. 42:1; 44:3; 59:21; 63:11; Ezek. 36:27; Hag. 2:5; Zech. 4:6; 7:12.) Luke does this through Jesus' teaching (Luke 11:13), citation of OT prophecy (Acts 2:17–21/Joel 2:28–32), and apostolic teaching (Acts 5:32; 11:17; 15:8). God the Father grants Jesus *the same authority as himself* to pour out the Spirit (Luke 24:49; Acts 1:4–5), which at Pentecost Jesus does in triumphant fulfillment of the Baptist's prophecy (cf. Acts 2:33; 1:4–5; Luke 3:16).

Luke accentuates his belief that Jesus is Lord of the Spirit in using the Joel citation as a point of transition in Peter's Pentecost sermon. After the glossolalia of the 120 within hearing of many Jewish onlookers (2:4, 6), this cosmopolitan group were amazed and perplexed to hear these Galilean believers speaking in the languages of their native countries (vv. 5–13). Peter attempts to resolve their bewilderment (v. 14; cf. their question in v. 12, Τί θέλει τοῦτο εἶναι;) by citing the Joel prophecy to explain to them what this phenomenon signifies: not a state of drunkenness but the coming of

---

[5] Stählin, "πνεῦμα 'Ιησοῦ," pp. 232–34; also Turner, "Jesus and the Spirit," pp. 36–40; Turner, "Spirit of Christ," pp. 179–81. Schweizer thinks that Jesus' Lordship over the Spirit is discernible as early as Luke 4. Luke wants to avoid the OT idea that "the Spirit stands over Jesus" ("πνεῦμα," *TDNT* 6, p. 404); Jesus is "not a *pneumatic*, but the *Lord* of the Spirit" (p. 405, my italic). On the other hand, Dunn, *Jesus and the Spirit*, p. 46 thinks that Luke intentionally waited until Acts 2:33 to express Jesus' Lordship over the Spirit so as not to imply that the Spirit was subordinate to Jesus before his exaltation and Pentecost.

the Spirit of God (2:17–20; Joel 2:28–31 [3:1–5]). Luke's version of the citation closely follows the LXX rendering of Joel 3:1–5 except for some mostly minor changes, which serve mainly to heighten the belief that the eschatological promise of the Spirit's outpouring is indeed the reason for these charismatic signs. In particular, Luke (1) historicizes the prophecy by replacing the more ambiguous μετὰ ταῦτα καί in Joel 3:1 with ἐν ταῖς ἐσχάταις ἡμέραις, λέγει ὁ θεός (Acts 2:17), thus emphasizing that with the Spirit's coming according to divine plan, "the new age" or "the last days" have begun (*contra* Haenchen, *Acts*, p. 179); (2) switches in Acts 2:17 (Joel 3:1) οἱ νεανίσκοι with οἱ πρεσβύτεροι, perhaps to give a better logical progression from sons and daughters to young men to old men; (3) adds in 2:18 (3:2) the particle γε, the possessive μου to τοὺς δούλους and τὰς δούλας, the verb (καὶ) προφητεύσουσιν, and in 2:19 (3:3) the adverb ἄνω and noun–adverb σημεῖα ... κάτω to place greater stress on the fact that the prophetic utterances of the believers at Pentecost signify the fulfillment of Joel's prophecy.[6] And as importantly, he uses the prophecy to direct their attention to the reason this has happened in the first place: Jesus' exaltation (in v. 21 κύριος = Jesus; cf. Joel 2:32).

The first four verses of the citation explain that the charismata reveal the eschatological presence of the Spirit and the dawning of the last days. The final verse introduces the topic for the rest of Peter's sermon: that Jesus' coming and ultimately his exaltation to God's right hand inaugurate the last days (so esp. 2:33–36). The Joel passage takes on significant christological meaning in that Peter transfers in v. 21 the agency of salvation from God (Yahweh) to Jesus.[7] As Lord of the Spirit, Jesus now pours out the promised Spirit upon believers.

Thus, on the basis of the fulfillment of the Baptist's prediction and Peter's use of the Joel citation in his Pentecost sermon, we can justifiably conclude that Luke brings to his work a conviction that, as with God the Father, Jesus is Lord of the Spirit.

---

[6] See further Rese, *Alttestamentliche Motive*, pp. 45–55; Bock, *Proclamation*, pp. 157–64.

[7] So, e.g., Haenchen, *Acts*, pp. 179, 186; Rese, *Alttestamentliche Motive*, pp. 54–55; Wilckens, *Missionsreden*, p. 59; Hubbard, "Commissioning Accounts," p. 195; Schneider, "Gott und Christus," p. 166; Dupont, "Apologetic Use," pp. 137–38; Roloff, *Apg.*, p. 55; Turner, "Spirit of Christ," pp. 174–84; Bock, *Proclamation*, pp. 164–67; Lincoln, "Theology and History," p. 206.

The work of Jesus and the Spirit

Luke also discloses his attitude toward Jesus and the Spirit in the way he describes in the Gospel their future work in the disciples' witness and demonstrates this in Acts, as a case in point, in the mission of the early church.

Luke parallels the Spirit's future enabling work for witness with that of Jesus himself – a feature not found in Mark, Matthew, or John – in the doublet Luke 12:11–12/21:14–15.[8] In the first instance, Jesus promises the disciples that when they stand trial before religious and civil authorities (v. 11), presumably for their faith, the Spirit will inspire their witness (v. 12). Whether Luke and Matthew (10:19–20) took over this saying from Q or from Mark 13:9, 11 is uncertain; but the presence of ἐπὶ τὰς συναγωγὰς καὶ τὰς ἀρχὰς καὶ τὰς ἐξουσίας in 12:11 suggests that Luke edited this logion with Mark 13:9 in mind; see also John 14:26. But in the second instance, Luke has in his version of the apocalyptic discourse[9] Jesus as the source of divine assistance in place of the Spirit.[10] Luke seems to anticipate in the doublet a thorough blending of the future ministry of the exalted Jesus with that of the promised Spirit. They will both be personally active in the church's witness.

Luke demonstrates this in Acts. E.g., concerning the Spirit, Peter

---

[8] Lampe, *God as Spirit*, pp. 70–71 all but admits this when he concludes that on this "occasion Luke comes close to identifying Jesus with the Spirit." See further our discussion on pp. 201–204 below.

[9] In all probability, Luke 21:5–36 is a loose editorialization of Mark 13 (Fitzmyer, *Luke X–XXIV*, pp. 1323–29) and perhaps supplemented with some similar version of the discourse (Marshall, *Luke*, pp. 752–58). For a more detailed source discussion of 21:14–15, see Fuchs, *Sprachliche Untersuchungen*, pp. 171–91.

[10] Whether this textual alteration stems from a Lukan redaction of Mark 13:11 (e.g., Fuchs, *Sprachliche Untersuchungen*, pp. 190–91) or reflects another version of the promise of divine assistance (e.g., Kremer, "Verheißung des Geistes, pp. 262–67) remains uncertain. On the redactional side, Schweizer, "πνεῦμα," *TDNT* 6, p. 398, n. 414 feels that Luke 21:14–15 reflects a Lukan christological heightening of Mark 13:11. Gräßer, *Parusieverzögerung*, p. 160 thinks this is esp. so in light of the apologetic defenses of Peter, John, Stephen, and Paul in Acts. Howard, *Ego Jesu*, pp. 229–30 agrees with Schweizer, but on the basis of Jesus' bestowal of the Spirit in Acts 2:33. It seems entirely possible, on the other hand, that Luke based this alteration on other sources he had at his disposal. In contrast to Mark 13:11 (and pars. Matt. 10:19–20; Luke 12:11–12), Barrett, *Holy Spirit*, pp. 130–32 thinks that Luke 21:14–15 represents the most original form of the saying; see also Kümmel, *Promise and Fulfilment*, p. 99, n. 40. However, Mahoney's suggestion in "Luke 21:14–15," pp. 220–21 that ἐγώ in v. 15 is derived from a Hebraic form reminiscent of Ps. 49:3 and Isa. 50:8 is not convincing. Nor is Ellis' conjecture in *Luke*, p. 244, that Luke got his material from a Christian prophet's oracle.

and Stephen's testimonies before the Jewish authorities show vividly the Spirit's empowering for witness in fulfillment of Luke 12:11–12. In Acts 4:8–22, Peter and John – filled with the Holy Spirit (πλησθεὶς πνεύματος ἁγίου, v. 8) – testify impressively about Jesus (cf. v. 13) before the ἄρχοντες τοῦ λαοῦ καὶ πρεσβύτεροι (v. 8; τοῦ συνεδρίου, v. 15). In Acts 5:27–40, Peter and the apostles again appear before the Sanhedrin. At the end of his speech Peter states, "we are witnesses of these things, and so is the Holy Spirit, whom God has given to those who obey him" (v. 32). The Spirit given at Pentecost is still present and bearing witness of God's saving plan in Jesus through them. Stephen also speaks powerfully through the agency of the Spirit (6:10!) to the members of the Synagogue of the Freedmen (6:8–15) and presumably in the same manner in his speech before the high priest (cf. 7:55).

Luke, however, also records a number of instances where Jesus appears directly to some of his followers in conjunction with the witness theme (e.g., to Stephen, 7:55–56; Ananias, 9:10–16; Paul, 9:4–5; 18:9–10; 22:7–10, 17–21; 23:11; 26:14–18). The first example occurs in Acts 6:10. Here Luke recounts that Stephen's opponents καὶ οὐκ ἴσχυον ἀντιστῆναι τῇ σοφίᾳ καὶ τῷ πνεύματι ᾧ ἐλάλει. George and Weiser believe that the expression ἀντιστῆναι τῇ σοφίᾳ recollects Luke 21:15 (cf. σοφίαν, ἀντιστῆναι) and that σοφίᾳ may well refer to the part Jesus played in empowering Stephen's witness.[11] Thus, in the phrase τῇ σοφίᾳ καὶ τῷ πνεύματι Luke shows in Stephen's defense the fulfillment of his Gospel doublet that both the Spirit and Jesus will strengthen the testimony of the disciples (12:12; 21:15). Some scholars question the christological association of Acts 6:10 with Luke 21:15. They argue that the emphasis in Luke 21:15 is upon the wisdom given by Jesus rather than upon Jesus himself; thus, σοφίᾳ in Acts 6:10 refers to the Spirit.[12] But in either case, as Luke's unmistakable reference to Luke 21:15 in Acts 6:10 makes clear, Jesus is *directly* responsible for this wisdom, whether in supplying it to Stephen through the Spirit or giving it himself without the Spirit's mediation.[13]

But a clearer example occurs in Acts 18:9–10. Here Luke records, in language reminiscent of OT theophany and prophetic calling,[14]

---

[11]   George, "Esprit saint," p. 121; Weiser, *Apg. 1–12*, p. 172; also Morris, *Luke*, p. 324.

[12]   So, e.g., Hengel, "Messianischer Lehrer der Weisheit," p. 167; Pesch, *Apg. 1–12*, p. 237.

[13]   See further Turner, "Jesus and the Spirit," p. 39.

[14]   For more lit. on Yahweh's parallel OT work, see Pesch, *Apg. 13–28*, p. 149, n. 16.

that Jesus appears to Paul in a vision in Corinth encouraging him to "fear not [μὴ φοβοῦ], but keep on speaking and not be silent [ἀλλὰ λάλει καὶ μὴ σιωπήσῃς], for I am with you [διότι ἐγώ εἰμι μετὰ σοῦ]." This passage is unparalleled in the NT. Here the exalted Jesus personally reassures Paul of his own continuing presence with him. According to the OT, the fact of divine presence connotes the supreme enabling and protective power and authority inherent in it (cf., e.g., Exod. 4:12).[15] The exalted Jesus' promise of his personal presence to Paul guarantees to him the same divine enabling. It will lead to the successful outcome of his preaching in Corinth whatever the opposition (so 18:12–17!). Therefore, in fulfillment of Luke 21:15, Jesus himself appears here as the divine agent empowering Paul's witness of him in the face of persecution.[16]

Moreover, in Acts 21:17–26:32 one would expect to find, in view of Luke 12:11–12, the Spirit empowering Paul's testimony as he stands trial before various religious and civil authorities. But Luke *never* directly or indirectly refers to the Spirit in this extended Acts passage. Instead, Jesus again appears as the divine agent directing Paul's witness (23:11). These chapters contain the only occasions in Acts where Luke specifically records a follower of Jesus being brought to trial before βασιλεῖς (Agrippa, 25:13–14, 24, 26; 26:2, 7, 13, 19, 26–27, 30) and ἡγεμόνας (Felix, 23:24, 26, 33; Festus, 26:30) on account of Jesus' name[17] and having opportunity to bear witness to them in fulfillment of Luke 21:12–13. In fact, Paul emphatically states in 26:23 that it is the resurrected Christ who is proclaiming the gospel to the Jews and the Gentiles through him. In this verse, Luke gives the impression that Paul's entire missionary career, in fulfillment of his divine commission (cf. 9:15–16 pars.), could be understood as a personal work of the Lord Jesus.[18]

This discussion takes on added christological importance as Jesus' work from heaven parallels Yahweh's. Some claim that Luke identifies the Spirit either as *representing* Jesus on earth[19] or, more specifically, as *mediating* his very presence.[20] In either instance, the

---

[15] See further Görg, "Redeform," pp. 214–40.
[16] See also O'Toole, "Risen Jesus," pp. 480–81.   [17] Ibid., p. 481.
[18] See further our discussion of Acts 26:23 on pp. 213–14 below.
[19] So, e.g., Lofthouse, "Holy Spirit," p. 336; Reicke, "Risen Lord," p. 162; Schweizer, "πνεῦμα," TDNT 6, pp. 405–406; Moule, "Christology of Acts," pp. 165, 179; Lampe, *God as Spirit*, p. 72; Krodel, "Functions of the Spirit," p. 36.
[20] So, e.g., Beasley-Murray, "Spirit," p. 477; Kränkl, *Jesus der Knecht Gottes*, pp. 180–81; MacRae, "Christology," p. 161; Stählin, "πνεῦμα Ἰησοῦ," p. 235;

Spirit is closely identified with Jesus. This picture conforms to the OT belief that the Spirit of Yahweh (*ruach yhwh*) appears as an extension of Yahweh himself. Luke, however, considers Jesus as *personally active* among his followers. In this case, as do the OT writers with Yahweh, Luke lays special stress at times on the fact that Jesus directly ministers to and inspires the witness of his people, apart from the Spirit.

In ch. 8, we looked in considerable detail at Luke's understanding of Jesus' relation to God. There we observed the similarity between what Jesus does from heaven in Acts and what Yahweh does from heaven in the OT. Yahweh reveals himself both through the mediation of the Spirit and directly through a number of self-manifestations. Similarly as Acts 18:9–10 illustrates, as with Yahweh Luke depicts Jesus as transcendent deity immanently expressing himself to his people (see also 7:55–56; 9:4–5, 10–16; 22:7–10, 17–21; 23:11; 26:14–18).

What is at stake here is the position typified by Lampe:

> *Luke therefore cannot say that Christ is personally present in the Church's mission*, nor, with Paul, that Christ dwells in the believer. The bond between the ascended Jesus and his people is close enough for a persecution of the Church to be a persecution of Jesus, but the link is external, constituted by the Spirit. *For Luke the risen Christ is no longer with his followers.* He appears in heaven, or from heaven, in special visions and theophanies. His Spirit is with men and in men, but Luke does not think, like Paul, of the Spirit as the mode in which Christ becomes personally present to them; still less does he think of the Spirit as that to which Christians are really referring when they speak of experiencing the presence of Christ; for Christ is one, in heaven, and the Spirit is another, on earth; it is "poured out" by the exalted Christ; it is a gift given, and not the giver.[21]

The weakness of Lampe's position is that he fails to consider the possibility that Luke intended to parallel the nature of Jesus'

George, "Esprit saint," pp. 521, 532; Turner, "Jesus and the Spirit," p. 39; Turner, "Spirit of Christ," p. 183; Recker, "Lordship of Christ," pp. 179, 186; also O'Toole, "Risen Jesus," p. 484 and lit. cited in n. 37.

21 Lampe, *God as Spirit*, p. 72 (my italic); similarly MacRae, "Christology," pp. 159–60.

heavenly work with that of Yahweh in the OT. As not all would agree with Lampe that, according to Luke, the Spirit does not mediate the exalted Jesus' presence on earth, Lampe's insistence that in Acts the exalted Jesus is not personally present in the church's mission because "Luke believed that the exalted Lord is not here but in heaven" (p. 71) is equally debatable. It minimizes, if not altogether misses, what Luke most likely thinks these special visions and theophanies signify christologically about the exalted Jesus.

Max Turner plausibly argues that "as the Spirit had mediated God's activity, and thus his presence, amongst his people, so, according to the perspective of Acts 2:33, the Spirit has now become the means of Jesus' presence and activity too."[22] But the Spirit is not Luke's sole means of expressing in Acts Jesus' continuing work in the church. Jesus' promise to inspire the disciples' witness in Luke 21:15 closely resembles Yahweh's promise to Moses in Exod. 4:12: "Now go, I will help you speak and will teach you what to say" (cf. also Isa. 50:4; 51:16; Jer. 1:9; and Yahweh to Balaam in Num. 22:35, 38; Mic. 6:5). Both promises suggest divine immanence via self-manifestation. We can see Yahweh's immanence borne out in Moses' ministry (see esp. Exod. 33:11, 18–23; Num. 12:8) and Jesus' immanence in Paul's ministry in Acts.

Thus, in contrast to Lampe, Luke's Spirit–Christ doublet in Luke 12:12/21:15 is expressive of what the Spirit will do on behalf of Christ in the mission of the church and in the fuller sense of what Christ himself will actively do alongside the Spirit. These categories are not mutually exclusive, for they parallel the work of Yahweh and his Spirit as depicted in the OT.

The unity of Jesus and the Spirit

In Acts 16:7, Luke sheds more light on his christological beliefs in relation to the Spirit. Here he carries the previous point a step further in uniquely fusing the two names together in the phrase "the Spirit of Jesus (τὸ πνεῦμα ᾿Ιησοῦ)." This title is unparalleled in the NT and for this reason is most likely the Lukan original. Bruce Metzger believes that the single NT usage of this phrase in 16:7 points to it as being the Lukan original (p^{74} X A B C^2 D E 33

---

[22] Turner, "Spirit of Christ," p. 183.

69 81* 326 467 vg syr^{p,h} cop^{bo} arm^{mss}) and thus best explains the three major textual variants as attempts to harmonize it with the more common τὸ πνεῦμα κυρίου (C* it^{gig} *al*), τὸ ἅγιον πνεῦμα (arm^{mss} Epiphanius) or with τὸ πνεῦμα dropping Ἰησοῦ altogether (H L P 81^c and most minuscules cop^{sa} arm^{mss} Ephraem Chrysostom *et al.*, followed by the TR).[23] Its closest parallel is in Phil. 1:19, "the Spirit of Jesus Christ (τοῦ πνεύματος Ἰησοῦ Χριστοῦ)" (also Gal. 4:6, "the Spirit of his son," τὸ πνεῦμα τοῦ υἱοῦ αὐτοῦ). Howard Marshall further observes that since the phrase occurs in narrative it probably reflects a deliberate Lukan viewpoint rather than a repetition of some stock phrase.[24]

Because Luke at times so closely parallels the work of the Spirit and Jesus in the church's mission, τὸ πνεῦμα Ἰησοῦ can rightly refer to the combined activity of both. In view of Jesus' promise of divine assistance in witness via the Spirit (Luke 12:11–12) and himself (21:14–15), and his injunction to testify to all the nations about him via "his name" (Luke 24:46–47) and in the power of the Spirit (Luke 24:47–49; Acts 1:8; 9:15), both Jesus and the Spirit could appear here as actively redirecting Paul toward Greece to achieve this end. In this sense, the Spirit and Jesus appear almost as interchangeable.[25] In addition, although most commentators believe that the designation refers to the Holy Spirit,[26] Martin Dibelius observes that this important juncture in the spread of the gospel was, in a sense, confirmed by the whole Godhead in the progression, "Holy Spirit (v. 6), Spirit of Jesus (v. 7), and God (vv. 9–10)."[27] Luke's close association of the work of the Spirit and of Jesus would certainly allow for this possibility.

In Acts 5:9 and 8:39, Luke speaks of "the Spirit of the Lord (τὸ

---

[23] So Metzger, *Textual Commentary*, p. 442. *Contra* Kilpatrick, "Spirit, God, and Jesus," p. 63, who prefers the last of the four positions for no other apparent reason than that τὸ πνεῦμα Ἰησοῦ only occurs in Acts 16:7 and thus, through implication, because of its "unparalleled" usage is probably not trustworthy.

[24] Marshall, *Historian & Theologian*, p. 181.

[25] Flender, *Redemptive History*, p. 142. *Contra* Wainwright, *Trinity*, p. 215, who asserts that Acts never associates Christ with the Spirit. Although he mentions Acts 16:7, he offers no argument in support of his view.

[26] E.g., Swete, *Holy Spirit*, pp. 105–106; Conzelmann, *Acts*, p. 127; Haenchen, *Acts*, p. 484; Beasley-Murray, "Spirit," p. 478; Penna, "Spirito di Gesù," pp. 241–61; Stählin, "πνεῦμα Ἰησοῦ," p. 232; George, "Esprit saint," pp. 510, 520, 526; Turner, "Spirit of Christ," p. 180; Marshall, *Acts*, p. 263; Chevallier, "Esprit saint," p. 16; Schneider, *Apg. 13, 1–28, 31*, pp. 205–206; Weiser, *Apg. 13–28*, p. 405; D. J. Williams, *Acts*, p. 269; Pesch, *Apg. 13–28*, p. 101; Bruce, *Acts* (NICNT), p. 307.

[27] As cited in Nock, *Gnomon* 25 (1953): 497, n. 3; also Krodel, *Acts* (ACNT), p. 301.

πνεῦμα κυρίου)." But as Gerhard Schneider notes, on the basis of Luke 4:18 and Acts 15:10, these passages probably refer to the Spirit of God rather than to the Spirit of Jesus.[28] The story of Ananias and Sapphira in Acts 5:1–11 substantiates this interpretation. Peter tells Ananias, "You have not lied to men but to *God*" (5:4), but to Sapphira, "How could you agree to test *the Spirit of the Lord*? (v. 9; cf. 15:10). These parallel expressions recall the close connection the OT makes between God and his Spirit. In fact, for Isaiah, this bond is so close that the Holy Spirit is occasionally thought of as identical to God's person (cf. Isa. 31:3; 34:16; 40:13; 63:10–14).[29] Luke's handling of the Ananias and Sapphira story mirrors this unity and interchangeability.

Eduard Schweizer's reference to a Jesus–Spirit parallel in Acts 10:14, 19 (par. 11:8, 12), however, is less clear.[30] In fact, if anything, it equates the Spirit with God. In 10:33, Cornelius asks Peter to tell him everything commanded to him "by the Lord (ὑπὸ τοῦ κυρίου)." It seems more logical that a Gentile would be referring to God here since the point of Peter's visit was to rectify his ignorance of Jesus. The alternate textual tradition of ἀπὸ τοῦ θεοῦ replacing ὑπὸ τοῦ κυρίου in 10:33 substantiates this.[31]

What, then, does the fusion of names in Acts 16:7 indicate to us about Luke's beliefs on the unity of Jesus and the Spirit? Some feel that since Luke presents Jesus as the Giver of the Spirit (Luke 24:49; Acts 1:5; 2:33), he at least functionally presents the Spirit's role as subordinate to that of the exalted Jesus.[32] Stählin thinks, however, on the basis of Luke's presentation of the work of Jesus and the Spirit "that one could speak of the Work and Workers as one and the same" (pp. 246–47, quot. p. 247), and hence, that "a subordination cannot clearly be maintained" (p. 246). I would suggest that Luke supports this same conclusion in his Gospel doublet 12:12/21:15, as illustrated above.

It seems arguably the case, therefore, that Luke regards the unity of Jesus and the Spirit in a way comparable to that of Yahweh and his Spirit. To what extent Luke believed that the

---

[28] Schneider, "Gott und Christus," p. 168; see also O'Neill, "Use of *KYRIOS*," pp. 158–59, 166; Seesemann, "πεῖρα, πειρ," *TDNT* 6, p. 32. Cf. Stählin, "πνεῦμα 'Ιησοῦ," p. 133.

[29] Lampe, "Holy Spirit," *IDB* 2, p. 629.

[30] See also Schweizer, "πνεῦμα," *TDNT* 6, pp. 405–406.

[31] See further Metzger, *Textual Commentary*, p. 378.

[32] E.g., Barrett, *Recent Study*, p. 67; Hull, *Holy Spirit*, pp. 173–75; Marshall, *Historian & Theologian*, p. 92; Dunn, *Jesus and the Spirit*, p. 46.

Spirit was subordinate to Jesus, if he thought in these terms at all, is not much clearer in his writings than in the OT's treatment of the Spirit and Yahweh, although in both testaments the idea may be hinted at in that both Jesus and Yahweh give the Spirit. We should, however, exercise caution in the way we read the thinking of later theologians on the subordination idea back into the consciousness of Luke himself. It is not certain that Luke ever thought in subordination terms, esp. if he believed that the Spirit mediated Jesus' presence. Luke's perception of Jesus' relation to the Spirit seems closely reminiscent of OT monotheism: as the Spirit of God was largely the point of contact between Israel and Yahweh in the OT, so is the Spirit, according to Luke–Acts, primarily the point of contact between Jesus and the church, and Jesus and the world.

Conclusion: the Spirit as christological apologetic

In this chapter, I have tried to show that in giving more extended treatment to the Baptist's prophecy, Luke has also made more explicit his beliefs concerning the relation of the Gift to the Giver. We have seen that Luke perceives Jesus' relationship to the Spirit as fundamentally similar to Yahweh's relationship to his Spirit in the OT. In view of this comparison, Vincent Taylor's belief that Luke reveals no special emphasis upon Jesus' relation to the Spirit proves gravely deficient. In fact, it is quite possible that *our* understanding of the issue would be noticeably impaired unless we read "the great New Testament writers" in light of Luke!

In addition, according to Luke, Jesus directly appeared at key junctures within the mission of the early church alongside the Spirit. Lampe's minimizing of Jesus' continued appearances to his followers in Acts borders on misreading Luke. It is at this very juncture that we perhaps see Luke's christology most profoundly, for it parallels how Yahweh communicated to people in the OT.

A powerful feature at work in the way Luke develops his work is that the Spirit's coming acts as a type of christological apologetic, not only as a literary feature of Luke–Acts, but as Luke considers the Spirit operative among his own readers as one and the same with the Spirit who was predicted by John, who anointed Jesus, who was given by Jesus and who is closely identified in work and unity with the exalted Jesus. The fact that the Spirit has been given and is present within believers accredits Jesus' life and teaching as authentic and reliable, demonstrates that Jesus is presently reigning at God's right hand, and stands as a "pledge" guaranteeing his future return. This aspect to Luke's writings would be especially important to his readers, since most of them had probably never seen the historical Jesus during his earthly career.

10

JESUS AND THE END OF HISTORY

Introduction

In ch. 7 we gave some attention to Mark's anticipation of Jesus' return[1] and to Luke's development of the place of eschatology in salvation history, more specifically to the *time* of Jesus' return.[2] There we argued that Luke supported Mark's eschatological anticipation of Jesus' imminent return; compelling evidence of this is the book of Acts, which, as we saw, exposits the sense of Mark 13:9–11. The thesis we shall test in this chapter is whether the presentation of Jesus' Lordship in Luke–Acts reveals a Lukan tendency to view Jesus' present reign as "a sign of the times" anticipating the end of history.[3] We shall take the representative position of Hans Conzelmann, who contends that Luke wrote on account of "the delay of the parousia," as our starting point and reassess the plausibility of the idea of a delayed parousia in Luke–Acts in light of the significance of Jesus' present Lordship.

---

[1] It is doubtful, however, whether the parousia is traceable in Mark to 16:7/14:28 as some would argue; cf. the discussion on pp. 92–93, 97–98 above. For more on Mark's eschatology generally, see Rasco, "Historia Salutis," pp. 308–309; Rigaux, *Testimony of St. Mark*, p. 174; Schweizer, "Eschatologie," pp. 43–48; Pesch, *Markus. 1, 1–8, 26*, p. 318; Pokorný, "Markus," pp. 1988–91; Geddert, *Markan Eschatology*.

[2] For a survey of the various ways scholars define NT eschatology, see Zmijewski, *Eschatologiereden*, pp. 22–37; Marshall, "Eschatology," pp. 264–69; specifically concerning the de-eschatologization of early Christianity, Aune, "Delay of the Parousia," pp. 88–95.

[3] My intention in this chapter is not to survey Lukan eschatology comprehensively. For a good review of the lit. and present state of the discussion, see Maddox, *Purpose*, pp. 100–102; Carroll, *Response*, pp. 1–30; see also lit. cited in Schneider, *Apg. 1–12*, p. 336; Fitzmyer, *Luke I–IX*, p. 267; Rese, "Lukas," pp. 2321–22; Bovon, *Luke the Theologian*, pp. 1–8a; van Segbroeck, *Luke*, p. 223.

A delay of the parousia?

In the seminal work, *Die Mitte der Zeit* (1953), Hans Conzelmann proposes that Luke wrote to appease the worries of a church stemming from an unexpected delay of Jesus' return:

> Luke's eschatology, compared with the original conception of the imminence of the Kingdom, is a secondary construction based on certain considerations which with the passage of time cannot be avoided. It is obvious what gives rise to these reflections – the delay of the Parousia. The original idea presupposes that what is hoped for is near, which means that the hope cannot be reconciled with a delay, as otherwise the connection with the present would be lost ... Eschatology as an imminent hope belonging to the present cannot by its very nature be handed down by tradition.[4]

Luke, Conzelmann thinks, sets out to rewrite the beginnings of Christianity in light of the delay. Luke does so by reinterpreting traditional material supporting an imminent return and by incorporating other material supporting that the "last days" have already arrived. The period of time in which the church now finds itself, Conzelmann calls "the epoch of the church":

> The Spirit Himself is no longer the eschatological gift, but the substitute in the meantime for the possession of ultimate salvation; He makes it possible for believers to exist in the continuing life of the world and in persecution, and He gives the power for missionary endeavour and for endurance. This change in the understanding of eschatology can be seen in the way in which Luke, by his description of history, depicts the nature of the Church, its relation to the world, and the course of the mission in its progress step by step, and in the way in which he repeatedly describes the Spirit as the power behind this whole

---

[4] Conzelmann, *Theology of St. Luke*, p. 97, also pp. 123, 133; Conzelmann, "Geschichte und Eschaton," pp. 210–21; Conzelmann, *Outline of Theology*, pp. 149–52; Conzelmann, *Acts*, pp. xlv–xlviii; and more generally, Conzelmann, "Present and Future," pp. 26–44, esp. pp. 37–41. For scholarly antecedents to Conzelmann's view of a Lukan non-eschatological vantage point in Acts, see, e.g., Dibelius, *A Fresh Approach*, p. 257; Vielhauer, "Paulinism of Acts," p. 47. For scholars supporting Conzelmann, see pp. 10–11, 45–49 above.

process. As far as the history of tradition is concerned, this means that Luke employs for his reconstruction of history the traditional material, which is stamped with the view that the last days have already arrived. (pp. 95–96)

Luke, Conzelmann argues, has consistently altered the eschatological stance of his sources – particularly Mark. For this reason he insists that any study of Lukan eschatology must, therefore, explain:

> The deliberate intention with which Luke recasts his sources, and also the fact that he does not preserve the early expectation, but eliminates it. We see the extent of this recasting if we make a comprehensive comparison with the sources, particularly with the Marcan passages. Such a comparison shows that it is not an adequate explanation of Luke's alterations to see them merely as "development," but that it is a question of a definite theological attitude to the problem of eschatology. Luke in fact *replaces* the early expectation by a comprehensive scheme of a different kind. (p. 96, my italic)[5]

Ernst Käsemann, in summarizing Conzelmann's position, sees in Luke–Acts primitive Christian eschatology giving way to a model of salvation history.[6] The concept of the parousia's delay lies at the heart of Conzelmann's proposed three-stage salvation-history scheme. William C. Robinson describes Conzelmann's formulation as "die klassische Lösung" ("the classical solution")[7] since it has so thoroughly dominated the subsequent field of Lukan studies. The question remains whether Conzelmann's theory does justice to Luke's perception of salvation history and the parousia, and of the corresponding implications for the church and the world.[8]

The main problem here involves Conzelmann's severing of eschatology from salvation history. As we have already established, in interacting with Mark's Gospel, Luke tends to explicate the theological traditions in Mark, rather than to refute them or to revise them radically. E.g., on the basis of Luke's exposition of the traditions paralleling Mark 13:9–11 in Acts, we have argued, *contra*

---

[5] For a fuller description of his proposed Lukan purpose, see pp. 45–49 above.
[6] Käsemann, "Problem of the Historical Jesus," p. 28.
[7] Robinson, *Weg des Herrn*, pp. 7–9.
[8] My critique applies to Flender's existential reinterpretation of Lukan eschatology as well; cf. also Ellis, *Eschatology*.

Conzelmann, that Luke's development of salvation history anticipates Jesus' imminent return. This means, in view of this conclusion, that Luke's presentation of Jesus' Lordship may itself appear
as "a sign of the times," anticipating the end of history. This factor,
although not as explicit in Mark, would reinforce Luke's solidarity
with Mark's eschatological stance and disclose valuable information concerning Luke's christological beliefs.

Jesus' Lordship: a sign of the times

In ch. 8 we argued that Luke considered the exalted Jesus as equal
to God the Father. The Lord Jesus' personal manifestations to the
church in Luke–Acts parallel the OT's way of describing the
immanency of Yahweh to Israel. Moreover, human responses to
Jesus as deity are virtually synonymous with those ascribed to
Yahweh. Hence, we concluded there that for Luke to speak of
Jesus' Lordship was tantamount to speaking about that of God the
Father and reciprocally, in many instances, to speak of God's rule
was equivalent to speaking about Jesus' Lordship.

One question, however, remains unanswered: How does Jesus'
Lordship in Luke–Acts coincide with the future dimension of
God's saving plan? The answer lies in Luke's understanding of
Jesus' relation to the church and the world, for he directly links his
perception of them to the eschatological significance of Jesus'
present Lordship.

Jesus' heavenly rule signals, for Luke, the expectation of a divine
verdict upon all people because of his death and resurrection. Jesus
is the nexus between God and man, either as Savior or Judge. This
polarity in function instills a sense of urgency to the gospel's
proclamation. Now is the time of salvation. But this period of
witness will not go on indefinitely. The ascended Lord will one day
return, and at that time as Judge. That Jesus in the meantime
appears, alongside the Father, sovereignly guiding the spread of the
gospel to the ends of the earth indicates that he too is personally
leading history toward its consummation in his return. The success
of the church's mission perhaps heightens this expectation.

In this section we shall examine whether, for Luke, the reality of
Jesus' Lordship itself anticipates the end of history in the sense
that it stands as "a sign of the times." Two points within Luke–
Acts are worth following up in this regard: (1) the connection of
promise and fulfillment to eschatology in reference to Jesus' work

as Lord, and (2) the reaffirmation of the early church's perception of the exaltation of Jesus.

Promise and Fulfillment

Since Conzelmann, scholars commonly accept that Luke had intentionally severed eschatology from promise and fulfillment. Zmijewski, e.g., insists that Luke's writings can only be thought of as eschatological in the sense that they reveal the continuation of promise and fulfillment in the church age, a period of time still separate from that of the last days.[9]

But this conviction doubtfully represents Luke's perspective. Conzelmann himself admits that Luke used for his alleged "reconstruction of history" traditional material stamped with the belief that the last days had arrived.[10] With regard at least to Jesus' promise of the Spirit, it seems that Luke was not predisposed to alter his sources. In Luke 12, a passage paralleling the expectant eschatological leaning of Mark 13 (esp. Luke 12:38–40, 41–48),[11] Jesus promises his followers that the Spirit will assist their witness; Acts, as we saw in ch. 9, only too clearly intends to report its fulfillment.

Therefore, to wrest the Spirit's coming and activity from the eschatological sense of Jesus' teaching – and that of Peter in Acts 2:17[12] – is to introduce a mare's nest of intractable difficulties in an attempt to understand Luke–Acts theologically. The many inconsistencies would make nonsense of Luke's own apparent desire to provide a focused and well-ordered account. The value of promise and fulfillment in Luke–Acts is the eschatological authority it bears. To remove the end-time implications from the promise-fulfillment theme in essence strips it of its scriptural significance and authority.

The issue now before us is whether the same holds true for Luke's depiction of Jesus: As his coming indicated the dawning of the new age, does the fulfillment of the promises he made to the church anticipate its consummation? In particular, does Luke's belief in Jesus' Lordship anticipate the parousia in the visibility he

---

[9] Zmijewski, *Eschatologiereden*, pp. 321–22.
[10] Conzelmann, *Theology of St. Luke*, p. 96.
[11] So Wilson, *Gentile Mission*, pp. 74–75; Bauckham, "Synoptic Parousia Parables," pp. 165–70; also Aune, "Delay of the Parousia," pp. 98–99.
[12] See further Mußner, "Letzten Tagen," pp. 263–65.

gives to Jesus' promise in Luke 21:14–15 that he will inspire his
followers' witness and in the summary statement of Acts 26:23 that
the exalted Jesus had, in effect, done this very thing?

Luke 21:14–15 as divine promise

Luke uniquely records in Luke 21:14–15 Jesus' promise to his
disciples that he will himself inspire their testimony when they
stand trial on account of their faith in him (cf. Luke 12:11–12;
Mark 13:11). We have already assessed the importance of this
passage for Lukan christology in relation to God the Father (ch. 8)
and the Holy Spirit (ch. 9). What is suggestive for our present study
is that the saying occurs within the context of Jesus' apocalyptic
discourse; it is included among the things which will take place in
the last days.

The key piece of evidence here is Jesus' prophetic self-claim in
Luke 21:15. It stands as perhaps the most revealing statement of
Luke's personal christological estimation of Jesus in the two
volumes. It represents, in fact, the only instance in the synoptic
tradition where Jesus, before his death, directly identifies himself
with a post-resurrection work among his disciples as their exalted
Lord. The way Luke illustrates its fulfillment in Acts implies that
this was *how – he believed, at least – the earthly Jesus had envisioned
it.*[13]

In Luke 21:15 Jesus announces to his disciples that he (ἐγὼ
γάρ)[14] will give them a στόμα καὶ σοφίαν which none of their
adversaries will be able to contradict. As we argued in ch. 9, Luke
understood Jesus' prophecy as compatible with a similar work he
forecasts of the Spirit in Luke 12:12; in so doing Luke ascribed to
him a level of supernatural authority only associated with deity in
the OT and otherwise in the synoptic tradition (cf. Mark 13:11;
Luke 12:12; Matt. 10:19).

What is of particular importance here is the time of its utterance:

---

[13] *Contra* the representative position of Bultmann, *History*, p. 327, who considers
Luke 21:15 as describing the Spirit's coming ministry, paralleling the sense of
Luke 12:12 – and more recently, Howard, *Ego Jesu*, pp. 229–30; Kremer,
"Verheißung des Geistes," pp. 263–64; Richard, *Composition*, pp. 283–85. Cf.
Schmithals, *Lukas*, vol. 1, pp. 201–202; Kühschelm, *Jüngerverfolgung und
Geschick Jesu*, pp. 205–206,290–91, who attribute stronger christological weight
to the verse.

[14] The phrase ἐγὼ γάρ is characteristic of Lukan style; outside Luke (three times)
and Acts (twice), it is common to Paul (seven times) and occurs once in John's
Gospel (8:42); so Fuchs, *Sprachliche Untersuchungen*, pp. 180–81.

Jesus announced it during his earthly career *before* his death; but, according to Acts, began to carry it out *after* his exaltation. This implies that the pre-resurrected Jesus knew beforehand of his coming exaltation and something of what he would do from heaven at that time. It is inconceivable from Luke's point of view that Jesus presumed that he would fulfill the promise to his followers sometime before his death. At this juncture, the disciples still had no inkling of what Jesus meant by his predictions of suffering. Luke even intimates that they were yet providentially not meant to know (e.g., Luke 18:34).[15] The resurrection must transpire first. Luke 12:12 indicates the same. The promise of the Spirit for witness (Luke 24:49; Acts 1:4–5, 8) and its fulfillment at Pentecost (Acts 2) also imply a post-resurrection milieu.

The witness motif supports the same conclusion. The reason for the persecution and court appearances ultimately arises from the disciples' allegiance to and confession of Jesus' name. In addition, the court appearances will provide them opportunity to testify about their faith. The substance of the evidence they will present essentially stems from their personal testimony, testimony rooted in their firsthand knowledge of Jesus' death and resurrection and their belief that Jesus currently reigns in heaven as evidenced by the Spirit of God among them. Thus, in accordance with Lukan usage, the witness motif receives its intended meaning only if it follows the passion and exaltation.

Luke, in effect, notes in this verse that Jesus envisioned a time corresponding to that of the post-Easter apostolic community. Jesus seems cognizant not only of the suffering and resurrection that lay before him but also of the future proclamation of the resurrection by his followers and of his heavenly session. Here Jesus consciously assumes divine prerogative before his glorification. Luke's documentation in Acts that the exalted Jesus fulfilled this promise, as we shall soon see, demonstrates that this is how Luke intended his readers to understand it.

It would appear, then, that Luke, at least as revealed in 21:15, believed the earthly Jesus to have had a reasonably formed messianic self-consciousness. And nothing in Acts would suggest otherwise. It pictures Jesus as learning nothing new about his own messianic dignity and status following the resurrection; on the contrary, it simply confirms that he has fulfilled what he predicted

---

[15] See further Squires, *Plan of God*, p. 114, n. 68.

of himself during his earthly career. This passage discloses something of what Luke believed the earthly Jesus to have known and said about his coming exaltation and activity as Lord.[16] Furthermore, Jesus' unique self-claim in Luke 21:15 as a prophetic element of the apocalyptic discourse raises the possibility that, for Luke, the fact of Jesus' coming Lordship will itself be "a sign of the times." The successful mission of the early church reinforces this claim.

Acts 26:23 as divine fulfillment

Acts 26:23 seems to touch on this very point. Standing trial before King Agrippa, Paul states, in line with Moses and the prophets, that "the Christ would suffer and, as the first to rise from the dead, *would proclaim light to his own people and to the Gentiles.*" But in contrast to Luke 21:15, the saying stands at the other end of the promise–fulfillment spectrum. It summarizes the leading part which the exalted Jesus has, in fact, played in the mission of the early church. Luke, in effect, reminds his readers that Jesus was true to this promise which he announced during his earthly ministry.[17]

Luke presents the exalted Jesus here as both the Proclaimer and the Content of that proclamation. In effect, Luke casts the entire witness motif in Acts as a personal work of Christ, especially in connection to Paul's missionary endeavors.[18] The mission of the church is the mission of Christ.[19] Jesus takes the gospel from Jerusalem to Rome, proclaims it to Jew and Gentile, defends its truthfulness before civil and religious authorities, and ultimately carries out its universal propagation. In this sense, the exalted Jesus is personally fulfilling his promises in Mark 13:9–11; Luke 12:11–12; 21:12–15; 24:46–47; Acts 1:8.

Since the church's mission is personified by the Lord Jesus and is being fulfilled according to his guidance, it takes on considerable eschatological importance. Charles Cosgrove observes that according to the theme of divine providence in Luke–Acts: "a

---

[16] Luke most likely preserves the reading of his source here and, accordingly, reflects early church belief rather than personally making up or rewriting traditional material. Kümmel, *Promise and Fulfillment*, p. 99, n. 40, in line with Barrett, suggests that the saying is in all probability original to Jesus himself. If this is true, it is quite suggestive of Jesus' self-consciousness; see further Wainwright, *Trinity*, p. 210; more generally Thüsing, *Erhöhungsvorstellung*, pp. 100–105, esp. p. 101.

[17] O'Toole, "Risen Jesus," p. 481–82; Chance, *Jerusalem*, p. 97.

[18] So Prast, *Presbyter und Evangelium*, pp. 326–27.

[19] Dupont, "Portée christologique," p. 129.

'deeschatologization' of the church's existence hardly seems to be in evidence, inasmuch as investigation into this overarching motif of the divine δεῖ uncovers at every point continuity between the time of Jesus, as a time of salvation, and the time of the church."[20] A similar parallel is true of Luke's development of Jesus' providential guidance of the church's early missionary activity. The Gospel and Acts show no shift in perspective. What Jesus predicts of his personal involvement in the church's mission in the Gospel comes to pass in Acts. C. F. D. Moule discerns numerous pieces of information in the Gospels and Acts which suggest that, "the post-Easter *interpretation* was only a *re-discovery* of what had been there in the teaching of Jesus himself."[21] Luke's association of divine providence and mission with Jesus' teaching especially exemplifies this. Luke shows continuity between the earthly Jesus' knowledge of his future Lordship and his subsequent active role as Lord. This unified perspective regarding Jesus' Lordship in Luke–Acts may further militate against an alleged de-eschatologization of Christian tradition by its author.

Jacques Dupont connects Acts 26:23 to Luke's development of Mark 13:10 in Luke 24:47 and Acts 1:8.[22] However, *contra* Dupont (pp. 133–34), Luke has not abandoned the eschatological position of his Markan source, but has only reexpressed it in the life of the early church. According to Mark 13:10, missionary activity is itself "a sign of the times." It represents, as in all strata of the NT, the salvation of the last days.[23] That Acts 26:23 fulfills to some extent its Lukan antecedents and its Markan counterpart is crucial. Luke's use of promise points to the fulfillment of eschatological hopes,[24] which in this case the church's successful mission to the Gentiles would notably heighten (p. 87).

This Lukan viewpoint accentuates the eschatological importance of Jesus' reign as Lord. Jesus' heavenly session, although temporary, is extremely important. His activity there evokes an expectation of the time when all things will be restored as God had announced through his prophets long ago (Acts 3:21a). That Acts shows him fulfilling some of these eschatological events further suggests that Luke believes that Jesus' Lordship itself appears as "a sign of the times" and anticipates his reappearance in the parousia.

---

[20] Cosgrove, "Divine δεῖ," p. 190.   [21] Moule, *Phenomenon*, p. 46 (his italic).
[22] Dupont, "Portée christologique," pp. 138–41.
[23] Pokorný, *Genesis of Christology*, pp. 161–62.
[24] Chance, *Jerusalem*, p. 91.

The perception of the exaltation

In a series of essays under the title *Erhöhungsvorstellung und Parusieerwartung in der ältesten nachösterlichen Christologie* (1969), originally appearing in *BZ* 11 (1967): 95–108, 205–22 and 12 (1968): 54–80, 223–40, Wilhelm Thüsing attempts to discern what Jesus' exaltation meant according to earliest Christian tradition. He concludes that the early church, in all probability, did not distance the parousia from Jesus' present exaltation.[25] Jesus' exaltation was not understood primarily as a divine corrective to the scandal of the cross, with the parousia pushed off to some indefinite time in the future. They stood side by side, in full view, without one diminishing the reality of the other. Implicit in the thought of Jesus' Lordship was the belief in his approaching return. The early church perceived the exaltation in terms of Jesus' resurrection, Lordship, and parousia, terms not identical in meaning but part of a unified, interrelated perception. Thüsing, moreover, thinks that the earthly Jesus identified himself with "the exalted one" in his teaching on the kingdom of God (p. 101). The idea of Lordship would necessarily comprise the past, present, and future dimensions of Jesus' existence (p. 100). Thus, for the early church to preach Jesus variously as Christ, Lord, Savior, or Judge would simultaneously call into view this monolithic understanding of what Jesus' exaltation necessarily entails.

To what extent, then, does Luke alter the early church's perception of Jesus' exaltation? His presentation will strongly reflect his own christological perceptions. I intend in this section to demonstrate that the affinity between Luke and these christological antecedents is surprisingly close and foundational for understanding Luke's christology. Even though he writes a history of the early church and chronicles in it the Lord Jesus' present work in its mission, this fact does not remove the importance of the parousia for Lukan eschatology or christology, or preclude a belief in Jesus' imminent return.[26]

Luke 22:69

A most interesting but unending cause of commentary in Lukan studies is the way the author handled the Sanhedrin's interrogation

---

[25] Thüsing, *Erhöhungsvorstellung*, pp. 89–91.
[26] *Contra* Vielhauer, "Paulinism of Acts," p. 47.

of Jesus during his trial (22:67–70). Precipitating the difficulties for
the exegete is the uncertain meaning of its Markan parallel (14:61b–
62). The emergence of an alleged delay of the parousia strand in
Lukan thought has further complicated a favorable reconciliation
of the two synoptic passages, and has negatively biased the view of
Lukan eschatology.

Our method for dealing with the Lukan context and Markan
parallel will be grounded again in our observation that where Luke
tends to fill out and enlarge upon Mark's somewhat compressed
account, Matthew often follows Mark except in instances where
clarity is needed. This factor coupled with Thüsing's proposal
concerning the view of the early church toward Jesus' exaltation
will, to a considerable extent, enable us to see a remarkably close
continuity between Mark and Luke (and Matthew for that matter),
christologically and eschatologically.

Mark 14:61b–62 records the high priest putting a single question
to Jesus and Jesus' reply. The high priest asks him if he is "the
Christ, the Son of the Blessed One." Jesus replies that he is. Jesus
adds, in melding together Ps. 110:1 and Dan. 7:13, that "you will
see the Son of Man sitting at the right hand of the Mighty One
[δυνάμεως] and coming on the clouds of heaven." This saying has
become a seedbed of controversy. The problem boils down to
whether the "sitting" of Ps. 110:1 and the "coming" of Dan. 7:13
represent two different ways of describing Jesus' enthronement,[27]
or whether the former pictures the enthronement and the latter
some form of near or distant eschatological judgment.[28]

According to Hebrew poetic style both positions are possible. A
good case can be made for the former on the basis of the apparent
synonymous parallelism of the two clauses: ἐκ δεξιῶν καθήμενον
τῆς δυνάμεως and ἐρχόμενον μετὰ τῶν νεφελῶν τοῦ οὐρανοῦ
form two ways of saying the same thing. On the other hand, the
two clauses also nicely follow a *synthetic parallelism* where the
second clause fills out and completes the idea of the first. This
would make sense of the juridical nature of the Markan context:
Jesus' position at the right hand of God ultimately supplies the
basis for a future judgment, at which time the roles will justifiably
be reversed.

---

[27] E.g., Glasson, "Reply to Caiaphas," pp. 88–89 and lit. cited on p. 89.
[28] E.g., Cranfield, *Mark*, pp. 444–45; Pesch, *Markus. 8, 27–16, 20*, p. 439; Beasley-
Murray, "Apocalyptic," pp. 420–29; Bock, *Proclamation*, pp. 141–42; Geddert,
Watchwords, pp. 189, 208–209, 212, 227.

The question then arises, in contrast to much of the scholarly discussion, need these two interpretations be mutually exclusive? Joachim Gnilka's moderating position seems best. He argues that while the coming of the Son of Man to the throne of God characterizes his exaltation, owing to its secondary position in the saying, it may also have in view Jesus' appearance as Judge at the parousia.[29] Although Vincent Taylor advocates solely the former position, his comment that "the emphasis lies on enthronement, and on enthronement as a symbol of triumph"[30] seems to support the latter view as well. Jesus' ultimate triumph as Lord will occur in the judgment of his enemies at his return.

This twofold understanding of Mark 14:62 is not contradictory theologically to Mark's point of view. Rather Mark apparently preserves *in nuce* the belief of the early church. The two positions, as Thüsing has shown, were quite compatible with the early church's perception of Jesus' exaltation.

In determining the christological significance of Luke 22:69, we must bear in mind that the high priest's question and Jesus' response in Mark 14:61b–62 largely concern Jesus' *identity*, which was defined functionally according to the kinds of things he would do. Luke, in 22:67–70, unpacks Mark's compressed account and expresses more clearly what exactly was being asked and said about Jesus' identity. Whether Mark's account was Luke's only source of information or whether he had other sources at his disposal is unknown and somewhat incidental to the discussion at hand. What is most important is that Luke knew Mark's Gospel and clarifies what was said there.

Luke achieves this by breaking down the high priest's question and Jesus' reply into two separate questions and answers, omitting an overt reference to Dan. 7:13 and substituting ἀπὸ τοῦ νῦν for the ambiguous ὄψεσθε. Mark's Gospel justifies such a move. In Mark, the ideas of messiahship and sonship do not seem strictly identical in meaning; nor do the Psalms and Daniel sayings appear of equal weight in reference to Jesus' identity. In Mark, the Son of Man saying from Dan. 7:13 was evidently interpreted in light of Ps. 110:1 – the comment, "sitting at the right hand," seems interjected into the Daniel citation. Ps. 110:1 underscores Jesus' unique sonship and thus enhances christologically the messianic sense of Dan. 7:13.

---

[29] Gnilka, *Markus. 8, 27–16, 20*, p. 282.   [30] Taylor, *Mark*, p. 569.

The essential point of the interrogation scene is Jesus' sonship. Luke's version makes more explicit what Mark tersely states. To the first question the Jewish leaders put to him concerning whether he is the messiah (22:67a), Jesus indirectly affirms through two rhetorical statements (vv. 67b–68). He further states matter-of-factly that as the messianic Son of Man he would from this point onward, or sometime in the near future – ἀπὸ τοῦ νῦν indicates that a change is imminent[31] – sit at God's right hand (v. 69). This reference to Ps. 110:1 shifts the emphasis from messiahship to sonship. The authorities then ask him, "Are you yourself in effect then claiming to be the Son of God?" (v. 70a), which Jesus again indirectly affirms (v. 70b).

The issue before us concerns Luke 22:69, where Luke omits Dan. 7:13. Did he omit the saying to correct Mark in view of the parousia's delay? Or does his concentration on Jesus' exaltation preserve in part the eschatological sense in Mark? The context forces us once again to consider what Jesus' Lordship means for Luke. And perhaps herein lies our clue.

Scholars commonly argue that the omission of the eschatologically suggestive phrase "coming on the clouds of heaven" in 22:69 reveals Luke's effort to rewrite tradition associating Jesus with an imminent return out of a personal belief that the parousia has been delayed.[32] This theory, however, is not defensible from the text in question for a number of reasons:

1. *The Markan reminiscence in Acts.* As we have seen in other cases, it is quite possible that here too Luke has edited his sources with Acts in mind.[33] The sense of the omitted phrase from Mark 14:62 implies that one day in the future the Jewish leaders will stand before Jesus, who at that time will pass judgment on them because they rejected him.

Luke, however, may have dropped Dan. 7:13 from his Gospel parallel so as not to confuse the final eschatological judgment with Stephen's vision recorded in Acts 7:55–56. The Acts passage recalls

---

[31] So Morris, *Luke*, p. 318.

[32] E.g., Conzelmann, *Theology of St. Luke*, pp. 84–85, n. 3; Gräßer, *Problem der Parusieverzögerung*, pp. 176–77; Rese, *Alttestamentliche Motive*, p. 199; Kränkl, *Jesus der Knecht Gottes*, p. 156; Wilson, *Gentile Mission*, pp. 67–68; Schneider, *Parusiegleichnisse*, pp. 93–94; Berchmans, "Lukan Christology," p. 18; George, "Eschatologie," p. 333; Maddox, *Purpose*, p. 108; Danker, *Jesus and the New Age*, p. 361.

[33] So, e.g., Weiser, *Apg. 1–12*, p. 190; Pesch, *Apg. 1–12*, p. 262, though their insistence that Luke was writing with a delay in view on the basis of Luke 22:69 is not necessary, as we shall see.

Jesus' twofold promise of vindication and judgment in Luke 12:8–9. Perhaps this resistance to the Spirit's prompting also illustrates what the unforgivable sin of blaspheming the Spirit means in Luke 12:10 and further signals Luke's use of Luke 12 at this juncture in Acts. In Stephen's vision, Jesus is described as the Son of Man standing at God's right hand and appears to Stephen as his advocate because of Stephen's faith in him. But to the Sanhedrin Jesus' position signifies that of judge because of their repeated disregard of the Spirit's testimony about him (Acts 7:51b) and ultimately their rejection of him. In this way, Jesus' twofold appearance as advocate and Judge in Stephen's vision suitably stands as a vivid portent of the deliverance and judgment yet to come. The Acts episode in conjunction with Luke 22:69 does not signal a delay of the parousia. Nor is Stephen's vision meant to historicize Jesus' promise of it.[34] It rather signals what is to come. A note of urgency is implicit in it. Stephen's plea for their pardon in v. 60 supports this.

2. *Omission of Dan. 7:13 in Luke 22:69.* The absence of the "coming" phrase in Luke 22:69 does not in and of itself indicate an imminent parousia or a distant one;[35] its omission merely emphasizes the reality of Jesus' sonship and approaching Lordship. As we discussed earlier, the primary concern of the episode according to the synoptic tradition is not eschatological judgment but the identity of Jesus. Luke merely accentuates this point.

3. *Broader use of the "coming" motif.* Luke does not hesitate to use the "coming" motif in other eschatological sections of Luke–Acts.[36] Luke 21:27 preserves Jesus' saying in Mark 13:26 almost verbatim: "they will see the Son of Man coming in a cloud with power and great glory." In addition to Mark, Luke 17:24, 26, 30; 18:8b stress the suddenness of the Son of Man's return. In Acts 1:11 the two messengers reassure the disciples that "Jesus, who has been taken from you into heaven, will come back in the same way you have seen him go into heaven," i.e., in the clouds (v. 9). Thus, whereas Mark only incorporates the "coming" motif explicitly in one other instance apart from 14:62, Luke does so six times! On the basis, then, of Luke's use of the motif in Luke–Acts, we can discover no immediately discernible reason why Luke should have been predisposed to avoid the use of it in 22:69.

---

[34] *Contra* Schneider, *Parusiegleichnisse*, p. 69.
[35] Maddox, *Purpose*, p. 108.
[36] Zmijewski, *Eschatologiereden*, p. 245.

4. *Juridical connotation of "Son of Man."* The title "Son of Man" in Luke–Acts carries with it a juridical meaning even where "the coming of the clouds" expression is not used (e.g., Luke 11:30; 12:8–9; 21:36; Acts 7:56).[37] The designation envisions a court setting with the Son of Man meting out judgment justly. Thus Luke in all probability retains the juridical aspect of Mark 14:62 by retaining the title in 22:69.[38]

5. ἀπὸ τοῦ νῦν. That Mark's version of Jesus' saying to the Jewish leaders – "you will see" (ὄψεσθε, 14:62) – is somewhat ambiguous is evidenced in the way both Luke (ἀπὸ τοῦ νῦν δὲ ἔσται ... καθήμενος, 22:69) and Matthew (ἀπ' ἄρτι ὄψεσθε, 26:64) attempt to amplify the idea implicit in it. In doing so, Luke and Matthew have provided us with a fairly reliable means of determining what Mark meant by his use of the term. The stress of ὄψεσθε according to Jesus' prediction is not the *time* of the return but the *fact* of it.[39] Its point is not so much whether Jesus will return in the lifetime of the Jewish authorities as to accent the inescapable fact that when he does return, they will see him as Judge.

The way Luke handles the Jewish authorities' culpability in Acts reinforces this assertion. Although Luke follows Mark in emphasizing the large-scale complicity among the Jewish authorities at Jesus' trial, he probably omits the "coming" motif to avoid giving the impression that all of them will face judgment because of it. His description in Acts of divine providence in the matter (3:17) and of the many conversions within their ranks (6:7) substantiates this. Hence, for Luke, Jesus' exaltation will etch in stone the destiny of his accusers; his exaltation undeniably reveals that the period of the last days has in fact begun and anticipates its denouement in the parousia.

On these grounds, then, it is arguable that Luke's expression ἀπὸ τοῦ νῦν refers to Jesus' exaltation and indicates little about a delayed parousia consciousness and a desire to reformulate the church age along some salvation-history scheme.[40] The emphasis clearly falls upon Jesus' enthronement, or perhaps better put, his

---

[37] Trites, *Witness*, p. 185; Fitzmyer, *Luke X–XXIV*, p. 1467; Marshall, *Luke*, p. 850; esp. Crump, *Jesus the Intercessor*, pp. 190–97.

[38] See also Ernst, *Lukas*, p. 619.

[39] *Contra* Wilson, *Gentile Mission*, p. 67 *et al.*

[40] Along with Flender, *Redemptive History*, pp. 100–101; Zmijewski, *Eschatologiereden*, p. 247. *Contra* Schneider, *Verleugnung*, p. 119; Schneider, *Parusiegleichnisse*, p. 69.

glorification – a process rather than a point in time, beginning with Jesus being handed over to death and culminating with his resurrection (see, e.g., Luke 9:51; Acts 2:23–36; 3:13–15, 18, 20–21; 4:10–11 etc.).[41] At issue here is Jesus' Lordship. Luke 22:69 places no temporal restrictions on the coming realization of his glorification. The impression given is that this exalted position will characterize the standing of Jesus evermore. The parousia will not alter this fact, and as such has nothing to do with the phrase ἀπὸ τοῦ νῦν.

6. *Sessio ad dextram Dei.* The two questions put to Jesus during this interrogation scene show an orderly ascension of christological revelation moving from the Jewish authorities' concept of what the messiah would be, to Jesus' self-identification as the messianic Son of Man, to the foundational reality that he is the Son of God. The last ascription forms the episode's climax.[42]

By retaining the "Son of Man" title in 22:69, Luke preserves the sense of Dan. 7:13 without detracting from the episode's primary focus on sonship (vv. 67–70) and Jesus' approaching exaltation to the right hand of God. Frederick Danker asserts that "in Luke–Acts the term 'Son of God,' in conjunction with the term 'Lord,' bears the main weight of Jesus' identity."[43] Luke firmly establishes this, as Fitzmyer observes, at the very outset of the Gospel.[44] The two questions posed to Jesus at his trial echo what the angel Gabriel announced about him at the time of his birth: "He will be great and will be called the Son of the Most High. The Lord God will give him the throne of his father David, and he will reign over the house of Jacob forever; his kingdom will never end" (1:32–33); "the holy one to be born will be called the Son of God" (v. 35b). Thus in the very first chapter of the Gospel Luke draws attention to Jesus' coming exaltation as the Son of God. The only thing that has changed by the time of Jesus' trial is that the time of the prophecy's fulfillment is now closer at hand.

What "sitting at the right hand of God" may have meant to the Jewish interrogators is a slightly different question and not directly

---

[41] So Voss, *Christologie*, p. 141; Ellis, "Present and Future Eschatology," p. 37, n. 2. *Contra* Lohfink, *Himmelfahrt Jesu*, p. 237.

[42] Rese, *Alttestamentliche Motive*, p. 199; Berchmans, "Lukan Christology," p. 18 *et al*. Schweizer's summation that the three titles are interchangeable is not convincing ("Lukanischen Christologie," p. 49); cf. also Jones "Servant," p. 156. The title is perhaps the most significant christological statement about Jesus in the NT; see further Marshall, *Work of Christ*, p. 28.

[43] Danker, *Jesus and the New Age*, p. 362.

[44] Fitzmyer, *Luke X–XXIV*, p. 1462.

related to our present study. Our concern here is Luke's perception of Jesus and whether he thought in terms of an alleged delayed parousia.

To stress Jesus' *sessio ad dextram Dei* does not supply *prima facie* evidence against the expectation of his future return. On the contrary, the ascription – pregnant with christological meaning – largely supports the opposite interpretation. It calls into mind the fullest picture of Jesus. It evokes images of all the things he has done, is doing, and will do. As we have seen in Acts, it stands as the epitome of any christological description of Jesus and establishes his relation to God and his Spirit, and as we shall see in the next section, to the world as well.

To the early church at least, the very mention of the exaltation would have stirred up a fuller picture of the theological significance of Jesus' present Lordship, *including the expectation of his return*. In all likelihood, Luke 22:69 clarifies the meaning of Mark 14:62. And in so doing, Luke shows close agreement with the christological beliefs of the early church. Jesus' *sessio ad dextram Dei* assumes the expectation of his return[45] and implicitly serves as a guarantee that the parousia will come about as promised (Luke 21:27; Acts 1:9–11; 3:19–21).[46] Moreover, the way Luke connects Jesus to the destiny of humankind substantiates the view that our discussion of Luke 22:69 reflects Luke's thinking and is not merely a piece of fanciful exegetical footwork.

Acts 17:31

This passage supports our proposition that Luke himself adhered to the early church's perception of Jesus' exaltation and in doing so shared their expectation of an imminent parousia. The chief factor here is *Jesus' resurrection*. We shall begin with Acts 17:31, focusing on Luke's connection of Jesus' resurrection to the final judgment, and conclude with an assessment of what Luke reveals here concerning his personal attitudes about Jesus as Lord.

Toward the conclusion of Paul's Areopagus speech as recorded in Acts, Paul calls his listeners to repentance because "God has set a day when he will judge the world with justice by the man he has appointed, giving proof of this to everyone by raising him from the dead" (Acts 17:31). This interplay among the themes of repentance,

---

[45] Zmijewski, *Eschatologiereden*, pp. 245–46.
[46] Bock, *Proclamation*, p. 142.

judgment, and resurrection suggests an overall Lukan viewpoint. Coupled with v. 30, 17:31 presents a sweeping redemptive historical picture involving the past, present, and future dealings of God with humanity: on the basis of Jesus' resurrection, God no longer excuses the past ignorance of humanity (shared by the Jews as well: cf., e.g., Acts 3:17; ch. 7; 13:27) and the present need to repent takes on immediate importance in view of Jesus' coming universal judgment. But does the passage have an imminent or delayed parousia in view?

In recent years, the delayed view has had sizeable support mainly on the grounds that the passage emphasizes *the fact and certainty* of the judgment rather than its *nearness*.[47] But such a polarization seems artificial to the sense of the passage itself.

To begin with, the meaning of vv. 30–31 more readily conforms to the imminence view found elsewhere in the NT – especially 1 Thess. 1:9–10; John 5:25–30; Acts 10:41–42. Gerhard Friedrich, e.g., points out the integral relation between Jesus' resurrection and eschatological work common to Luke and Paul: "In 1. Thess. 1,9f. und Act. 17,31 werden Auferweckung und eschatologisches Wirken Christi zusammengefaßt: in Act. 17 ist Christus der eschatologische Richter, in 1. Thess. 1 der eschatologische Erretter. Beide Aussagen stehen nicht im Widerspruch; denn der Richter der Welt ist der Erretter der Glaubenden" ("1 Thess. 1:9–10 and Acts 17:31 unite Christ's resurrection and eschatological work. In Acts 17, Jesus is the eschatological judge; in 1 Thess. 1, he is the eschatological savior. The statements are not contradictory: the judge of the world is the savior of believers").[48]

Here the fact of Jesus' resurrection gives comfort or warning as the case may be in regard to the coming judgment. In both instances, it establishes beyond doubt that the final judgment will occur. The need for appropriate response in conversion or perseverance is preeminent. These parallels indicate a shared eschatological viewpoint between the two writers. Nothing in Acts 17:31 necessarily indicates otherwise.

Accordingly, the promise of universal judgment bestows a sense of urgency upon the present situation – both to Paul's listeners and

---

[47] See, e.g., Conzelmann, *Acts*, p. 146; Vielhauer, "Paulinism of Acts," pp. 45–48; Kaestli, *Eschatologie*, p. 69; Kränkl, *Jesus der Knecht Gottes*, pp. 147, 205, 209; Wilson, *Gentile Mission*, p. 79; Wilckens, *Missionsreden*, pp. 98–99; Gräßer, *Problem der Parusieverzögerung*, p. 214; Weiser, *Apg. 13–28*, p. 476.

[48] Friedrich, "Tauflied hellenistischen Judenchristen," pp. 240–41; also (with qual.) Schneider, "Urchristliche Gottesverkündigung," pp. 285–87.

to Luke's readers. The concern for a prompt response to the message would logically suggest that Jesus, as Lord, was expected. Here the imminent expectation of Jesus' final judgment provides the *motive* of repentance.[49] Knowing that God has already appointed a day and a person to judge all people[50] firmly establishes *now* as the time to respond for or against the gospel message.[51] The appeal of Acts 17:31 goes hand in hand with Luke's incorporation of the themes of Mark 13:9–11 in Acts. The witness motif stands as an eschatological sign, simultaneously exhorting people to repent and warning them of the coming judgment.[52] To distance the coming judgment from Paul's gospel appeal to some remote time in the future defuses the punch of Paul's address.[53]

The association, therefore, of Jesus' resurrection to the nearness of the parousia and final judgment as presented in Acts 17:31 in all probability mirrors Luke's own theological viewpoint. Howard Marshall, e.g., believes that Acts 17:31 clearly establishes "that in Acts the hope of the parousia and the associated judgment is an accepted part of the author's theology."[54] In contrast to the tendency in Lukan critical study of distancing the eschatological viewpoint of Luke–Acts from its traditional antecedents, Luke shows here solidarity with the expectation of the early church.

But we can take this still further. Thüsing argues that early Christian tradition considered the confession that Jesus had been raised from the dead an eschatological claim because of its relevance for all people.[55] Jesus' resurrection and conferral of the Spirit represented the dawning of the eschaton. The exalted Jesus was thought to be presently at work in heaven, actively leading history to his return.[56] For these reasons, the early church believed that the resurrection and exaltation demonstrated that they were now living in the last days. To what extent, then, does Luke–Acts preserve this early Christian teaching?

Emmeram Kränkl, typical of the delayed-parousia school, insists that Luke is at variance with these beliefs. Acts 17:31, he believes,

---

[49] Kümmel, "Urchristentum," pp. 208–10; also Maddox, *Purpose*, p. 130.
[50] Marshall, *Acts*, p. 290.
[51] Neil, *Acts*, p. 192.
[52] See also Munck, *Acts*, p. 173.
[53] *Contra* Conzelmann, *Theology of St. Luke*, pp. 110–11.
[54] Marshall, *Historian & Theologian*, p. 176.
[55] Thüsing, *Auferweckung*, pp. 119–21.
[56] Cf. ὃν δεῖ οὐρανὸν μὲν δέξασθαι (Acts 3:21). Mußner, "Apokatastasis," p. 294 reminds us that v. 21 only expressly states that it is God's will for Jesus to remain in heaven; it says nothing about a delay.

typifies Luke's altered perspective: "Die Auferweckung Jesu ist also bei Lukas nicht Zeichen des Ein- und Anbruchs des Eschaton wie in der frühchristlichen Christologie, sie hat nun vielmehr Beweis-funktion" ("Jesus' resurrection, therefore, does not signal for Luke the inbreaking and beginning of the eschaton as in the christology of early Christianity; rather, it now functions as a proof").[57] This assessment, however, seems doubtful. The verse nowhere lends itself to such an interpretation. Without the possibility of an imminent judgment, Paul's appeal loses its urgency, and the proof loses its overriding relevance to the situation at hand. Elsewhere in Acts, as we shall see, Luke repeatedly links the resurrection motif to the eschatological role of the exalted Jesus as Savior, Lord, and Judge.

It seems quite reasonable to suppose that Luke himself consid-ered Jesus' resurrection to be full of eschatological meaning. E.g., Jürgen Roloff asserts in reference to Acts 17:31 that God's raising Jesus from the dead demonstrates "da er sein endzeitliches Handeln begonnen hat, und Jesus ist der, der dieses Handeln vor aller Welt repräsentiert" ("that he has begun his end-time activity and that Jesus is the one who represents this activity to all the world").[58] Luke reiterates this pattern elsewhere in Acts to describe the different dimensions of Jesus' Lordship: e.g., his exaltation (2:33–36; 5:30–31), his role as Savior (3:15–16, 26; 4:10–12; 10:40, 43; 13:37–39), as the Hope of the believer (4:2; also 23:6; 24:15), and as the end-time Judge of the unrepentant (10:41–42; also 24:25).

In close conformity to early church tradition, Jesus' exaltation, Lordship, and parousia, according to Luke, are inextricably bound to the belief that Jesus' resurrection bears witness that the last days have begun.[59] The urgency of right response to the gospel message becomes preeminent. Luke reminds his reader in no uncertain terms that humanity is sinful, that only in Jesus can salvation be found,[60] and that those who reject this salvation will be lost.[61] Here again, Jesus' Lordship stands as "a sign of the times."

---

[57] Kränkl, *Jesus der Knecht Gottes*, pp. 147,209 (quot. p. 147).
[58] Roloff, *Apg.*, p. 266.
[59] The closest extra-biblical parallels to a messianic figure comparable to Luke's christological portrait of Jesus' Lordship as an eschatological indicator come from Test. Jud. 24:5–6; Test. Levi 18:9, although obscure. See further Chance, *Jerusalem*, p. 97.
[60] Cf., e.g., Guthrie, *Theology*, pp. 199–200, 231.
[61] Green, *Meaning of Salvation*, p. 127, n. 2.

Conclusion: the unity of eschatology and salvation history

The scarlet thread connecting the various sections of ch. 7 and this inquiry is that the author of Luke–Acts shows fidelity to the eschatological position of his sources and of early church tradition.[62] Luke neither subordinates eschatology to a model of salvation history nor abandons salvation history for some existential redefinition of eschatology. Both complement his desire to enunciate the significance of Jesus according to God's saving plan. The textual evidence confirms this summation.

If Luke had sensed a delay of sorts – perhaps unconsciously via his theological environment[63] – to respond literarily by no longer considering the church to be in the last days would seem an uncharacteristically bold move for one normally showing allegiance to early church tradition. Other church leaders would most likely have looked askance at anyone so drastically redefining the traditional stance of apostolic teaching.[64] Even toward the end of the first century, the belief in an imminent expectation had not been substantially redefined or dropped from church theology, as the very existence of John's Apocalypse would prove.[65]

Although the prospect of the apostles' deaths (e.g., for Paul, Phil. 1:22–24; 2 Cor. 5:1–10; cf. 1 Thess. 4:13–17[66]) – may have forced the church to enlarge its horizons, it is doubtful whether it produced a delayed consciousness. David Flusser shows that among religious movements, both ancient and modern, an acute eschatological expectation is not diminished even if the expectation goes unfulfilled.[67] First-century Christianity was no exception. It is doubtful whether an exaltation christology was a by-product of a gradual lessening of eschatological tension (pp. 60–61).

In contrast, therefore, to some pervasive tendencies within Lukan critical studies, the center of Luke's theology is not eschatology or salvation history but christology. "Luke's (and the early Christian's) eschatology," Hans F. Bayer concludes, "is heavily influenced and shaped by a vital christology."[68] Jesus as the Lord

---

[62] See further Kümmel, "Futurische und präsentische Eschatologie," pp. 118–26 and lit. cited on p. 125, nn. 1–2; Rasco, "Historia Salutis," pp. 308–16, esp. p. 314.

[63] So Marshall, "Gospel," pp. 290–91; also Aune, "Delay of the Parousia," p. 101.

[64] See further Marshall, "Gospel," pp. 290–91.

[65] See also the reply to Conzelmann in this regard on pp. 45–46 above.

[66] Fitzmyer, *Luke I–IX*, p. 234.

[67] Flusser, "Salvation Present and Future," pp. 46–61.

[68] Bayer, "Christ-Centered Eschatology," p. 250.

of history is leading it to its consummation in his return.[69] The personal work of the exalted Jesus does not oppose the Father or Spirit's corresponding work, but complements their divine activity. It becomes, in effect, another way of speaking about it. In consonance with early church christology, Jesus' Lordship and his resurrection and exaltation ostensibly stand as "a sign of the times" anticipating his return.

Therefore, Conzelmann's view that Luke wrote in response to the parousia's delay seems remote to the evangelist's intentions. In fact, the scheme seems more a rewriting of Luke–Acts than reflecting Luke's rewriting of early church tradition. The belief that a time interval separates Jesus' exaltation from the parousia does not give Luke the freedom to rewrite biblical history according to a "non-eschatological" paradigm. As we have seen, the time interval itself seems traceable to traditional material. Luke seems focused on explicating the "already" and "not yet" of Jesus' eschatological teaching: he traces out Jesus' announcement of it in his Gospel and details in Acts the fulfillment of some of the announced events anticipating his return.

The common denominator in this is the Lord Jesus himself. The last days have been inaugurated with his coming and will be consummated with his return. For the interval, Jesus reigns as Lord leading history to its full realization of eschatological hope in the parousia, as Savior offering the hope of resurrection life to all who believe in him, and as Judge warning those who refuse to repent of the final coming judgment. Standing behind all of this, for Luke, is Jesus' ever-present urging: "You must be ready at all times, because the Son of Man will come at an hour when you do not expect him" (Luke 12:40).

In part 3, we have seen that Luke discloses his christological beliefs in the way he describes Jesus' relation to the Father (ch. 8), the Spirit (ch. 9), and the end of history (ch. 10). These studies indicate that Luke had approached his writing with the christological conviction that Jesus is Lord. But in contrast to Conzelmann's diminished understanding of it, the textual evidence most likely suggests that Luke considered Jesus' heavenly reign as equal to the Father's: the exalted Jesus appears, in the cosmological sense, as the Father's co-equal, ruling over Israel, the church, and the world,

---

[69] So in this sense Ernst, *Herr der Geschichte*, pp. 87, 112.

and leading sacred and world history to its consummation in his return.

But Luke's christology has another dimension to it. Luke develops his story of Jesus according to a two-stage humiliation–exaltation christology. In fairness to those who see a subordination christology in Luke's writings, the notion that Jesus must depend upon God during his earthly career and for his exaltation suggests that Jesus is subordinate to the Father. How, then, does this Lukan christological strand balance with his personal convictions about Jesus' supreme Lordship, convictions which he believes Jesus himself was to some degree aware of during his earthly career (cf., e.g., Luke 21:15)?

Our concern in ch. 11 will be to examine how Luke reconciles these two apparently contradictory christological strands of Lordship and subordination in Luke–Acts and then to explore the ethical implications which his resolution holds for Christ's followers – implications which are themselves christologically revealing.

PART 4

Luke's christology and Jesus' humiliation–exaltation

11

JESUS AND SERVANTHOOD

Introduction

Church tradition has from antiquity accepted Luke's intimation of personal involvement in Paul's travels in the we-sections of Acts, and Paul's allusion to a certain traveling companion named Luke (Col. 4:14; 2 Tim. 4:11; Phile. 24) as corroborating evidence that this Luke wrote Luke–Acts. But many scholars in the modern era find this traditional view unacceptable – a most persuasive piece of evidence against it being the incompatibility between the christologies of Luke and Paul. Luke's christological portrait, many claim, lacks originality and uniformity, and shows none of the freshness and vitality of Paul's christology. Its virtual silence on the saving significance of Jesus' death offers the most compelling evidence of its dissimilarity to Paul: Luke gives a false picture of Paul's christology and his own surprisingly differs from Paul's if he was his colleague.

But in view of the special "hero-like" status which the author of Acts assigns to Paul, coupled with his supposed personal association with the apostle, modern scholars are right to expect to find a high degree of compatibility between their christologies. In this chapter I should like to demonstrate that this is indeed the case. We shall examine a Pauline parallel which, in principle, explains Luke's main writing concern and reason for his expressed christology, and reconciles the apparent tension between his Lordship and subordination christologies. The connecting christological theme is the *servanthood* of the *Lord Jesus*. We shall evaluate the representative position of Philipp Vielhauer, which sees Luke and Paul's christologies as incompatible, in light of the close correlation between the "humiliation–exaltation" christology of Philippians and Luke–Acts.

Luke and Paul: incompatible christologies?

Philipp Vielhauer, in his essay, "On the 'Paulinism' of Acts,"[1] believes that Luke misrepresents Paul theologically. He defines his inquiry as follows:

> The following discussion poses the question whether and to what extent the author of Acts took over and passed on theological ideas of Paul, whether and to what extent he modified them ... The way in which the author presents Paul's theology will not only disclose his own understanding of Paul, but will also indicate whether or not he and Paul belong together theologically. (p. 33)

Vielhauer's method is to assess theologically Luke's estimate of Paul by comparing the topics of natural theology, Jewish law, christology, and eschatology in Paul's speeches in Acts to Paul's letters (p. 34). He discerns a theological distinction between the two writers:

> The author of Acts is in his Christology pre-Pauline, in his natural theology, concept of the law, and eschatology, post-Pauline. *He presents no specifically Pauline idea.* His "Paulinism" consists in his zeal for the worldwide Gentile mission and in his veneration for the greatest missionary to the Gentiles. The obvious material distance from Paul raises the question whether this distance is not also temporal distance, and whether one may really consider Luke, the physician and travel companion of Paul, as the author of Acts. *But of greater importance than the question of authorship is that of the author's distinctive theological viewpoint and his place in the history of theology.* (p. 48, my italic)[2]

Vielhauer concludes that the Paul of Acts is incompatible theologically with the Paul of the epistles. This verdict, in effect, draws into question the integrity of Luke's entire presentation of Paul and the general historical reliability of his writings.

With the addition of Ernst Haenchen's work, which charts the historical discrepancies of Luke's portrait of Paul[3] left undiscussed

---

[1] Originally appearing as "Zum 'Paulinismus' der Apg.," *EvTh* 10 (1950–51): 1–15; the English version appearing in *PST* 17 (1963) and *Studies in Luke–Acts* (1966) (my quots. are from *SLA*).

[2] A position he later affirms in *Geschichte*, p. 391.

[3] Haenchen, "Luke and Paul," in *Acts*, pp. 112–16; regarding Haenchen's loyalty to Vielhauer's position, see ibid., p. 48.

by Vielhauer (p. 34), many Lukan scholars have come to accept this position as the definitive statement on Luke's relation to Paul. Commentators now often perceive Luke as living at least one generation removed from Paul and being nearly, if not fully, non-conversant with the historical and theological content of his letters.[4] Perhaps the most influential advocate of this position is Hans Conzelmann, whose thesis that Luke rewrote early Christian theology on account of the delayed parousia becomes in many ways a logical outworking of Vielhauer's conclusions.[5]

But Vielhauer's position has not gone uncontested. Numerous German and English responses have come forth. The substance of these replies primarily takes one of two forms. The first group, closer to Vielhauer, agree that Luke did not know Paul personally but want to see a positive link between their writings.[6] The second group are more critical. They think that Luke as Paul's traveling companion best explains the evidence despite some apparent theological and historical discrepancies.[7]

We shall limit our reply to Vielhauer's christological comparison. Vielhauer isolates four separate christological emphases in Paul notably absent from Acts: the cross as atoning, the preexistence of Christ, the "in-Christ" formula, and the presence of the whole of salvation in Jesus (a point he leaves largely undefined) (pp. 43–45). Because of these omissions, he concludes that the christology of Acts is pre-Pauline.

His assessment, however, is questionable from a Lukan and Pauline perspective. Within Luke–Acts, Vielhauer studies only the

---

[4] E.g., Bultmann, *Theologie*, pp. 469–70; Roloff, "Paulus-Darstellung," pp. 510–31 and lit, cited on p. 515, n. 17; Weiser, *Apg. 1–12*, pp. 39–40 and German lit. cited therein; Maddox, *Purpose*, pp. 67–68 (although with qual., he considers Luke "a relatively junior member of Paul's traveling group," cf. pp. 6–7); see also lit. cited in Gasque, *Interpretation*, p. 287, n. 78; Kränkl, *Jesus der Knecht Gottes*, p. 67, n. 13; Lüdemann, *Acts*, p. 6.

[5] So Conzelmann, *Theology of St. Luke*, p. 81; Conzelmann, "Development of Early Christianity," pp. 307–309; Conzelmann, *Acts*, pp. xlv–xlviii.

[6] Eltester, "Lukas und Paulus," pp. 1–17; Borgen, "From Paul to Luke," pp. 168–82; Barrett, "Acts of Paul," pp. 86–100; Wilckens, "Interpreting," pp. 69–77 and lit. cited on p. 81, n. 56 (although he critiques Vielhauer only on eschatology); Fitzmyer, *Luke I–IX*, pp. 27–29 and lit. cited therein; Aejmelaeus, *Rezeption*, pp. 217–19.

[7] Siotis, "Paul's Collaborator," pp. 105–11; Ellis, *Luke*, pp. 40–51; Bruce, "Paul of Acts," pp. 282–305; Jervell, "Problems of Traditions," pp. 19–39; Jervell, "Unknown Paul," pp. 52–67; Jervell, "Paul in Acts," pp. 68–76; Hemer, *Hellenistic History*, pp. 308–34; Morris, *Luke*, pp. 20–24; Gasque, *Interpretation*, pp. 283–91; Gasque, "Fruitful Field," p. 131 and n. 61; Marshall, "Luke's View of Paul," pp. 41–51.

christology of Paul's speeches in Acts – particularly 13:13–43 and 26:22–23 – making what he finds there stand for Luke's christology in full. It is true that the christology of these two passages is not representative of Paul's christology. But Vielhauer fails to consider Luke–Acts as a whole and whether it parallels any of Paul's letters. He assumes *a priori* that it does not. Otto Bauernfeind warns against such an approach: "Any theological comparison between the two writers must keep Luke's entire work in view."[8]

Within Paul's writings, Vielhauer claims that "the cross as saving" underlies the whole of Paul's christology (pp. 44–45). In support of this, he cites in passing Rom. 5:6–11; 2 Cor. 5:14–21; 6:2. Although "the cross as saving" does form the center of Paul's christology, one should also consider whether the theme is explicitly expressed and stands as the "featured" christology in each of his letters.[9] Vielhauer's judgment that the christologies of Luke and Paul are incompatible may well oversimplify the NT picture.[10] How, then, are we to understand the lack of reference to the saving significance of the cross in Luke–Acts? Since Luke–Acts, e.g., contains minor treatment of the vicarious nature of Jesus' death, does it follow that its author was unfamiliar with Paul's teaching, misunderstood it, ignored it, or did not agree with it?

"Jesus' death as saving" – an invalid criterion

The only substantial references to Jesus' death as atoning in Luke–Acts occur in Luke 22:19–20 and Acts 20:28; unfortunately, in both cases even the actual wording of the text is embroiled in controversy.[11] Luke omits Mark 10:45 (Matt. 20:28).[12] In contrast, Paul visibly centers his christology and soteriology on the theme. He writes, e.g., that Jesus' death on the cross:

1.   forms the basis of salvation (1 Cor. 1:18; 1 Thess. 5:9–10; [Col. 1:20–22]);

---

[8]   Bauernfeind, "Entscheidung," pp. 381–82.
[9]   For an excellent discussion of the "vicarious" nature of Jesus' death in Luke–Acts in Isaiah's Servant of the Lord, see France, "Servant of the Lord," pp. 26–52; more briefly, Higgins, *Jesus and the Son of Man*, pp. 196–97; Long-enecker, *Christology*, pp. 105–107.
[10] Cf. also Gasque, "Fruitful Field," p. 131 and n. 61.
[11] See, e.g., Metzger, *Textual Commentary*, pp. 173–77, 480–82.
[12] See further our discussion of Mark 10:45 on pp. 146–48 above. For more on the absence of the idea of Jesus' death as atoning in Luke–Acts, see Hengel, *Atonement*, p. 34; Green, "God's Servant," pp. 1–7.

2. makes salvation available to all people (Rom. 5:10; 2 Cor. 5:21; Gal. 1:4; 3:13; [Eph. 1:7]);
3. is for sin (Rom. 6:10; 1 Cor. 15:3; 2 Cor. 5:21; Gal. 1:4);
4. satisfies God's justice (Rom. 3:23–26; Gal. 3:13);
5. is undeserved (Rom. 4:25; 5:8; 8:32; Gal. 1:4; 2:20; [Eph. 5:25; Titus 2:14]);
6. is substitutionary (Rom. 5:6–8; 2 Cor. 5:14–15; 1 Thess. 5:10);
7. forms the basis of justification (Rom. 3:25; 5:9; [Eph. 1:7; 2:13; Col. 1:20]);
8. reconciles to God (Rom. 5:6–11; 2 Cor. 5:18–19; [Eph. 2:15–16; Col. 1:19–22]);
9. frees from God's wrath (Rom. 5:9);
10. ransoms from death ([1 Tim. 2:5–6]);
11. destroys the power of death (Rom. 6:9);
12. redeems (Rom. 3:23–25; Gal. 1:4; 3:13–14; [Eph. 1:7; Col. 1:14; Titus 2:13–14]);
13. is an atoning sacrifice (Rom. 3:25; 5:1);
14. is a payment, purchasing the believer back from the power of sin and death (1 Cor. 6:19–20; 7:23);
15. is a sin offering (Rom. 8:3);
16. models the passover lamb sacrifice (1 Cor. 5:7).[13]

The lack of similar teaching in Luke–Acts seems to vindicate Vielhauer's claim that the main christological difference separating Acts from Paul is "the understanding of the cross" (p. 44). But does this judgment adequately summarize the christology that Paul features in each of his letters?

A striking feature of the Philippian correspondence is that Paul, in contrast to his other letters, writes little about the atoning value of Jesus' death. Only two possible allusions to it occur in the letter: "He humbled himself and became obedient to death – even death on a cross!" (2:8b); "Many live as enemies of the cross of Christ" (3:18b). But even here most believe that the idea if present is more assumed than explicated. E.g., concerning 2:8b, Arland Hultgren writes: "The hymn in fact does not speak of his bearing of sin or delivering humanity from sin or cosmic powers, in spite of the fact that it speaks of his death (2:8); his redemptive work can only be inferred from it."[14] About 3:18b, Jean-François

---

[13] For more on Jesus' death as saving in Paul, see *TAB*, pp. 458–66; Taylor, *Atonement*, pp. 79–147.

[14] Hultgren, *Christ and His Benefits*, p. 142; see additionally, Hofius, *Christus-*

Collange writes: "The expression is unfortunately vague, though that is no reason for thinking Paul was not alluding here to some definite doctrine."[15]

But despite the scantiness in Philippians of this standard Pauline teaching, no scholar concludes that its christology is not Pauline. Nor do scholars conclude that Paul reflects here a theological shift in perspective. Rather most feel that the situation to which he writes has largely influenced what he chooses to say about Christ.[16]

In returning to the issue of christological compatibility, we find that even for Paul Jesus' death as saving, although implied, does not uniformly stand out as his featured christology. May Luke–Acts not represent a similar tendency, especially if its christology closely resembles that of Philippians? To make, therefore, explicit reference to the saving significance of Jesus' death the key for determining the compatibility of Luke and Paul's christology may misrepresent Paul and belittle the christological affinity between Luke–Acts and Philippians – an affinity bound to Jesus' humiliation and exaltation.

In Paul's letter to Philippi, the Christ hymn (2:5–11) forms its richest christological statement (containing twelve of the letter's seventy-three references to Jesus). The attention Paul devotes to Jesus' humiliation and exaltation, to the virtual exclusion of a soteriology of the cross, gives the hymn and letter an unmatched christological distinctiveness in comparison to his other writings and to much of the NT itself. This is not to say that the humiliation–exaltation pattern does not occur elsewhere in Paul (cf. 2 Cor. 5:21; 8:9; Gal. 3:13; 4:4–5; also Col. 1:15–20; 1 Tim. 3:16) or the NT (Heb. 1:2–4; 2:9, 17; 5:7–9; 1 Pet. 3:18–22) – though in most of these cases it occurs alongside a statement on the cross as saving – or that the cross as saving has no bearing on what he writes concerning the cross and Jesus' death in Philippians. Rather Paul probably knows that his readers are familiar with the teaching.

hymnus, p. 17; Guthrie, *Theology*, pp. 344–45; Marshall, *Historian & Theologian*, p. 120; Hengel, *Atonement*, p. 71; Hurtado, "Jesus as Lordly Example," p. 123; Kim, *Origin*, pp. 148–49.

15 Collange, *Philippians*, p. 137.

16 A situation perhaps more governed by Paul's concern "to reinforce family ties" with the Philippians rather than by "some major heresy or conflict within the church"; so Alexander, "Hellenistic Letter-Forms," pp. 99–100. However, cf. Mengel, *Philipperbrief*, pp. 289–96; Silva, *Philippians*, p. 21; O'Brien, *Philippians*, pp. 36–38; Peterlin, *Disunity* (forthcoming), who sense a pronounced struggle among the Philippians, as is reflected in Paul's appeal for unity (esp. Phil. 1:27–30).

Therefore, on its basis he addresses the issues of spiritual maturity and perseverance. Within the letter, the Christ hymn makes simultaneously a christological and ethical statement.[17] It challenges the readers to conform themselves to the kind of attitudes and patterns of behavior which Jesus exhibited in his humiliation and exaltation, i.e., his obedience to and dependence upon God.

The states of Jesus' Lordship

For Paul, to understand fully the meaning of Jesus' Lordship is to understand his servanthood. The hymn affirms this.[18] The servanthood concept indicates a humbling from a previous position of exaltation associated with Jesus' preexistence. The hymn naturally suggests it.[19] The meaning of Jesus' humiliation and exaltation is most remarkable: God's co-equal humbled himself to restore a sinful humanity back to God. Yet, as N. T. Wright asserts, it was the very attribute of preexistence which uniquely qualified Jesus to do so (p. 345). Knowledge of Jesus' preexistence strikes in bold relief the christological and ethical dimensions of Jesus' humiliation. It highlights his willing submission to the Father's will. Moreover, his exaltation does not indicate a "new" state as much as a "return" to what he was before. What is new is that he now appears *as the exalted servant of God* (p. 346, n. 92). We shall evaluate the extent to which Luke–Acts parallels the states of Jesus' servanthood and Lordship as presented in the Christ hymn and the letter.

Philippians

The Christ hymn naturally suggests "a straightforward statement contrasting Christ's pre-existent glory and post-crucifixion exaltation with his earthly humiliation."[20] Its basic structure consists of

---

[17] Caird, *Letters from Prison*, p. 104 insists that "to isolate these verses from their context is to remove them from the epistle." Similarly Stanton, *Jesus of Nazareth*, p. 106 thinks that within the hymn the two themes are "inextricably woven together." *Contra* Käsemann, "Kritische Analyse," pp. 51–95; Martin, *Carmen Christi*, pp. 289–91 *et al.*

[18] The hymn, however, also presupposes a significant amount of christological teaching, as does Paul in that he omits further doctrinal exposition of it in the letter; so Beare, *Philippians*, pp. 29–30.

[19] So esp. Wright, "ἁρπαγμός," pp. 321–52. *Contra*, Dunn *et al.*; see my reply to Dunn in the next note.

[20] Dunn, *Christology in the Making*, p. 114. But his attempt to dismiss this

two parts: Jesus' humiliation (vv. 6–8) and exaltation (vv. 9–11).
The hymn's four independent verbs graphically illustrate this:

ἑαυτὸν ἐκένωσεν (he emptied himself, v. 7)

ἐταπείνωσεν ἑαυτόν (he humbled himself, v. 8)

ὁ θεὸς αὐτὸν ὑπερύψωσεν (God highly exalted him, v. 9)

[ὁ θεὸς] ἐχαρίσατο αὐτῷ (God freely gave to him, v. 9).[21]

The first two verbs have Jesus as the subject; the last two have God.
This implies that Jesus' humiliation was by his own act and his
exaltation by God's act (Hawthorne, p. 77).

The humiliation–exaltation pattern appears again in 3:10–11.
Here Paul personally identifies himself with Jesus' humiliation and
exaltation: "I want to know Christ and the power of his resurrection [exaltation] and the fellowship of sharing in his sufferings
[humiliation], becoming like him in his death [humiliation], and so,
somehow, to attain to the resurrection from the dead [exaltation]."
Paul perhaps also anticipates the two stages in 2:5. In light of the
subsequent hymn, the designation ἐν χριστῷ Ἰησοῦ in 2:5 may
suggest inclusively both states of Jesus as well. Ἰησοῦ may
specifically turn the reader's attention to Jesus' life, as the hymn
would then serve to illustrate.[22] This instance, however, is less
clear.

These passages (2:5–11; 3:10–11) also indicate that Paul did not
consider the states of Jesus' humiliation and exaltation as fully
distinct from each other. Although they legitimately define separate
periods of time, the earthly and heavenly spheres of Jesus' existence, to understand Jesus' Lordship fully is to see him simultaneously in light of his humiliation and exaltation. The hymn
thoroughly impresses upon the reader the Lord Jesus' serving
nature in his willingness to carry out this divine plan.

---

traditional definition is not convincing (see pp. 114–21). He fails to consider how
his proposed Adam christology would fit with Phil. 2:5 and gives minimal
treatment (one sentence) to how it would enhance Paul's ethical exhortation in
the rest of the letter; cf. Fowl, *Story of Christ*, pp. 50–52, 70–73. On the other
hand, even if an Adam christology does, in part, describe the hymn's imagery,
there is no governing reason why it must preclude the idea of preexistence; so esp.
Martin, *Carmen Christi*, pp. xxi, 116–19; Wright, "Adam," pp. 373–84. Moreover, Dunn's exegesis itself appears loaded with presuppositions (cf. his citing of
J. Murphy-O'Connor, p. 114); and is also somewhat selective, as is esp. apparent
in his failure to reckon with the significance of the phrase καὶ σχήματι εὑρεθεὶς
ὡς ἄνθρωπος in v. 7, if Jesus were *only human*; so O'Brien, *Philippians*,
pp. 263–68; Hooker, "Philippians 2:6–11," pp. 161–64.

21 Hawthorne, *Philippians*, p. 77.
22 Hooker, "Philippians 2:6–11," p. 154.

Luke–Acts

Luke exhibits a similar structure in the standard two-book division: Luke–Acts. The Gospel delineates Jesus' humiliation; Acts focuses mainly upon his exaltation. Luke in his Gospel unmistakably presents Jesus' humiliation in terms of "the divine δεῖ" as it refers to his approaching passion. As Cosgrove argues: "Jesus is *no passive pawn* of divine necessity in Luke's Gospel; he is *the executor* of that necessity."[23] Luke emphasizes consistently that Jesus is in control of his own fate. He knows that death awaits him in Jerusalem. But according to divine plan, he allows nothing to deter him (see, e.g., Luke 4:30; 9:31; 9:51; 23:46). Jesus' way to the cross for Luke is clearly the way of humiliation. As with Phil. 2:8, the lowest point of Jesus' earthly career, but nevertheless its primary objective, is the cross.

Luke, moreover, makes a special effort in Acts to stress that the cross was not the end but the way to exaltation. He uniquely forecasts this in Luke 9:51: "As the time approached for [Jesus] to be taken up to heaven ..." (also 9:31; 22:69). Gerhard Lohfink observes that here "Luke has a complex event in view, which includes the resurrection and ascension."[24] The meaning of Jesus "being lifted up" (ἀναλήμψεως) seems to be a double one referring to his suffering and exaltation. For Luke the resurrection and ascension synonymously express the exaltation. This is most apparent in Acts 2:33 and 5:31. Here Jesus' exaltation (ὑψόω) to God's right hand replaces, but is equivalent to, his resurrection and ascension and is closely reminiscent of its cognate ὑπερυψόω in Phil. 2:9.[25]

Mary's comment in Luke 1:52: "[God] has brought down rulers from their thrones but has lifted up [ὕψωσεν] the humble [ταπεινούς]"; and Jesus' words in Luke 14:11 (and 18:14): "For everyone who exalts [ὑψῶν] himself will be humbled [ταπεινωθήσεται], and he who humbles [ταπεινῶν] himself will be exalted [ὑψωθήσεται]" perfectly epitomize Jesus, the humble obedient servant whom God made both Lord and Christ. Paralleling Phil. 2:9, the vindication of Jesus' humiliation was God's exaltation of him.[26] Thus, Luke's two volumes respectively stress that Jesus

---

[23] Cosgrove, "Divine δεῖ," p. 180 (my italic).

[24] Lohfink, *Himmelfahrt*, p. 217.   [25] Fitzmyer, *Luke I–XX*, p. 828.

[26] As it also affirmed the finality of God's saving plan in Jesus; see further Wright, "ἁρπαγμός," p. 346.

voluntarily gave up his own life, dying on a cross, and that God raised him from the dead, exalting him to his own right hand. The book division of Luke–Acts corresponds to the twofold structure of Phil. 2:6–11.[27]

But in contrast to some scholarly opinion, it is doubtful that Luke considered the states of Jesus' humiliation and exaltation as mutually exclusive periods of salvation history, owing in part to some new rank or dignity bestowed upon him at his exaltation.[28] Luke's Gospel suggests the contrary. The earthly Jesus seems personally aware that he already possesses a divine rank and nature belonging otherwise to God alone.[29]

Jesus, e.g., describes himself in a Father–Son relation with God (Luke 10:21–22), where as the Son he has special knowledge of the Father in a way strongly resembling the absolute sense of sonship in John's Gospel.[30] He knows and controls his destiny, as is seen in his departure through the midst of the angry crowd about to push him over a cliff (Luke 4:30),[31] or when he had "set his mind" on going to Jerusalem to face death there (Luke 9:51). Luke 21:15 provides perhaps the clearest example. Jesus reveals knowledge of his future work as exalted Lord in strengthening the testimony of his followers. We have seen in chs. 7 and 10 that Acts reaffirms this interpretation.

As in Philippians, the unifying feature in Luke–Acts is *Jesus' willingess to carry out the Father's will*. The humiliation reveals his obedience, even to the point of death on a cross, and the exaltation reveals God's affirmation of it in raising him from the dead. Both aspects mutually describe what Jesus' Lordship means, i.e., Jesus' willingness to give up his own life to make salvation available to all people.

The question remaining is whether this similarity is coincidental

---

[27] *Contra* Conzelmann, *Theology of St. Luke*, p. 171, who thinks that Luke attaches no cosmological significance to the κύριος designation in his writings as does Paul in Phil. 2:6–11.

[28] *Contra* Conzelmann, *Theology of St. Luke*, pp. 16, 27–29, 80–82, 156–57, 170, 180, who thinks that Jesus' earthly ministry represents a past era fully separate from the present church age (esp. p. 82). But cf. Schnackenburg, "Christologie," pp. 299–300, 307–308.

[29] For more on the possible significance of Jesus' teaching and prayer in this regard, see Schnackenburg, "Christologie," pp. 302–303; Crump, *Jesus the Intercessor*.

[30] Ellis, *Luke*, pp. 158–59; Marshall, *Luke*, pp. 435–38; Stein, *Luke*, pp. 312–14.

[31] But to conclude with Ernst, "Christusbild," p. 108, that according to Luke 4:30, "Luke never depicts Jesus in his earthly activity as the Humiliated One" is to overstate the evidence as well. Cf. Schnackenburg, "Christologie," p. 302.

or suggests a deliberate effort on Luke's part to provide his readers with written instruction similar to Paul's intentions for the Christ hymn in Philippians. In what sense does Jesus' life stand as a continuing summons and ethical standard for those following him? And how does walking as Jesus walked itself reveal christologically the Savior to a world that has never seen him?

The ethics of Jesus' Lordship

The summons to follow Jesus is not so much to imitate or emulate his life. Because of his unique status as God's Son, much of what he has done during his earthly life and his reasons for doing so lie utterly beyond human imitation. Rather, the summons is to *conform to his likeness*, particularly his submission and obedience to the Father. This is apparently how Paul understood the Christ hymn and wanted his readers to apply it.[32] To what extent, then, does this same christological motive find a fitting parallel in Luke–Acts?

Philippians

The aspect of the Christ hymn which most suitably suggests an ethical model for Christian living is Jesus as servant: Jesus μορφὴν δούλου λαβών (2:7). But commentators are divided on the exact meaning of δούλου.[33] Does it primarily refer to an acceptance of bondage under the powers of the world,[34] the obedient last Adam,[35] a righteous sufferer, whose death was not associated with atoning merit,[36] taking on the form of a slave, i.e., the deprivation of all rights,[37] a condition of service compared to one of equality

---

[32] But this is not to lessen the hymn's soteriological teaching. Salvation and ethics are inseparable. Paul makes this association himself (Phil. 2:12). For more on the hymn's soteriological value, see Schnackenburg, "Christologie," p. 315; Deichgräber, *Gotteshymnus und Christushymnus*, pp. 119–20; Marshall, *Historian & Theologian*, p. 174; Wright, "ἁρπαγμός," p. 346.

[33] See also Martin, *Carmen Christi*, pp. 169–96; O'Brien, *Philippians*, pp. 218–24.

[34] Käsemann, "Kritische Analyse," pp. 72–74; Fuller, *Foundations*, pp. 209–10; Gnilka, *Philipperbrief*, pp. 119–20, 140–41; Beare, *Philippians*, pp. 82–83; Caird, *Letters from Prison*, pp. 121–22; Hofius, *Christushymnus*, pp. 62–63; Barth, *Philipper*, p. 42; Craddock, *Philippians*, p. 41.

[35] Hooker, "Philippians 2:6–11," pp. 161–63; Dunn, *Christology in the Making*, p. 115; Wright, "Adam," pp. 373–84.

[36] Schweizer, *Erniedrigung und Erhöhung*, pp. 97–98.

[37] Moule, "Further Reflexions," pp. 268–69.

with God[38] or Isaiah's Servant of the Lord?[39] Currently no consensus exists.

The difficulty in interpretation stems from the poetic nature of the hymn itself. The interpreter encounters in nearly every line of the hymn some obscurity,[40] mainly owing to its brevity and possibly to a degree of poetic license, where its author simultaneously incorporates different images to depict in fuller measure the meaning of Christ's incarnation. Furthermore, no verbal parallels, biblical or extra-biblical, have been found for the hymn as a whole.[41] These factors make the task of locating a conceptual background for the servant idea extremely difficult.

The best textual evidence we have, and perhaps the most suggestive, comes from Isa. 45:23b: κάμψει πᾶν γόνυ καὶ ἐξομολογήσεται πᾶσα γλῶσσα (LXX). Phil. 2:10–11 reproduces this citation almost verbatim (except that it alters the mood of the verbs from the future indicative in Isaiah to the subjunctive, perhaps owing to a shift in perspective, at God's initiative, where universal homage is now attributed to Jesus Christ instead of Yahweh, cf. τῷ θεῷ, Isa. 45:23b). The citing of the Isaiah passage in the hymn provides an important clue. It directs us to a Jewish source as the probable background of the servant concept rather than to a gnostic redeemer-myth or some oriental divine man concept.[42] It also specifies the significance of Jesus' exaltation. He is worshiped as deity. Phil. 2:10–11 substitutes Jesus for Yahweh (cf. τῷ θεῷ, Isa. 45:23b LXX) as the object of divine worship. In this sense, at least, Jesus appears again as God's co-equal (cf. 2:6). The presence of the Isaiah citation in vv. 10–11 also raises the probability that the hymn was understood in light of the four surrounding servant songs (42:1–4; 49:1–7; 50:4–9; 52:13–53:12).[43] The role which the

---

[38] Collange, *Philippians*, pp. 101–102; Bruce, *Philippians*, p. 46; Hurtado, "Jesus as Lordly Example," pp. 113–26; Hawthorne, *Philippians*, p. 87; Fowl, *Story of Christ*, pp. 57–59, 63–64; O'Brien, *Philippians*, pp. 223–24.

[39] Lohmeyer, *Philipper*, p. 94; Jeremias, *Servant of God*, pp. 97–99; Martin, *Carmen Christi*, p. 195 (with qual.); Hendricksen, *Philippians*, p. 109; Ernst, *Philipper*, p. 68; Wagner, "Scandale de la croix," pp. 177–87; Silva, *Philippians*, p. 125 (with qual.); Marshall, "Development of Christology," pp. 159–61.

[40] E.g., note the repeated admissions along these lines in Fowl's discussion of the hymn in *Story of Christ*, pp. 49–75.

[41] Hawthorne, *Philippians*, pp. 78–79 sees conceptual and structural parallels with John 13:3–17, although he readily admits that the specific verbal links are slight.

[42] See further Schweizer, *Erniedrigung und Erhöhung*, p. 97; Marshall, "Christ-Hymn," pp. 119–20 in summary of Martin, *Carmen Christi* (1st ed.); Hurtado, "Jesus as Lordly Example," p. 118.

[43] Silva, *Philippians*, p. 125.

'ebed concept evidently played in forming Jesus' self-understanding and the church's understanding of him increases the likelihood of this position.[44]

The strongest parallel between Isaiah's fourth servant song and the Philippian Christ hymn is the shameful abasement which the servant would undergo and his subsequent glorification (also Isa. 50:4–9). Hawthorne, however, contends that δοῦλος in Isa. 52:13 is an honorific title and would contradict the extreme abasement of Jesus as δοῦλος in Phil. 2:7. For this reason he believes that the fourth servant song could not have influenced the hymn's conceptual background.[45] But OT scholars widely accept Isa. 52:13–53:12 "as a liturgy framed by two sayings of Yahweh (52:13–15 and 53:11b–12)"[46] with 52:13–15 briefly summarizing what follows in the rest of the song.[47] Isa. 52:13 does not minimize the servant's utter humiliation. Rather, the term δοῦλος rightly stands as an honorific title because of the complete humiliation inherent in the designation itself. This description coincides well with what the hymn describes of Christ in Phil. 2.[48] Other Jewish images probably also influenced the servant concept of the hymn, especially the suffering righteous one (Ps. 16, 22, 40, 69; Wisd. Sol. 2–5)[49] and a second Adam parallel.[50]

Thus, although the suffering and vindication of Isaiah's servant of Yahweh in 52:13–53:12 may provide the primary conceptual background of the Christ hymn, the hymn's ambiguity may well be

---

[44] Jeremias, *Servant of God*, pp. 94–106; France, "Servant of the Lord," pp. 26–52; Black, "'Son of Man' Passion Sayings," pp. 1–8; Wolff, *Jesaja 53*; Hengel, *Atonement*, pp. 59–60, 71–75 and lit. cited on p. 96, n. 63; also Marshall, "Development of Christology," pp. 159–61. *Contra* Hooker, *Jesus and the Servant*; Jones, "Servant," p. 149, who largely depends on the arguments of Hooker; for a convincing reply to Hooker, see France.

[45] Hawthorne, *Philippians*, p. 87.

[46] Wolff, *Jesaja 53*, p. 30; also von Rad, *Theology*, vol. 1, pp. 255–57; Beauchamp, "Quatrième chant du serviteur," pp. 327, 332–35.

[47] E.g., Lindsey, *Servant Songs*, p. 99 comments: "Unlike scholarly opinion on the other Servant songs, there is a general agreement on the extent of the fourth song: 52:13–15 constitutes an introduction or prologue to 53:1–12." See also Motyer, *Isaiah*, pp. 422–24.

[48] Westermann, *Isaiah 40–66*, p. 258 similarly comments: "Expressions referring to Jesus' exaltation ... probably go back to [Isa. 52:13 and the fourth servant song]."

[49] E.g., Schweizer, *Erniedrigung und Erhöhung*, pp. 21–33, 97; Georgi, "Vorpaulinische Hymnus," pp. 276–81; Sanders, *Christological Hymns*, pp. 70–74.

[50] E.g., Wright, "Jesus Christ is Lord," pp. 57–62. Wagner, "Scandale de la croix," pp. 183–84 argues that although the hymn portrays Jesus in light of Isa. 53, it probably simultaneously envisions Jesus as the second Adam.

deliberate in order to depict Jesus' humiliation and exaltation through numerous Jewish images.

Vv. 9–11 are also instructive ethically.[51] Scholars have given little attention to the second half of the Christ hymn in this regard.[52] The corollary to Jesus' becoming a servant is his *dependence upon* God for his exaltation (cf. Heb. 12:2). In becoming a servant, Jesus willingly set aside some personal freedoms, even to the point of depriving himself of his rights as a person (so v. 7a, ἀλλὰ ἑαυτὸν ἐκένωσεν). "The statement," Moule comments, "that Jesus so completely stripped himself of all rights and securities as to be comparable to a slave, constitutes a poignant description of his absolute and extreme self-emptying – even of basic human rights."[53] Jesus μορφὴν δούλου λαβών became *fully dependent upon God for his future glorification.* Jesus relied upon God for restoration to his former state (cf. v. 6), although Jesus himself was never uncertain of the outcome. Vv. 9–11 depict God, as virtually everywhere else in the NT, as the divine power behind Jesus' resurrection/exaltation.

This idea translates into Christian practice as perseverance in the faith, i.e., steadfastness, persistence, patient endurance, standing firm, and so on. This common NT teaching is especially pertinent for the Philippian church, "for the fact that Christ is exalted is an indication that God is at work in their midst."[54] Christian suffering, persecution, and martyrdom find their most fitting parallel in Jesus' own humiliation (Phil. 1:29–30; 2:5, 12; 3:10b); similarly, the corresponding Christian hope of resurrection from the dead becomes inseparably rooted in God's exaltation of Jesus (1:9–11, 27–30; 2:5, 12; 3:10a, 11, 20–21). Believers must also rely continually upon God (and Jesus, cf. 3:21), but, as with Jesus, the outcome is never in question (cf., e.g., 3:20). God will not fail them (1:6).

The passages which perhaps best reveal the relevance of the Christ hymn within the letter are those linking it to its surrounding context. Phil. 2:5 introduces the hymn and connects it to the foregoing humility theme; 2:12, in effect, summarizes it and connects it to Paul's exhortation on proper Christian conduct. Both verses reveal Paul's intent to feature Jesus' life as the ethical model

---

[51]   *Contra* Käsemann, "Kritische Analyse," pp. 57–62, 91; followed by Martin, *Carmen Christi*, p. 88 *et al.*

[52]   But cf. Marshall, "Philippians 2:5–11," pp. 117–19; Stanton, *Jesus of Nazareth*, pp. 102–103; Fowl, *Story of Christ*, pp. 77–101.

[53]   Moule, "Philippians 2:5–11," pp. 268–69.

[54]   Stanton, *Jesus of Nazareth*, pp. 102–103.

for Christian living, which apparently is his main reason for
including the Christ hymn in the letter.

A relatively recent debate in the study of the Christ hymn
concerns whether its introductory verse (2:5) refers to an ethical
exhortation to believers to conform (rather than "to imitate")[55]
their lives to the pattern set for them by Jesus Christ[56] or to a
kerygmatic exhortation to believers to adopt an attitude toward one
another that would befit their union with Christ.[57] The issue is not
as black and white as many commentators would suggest. The
former more traditional position makes sense of the verse in stating
how Paul intended the hymn to coincide with his ethical appeal.[58]
Paul's personal desire to participate in Jesus' sufferings and resurrection (3:10–11) parallels his appeal to the Philippian church in 2:5.
He challenges them to set for themselves the same goal which he has
set for himself: to conform to the kind of attitudes and behavior
which characterized Jesus' life as illustrated in the hymn, a Christ-
likeness which he had already begun to personalize in his own life.[59]

Furthermore, Philippians contains no single meaning of
the "in Christ" statements.[60] This undermines the belief that ἐν
χριστῷ Ἰησοῦ in v. 5 should be understood exclusively as union
with Christ. A position better reflecting Paul's own thinking, in
contrast to the "either–or" stance, is a blending of the two
interpretations (so Rom. 15:1–7; 1 Cor. 10:31–11:1; 2 Cor. 8:9; 1
Thess. 1:6). Life in Christ would naturally demand conformity to
the pattern set by Jesus.[61]

---

[55]   See further Marshall, "Christ-Hymn," p. 119; Dahl, "Form-Critical Observa-
       tions," p. 34; Hooker, "Philippians 2:6–11," pp. 155–56. About Jesus as
       "exemplar," i.e., a shared norm, see Fowl, *Story of Christ*, pp. 92–95.
[56]   E.g., Fowl, *Story of Christ*, pp. 49–101; O'Brien, *Philippians*, pp. 203–205, 253–62.
[57]   E.g., Caird, *Letters from Prison*, p. 118; Craddock, *Philippians*, pp. 38–39;
       Thüsing, *Gott und Christus*, pp. 49–51; Silva, *Philippians*, pp. 107–12.
[58]   For more detailed support of this view, see Marshall, "Christ-Hymn,"
       pp. 117–19; Moule, "Philippians 2:5–11," pp. 265–66; Hawthorne, *Philippians*,
       pp. 79–81; O'Brien, *Philippians*, p. 205.
[59]   Hence, *contra* Martin, *Carmen Christi*, p. 88 *et al.*, the ethical interpretation does
       not necessarily render Phil. 2:9–11 as irrelevant.
[60]   Marshall in a lecture entitled "In Christ" (1989), discusses five classifications of
       the phrase in Philippians with the technical usage forming only one of the
       categories; see also Nagata, *Philippians 2:5–11*, pp. 345–46.
[61]   Hooker, "Philippians 2:6–11," pp. 152–57, esp. p. 154; also Larsson, *Christus als
       Vorbild*, p. 260 (as cited in Martin, *Carmen Christi*, p. 87); Strecker, "Redaktion
       und Tradition," pp. 66–68; Moule, "Philippians 2:5–11," p. 262; Schnackenburg,
       "Christologie," p. 311; Ernst, *Philipper*, p. 95; Collange, *Philippians*, p. 95; Barth,
       Philipper, pp. 40–41; Nagata, *Philippians 2:5–11*, pp. 338–50; implicit in Hurtado,
       "Jesus as Lordly Example," pp. 120–21.

This would also mean that interpreting ἐν ὑμῖν in v. 5 exclusively as "interaction with other believers"[62] or "an attitude directed toward the inward self"[63] is foreign to Paul's thinking. Greek grammar permits either translation.[64] In addition, Paul's call to his readers to obey his instructions – as Christ's messenger – immediately after the hymn in 2:12 supports his conscious linking of proper Christian conduct to Jesus' life made in v. 5.[65] Paul undoubtedly intended his readers to work out their salvation individually and corporately. The two dimensions – personal obedience toward God and proper Christian conduct toward other believers – logically require each other.[66] The textual links (2:5, 12) sum up succinctly Paul's most ardent appeal to the Philippian church: that as individuals and as a group, they should remember that union with Christ demands continual conformity to the pattern set by Jesus himself.

Paul's christology in the hymn and the letter thus appears mostly in support of this main writing concern. He assumes a sizeable amount of christological teaching. It was unnecessary to write more. He was not countering or correcting a faulty christology. Rather, on the basis of what the readers had already known intellectually and experientially about Christ, he used the writing occasion to encourage the church not to compromise its faith.

Toward this end Paul most likely used the hymn to epitomize the Christ-like "attitude" (2:5, φρονεῖτε; or "example" 3:17a, συμμιμηταί μου γίνεσθε; "pattern," 3:17b, τύπον) after which the readers were to model their lives (also 1:8, 27a, 29–30; 3:7–11). His stated aim was to encourage their spiritual development (1:9–11a). But in contrast to the other examples he cites (e.g., Paul himself, 1:3–30; 2:17–18; 3:4–16; 4:11–13; Timothy, 2:19–23; Epaphroditus, 2:25–30; "those among them," 3:17b), Paul exhorts his readers in ch. 2 to more than simple emulation of Jesus' attitude and behavior.

---

[62] A position generally subscribed to by those taking a strictly "incorporation" line e.g., Collange, *Philippians*, pp. 94–95; Thüsing, *Gott und Christus*, p. 50; Silva, *Philippians*, pp. 107–109.

[63] Lightfoot, *Philippians*, p. 110; Vincent, *Philippians*, p. 57. Hawthorne, *Philippians*, p. 81 also allows for this meaning.

[64] Lightfoot, *Philippians*, p. 110.

[65] See further O'Brien, *Philippians*, p. 275. *Contra* Käsemann, "Kritische Analyse," pp. 76–81, who believes that Paul saw no immediate ethical relevance for the Philippian church stemming from the example of Christ's obedience within the hymn itself. Cf. Hurtado, "Jesus as Lordly Example," p. 125; Fowl, *Story of Christ*, p. 96.

[66] See further Lightfoot, *Philippians*, p. 73; Gnilka, *Philipperbrief*, p. 110.

They were to conform to Jesus' very likeness, a process begun in this life (2:12; also 1:9–11; 3:12–17) and brought to perfection at his return (1:10; 2:14–16; 3:20–21). Paul connects the goal of Christian living to the parousia.[67] In this way he fuses ethical conformity to Jesus with the saving gospel event (Hooker, pp. 155–57).

In summary, Paul features in Philippians how Jesus' life stands as *the ethical model for Christian living*. The Christ hymn illustrates this. But this emphasis in no way invalidates the importance of Jesus' atoning work. Even though the standard Pauline teaching on Jesus' death as saving receives minor attention in the letter, it supplies Paul with his basis for establishing Jesus' life as an ethical model for his readers. The summons is not to imitate or emulate but to conform to the attitudes and behavior characterizing Jesus in his humiliation and exaltation. Jesus' saving work is not repeatable. As "the preexistent one become flesh," his sacrificial death stands alone as God's perfect saving plan for humanity. On these grounds, however, the whole of Jesus' life in his humiliation and exaltation becomes a guideline for Christians to follow. The servanthood of the Lord Jesus becomes the ethical norm for Christian living.

Luke–Acts

We saw in chs. 8–10 the importance of Jesus' Lordship in Luke's christology. But is this picture complete? To what extent does Luke–Acts manifestly illustrate how the serving nature of the Lord Jesus furnishes believers with a preeminent ethical model to follow? How would this christological theme pertain to his reason for writing? And how would it affect his meager treatment of the vicarious nature of Jesus' death?

Jesus and servanthood in Luke–Acts

Luke is apparently particularly interested in his Gospel and Acts to depict Jesus' servanthood against the backdrop of his Lordship. His writings display an overriding concern to provide a greatly expanded description of Jesus' humiliation and exaltation, some-what analogous to Paul's use of the Christ hymn in Philippians. He repeatedly draws attention, e.g., to Jesus' servanthood from every

---

[67] Hooker, "Philippians 2:6–11," p. 156.

stage of Jesus' life – his birth, ministry, death and resurrection – and from the preaching of the early church. He powerfully sharpens his depiction by stressing the connection of Jesus' servanthood to various OT portraits. These include the Davidic messiah, Daniel's Son of Man, Isaiah's suffering servant, the Deuteronomic prophet-like Moses, and the rejected prophet.

1. *The birth narratives.* The birth narratives immediately immerse the reader in an OT atmosphere of service. Mary calls herself "the Lord's servant" (Luke 1:38), closely paralleling Hannah's self-designation in 1 Sam. 1:11, 16, 18.[68] David (Luke 1:69; cf., e.g., 2 Sam. 7; Ps. 132:11; Isa. 37:35) and Israel (Luke 1:54; cf. Ps. 136:22; Isa. 41:8; 44:21) are also called "servant," meaning "servant of God."[69]

In OT usage, servanthood connotes piety (Zimmerli, pp. 18–19). Simeon, who is described as "righteous and devout" (Luke 2:25) and calls himself "servant" (v. 29), personifies this OT description of the pious servant of the Lord; the same also holds true for Zechariah and Elizabeth (1:6) and Anna the prophetess (2:37).

Servanthood in the OT also denotes humbleness/humility, as is most clearly seen in Mary's Magnificat (1:46–55; e.g., Isa. 50:4–9; 52:13–53:12). She praises God, for he has (1) "scattered those proud in their inmost thoughts" (v. 51b); (2) "brought down rulers from their thrones" (v. 52a); and (3) "sent the rich away empty" (v. 53b). In contrast, he has (1) "been mindful of the humble state of his servant [Mary]" (v. 48a); (2) "extended mercy to those who fear him" (v. 50); (3) "lifted up the humble" (v. 52b); (4) "filled the hungry with good things" (v. 53a); and (5) "helped his servant Israel, remembering to be merciful to Abraham and his descendants forever" (vv. 54–55). The lowliness of Jesus' birth also superbly displays this.[70] He was laid in a manger (2:7, 12) and visited by shepherds (2:8–20) – not exactly how one would have envisioned the messiah's coming.[71] In contrast, Matthew deliberately underscores the kingly side of Jesus' birth; he makes no mention of the inn and manger story (cf. Matt. 1:25; 2:11) or of a visit by shepherds but one by magi (cf. 2:1–12), who, as is commonly thought, were associated with royal courts as advisers to the throne!

OT servanthood also signifies obedience (Ps. 69:36; Isa. 56:6). Zechariah declares that "God's raising up of the horn of salvation"

---

[68] Fitzmyer, *Luke I–IX*, p. 352.   [69] Zimmerli, *Servant of God*, pp. 46–47.
[70] Marshall, *Luke*, p. 108.   [71] Fitzmyer, *Luke I–IX*, p. 410.

will "enable us to serve him [λατρεύειν αὐτῷ] without fear in holiness and righteousness before him in all our days" (1:74b–75). λατρεύειν αὐτῷ means here more than priestly service or acts of worship. "It refers analogously to the entire way in which God's people were to conduct themselves."[72] As in the OT, "obedience for Luke is the true cult."[73]

Lastly, Luke emphasizes the OT tendency to link servanthood with salvation (Isa. 49:5–7; 53:11–12; Zech. 3:8–9). E.g., Zechariah says: "[God] has raised up a horn of salvation for us in the house of his servant David" (1:69); the idea also appears in the angel's declaration to the shepherds at the time of Jesus' birth (2:12), Simeon's song (2:29–32), and Anna's comments to the people of Jerusalem (2:37b–38).

Luke places Jesus' birth within an OT context of servanthood. The main characters exemplify what it means to be "a servant of God." But how does he fit Jesus into this environment of obedient service? Does Jesus appear like these others as human servants of the Lord, or does he appear more on the godward side as "the servant of the Lord"? Luke mentions in 1:69: καὶ ἤγειρεν κέρας σωτηρίας ἡμῖν ἐν οἴκῳ Δαυὶδ παιδὸς αὐτοῦ (cf. 2 Sam. 7:26; 1 Chron. 17:24). Jesus was born to a parentage with a longstanding reputation of servanthood and one from which the messiah was expected to come. In the OT and Judaism, however, David never appears as a suffering humiliated servant. Nor does the promised messiah. The designation is honorific and associated with kingly rule where David (2 Sam. 3:18) and his promised offspring (Ezek. 34:23–24; 37:24–25) would rule as servants of Yahweh "with the special office of saving the people of God out of the hands of its enemies" (2 Sam. 7:12–16; Jer. 33:15–16).[74] In keeping with this description, Luke anticipates in Jesus a fulfillment of scripture, where as the messiah Jesus will make salvation available both to Jew and Gentile (2:29–32; also Acts 3:26!).

But in contrast to the OT-like environment of servanthood in which Jesus was born, Luke uniquely heightens the godward side of Jesus in his obedient service to God. Jesus' first words in Luke are ἐν τοῖς τοῦ πατρός μου δεῖ εἶναί με (2:49).[75] In these words Luke probably discloses Jesus' unique relation with the Father, one

---

[72] Ibid., p. 385.   [73] Schürmann, *Lukas. 1, 1–9, 50*, p. 88.
[74] Zimmerli, "παῖς θεοῦ," *TDNT* 5, p. 664.
[75] In support of the "in my father's house" translation, see lit. cited in Sylva, "Cryptic Clause," p. 133, n. 4.

incomparable to any of God's servants of old.[76] The fact that his parents "did not understand what he was saying to them" (v. 50) and that "Mary treasured all these things in her heart" (v. 51) reinforces a special claim to sonship.[77] It seems no coincidence for Luke, therefore, that the saying stands at the head of all that Jesus goes on to say and do in Luke–Acts. It marks his special relation to the Father and anticipates his complete obedience to the Father's will.[78]

Simeon's prophecy to Mary that "this child is destined to cause the falling and rising of many in Israel, and to be a sign that will be spoken against, so that the thoughts of many hearts will be revealed. And a sword will pierce your own soul too" (2:34–35) foreshadows the fact that Jesus' obedient service to the Father will end in suffering rather than kingly rule. This portrait stands in marked contrast to Matthew's birth narrative.

2. *Jesus' ministry.* In Luke's Gospel especially, Jesus thoroughly describes himself and his mission in terms of several well-known OT images of divine agents. The more important ones include the Davidic messiah, Daniel's Son of Man, the Deuteronomic prophet-like Moses and Isaiah's suffering servant. What, however, was unknown to pre-Christian Judaism but unique to Jesus is the way he identified himself as the suffering messiah and the suffering son of man. According to Luke, at least, in all probability Jesus' understanding of his mission in terms of Isaiah's suffering servant and the Deuteronomic prophet-like Moses had largely influenced this merging of images.[79]

[76] Cf. Bovon, *Lukas. 1, 1–9, 50*, pp. 160–61, who draws upon Winter, "Targum Yerushalmi," pp. 145–79. But in reply to Winter, see Marshall, *Luke*, p. 129.

[77] So esp. Laurentin, *Jésus au temple*; Marshall, *Luke*, pp. 128–30; Fitzmyer, *Luke I–IX*, pp. 437–39, 443–46; Schürmann, *Lukas. 1, 1–9, 50*, pp. 136–38; Nolland, *Luke 1–9:20*, pp. 131–35.

[78] See further Cosgrove, "Divine δεῖ," p. 175.

[79] It is commonly held that the fusing of OT christological portraits to Isaiah's suffering servant is already hinted at in the account of Jesus' baptism, where in Luke 3:22 (Mark 1:11) Jesus' sonship as a possible messianic designation stemming from Ps. 2:7 appears, on the basis of the words ἐν σοὶ εὐδόκησα, to be fused with Isaiah's Servant of the Lord according to Isa. 42:1 – a connection already made in Judaism; so, e.g., Marshall, "Son of God," pp. 121–33; Marshall, *Luke*, pp. 156–57. Thus as Morris, *Luke*, p. 110 observes: "This combination [in Luke's Gospel] was to determine much of his ministry" (also Acts 4:27). See further, e.g., Fitzmyer, *Luke I–IX*, pp. 485–86; Bock, *Proclamation*, pp. 99–105 (with qual.); Nolland, *Luke 1–9:20*, pp. 162–65. Judaism also had most likely already associated a similar mediating role with the Deuteronomic "prophet-like Moses"; see, e.g., von Rad, *Theology*, vol. 1, pp. 261–62; Moessner, *Lord of the Banquet*, pp. 46–79, 260–88.

The key passage in this regard is Luke 4:16–30. Whether Luke is following another source here – perhaps the more original with Mark representing an abridged form[80] – or greatly revising Mark 6:1–6 (Matt. 13:53–58), the point remains the same: in contrast to Mark, he assigns the episode thematic importance for both the Gospel and Acts.[81]

Its placement in the Gospel indicates its importance for Luke. Whereas Mark and Matthew mention the episode well into Jesus' ministry, Luke shifts it to the beginning. After Jesus' temptation (Luke 4:1–13) and a brief summary of his Galilean ministry (4:14–15), Luke follows with the Nazareth story. In Luke's Gospel, the story introduces Jesus' public ministry. It is only after the story that we see Jesus healing the infirm, raising the dead, exorcizing demons, proclaiming the good news, and calling disciples. Luke directly links these episodes to the Nazareth story.

The Nazareth story has "topic-sentence" status. It describes *what* Luke will say in the Gospel and Acts about Jesus' earthly work; and as importantly, it discloses *how* he intends to portray Jesus to his readers in the entirety of his writing. The story embodies Luke's reason for writing: to supply his readers with a model of servant-hood taken from Jesus' life, illustrating to them "how they can and should live as Jesus lived." To this end the Nazareth story appears, as some have defined it, as "an inaugural address,"[82] "a frontis-piece,"[83] or "an introduction"[84] to the whole of Luke–Acts.[85]

Luke brings together a number of ideas here – most of them unique to his version of the Nazareth account – that express his interest in the servant theme. On the basis of Jesus' reading of Isa. 61:1–2 and 58:6 (4:18–19), which is understood as self-proclama-tion, Luke stresses that Jesus has come to serve: "to preach the good news to the poor, to proclaim freedom for the prisoners and recovery of sight for the blind, to release the oppressed and to proclaim the year of the Lord's favor."[86] In 7:22 Luke discloses

---

[80] Marshall, *Luke*, p. 180. [81] See, e.g., Kimball, *Exposition*, p. 97.

[82] E.g., George, "Prédication inaugurale," pp. 17–29; Muhlack, *Parallelen*, pp. 117–39.

[83] Cosgrove, "Divine δεῖ," p. 179.

[84] Lampe, "Portrait of Christ," p. 167; Navone, *Themes*, p. 189.

[85] For other survey discussions of the programmatic nature of Luke 4, see Green, "Jesus on the Mount of Olives," p. 41 and lit. cited on p. 47, n. 47; Tannehill, *Luke*, pp. 61–68.

[86] For a more detailed discussion of Jesus as preacher and healer and of his ministry to the oppressed in conjunction with Luke 4:18–19, see Tannehill, *Luke*, pp. 75–139.

what this evidently looked like in Jesus' ministry. In replying to John's question concerning whether he was the expected messiah (7:20; cf. 3:15), Jesus says "the blind receive sight, the lame walk, those who have leprosy are cured, the deaf hear, the dead are raised, and the good news is preached to the poor." Jesus confirms here that what he announced about himself in Nazareth he is, in fact, doing.[87] Luke repeatedly draws attention to this point throughout Jesus' public ministry. Jesus' preaching the good news (Luke 4:43–44; 5:31–32; 6:17–18; 7:22; 8:1; 9:11; 16:16–17), healing the sick (Luke 4:38–40, 42; 5:12–16, 17–26; 6:6–11, 18–19; 7:1–10, 12–17, 21–22; 8:2–3, 41–56; 9:11; 13:10–13; 14:1–6; 17:11–19; 18:35–43; Acts 2:22), and exorcizing demons (Luke 4:31–37; 4:41; 5:29–32; 6:18; 7:21–22; 8:2, 26–39; 9:37–43; 11:14; Acts 2:22; 10:38) reveal his self-fulfillment of Isa. 61:1–2 (58:6) and explicate his serving character as the messiah (and Son of Man, 19:10).

The foreboding of future suffering in Luke 4:22–30 also anticipates Luke's servanthood theme. The resulting ill will of Jesus' hometown toward him is typologically important for Luke.[88] It casts the whole of Jesus' ministry in the shadow of the cross. In addition to the four passion predictions Luke has taken over from Mark – in reference to the suffering of the Son of Man ([1] Luke 9:44; Mark 9:31; Matt. 17:22–23; [2] Luke 18:31–33; Mark 10:33–34; [3] Luke 22:22; Mark 14:21; Matt. 26:24) and "the baptism he would undergo" (Luke 12:50; Mark 10:38) – he considerably expands this by drawing from a wealth of OT imagery. E.g., his melding of Peter's confession with the subsequent passion prediction in effect asserts that both the Christ and the Son of Man will suffer (Luke 9:22; not as explicit in Mark 8:31; and even less so in Matt. 16:21). He uniquely combines Jesus' anticipated suffering with the OT portraits of the Son of Man (11:29–32, as the rejected sign; 17:25), the rejected prophet (13:33), and the prophet-like Moses (Luke 9:31). It forms the destination of the travel narrative (9:51) and is used in normal self-reference at the time of the Last Supper (22:15). Moreover, it links Jesus as messiah and prophet

---

[87] See similar summary statements in Luke 13:32; 16:16–17; 19:37. Moreover, as with the Nazareth account, much of the imagery in 7:22 is drawn from Isaiah as well (cf. Isa. 26:19; 29:18–19; 35:5–6; 61:1). The only exception is "the cleansing of the lepers," which Marshall, *Luke*, pp. 291–92 argues was perhaps influenced by the Elisha typology; cf. 2 Kings 5; Luke 4:27.

[88] But as Brawley, *Jews*, p. 17 argues, such a conclusion does not necessarily make Jesus (or Luke) anti-Jewish.

with Isaiah's suffering servant[89] and the Deuteronomic prophet-like Moses[90] in Luke 4:18–19.

Luke, moreover, affirms in the Nazareth story that Jesus' mission as servant is according to divine plan. As Cosgrove points out, Jesus does not appear here as a "passive pawn of divine necessity."[91] In Nazareth, in fact, he stirs up the trouble. He turns the listeners' praise into hostility. As elsewhere in the Gospel Jesus appears as "the executor of the divine δεῖ"; he knows he will be rejected and suffer, but in obedience to his Father's will, "he virtually engineers his own passion" (p. 179). Jesus knows God's will for him. The hallmark of servanthood, as exemplified in the Nazareth story, is Jesus' willing submission to God's plan and his actively leading it to completion in his suffering and death.

A final comment in reference to Jesus' ministry is that Luke draws special attention to Jesus' servanthood through his teaching. Luke has all of Jesus' sayings pertaining to the servant theme found in Mark and Matthew: he takes over two similar sayings in Mark ([1] Luke 9:46–48; Mark 9:33–37; cf. Matt. 18:1–5; and esp. [2] Luke 22:24–27!; cf. Mark 10:41–45; Matt. 20:24–28) and shares one in common with Matthew (Luke 16:13; Matt. 6:24). He also adds three of his own (Luke 12:37; 14:7–13; 17:7–10). In Jesus' story of the servants waiting for their master to return from a wedding banquet (12:35–38), illustrating to his followers the need to be ready at all times for the Son of Man's coming (v. 40; cf. Mark 13:33–37; Matt. 25:1–13), Luke additionally records in v. 37: "It will be good for those servants whose master finds them watching when he comes. *I tell you the truth, he will dress himself to serve, will have them recline at the table and will come and wait on them*" (cf. John 13:4–5). Whatever the background to the saying, the message here is clear as it relates to Jesus. His description of himself in

---

[89] Seccombe, "Luke and Isaiah," pp. 252–59; Bock, *Proclamation*, pp. 108–10; Radl, *Lukas*, pp. 89–90; Green, "Death of Jesus," pp. 18–28; also France, "Servant of the Lord," pp. 42–43 and earlier lit. in n. 84. France's comment "that nowhere in Is. 40–66 is the first person used by the prophet in describing his own work, but it is used both in Is. 61, and in the second and third Servant Songs" and hence would likely connect Isa. 61 with the servant songs (p. 43, n. 84) is compelling.

[90] E.g., Miller, "Deuteronomic Portrait of Moses," pp. 251–55; Moessner, *Lord of the Banquet*, pp. 46–79, 260–88; Turner, "Jesus and the Spirit," pp. 26–28 and lit. cited on p. 27, n. 104; also lit. cited in Crump, *Jesus the Interecessor*, p. 47, n. 75. For a convergence of the portraits of Jesus as the messiah, prophet-like Moses, and Servant of Yahweh in Luke 4:18–19, see Marshall, *Historian & Theologian*, pp. 125–28.

[91] Cosgrove, "Divine δεῖ," pp. 179–81.

future terms, possibly in allusion to the Lord's banquet at his return (cf. Luke 13:29; 22:27–30; Rev. 19:9),[92] stems from how he perceived himself during his earthly career. Jesus says: "For who is greater, the one who is at the table or the one who serves? Is it not the one who is at the table? *But I am among you as one who serves*" (22:27). To see the Lord Jesus aright is to see him as a servant. Thus, in terms of Isa. 61:1–2 (Luke 4:18–19), Luke demonstrates how this is so in Jesus' earthly ministry.

3. *Jesus' passion.* Regarding Jesus' passion, Luke uniquely describes the lowest point of Jesus' humiliation, his death, and conversely his divine vindication in exaltation, his resurrection and ascension. On the eve of his death, Jesus tells his followers that he was about to suffer. In addition to the statement that "the son of man will go as it has been decreed" (Luke 22:22; Mark 14:21; Matt. 26:24), Luke uniquely adds in 22:15 an "I saying" of Jesus. Here Jesus plainly states his desire to eat the Passover meal with his disciples before he suffers (πρὸ τοῦ με παθεῖν). This saying explicitly and concisely draws together all of Jesus' prior pronouncements and allusions to his approaching suffering. It accentuates the event about to take place.

The only overt citation of Isa. 53 in the synoptic tradition occurs in Luke's Last Supper discourse (22:37; cf. Isa. 53:12). Its location in Luke's Gospel speaks volumes. When Jesus stands on the brink of death, he calls to mind the OT image of Isaiah's suffering servant in the words καὶ μετὰ ἀνόμων ἐλογίσθη. The expression, according to Luke, powerfully reveals the extent of Jesus' humiliation. This same Jesus, who at birth Gabriel had forecasted would be called Son of the Most High, whom the angels praised as Christ the Lord, whom God declared his Beloved Son, whom the evil spirits identified as the Holy One of God, who Peter claimed was the Christ of God, with whom Elijah and Moses spoke while he appeared to them in his transfigured Glory, and who considered himself the Spirit's equal (cf. Luke 21:15), was to die the ignoble death of a criminal.

Luke uses the citation mainly for contrast. Although innocent, Jesus was to be counted among transgressors (ἀνόμων, i.e., the lawless, the rebellious), who were, according to Isaiah, the whole human race.[93] It also reveals the extent of Jesus' obedient service. Jesus knows what is before him: his death will have universal implications and form the lowest point of his humiliation. At issue

---

[92] Fitzmyer, *Luke X–XXIV*, p. 988.
[93] See esp. Knight, *Deutero-Isaiah*, p. 243.

here is not whether Jesus' death was vicarious or not. For the emphatic nature of Jesus' self-identification with the Isaiah passage – considered as "one of the strongest fulfilment formulae ever uttered by Jesus" – naturally suggests that Jesus, at least according to Luke, has all of Isa. 53 in view.[94] Luke points out here that the depth of Jesus' suffering parallels the depth of his obedience. He undeservedly but willingly approaches the cross in full recognition of what lay before him. As importantly, then, Luke's audience reads this in full knowledge of who Jesus is and most probably in full knowledge of the soteriological interpretation of his death as saving![95]

The force of Luke's post-resurrection account lies in Jesus' appearance as the glorified servant. Luke pictures for the first time in his Gospel – and the only time in the synoptic tradition – the disciples coming to understand the true christological meaning of Jesus, a meaning inseparably linked to his suffering. In ch. 24 the suffering motif appears at three prominent points: the two messengers to the women at the tomb (24:7), Jesus to the two disciples on the Emmaus road (vv. 25–27), and Jesus to the twelve in Jerusalem (vv. 44–46). In the first instance Jesus appears as the suffering Son of Man, in the other two as the suffering Christ. The first saying essentially rehearses Jesus' Son of Man passion predictions (esp. 9:22; 18:31–33). The other two form the only occasions in the synoptic tradition where Jesus explicitly states that "the Christ" would suffer. The divine illumination for his followers in the latter two instances comes in the recognition that Jesus as the Christ had to suffer before being glorified.

The most illustrative of these instances for our discussion is the Emmaus episode. The *crux interpretum* is that Jesus' messiahship would ultimately entail suffering. It was of divine necessity, as Jesus had intimated. But such a concept was apparently virtually non-existent in pre-Christian Jewish literature.[96] This may partially explain why Jesus' followers could not make the connection between his death and a saving work of God (24:20–21). The concept of a

---

[94] France, "Servant of the Lord," pp. 30–32 (quot. p. 31); also Taylor, *Passion Narrative*, p. 138; Seccombe, "Luke and Isaiah," pp. 256–58.

[95] In view of the strong probability of presumed knowledge of the cross, to conclude as does Hultgren, *Christ and His Benefits*, pp. 85–89, that, for Luke, "the cross is not regarded as the decisive moment at which sin or sins and their consequences were borne once for all for the benefit of others" (p. 86) seems less compelling.

[96] Hengel, *Atonement*, pp. 40–44; Marshall, *Luke*, pp. 896–97; Fitzmyer, *Luke I–IX*, p. 200 *et al.*

suffering Christ most likely resulted from Jesus' fusing, according
to Luke at least, the portrait of David's messiah with Isaiah's
suffering servant[97] and the Deuteronomic prophet-like Moses. This
principle of inclusion sheds more light, then, on the meaning of ἐπὶ
πᾶσιν οἷς ἐλάλησαν οἱ προφῆται in v. 25.

The principle of inclusion, therefore, involves an unusual fusing
of diverse, apparently unrelated OT portraits to Jesus' person and
work. For Luke especially, Jesus did this to teach his followers
how he had in an entirely unexpected way personally become
their salvation.[98] As David's messiah, he powerfully intervened
on behalf of Israel – and the world – but not in delivering them
from their enemies as expected but in taking on the role of a
servant, who would be humiliated to the point of death on a
cross.

4.   *Early church preaching.*   In the early church preaching in Acts,
Luke also features Jesus' obedient service and his humiliation-
exaltation in the message preached: e.g., Peter's speech at Pentecost
(2:14–36, vv. 21–36), in Solomon's Colonnade (3:12–26, vv. 13–18,
20, 22–26), and before the Sanhedrin (4:8–12, vv. 10–11, also vv.
24–30; 5:29–32, vv. 30–31); and to Cornelius (10:34–43, vv. 36–43);
Stephen's speech (7:2–53, vv. 51–53, also vv. 54–60); Philip's speech
(8:30–35); and Paul's speech at Pisidian Antioch (13:16–41, vv. 16–
37), before the Areopagus in Athens (17:22–31, v. 31) and King
Agrippa (26:2–23, v. 23!).

In view of Jesus' explanation that the Christ must suffer (Luke
24), Luke also implies the suffering and humiliation–exaltation
themes in his summary statements in Acts that "Christ is being
preached" (8:5; 9:22; 17:3; 18:5; 18:28; 24:24; 28:31). E.g., according
to Acts 17:2–3, Paul customarily went to the synagogue "to explain
and prove that the Christ had to suffer and rise from the dead."
Within Acts, even to mention merely that Christ was preached
seems intended to call forth in the reader's mind the image of the
serving nature of the Lord Jesus as the Christ.

The same conclusion may also hold true for speeches which
mention Jesus as servant. "For Luke, the primary ... significance
of the Servant is to be found in the fact that he suffers."[99] Peter
explicitly refers to Jesus as "the Servant of God" (ὁ παῖς τοῦ θεοῦ),

---

[97] Fitzmyer, *Luke I–IX*, pp. 200, 212.
[98] For more on the concept of redemption in Luke–Acts, see Marshall, "Develop-
      ment of Redemption," pp. 239–41.
[99] Franklin, *Christ the Lord*, p. 61.

on two occasions (3:13, 26; 4:27, 30). The connection in these contexts between Jesus' servanthood and suffering recalls the Gospel fusing of Jesus with the Isaianic and Deuteronomic images. Acts 3:18, e.g., is reminiscent of Jesus' very words: "But this is how God fulfilled what he had foretold through *all the prophets, saying that his Christ would suffer*" (also 26:23; cf. Luke 24:25–27, 44–46). Philip explains Jesus to the Ethiopian eunuch in terms of Isaiah's suffering servant (8:32–35; Isa. 53:7–8) – at least in underscoring Jesus' humiliation and innocent suffering (cf. Luke 22:37).[100] Peter and Stephen speak of Jesus as "the prophet-like Moses" (3:21–23; 7:37; cf. Deut. 18:15). Peter (3:14), Stephen (7:52), and Paul (22:14) refer to Jesus as the Righteous One. Δίκαιος probably links up here to some degree with the δικαιῶσαι δίκαιον of Isa. 53:11,[101] rather than only with the more general righteous sufferer of Judaism.[102]

But if Jesus' servanthood was so important to Luke, why did he refrain from introducing much atonement language in the speeches? The answer most likely has to do with his desire to show how Jesus' life stands as an ethical model for believers. As with Paul's Philippians correspondence, Luke's readers probably also know full well the atoning value of Jesus' death. Their faith is undoubtedly premised on it (so Luke 22:19–20; Acts 20:28). Luke probably consciously avoids much reference to it so as not to confuse Jesus' death as saving with the deaths of the believers, he documents in Acts (Stephen, James) – or the death of any believer for that matter. Jesus' death is unique in this regard. Luke writes to show how Jesus' conformity to the cross was imaged in especially Peter, Stephen, and Paul's ministries. Luke goes to great lengths to show that Christian witness is more than verbally confessing Christ; it is "living as the master lived." We see a good example of this in the way Paul identifies Jesus (26:23) with himself as "servant and witness" (26:16–18). Herein lies a primary reason why Luke wrote: to show *how the life of the believer should image the message preached*, a writing aim that has everything to do with living as Jesus lived. The following three points further substantiate this.

---

[100] So Hooker, *Jesus and the Servant*, pp. 113–14.

[101] Franklin, *Christ the Lord*, pp. 62–63; Rigaux, *Dieu l'a ressuscité*, p. 80; Seccombe, "Luke and Isaiah," p. 257; Green, "Death of Jesus," pp. 19–21.

[102] Cf., e.g., Schweizer, *Erniedrigung und Erhöhung*, pp. 21–33, 53–62; Karris, "Jesus' Death," pp. 68–78, 187–89.

The sayings of Jesus and discipleship

A peculiarity of the speeches in Acts is that except for two general allusions (11:16; 20:35), none mention any logia of Jesus. Nor does Luke intimate in the book that the early church did so.[103] Acts gives the impression that the early church did not incorporate dominical sayings into its preaching and teaching. But the very existence of the gospel tradition itself suggests otherwise, a tradition which Luke, of course, knew well. It also seems that the disciples, especially those who were with Jesus from John's baptism to the ascension, would have appealed to it in defending the gospel before Jewish authorities or would have used it in substantiating and supplementing Christian teaching. Why, then, did Luke, who obviously had considerable sayings material at his disposal, refrain from using any of it in the testimony of Jesus' followers about their Lord? The answer most probably lies in Luke's desire to depict what it means to follow Jesus.

From a synoptic comparison of Mark and Luke, we see that Luke's Gospel contains considerably more teaching of Jesus. Its uniform emphasis is on *discipleship*. Ernest Best strongly argues for a positive role of discipleship in Mark.[104] Mark equates the disciples with the church and, accordingly, sees Jesus' actions and sayings as correlated to Christian living. Luke greatly expands this picture. He sharpens a number of Markan sayings on discipleship and supplements his Gospel with much new material on this theme – sayings shared with Matthew not found in Mark (Q) and sayings unique to Luke (L).[105]

In addition to the Markan sayings on discipleship which Luke has retained relatively unchanged (e.g., the interpretation of the parable of the sower, Luke 8:11–15; Mark 4:13–20; Matt. 13:18–23; the call to follow Jesus Luke 9:23–27; Mark 8:34–9:1; Matt. 16:24–28; the story of the rich young ruler, Luke 18:18–23; Mark 10:17–22; Matt. 19:16–22; and Jesus' teaching on riches and rewards of discipleship, Luke 18:24–30; Mark 10:23–31; Matt. 19:23–30), he shows a tendency to sharpen other sayings in Mark where the discipleship aspect is less clear. First, in the parable of the sower (Luke 8:4–8; cf. Mark 4:1–9; Matt. 13:1–9), Luke slightly alters Mark to emphasize the need to respond rightly to God's

---

[103] See further Robinson, "Theological Context," p. 31 and lit. cited in n. 46.
[104] Best, "Role," pp. 396–401.
[105] See also Martin, "Salvation and Discipleship," p. 380.

word.[106] Second, in the illustration of "a lamp on a stand" (Luke 8:16–18; cf. Mark 4:21–25), Luke specifically mentions the disciples as Jesus' audience and combines the story with the preceding saying on discipleship (Jesus' interpretation of "the parable of the sower," 8:11–15), whereas Mark directs the saying to the crowds and loosely connects it to the similar foregoing episode (Mark 4:13–20).[107] Third, in Jesus' teaching on "true greatness" (Luke 9:46–48; also Matt. 18:1–5; cf. Mark 9:33–37), Luke alters Mark to make the main lesson of the story, "for he who is least among you all, he is the greatest," its fitting climax as well.[108] Fourth, "Jesus' blessing of the little children" Luke places in a series of dominical sayings specifically related to discipleship (Luke 18:15–17; cf. 18:1–8, 9–14, 18–30), whereas Mark (10:13–16; also Matt. 19:13–15) places it after a couple of sayings on marriage and divorce (Mark 10:1–9, 10–12; also Matt. 19:1–9, 10–12).[109] The last and perhaps the most influential example, as we have already seen, is Luke's reshaping of Mark's Nazareth story in content and narrative sequence for his Gospel and Acts.

Luke has also incorporated into his Gospel a large collection of sayings and incidents attributed to Jesus not found in Mark on the theme of discipleship. This holds true for *all* of the Q material and *all* of the L material associated with Jesus' teaching. It also includes *all* the healing incidents of Jesus' ministry of L, further revealing Luke's intended use of Jesus' self-fulfillment of the Isaiah citations in 4:18–19, a passage also unique to Luke. Luke 7:22; 16:16–17 (Q) and 13:32 (L) also resemble Jesus' self-pronouncement in the Nazareth episode. Jesus' healing of the centurion's servant (7:1–10 Q), the widow of Nain's son (7:12–17 L), the crippled woman (13:10–17 L), the man suffering from dropsy (14:1–6 L), and the ten lepers (17:12–18 L) each illustrate and substantiate his claim at Nazareth that he would heal the sick.

In supplementing Mark on Jesus' teaching, Luke has selected sayings relating to discipleship. He has done so to give his readers a clear and rich statement on what it means to follow Jesus. Luke strengthens this picture in Acts by showing the disciples powerfully *imaging* Jesus' message in their own ministries. While the disciples

---

[106] So, e.g., Marshall, *Luke*, pp. 318–19; Nolland, *Luke 1–9:20*, p. 376.
[107] So, e.g., Marshall, *Luke*, p. 327; Fitzmyer, *Luke I–IX*, pp. 718–19.
[108] So, e.g., Marshall, *Luke*, p. 395; Schneider, *Lukas. 1–10*, pp. 222–23; Fitzmyer, *Luke I–IX*, pp. 815–16.
[109] So, e.g., Marshall, *Luke*, p. 681.

had difficulty following Jesus during his earthly ministry, because of human and divine factors, Acts depicts a different story altogether. The nature of the speeches themselves illustrates this. Here the disciples appear boldly preaching, ably defending themselves, and successfully testifying about Jesus in their own words. Because of the Spirit's presence within them, their words and actions now carry divine authority. Jesus still speaks, but now through them (cf. Acts 1:1). As he came speaking with authority, so now do his followers!

In Acts, Luke exemplifies in writing the pattern of Christ-like discipleship in the lives of Peter, Stephen, and especially Paul. The early church's preaching and life powerfully image Jesus' teaching on discipleship and life. The disciples had become like their master in public debate, preaching the good news, going to outsiders (Gentiles), exorcizing demons, healing the sick, strengthening his followers, standing trial, and so on. Luke–Acts reveals no gulf between the earthly Jesus and the resurrected Christ – Jesus Christ is still speaking, only now through his disciples (e.g., Acts 26:23).

Within Luke's Gospel, therefore, we can satisfactorily explain the reshaping of the Nazareth episode and inclusion of extra sayings of Jesus as a deliberate attempt to expound the theme of Jesus' servanthood and teaching on discipleship. One other prominent but unique literary feature of Luke's Gospel, which we can explain on similar grounds, is *the way of Jesus* as particularly seen in his journey to Jerusalem in 9:51–19:27.

The way of Jesus and discipleship

Scholars have well observed Luke's connection between the travel narrative and discipleship.[110] But what remains less certain is how it reveals, or at least conforms to, Luke's overall reason for writing.[111] Its prominence within the Gospel narrative suggests that it is an important piece of the puzzle.

On this matter, William C. Robinson's Basle dissertation, *Der*

---

[110] E.g., Lampe, "Portrait of Christ," p. 173; Robinson, "Theological Context"; Robinson, *Weg des Herrn*; Brown, *Apostasy and Perseverance*, pp. 131–45; Navone, *Themes*, pp. 188–98; Radl, *Paulus und Jesus*, pp. 103–31; Fitzmyer, *Luke I–IX*, pp. 241–43; Schneider, *Lukas. 1–10*, pp. 226–28 and extensive lit. cited on p. 226.

[111] See esp. Moessner's survey of its various interpretations in *Lord of the Banquet*, pp. 21–33.

Weg des Herrn (1964), has become a representative statement.[112]
Luke, he argues, intended to portray the movement of Jesus to
Jerusalem and of the gospel to Rome as two consecutive but
distinct periods of *the way of the Lord* in salvation history (pp. 8,
33–36). By depicting the worldwide advance of the Christian
message as a divinely planned and directed journey mutually
related to the way of Jesus to Jerusalem, Luke had hoped to
reassure his readers of the legitimacy of Christianity as "the true
Israel" (p. 37). But in contrast to Conzelmann, he believes that the
parousia's delay is circumstantially evident in Luke–Acts, but not
the author's primary concern (pp. 37, 45).

Robinson thinks that the keystone of Luke's theological emphasis is "the time of divine visitation" as derived from the LXX
(pp. 8–9, 50, 55–56). The way of the Lord is the way of God (pp.
42, 58). Luke, he believes, intentionally fashioned Jesus' ministry
according to the way he saw God at work in his own day. The
course of Jesus' ministry, as primarily seen in his journey to
Jerusalem and secondarily in Paul's journey to Rome, would
exemplify to Luke's own contemporaries the way of Christian
mission.

The critical weakness of his argument for the present study is the
subordinate role he assigns to Luke's christology and pneumatology in relation to *the way of the Lord* (p. 67). For Robinson,
God is the focal point. But for Luke, it is Jesus! John the Baptist
announces in the words of Isa. 40:3 that he has come to "prepare
the way for the Lord, to make straight paths for him" (Luke 3:4;
Mark 1:3; Matt. 3:3). The synoptic writers uniformly have αὐτοῦ in
the second clause in place of τοῦ θεοῦ ἡμῶν (LXX). The meaning
here is clear. The Synoptics more precisely identify *the way of
Yahweh* as *the way of Jesus*.[113]

Luke apparently intended this meaning, moreover, to hold true
for the whole of his writings, not just for Jesus' earthly ministry.[114]
He prefaces Acts, e.g., with the words that in the Gospel he wrote
"about all that Jesus began (ἤρξατο) to do and to teach" (1:1).
Apparently Luke believes that even after the exaltation Jesus

---

[112] See also Robinson, "Theological Context," pp. 20–31; esp. followed by Brown,
Apostasy and Perseverance, pp. 131–45 (with qual.) and Navone, *Themes*,
pp. 188–98.

[113] Robinson, *Weg des Herrn*, p. 39 fails to note this in discussing Isa. 40:3. But cf.
Brown, *Apostasy and Perseverance*, p. 132.

[114] *Contra*, e.g., Robinson, *Weg des Herrn*, pp. 66–67; Brown, *Apostasy and
Perseverance*, pp. 131–32, 134–42; Navone, *Themes*, pp. 196–98.

personally continues to minister in word and deed. For this reason
Luke can describe Paul's summary of his missionary campaigns in
Acts 26:23 as a work of Jesus himself. For Paul to persecute the
followers of the Way (9:2) was, in effect, to persecute Jesus (vv. 4–
5). Luke perhaps also intends to parallel Paul's journey to Jerusalem (Acts 19:21) with Jesus' journey (Luke 9:51).[115]

Luke seems convinced that Jesus' entry into history fulfills the
way of the Lord and becomes the watershed of salvation history.
The way of the Lord comes to mean more precisely *the way of Jesus*
and ultimately *the way of salvation*. But that this emphasis reveals
Luke's effort to periodize the time of Jesus and the church
according to some scheme of salvation history because of the
parousia's delay is doubtful. His concern was not so abstract. He
more likely wanted to depict in straightforward terms for the
believer what following Jesus would entail. Simply put, it means
following Jesus to the cross. Jesus' voluntary obedience to the
Father's will becomes the single most important personal attribute
to which his followers were to conform. For Luke's readers, then,
the way to the cross is the pattern for Christian living.

The principal passage is Jesus' journey to Jerusalem (Luke 9:51–
19:27). The value of this block of material is that Luke takes it from
Jesus' own life, both for confirming the pattern of voluntary
obedience and for supplying teaching on discipleship. Mark 10:32
most likely forms its conceptual background, especially in the
words ἦσαν δὲ ἐν τῇ ὁδῷ ἀναβαίνοντες εἰς Ἰεροσόλυμα, καὶ ἦν
προάγων αὐτοὺς ὁ Ἰησοῦς.[116] Mark undoubtedly understood Jesus'
way to Jerusalem as the way to suffering (cf., e.g., the repetition of
ἀναβαίνοντες εἰς Ἰεροσόλυμα, 10:32, to ἀναβαίνομεν εἰς Ἰεροσόλυμα, v. 33a, the latter a preface to his passion prediction in vv.
33b–34); that Jesus leads the way signifies as well the pattern to
which his followers were to conform. Luke apparently formalizes
Mark 10:32 into an episodic travel account (cf. also Luke 23:5).
The large collection of dominical sayings on discipleship (9:51–
18:14 is not common to Mark) and the lack of geographical detail
(the only specific place named in narrative comment from 9:51 until
Luke joins up with Mark's account in 18:35 is Jerusalem, the city of
Jesus' destiny, 13:22; 17:11) suggest that he has created a literary
vehicle composed of traditional material from Jesus' life and

[115] See further, e.g., Radl, *Paulus und Jesus*, pp. 103–26.
[116] See further Robinson, *Weg des Herrn*, pp. 38–39. For its meaning about discipleship in Mark, see Schweizer, *Erniedrigung und Erhöhung*, pp. 12–13.

teaching to convey what discipleship means. That the cross looms over the whole account (cf. 9:51), the destiny toward which Jesus voluntarily and obediently moves, is itself indicative of Luke's intention: *the way of the Lord is the way of Jesus; the way of discipleship is to follow Jesus in that way.*

Luke uniquely enhances this Gospel picture by associating the way of Jesus and the travel narrative with the OT exodus motif. At Jesus' transfiguration – itself an image of Mt. Sinai – Moses and Elijah appear and speak about Jesus' approaching ἔξοδον in 9:31, i.e., the death he would soon undergo in Jerusalem.[117] The term ἔξοδος recalls Moses' leading of Israel out of Egypt. Luke parallels Jesus' approaching passion with perhaps the greatest OT example of God's saving work in Israel's history. This powerful OT image superbly defines Luke's soteriological emphasis, one which in Luke–Acts is inseparable from *the way of Jesus* and the author's discipleship interests.

E. M. B. Green summarily defines the OT conditions of salvation as "a humble recognition of our total inadequacy to save ourselves, a firm trust in God and prayer to him in an attitude of willingness to obey his will" (Green, *Salvation*, p. 25). Two factors stand out here. First, salvation comes only from God. Second, willing obedience is the necessary human response. The exodus represents Yahweh's redemption of Israel. Israel, in turn, is now to live in a way befitting the person, teaching and work of Yahweh its Redeemer. Jer. 7:23, in referring to the exodus, nicely sums it up: "Obey me, and I will be your God and you will be my people. *Walk in all the ways I command you* [καὶ πορεύεσθε ἐν πάσαις ταῖς ὁδοῖς μου, αἷς ἂν ἐντείλωμαι ὑμῖν, LXX], that it may go well with you" (also Deut. 5:33). Here the way of the Lord describes the pattern of divine deliverance and corresponding obedience.

In Luke–Acts, the author asserts that divine deliverance comes only through Jesus' suffering, death, and resurrection. The exodus motif in Luke 9:31 seems intended to make this clear. In Luke's case, however, the divine deliverer is Jesus! "Salvation is found in no one else, for there is no other name under heaven given to men by which we must be saved" (Acts 4:12). In this, Jesus and Moses are not parallel figures. The OT *never* attributed Israel's redemption

---

[117] Luke's journey account seems replete with imagery descriptive of Israel's journey according to Deuteronomy. See, e.g., Evans, "Central Section," pp. 37–53; Minear, *To Heal and To Reveal*, pp. 102–21, esp. pp. 110–11; Moessner, *Lord of the Banquet*, pp. 46–70.

from Egypt to Moses, but *always* to God (cf. esp. Hos. 12:13 to 13:4–5; also Ps. 77:13–20; 105:1–45); but Luke–Acts attributes salvation *both* to God (Luke 1:47) and Jesus (Luke 2:11; Acts 5:31; 13:23).

In conformity to the OT picture of salvation and obedience, Luke summons Jesus' followers to live according to the person, teaching, and work of their divine deliverer. But in this instance the pattern of obedience is revealed in the person of the divine deliverer himself: in the servanthood of the Lord Jesus. For Luke, the way of the Lord images the OT exodus pattern of divine deliverance and corresponding obedience; but what is different is that both elements are fulfilled in Jesus.

Luke–Acts attests to the reality that in Jesus divine deliverance is ultimately fulfilled and that in Jesus the "how to" of discipleship is ultimately displayed. The account of Jesus' journey to the cross provides the most illustrative statement. Thus to conclude from Luke's travel narrative that,

> For Luke Christian discipleship is portrayed not only as the acceptance of a master's teaching, but as the identification of oneself with the master's way of life and destiny in an intimate, personal following of him. Because of the geographical perspective in the Gospel, the "following" has a pronounced spatial nuance: The disciple must walk in the footsteps of Jesus[118]

hits at the author's intention for Luke–Acts itself.

In fitting parallel, *the way of Jesus* is, according to the Christ hymn in Phil. 2, *the way of voluntary humiliation* even to the point of death on a cross and *depending on God's* raising him from the dead, returning him to his former exalted position. Discipleship, then, is following in the master's footsteps of willing obedience and having the same hope of resurrection. Similarly for Luke, the fact that the disciples made converts and that the gospel spread from Jerusalem to Rome shows that Jesus' followers were obediently personalizing their master's teachings and the eschatological hope which their obedience nurtured. The Christian movement can, therefore, without compromise be called "The Way" (Acts 9:2; 19:9, 23; 22:4; 24:14, 22), for it is none other than *the way of Jesus*.

---

[118] Fitzmyer, *Luke I–IX*, pp. 241–43 (quot. p. 241).

Jesus and The Acts of the Apostles

The one remaining monumental feature of Luke's writings, which we have yet to consider, is the book of Acts itself. What was Luke's primary reason for writing it? I believe that the thesis that I am proposing adequately explains why he did so.

The title "The Acts of the Apostles" for Luke's second volume has come under fire among Lukan scholars as seemingly irrelevant to the content of the book and to the author's intention for the double work as stated in the Gospel preface.[119] The designation, e.g., tells us little about "The Acts of *all* the Apostles." We read only of Peter and Paul, the latter not one of the twelve and mentioned only in passing as an apostle (14:4, 14). "The traditional designation of "The Acts of the Apostles',' William Willimon concludes, "fails to tell us much about the purpose of the work at hand."[120]

Contrary to this perspective, I believe that a more positive view is possible. Luke's main focus for Acts was to substantiate the pattern of Christian discipleship as imaged in Jesus' life as in the Gospel. The Acts of the Apostles, therefore, continues Jesus' life and teaching, but now through the life and work of the early church. Paul's letter to the Philippians stands as a suitable NT parallel to this literary endeavor. The fact that Luke focuses on a select number of individuals, most not of the twelve, does not mitigate against the book's title; instead, he underscores in several concentrated cases what was typical of the apostles and leaders of the early church, as he seems to have done with Jesus' teaching and work in the Gospel as well.

A key idea here is that of witness. We saw in ch. 7 that the term "witness" in Acts can rightly be understood as the presentation of facts – i.e., evidence – to authenticate the viability of the Christian movement as a work of God in the last days and as a gospel confession of Jesus as savior. But Luke apparently understands these meanings as part of a deeper, more encompassing definition of witness.

Acts 1:1 is instructive in this regard. Luke informs Theophilus that in the first book he recounted for him all that Jesus "began" (ἤρξατο) to do and teach. The verb is important. Its suggests that all that follows continues Jesus' ministry, only now through the

---

[119] So, e.g., Pesch, *Apg. 1–12*, pp. 22–23.
[120] Willimon, *Acts*, p. 8.

disciples.[121] Luke, however, does not mean by this that the disciples would merely carry on in the spirit of Jesus' ministry but that they themselves, now empowered with his Spirit, would image him. As the resurrected Jesus "gave his followers many convincing proofs that he was alive" (Acts 1:3), so now his followers become that proof to the world (so 1:8!). Jesus reigns in heaven and at present is no longer visible in the world as he was during his earthly career. But to see his followers is tantamount to seeing Jesus himself!

It is doubtful, however, whether Luke or his readers understood Acts as an idealization, i.e., a fictitious picture, of early Christianity.[122] Luke certainly exercised some editorial freedoms (e.g., in the speeches) to emphasize certain elements best suiting his literary objectives. *But that this material was largely fiction based on a few scraps of early church tradition would be counterproductive to his literary effort. Rather the strength of his work is that what he documents had actually happened in the early church and was, in fact, perhaps still verifiable to his audience.* He was not creating idealized examples of Christian disciples, but more likely documenting "flesh and blood examples."

Furthermore, if Luke in fact wrote to assure his readers of things they had been taught (Luke 1:4), his writings most likely represent a selected portion of that teaching. For this reason, it is doubtful whether Luke meant to give the impression in Acts that Paul's missionary work was trouble-free. This apparent dichotomy between Acts and Paul's own writings may have arisen as a simple accident of history, largely stemming from our ignorance of the amount of knowledge that Luke had in common with his readers. Many of the difficulties Paul faced, as mentioned in his writings, were probably well known to Luke's readers – even if Paul himself was not, as many would argue – given the extent of Paul's travels, the many major cities where he had worked, and the many personal and sometimes influential contacts he had made along the way.[123]

We should read Acts against this backdrop. Luke focuses on

---

[121] Recently, e.g., Franklin, *Christ the Lord*, p. 64 and n. 29; Marshall, *Acts*, p. 56; O'Toole, *Unity*, p. 63; Ogilvie, *Acts*, p. 24; see also Dörner, *Heil Gottes*, p. 110, n. 110 for further lit. in this regard. For a brief summary of other possible readings, see Roloff, *Apg.*, p. 19.

[122] Cf., e.g., Talbert, *Luke and the Gnostics*, p. 92.

[123] This factor should not be ignored in assessing Luke's treatment of Paul in Acts; cf., e.g., Lentz, *Portrait of Paul*, p. 107.

episodes from the life and ministry of a number of individuals and incidents illustrating how the early church imaged Jesus. Although his readers may not be able to emulate their specific deeds in every instance for whatever reason – i.e., miracles, tongues, visions, and so on – they can emulate the apostles' conformity to Jesus' behavior and attitudes so that Jesus will be revealed in them as well.

Modern research has taken great interest in pointing out the many parallels between Jesus and the early church's witness in Luke–Acts.[124] The parallels pertain to Jesus' person, work, and life.[125] Peter, Stephen, and Paul stand in Acts as Luke's primary examples. Luke uses the same vocabulary and concepts to describe Jesus and his followers (esp. O'Toole, pp. 79–82). In fact, as Jesus appears as "the prophet-like Moses," his followers appear as "prophets-like Jesus."[126]

Since others have already pointed out many of these parallels, it is unnecessary to rehearse them in detail here. Instead, we shall note how Luke develops the themes of Luke 4:16–30 in Acts. This examination will sufficiently illustrate how these parallels reveal his literary intentions for Acts.

The Nazareth story has almost as much relevance for describing the church's witness in Acts as it does for Jesus' ministry in the Gospel.[127] As Jesus proclaimed the good news and hinted at its universal appeal, healed the sick and demon-afflicted, and encountered hostility because of the message he preached, so does the church. This equation seems deliberate on Luke's part. Jesus becomes the paradigm for the church. He revealed in his life and passion work mainly to Jews in Palestine how the reality, meaning, and significance of these elements were fulfilled in him; the church

---

[124] Lampe, "Portrait of Christ," pp. 174–75; Simon, *Stephen*, pp. 20–26; Scharlemann, *Stephen*, pp. 86–90; Dietrich, *Petrusbild*, pp. 327–32; Reicke, "Jesus in Nazareth," pp. 51–53; Stolle, *Zeuge als Angeklagter*; Mattill, "Evans," pp. 15–46; Radl, *Paulus und Jesus*; Minear, *To Heal and To Reveal*, pp. 122–47; Muhlack, *Parallelen*; Maddox, *Purpose*, pp. 79–80; Cosgrove, "Divine δεῖ," pp. 172–87; O'Toole, "Parallels," pp. 195–212; O'Toole, *Unity*, pp. 62–94; Talbert, "Discipleship," pp. 62–75; Talbert, *Literary Patterns*, pp. 16–18; Talbert, *Reading Luke*, pp. 54–57, 186–87; Tannehill, *Luke*, pp. 60–73; Brawley, *Jews*, pp. 24–25; Moessner, *Lord of the Banquet*, pp. 296–307; Moessner, "Parallels," pp. 250–53; Barrett, "Imitatio Christi," pp. 251–62.

[125] See further O'Toole, *Unity*, pp. 62–94.

[126] Minear, *To Heal and To Reveal*, pp. 122–47; also Moessner, *Lord of the Banquet*, pp. 296–307.

[127] E.g., Radl, *Paulus und Jesus*, pp. 82–100; Muhlack, *Parallelen*, pp. 117–39; Talbert, *Reading Luke*, pp. 55–56; Cosgrove, "Divine δεῖ," pp. 179–83; Brawley, *Jews*, pp. 24–25.

revealed them, in his name, to the rest of the world. Although many throughout the world had never known the earthly Jesus or at least had never met him, they now learn of him and see him through the lives of his followers.

A most outstanding piece of evidence supporting Luke's deliberate use of the Nazareth story to parallel the early church's witness in Acts with Jesus' ministry in the Gospel is *the working of miracles.*[128] Luke mentions that the apostles (2:43; 5:12), Stephen (6:8), Philip (8:6–7, 13), and Barnabas (14:3) worked miracles in addition to Peter and Paul, but he specifically illustrates them within the ministries of Peter (3:1–10; 5:1–11; 9:32–35; 9:36–42) and Paul (13:4–12; 14:8–11; 16:16–19; 20:7–12; 28:7–8).[129] In describing some of these, he details that the lame beggar in Jerusalem was forty years old (4:22) and crippled since birth (3:2); that Aeneas of Lydda was a paralytic, bedridden for eight years (9:33); that Dorcas (Tabitha) of Joppa was dead, her body already being prepared for burial (9:37); and that the lame man in Derbe had never walked (14:8). According to Luke, the healings defy normal explanation. But he, nonetheless, seems convinced that they genuinely happened; he gives the impression that they were not made up, fraudulent, or explainable on psychosomatic grounds. His reserved manner of documenting these incidents further implies that, if pressed, others could substantiate the validity of these happenings as well: the two lame men were well known by the inhabitants of their cities (3:2, 9–10; 4:14; 14:8, 11) and Luke specifically mentions the other two by name and place of residence. "It is reasonable to insist," Hemer comments, "that Luke needed to authenticate his case [about miracles] before educated and sophisticated readers, fully capable, *mutatis mutandis*, of subjecting him to keenly critical assessments."[130]

For Luke the only satisfactory explanation is Jesus. As miracles had revealed and confirmed Jesus' person and work in his earthly life, they continue to do so to people now through his followers (so also esp. Heb. 2:2–3).[131] Luke features Peter and Paul as his two outstanding examples (so esp. Acts 5:15–16; 19:11–12).

---

[128] For a good discussion of miracles in Acts, see Hemer, *Hellenistic History*, pp. 428–43.

[129] For a comprehensive listing of the specific miracles performed and of summary references to the working of miracles in Acts, see, e.g., Pesch, *Apg. 1–12*, pp. 141–48; Hemer, *Hellenistic History*, pp. 433–38.

[130] Hemer, *Hellenistic History*, p. 440, also p. 85.

[131] In this sense, the revelatory value of miracles in the Gospel and Acts, for Luke, is

In connection to the Nazareth story, a similar comparison holds true for the suffering of hostilities. Luke concentrates here as well on the "acts" of Peter and Paul (and Stephen).

Luke also closely images Jesus' voluntary submission to God's will with believers in Acts. We have seen in connection to the Nazareth story Luke uniquely highlighting two elements in this regard: (1) Jesus knows that he will suffer and die, and (2) he actively brings it about. Acts reiterates these same traits of obedience to God but now in the lives of Jesus' followers. Luke's chief examples are Peter, Stephen, and Paul. Peter's exclamation to the Sanhedrin, "We [all the apostles] must obey God rather than men!" (5:29; also 4:18–20), characterizes the tone of his entire ministry as portrayed in Acts. Stephen strikingly resembles Jesus in his ministry, death, and hope of resurrection. Paul obediently fulfills his Damascus road appointment as "servant and witness" (26:16) in taking the gospel to the Gentiles (26:16). The many parallels Luke draws between Jesus' life and these men impressively reinforce this point.[132]

Luke, furthermore, develops pneumatology and soteriology in Acts to substantiate the correspondence between the obedience of Jesus and his followers to God's plan. E.g., concerning the Spirit, Peter says to the Sanhedrin: "We are witnesses of these things [God's plan in Jesus], and so is the Holy Spirit, whom God has given to those who obey him" (Acts 5:32, cf. v. 29). The Spirit's presence among believers in Acts, in effect, reveals their obedience in accepting/believing the gospel. Thus the promised Spirit (Luke

virtually identical. Conzelmann's belief in *Theology of St. Luke*, p. 193, n. 2, followed by Schneider, *Apg. 1, 1–8, 40*, p. 308, that miracles recede to secondary importance in Acts because of hermeneutical implications owing to Luke's alleged demarcation between the periods of Jesus and the church is doubtful.

[132] In reference to Peter: Dietrich, *Petrusbild*, pp. 327–32; Minear, *To Heal and To Reveal*, pp. 141–42; Muhlack, *Parallelen*, pp. 27–31, 39–54, 125–31; O'Toole, "Some Observations," pp. 85–92; Moessner, "Parallels," pp. 250–53. In reference to *Stephen*: Simon, *Stephen*, pp. 20–26; Hasler, "Jesu Selbstzeugnis," pp. 36–47; Scharlemann, *Stephen*; Minear, *To Heal and To Reveal*, p. 140; O'Toole, *Unity*, pp. 63–67; Moessner, "Parallels," pp. 250–53; Moessner, *Lord of the Banquet*, pp. 299–301. In reference to *Paul*: Reicke, "Jesus in Nazareth," pp. 51–53; Stolle, *Zeuge als Angeklagter*; Mattill, "Evans," pp. 15–46; Radl, *Paulus und Jesus*; Minear, *To Heal and To Reveal*, pp. 142–47; Muhlack, *Parallelen*, pp. 31–36, 131–35; Talbert, *Reading Luke*, pp. 186–87; Maddox, *Purpose*, pp. 79–80 (with qual.); Cosgrove, "Divine δεῖ," pp. 172–87; O'Toole, *Unity*, pp. 67–72; Moessner, "Parallels," pp. 250–53; Moessner, *Lord of the Banquet*, pp. 297–99; Kilgallen, "Persecution," pp. 157–59. In reference to *Philip*: Minear, *To Heal and To Reveal*, pp. 140–41; Spencer, *Philip*, esp. pp. 104–107 and lit. cited in O'Toole, "Parallels," p. 196, n. 5.

3:16–17; 24:49; Acts 1:4–5) now often operates in them as he did in Jesus (Luke 3:21–22; 4:18).[133] Accordingly, refusing to believe the gospel is tantamount to disobeying the Spirit of God (so, e.g., Acts 7:51–53). Moreover, as we have seen with the exodus motif in the OT, Luke at times considers salvation and obedience as virtually synonymous themes. E.g., Luke writes that "many priests became obedient to the faith" (Acts 6:7). As Israel was to obey God in light of his redemption of them from Egypt (cf. Jer. 7:23), in Acts Israel must now do the same in light of God's final redemption of all humankind in Jesus. To become obedient to the faith is to believe in the gospel (also a common NT perspective; e.g., Rom. 15:18; 16:26; 2 Thess. 1:8; Heb. 5:9; 1 Pet. 4:17; 1 John 2:3; 3:24). In doing so, the Israelites too become disciples, i.e., followers, of Jesus. Jesus' announcement in Luke 4:18 that he would bring sight to the blind, merged with the hinted at universal appeal (vv. 24–27),[134] foreshadows metaphorically in Acts the perception of divine revelation and salvation by all nations (so esp. Acts 13:47; 26:18, 23).[135] Luke records in Acts twenty-seven separate instances of people responding in faith.[136] The conversions prove the disciples' obedient service to God and image Jesus' work (e.g., 26:22–23).

The act of proclamation itself shows a similar correspondence. E.g, Peter replies to the Sanhedrin: "Judge for yourselves whether it is right in God's sight to obey you rather than God. For we cannot help speaking about what we have seen and heard" (Acts 4:19–20; also, e.g., 5:29–32; 26:19–20). Acts contains thirty-nine occurrences of preaching and defending this message.[137] Here again the likely Gospel antecedent is Luke 4:18. Jesus identifies himself as *the proclaimer of the good news* in Isa. 61:1 (see also Luke 4:43; 7:22;

---

[133] See further, e.g., Tannehill, "Mission of Jesus," pp. 68–69; Talbert, *Reading Luke*, pp. 55–56; O'Toole, *Unity*, pp. 79–80; Brawley, *Jews*, p. 24; in reference to Pentecost in particular, see the extensive lit. cited in Menzies, *Early Christian Pneumatology*, p. 162, n. 1. But this is not to overlook the differences as well. For a helpful caution in this regard, see Turner, "Jesus and the Spirit," pp. 3–42.

[134] See esp. Dupont, "Theological Significance," p. 22.

[135] See esp. Tannehill, *Luke*, pp. 66–67; also Hamm, "Sight to the Blind," pp. 457–77; Crump, *Jesus the Intercessor*, p. 41.

[136] Acts 2:41; 3:16; 4:4; 5:14; 6:7; 8:13; 9:31; 9:35; 9:42; 10:44–48 (11:17); 11:21; 11:24; 13:12; 13:48; 14:1; 14:8–10; 14:21; 16:5; 16:13–14; 16:31–34; 17:4; 17:12; 17:34; 18:8; 19:20; 21:20; 28:24.

[137] Acts 2:14–39; 3:11–26; 4:1–2, 8–12, 18–20; 4:31; 4:33; 5:29–32; 5:42; 6:2–4, 7; 7:2–53; 8:4; 8:5–6; 8:25; 8:40; 9:22, 27; 9:28–29; 10:34–43 (11:13–15); 11:20; 13:5; 13:16–41; 14:3; 14:6–7; 14:21; 14:25; 16:13; 16:32; 17:13; 17:16–31; 18:4–5; 18:19–21; 18:28; 19:8–10; 20:24; 22:3–21; 23:1–6; 24:10–21; 25:8–11; 26:2–29; 28:23; 28:31.

8:1; 16:16). And as anticipated in Luke 2:10–11, "the good news that will be for all people" is that Jesus is the Savior, the Christ, and the Lord.

For this reason, Luke probably deliberately describes the gospel in Acts as "the good news" (13:32), "the good news about Jesus" (8:35), "the good news about Jesus and the resurrection" (17:18), "the good news about the Lord Jesus" (11:20), "the good news of peace" (10:36), "the good news of the kingdom of God" (8:12), and "the good news that Jesus is the Christ" (5:42). He does this to parallel the preached message of Jesus' followers in Acts with what Jesus announced of himself in the Gospel. The disciples' preaching in Acts discloses once again their obedient service to God.

Therefore, in light of Luke 4, the conclusion of Luke's Gospel in Jerusalem and Acts in Rome indicates that both Jesus and his followers obeyed the divine plan. Through his thematic handling of the Nazareth story in the Gospel and Acts Luke shows how Jesus's life becomes a model for believers to follow.

Conclusion: discipleship and christology

Jacob Kremer writes that in Acts, "Christian missionaries are in essence 'witnesses of Christ.' "[138] I have sought to show that this is true in the legal sense of presenting evidence, in the kerygmatic sense of proclaiming the gospel, and, as importantly, in the way believers image Jesus to a world that has never seen him. "Luke presents the reader of his two-volume work with a consistent picture of what it means to be a Christian disciple. Jesus and his way of life are presented as examples for Christian disciples to emulate."[139] Luke's main literary concern was to give his readers a tract on Christian discipleship drawn from Jesus' life, work, and teaching, and personified in the early church.

Luke–Acts reveals an inseparable union between Jesus and the church: what Jesus began to do and teach in the Gospel he now carries on through his followers.[140] Acts exemplifies what it means to conform to the attitudes and behavior characterizing the Lord Jesus' obedient service to the Father as portrayed in the Gospel. The corollary to Jesus' servanthood is Christian discipleship. This also means that to see Jesus' followers is to know something about

---

[138] Kremer, "Weltweites Zeugnis," p. 160.
[139] Sweetland, *Journey*, p. 83, also p. 107.
[140] See further Schnackenburg, "Christologie," p. 300.

who Jesus is and what he has done! In Luke–Acts, discipleship is revealing of christology.

Herein lies Luke's special contribution to first-century Christian literature, especially in light of the addition of Acts. In contrast to Ernst Haenchen's claim that Acts "had no 'life-situation' in the church at all,"[141] Luke writes to teach readers, who most likely had never seen Jesus, how they too are to follow him as disciples. Fellowship with Christ means nothing short of following Christ, and following Christ is to walk in his footsteps.[142]

In returning, then, to the issue of christological compatibility between Luke and Paul, we have seen that the christological emphases of Luke–Acts and Philippians are remarkably similar. In these instances, the authors seem to share similar motives in writing; they attempt to show their readers *how believers are to image the servanthood of the Lord Jesus*. Believers are to image the message preached.[143] In particular, Jesus' humiliation and exaltation in Philippians, as epitomized in the Christ hymn, closely parallel the literary structure and christological emphases in Luke–Acts. The Lord Jesus' obedience in becoming a servant depicts the supreme pattern for believers to follow. A valuable feature of Luke–Acts is the way Luke depicts this teaching from Jesus' life and shows Peter, Stephen, and Paul's conformity to it.

This reason for writing additionally suggests that, like Paul in Philippians, Luke presupposed a doctrinal understanding of Jesus' death as saving rather than stressing some other soteriological viewpoint or actual bias against it. But incidentally even in this regard, the two writers closely resemble each other. As Howard Marshall has pointed out, Paul and Luke present in these respective instances the belief that the resurrection is saving in its own right.[144] Moreover, they both seem convinced that the saving importance of Jesus' death and resurrection is not repeatable. And on that basis, they exhort their readers to live as Jesus lived.

Hence, Vielhauer rightfully insists that the cross as atoning is foundational to Paul's christology and soteriology. But in view of the Luke–Acts and Philippians parallel, to demand that the evidence indicates an incompatibility between their christologies is mistaken.

---

[141] Haenchen, *Acts*, p. 9.   [142] Schweizer, *Erniedrigung und Erhöhung*, p. 76.

[143] But in doing so, neither writer compromises the uniqueness of Jesus' person and work; as Christ, Lord, and Savior, Jesus is inimitable. See further Schweizer, *Erniedrigung und Erhöhung*, pp. 126–27.

[144] Marshall, *Historian & Theologian*, p. 174.

Conclusion

12

THE CHARACTER AND PURPOSE OF
LUKE'S CHRISTOLOGY

Luke–Acts is extremely rich in christological material despite its lack of the typical Pauline phrases on atonement and union with Christ, the Markan ransom concept and the Johannine *logos* concept. Our intention in this work was to learn something of the author's personal christological convictions and why he wrote what he did about Jesus and christology in Luke–Acts.

In ch. 1 we saw that little consensus exists among Lukan scholars on this issue. There we evaluated eighteen proposals on what scholars think was Luke's *controlling* christology – a christology regulating what he writes about Jesus for the entirety of his two-volume work. These proposals ranged from christologies emphasizing Jesus' humanity and exemplary functions to ones emphasizing his subordinate relation to God, function as Savior, and authoritative status as Lord. Most of these characterizations represent genuine strands of Luke's christology (with perhaps the exception of Talbert's anti-gnostic christology, Conzelmann's christology adapted to the delay of the parousia, Braun's subordination christology, and Flender's dialectical christology). But we questioned there whether the majority of these *Leitmotive* could singly stand as his controlling christology in support of a leading literary concern.

It was our stated objective to see if we could discover whether *a single overriding concern explained the character and purpose of Luke's expressed christology*. We set for ourselves a way of cross-checking a proposal's validity against the broader context of Luke–Acts itself. For a concern to be controlling it should (1) coincide with Luke's purpose in writing, (2) plausibly explain his redactional motives, formulation of the Acts' speeches, and unique literary features of Luke–Acts, (3) resolve the ostensible christological tension within Luke–Acts between Jesus' Lordship and subordination, and above all (4) explain the character and purpose of Luke's diverse christologies.

We maintained from the outset the belief that Luke's literary concerns greatly influenced the kinds of material he incorporated into his writings. Luke states in his Gospel preface that he intended to provide his readers with a studied and well-organized account (1:3) to reassure them of what they had already been taught (v. 4). Although he says nothing explicitly about this intention in the rest of the work, Luke's stated aim greatly diminishes the possibility that he would have deliberately included material contradicting or confusing *his writing intentions*. This then obligates the modern reader to identify a writing concern which adequately explains Luke's expansive treatment of the beginnings of Christianity, without explaining away or ignoring, for one reason or another, any portion of the Gospel or Acts not conforming to the proposed concern.

The five principal proposals we examined in ch. 2 on why Luke wrote falter at this point in particular. They either lack strong textual grounds or ignore material suggesting a contrary position. We have sought to detect a Lukan concern that would account for his entire two-volume work. This would include satisfactorily explaining why Luke, in contrast to Mark (and Matthew, for the most part), began his story with a birth narrative, gave programmatic importance to the Nazareth story, added more of Jesus' teaching, developed a travel narrative, referred as he did to the cross, resurrection, ascension, and exaltation, as well as why he wrote an Acts of the Apostles, featured Peter, Stephen, and Paul in it, mentioned Jesus as he did in the preaching of the early church, and ended his account with an expanded treatment of Paul's imprisonment and trial scenes. The proposal should, moreover, be compatible with other important themes which seem integral to Luke's writing purposes (esp. religious apology, definition of Christian self-understanding, and evangelism).

In ch. 1 we observed that one particular clue was worth following up in this regard – the relation of Luke to Mark and Paul. He implicitly professes contact with these two NT writers through his use of Mark's Gospel and his contact with Paul in the we-sections of Acts. Furthermore, if, as we argued in ch. 2, Luke writes to reaffirm rather than to inform his readers about the birth of the church, this factor would considerably increase the possibility that both he and his readers shared many of the same christological beliefs. It is doubtful that he records everything he knows about Jesus' life and ministry, and christology. In all probability, he drew material which particularly strengthened his writing concerns from traditions he shared with his readers. His writing purposes very likely governed what he says christologically – a point of view which the remaining chapters of this work have substantiated.

This position enhances the possibility that he presupposes among his readers a much broader grounding in christology than he gives us in the work itself. This may, in part, explain his limited handling of the cross as saving and his virtual silence on Jesus' preexistence and the believer's union with Christ. It warns us against interpreting what Luke does and does not say too precisely – in the sense that what we read in Luke–Acts either represents his full understanding of Christ or suggests viewpoints which he endorses in opposition to other NT writers. It, in turn, warns us against constructing models too rigid to support other NT points of view (e.g., his relation to Mark's eschatology or to Paul's soteriology).

In ch. 3, we set out a possible *Sitz im Leben* for Luke's church. There we concluded on the basis of the evidence within Luke–Acts itself that Luke most likely wrote sometime *c*. AD 62–80. The life situation of his readers was probably one characterized by church issues involving spiritual maturity and perseverance, perhaps in the face of external Jewish hostility. Luke–Acts may represent a written charge to readers, somewhat akin to Paul's charge to the Ephesian elders in Acts 20:29–31, to persevere in the faith. In ch. 11, we defined more precisely what his writing concern was: to encourage fellow believers *to live as Jesus had lived*. A most intriguing NT parallel was Philippians and the Christ hymn in Phil. 2. As with Paul in his letter to the Philippians, Luke's featured christology is *the servanthood of the Lord Jesus Christ*.

In chs. 4–7 we observed that in the process of revising Mark Luke reveals something of his own christology. We saw this especially in his interaction with three fragmentary christological themes in Mark – Jesus' resurrection, giving of the Spirit, and role in salvation history. For Mark's purposes, his work was undoubtedly effective. Knowledge of what his readers already knew about Jesus' life and christology allowed him to treat these foundational christological themes in the cursory way he did. But for Luke the themes were fundamentally related to his concern to show how Jesus' humiliation and exaltation provide believers with a model of servanthood for discipleship. His writing aims demanded considerable discussion of them.

At this juncture, we distinguished between the *form* of Luke–

Acts, i.e., a revision and expansion of Mark, and the *area* of Luke–Acts, i.e., the specific issues treated, especially christology and discipleship, so as not to confuse Luke's specific reason for writing with the resulting matter of how he literarily intended to respond to it. Although Gospel writing most likely had no fixed literary form at the time Luke wrote, he took Mark as the general form for his Gospel; but the "looseness" in Gospel writing also permitted him the freedom to improve on the form of Mark's presentation for addressing his own writing concerns and to add the book of Acts, where he demonstrates the fulfillment and some of the implications of these christological themes for his readers.

In chs. 5–7 we examined Luke's handling of the major fragmentary christological themes in Mark as evidenced in Mark 9:9–10; 14:28/16:7; 16:1–8 in relation to the resurrection (ch. 5), Mark 1:8 in relation to Spirit baptism (ch. 6), and Mark 1:17; 9:9–10a; 10:45; 13:10; 14:9 in relation to salvation history (ch. 7). In each of these instances we noted that the content of Luke's Gospel reveals a deliberate improvement on the Markan theme within the limits imposed by a Gospel and that the idea of writing a second volume and some of the content and shaping of that second volume also evidences this Lukan revision.

In ch. 5 we saw that Luke heightens the role of divine providence and scriptural fulfillment concerning Jesus' passion and resurrection. Jesus' suffering was not accidental but according to divine plan. Its proof is God's raising of Jesus from the dead. In ch. 6 we observed that in developing the fulfillment of the Baptist's prophecy that "the Coming One will baptize with the Spirit" Luke gives considerably more attention to John's prophecy and to its attending christology. To write about the prophecy's fulfillment in effect requires one to write about Jesus' exaltation, i.e., his heavenly enthronement by the Father's side. In ch. 7 we explored the significance of the teaching of Mark 13:9–11 (and Lukan pars.) for the content and shaping of Acts. Acts documents their fulfillment and thus itself stands as evidence eschatologically supporting Jesus' expected imminent return.

Moreover, as we touched on at the close of these chapters, implicit in each of the themes was a key *relational* dimension: from ch. 5, the relation of "the Resurrected One" to "the One who raises him from the dead"; from ch. 6, the relation of "the Giver" to "the One Given"; and from ch. 7, the relation of "the Savior" to "salvation history and its consummation in his return."

Accordingly, in chs. 8–10, we examined what Luke discloses to us about his understanding of Jesus' relation to God the Father (ch. 8), the Holy Spirit (ch. 9), and the end of history (ch. 10). In contrast to Conzelmann's attempt to diminish the present nature and extent of Jesus' heavenly reign in Luke–Acts, we found that Luke apparently approached his work with a strong – and remarkably high – christological conviction concerning Jesus' Lordship. Luke repeatedly describes the person and activity of the exalted Jesus in language reminiscent of Yahweh in the OT. Scholars have often observed that Luke depicts the nature of Jesus' Lordship functionally rather than ontologically. But if in fact "the thought of the OT is interested in the activity of God rather than in the metaphysical problem of his being," as Lampe suggests,[1] would not Luke's presentation of Jesus as Lord also strikingly conform to this same writing emphasis? May not the kinds of conclusions we draw about God's nature and being in the OT on the basis of his activity illustrate how Luke understood the nature and being of Jesus' Lordship on the basis of his heavenly work?

At the Gospel's end and in the beginning of Acts Luke describes Jesus' return to heaven. He makes it clear that Jesus is no longer on earth guiding his followers as he had done during his earthly career. But Luke is also careful to point out that as Lord, Jesus continues to be immanently involved with his people. In ch. 8, we had argued that evidence for this lies in the way Luke parallels Jesus with Yahweh as immanent deity appearing through self-manifestation to his people. The three essential characteristics describing the nature of Yahweh's divine presence in the OT – his invisibility (i.e., transcendence), uniqueness, and personal presence and activity – closely parallel Luke's depiction of the exalted Jesus in Acts. It seems that Luke consciously describes the exalted Jesus as the Father's co-equal by showing how Jesus' heavenly work uniquely images Yahweh's. Luke apparently does not do this out of a response to some question or attack on Jesus' divine identity, but out of a personal conviction of who Jesus is.

In ch. 9 we observed that Luke pictured Jesus' relation to the Spirit in terms similar to those used of Yahweh and his Spirit in the OT. The OT clearly states that the Spirit is always closely associated with Yahweh and exclusively given by him. But according to Acts 2, Luke identifies Jesus instead of the Father as the means of

[1]   Lampe, "Holy Spirit," *IDB* 2, p. 629.

salvation (2:21; Joel 3:5 LXX) and the Giver of the Spirit (2:33). In Luke–Acts, Jesus appears alongside Yahweh as Lord of the Spirit. Luke also parallels the work of Jesus and the Spirit to that of Yahweh and his Spirit. In Acts the exalted Jesus guides the church both through his Spirit and personal manifestation at critical junctures in its mission (cf., e.g., Luke's explication of the Spirit–Christ doublet, Luke 12:12 – 21:15, in Acts). Furthermore, the unity of Jesus and the Spirit according to Acts 16:7 resembles the unity of Yahweh and his Spirit.

Lastly, in view of our discussion in ch. 7 that Luke did not abandon the expectation of Jesus' imminent return but, in fact, had preserved the eschatological sense of Mark 13:9–11 in Acts, we defended in ch. 10 the claim that Jesus appears in Acts as the Lord of world history, who is presently actively leading it to its consummation in his return. For Luke, the successful universal mission and witness of the church confirms this belief. According to Luke, the exalted Jesus now appears as Lord of the whole world: he presently reigns as *Lord* leading the course of world history to its anticipated end in his return, as *Savior* offering the hope of resurrection life to all who believe in him, and as *Judge* warning those refusing to believe the gospel of the final judgment to come.

On the basis of our findings in chs. 8–10, Luke apparently believed that the exalted Jesus shares a divine status equal to the Father's, a reality which, according to Luke, Jesus had apparently known about even during his earthly career (cf. Luke 21:15). The weight of the evidence from these chapters supports this conclusion as a feasible one, if not the probable one. The Lord Jesus seems for Luke as much God as the Father is on the basis of the kinds of things he does and says from heaven. E.g., in directing Paul's mission to the Gentiles in Acts, the exalted Jesus appears, as we have seen, as supreme in knowledge and power and guarantees his presence to Paul despite whatever difficulties Paul would face (e.g., Acts 18:9–10). That Paul arrives safely in Rome and freely preaches the gospel to all who would hear him there (cf. 28:30–31) is itself witness to this divine reality (cf. 23:11). For Luke, the Lord Jesus reigns supreme as the Father's co-equal over Israel, the church, the powers of darkness, and the world.

In ch. 11 we observed that the Christ hymn in Phil. 2 provides a fitting literary parallel to Luke's humiliation–exaltation christology. Many believe that Luke and Paul's christologies are incompatible, mainly on the grounds that Jesus' death as saving is slimly attested in Luke's writings. But the christological affinities between Luke–Acts and the Philippian letter are striking. Neither author makes much reference to the vicarious nature of the cross, but both arguably assume it in their works; and, in turn, both place the primary christological focus on *the servanthood of the Lord Jesus as the ethical model for Christian living.*

The christology of the Christ hymn in Phil. 2 finds many parallels in Luke–Acts. We have seen this in two ways. First, as with the body of the hymn in Phil. 2:6–11, Luke similarly structures the two volumes according to the states of Jesus' humiliation and exaltation. Second, as with Paul's preface to the hymn in Phil. 2:5, Luke shapes the content of both volumes according to the idea of discipleship: living as the master lived. Acts exemplifies through the lives of Peter, Stephen, and especially Paul what it means for believers to conform to the kind of attitudes and behavior characterizing the servanthood of the Lord Jesus as portrayed in the Gospel.

To sum up my proposal concerning a primary literary objective of Luke: he writes to show his readers how Jesus' life stands as the ethical model for Christian living and how the early church has imaged his likeness in their own life and witness. According to Luke, *the corollary to the Lord Jesus' servanthood is Christian discipleship.*

In closing, the results of the work suggest a number of observations and ramifications for Lukan and NT christology. First, the proposal on Luke's purpose conforms well to the six criteria for determining purpose as outlined in ch. 2 and *plausibly accounts for all the material recorded in Luke–Acts.*

1.   *Readers.*   Luke's literary intention and techniques would in all probability be readily comprehensible to most Christian readers. Such an appeal to Christian living on the basis of Jesus' life was perhaps fairly common within first-century Christian teaching and was probably already a familiar teaching to Luke's readers. Paul's similar use of the Christ hymn in Philippians strengthens this position.

2.   *Concrete occasion.*   In view of the likelihood that Luke wrote in response to church issues involving spiritual maturity and perseverance, such an appeal to Christian living also supplies a concrete occasion, under fairly normal circumstances, which would plausibly "call for the sort of book Luke wrote."[2]

---

[2]   Barrett, *Recent Study*, p. 53.

3. *Author's stated aim.* The author's stated aim to reaffirm what his readers had been taught coincides well with this proposal. Luke makes his point by communicating to his readers what they had most probably already known about discipleship and the need to follow Jesus, but in a very original way! Such a proposal, moreover, would allow for numerous secondary aims – such as an interest in evangelism, religious apology, and defining the relations between Judaism and Christianity – in assisting this principal aim, and they would merit further comment in their own right.

4. *Broad textual support.* We have also seen that in comparison to the other proposals on Lukan purpose, the thesis finds broad textual support in the multiple themes of the work, the breadth of the work, Luke's literary ingenuity, and fidelity to tradition.

5. *Unity of Luke–Acts.* Luke's main literary concern to provide his readers with an illustrated tract on Christian discipleship taken from Jesus' life, work, and teaching, and from the early church's imaging of him in their own life and ministry supports the belief in the unity of Luke–Acts: it accounts for the many *parallels* between the two books and clearly shows how Luke designed the book of Acts as a *continuation of and sequel to* the Gospel.

6. *Theological interest.* This proposal also recognizes the author's interest in theology. Luke writes according to a theological *Tendenz*. In view of the christological character and purpose of his writing concern, the whole of Luke–Acts appears as a theological treatise. In writing up his work, Luke combines various pieces of christological tradition, some ancient and some from his own day. However, as I have argued, such a theological interest need not be based, in part, on some kind of reinterpretation of Mark or Paul; rather, it may mostly reflect an accentuation and development of various theological themes integral to their writings. Nor does Luke give us any *prima facie* evidence for dismissing the historical verifiability of that which he reports; in fact, it is perhaps on "the matter of fact reality of history" that he premises his theological statements, for this is what grants them their verity and authority.[3]

Second, in reference to Mark, we have observed that Luke employs Mark's Gospel in the service of his own writing concerns. Via redaction and the book of Acts, we have seen how Luke had deliberately expanded Mark's account – mainly to supplement important details and to reexpress certain themes – according to his

---

[3] Hemer, *Hellenistic History*, pp. 84–85.

own writing purposes. But in so doing, as the study has affirmed, Luke shows allegiance to the theological stance of the synoptic tradition as expressed in Mark.

Third, an important corollary to my proposal in reference to the relation between Luke and Paul is that, as regards christology, Luke is not as incompatible with Paul as is sometimes assumed. According to my work, Luke's christology is not *ipso facto* simpler than Paul's, nor is it Pauline christology simplified; on the contrary, it is perhaps closer to Paul than many scholars are willing to admit and appears as a notable christological expression in its own right.

Fourth, my proposal on Lukan purpose reconciles the christological tension in Luke–Acts between Jesus' sovereign Lordship and his apparent subordination to the Father, where the servant Jesus must *depend upon the Father* both during his earthly career and for his resurrection and exaltation. As in Paul's letter to the Philippians, the fact of Jesus' sovereign Lordship (perhaps also understood by Luke in Jesus' status as God's Son) reveals the extent of his humiliation. But it is doubtful that Luke supports a subordination christology in the sense that Jesus, either in his earthly or heavenly state, is *inferior* to the Father *in being and status* for even in his humiliation he appears as "the executor of his own destiny."[4] Luke presents Jesus in his earthly ministry as *voluntarily* submitting to the Father's will and *purposefully* carrying it out. The earthly Jesus, moreover, according to Luke, seems cognizant of his future work as Lord in the witness of his followers at a time following his exaltation (cf. Luke 21:15), as Acts would affirm. Factors such as God's raising Jesus from the dead, making him Lord and Christ, and granting him the right to give the Spirit are perhaps better explained in terms of his *dependency* upon the Father because of his humiliation rather than in terms of an inherent inferiority. Therefore, these factors, when considered together with Luke's writing concern, at least as defined here, strengthen the belief that a subordination christology was foreign to his thinking.

Lastly, in contrast to Wilson's view that Luke fails to integrate the various christological strands into an overall scheme, the study supports just the opposite conclusion. *There is a unity or coherence to his christology.* It is the servanthood of the Lord Jesus. His main or controlling christological concern was to demonstrate for his readers that during his humiliation the earthly Jesus behaved

[4] Cosgrove, "Divine δεῖ," p. 180.

among his people as one who serves (Luke 22:25–27); and as exalted Lord and the Father's co-equal, Jesus continues to come in service to his people, strengthening and encouraging them in their witness of him to the world, a heavenly work, as we have seen, not unlike that of Yahweh in the OT (cf., e.g., Exod. 4:12). Moreover, that Jesus' followers resemble him in their own ministries in Acts means that they too are now imaging his servant-like character in their witness of him (cf. Luke 22:26). For this reason Paul can rightly insist that his missionary work to the Jews and Gentiles was in reality a work of the resurrected Christ himself (Acts 26:23). Much of Luke's expressed christology seems to be in the service of this theme. And it is possible that he expected his readers to take such "an overall view"[5] of his christological description of Jesus as well.[6] This proposal offers us a Lukan writing concern which plausibly explains (1) his purpose in writing, (2) the literary features of his two-volume work, (3) the apparent tension between Jesus' Lordship and subordination (i.e., humiliation), and, above all, (4) the character and purpose of his christology.

In Luke 6:40 Jesus instructs his disciples: "A student is not above his teacher, but everyone who is fully trained will be like his teacher." Luke writes to show how this is so.

[5]   The phrase taken from Hengel, "Chronology," p. 38.
[6]   So Lampe, "Lucan Portrait of Christ," p. 160; Talbert, "Anti-Gnostic Tendency."

BIBLIOGRAPHY

Achtemeier, Paul J. "'He taught them many things': Reflections on Marcan Christology." *CBQ* 42 (1980): 465–81.

Adebola, S. O. M. "The Christology of Luke–Acts." Diss., Oxford University, 1971.

Aejmelaeus, Lars. *Wachen vor dem Ende. Die traditionsgeschichtlichen Wurzeln von 1. Thess 5:1–11 und Luk 21:34–36.* SESJ 44. Helsinki: Kirjapaino, 1985.

Die Rezeption der Paulusbriefe in der Miletrede (Apg 20:18–35). STAT 232. Helsinki: Academia Scientiarum, 1987.

Aland, Kurt. "Bemerkungen zum Schluss des Markusevangeliums." In *Neotestamentica et Semitica*, ed. E. E. Ellis and M. Wilcox. Edinburgh: Clark, 1969, pp. 157–80.

"Der Schluß des Markusevangeliums." In *L'Evangile selon Marc*, ed. M. Sabbe. BEThL 34. Gembloux: Duculot, 1974, pp. 435–70.

Alexander, Loveday. "Hellenistic Letter–Forms and the Structure of Philippians." *JSNT* 37 (1989): 87–101.

The Preface to Luke's Gospel: Literary Convention and Social Context in Luke 1.1–4 and Acts 1.1. SNTSMS 78. Cambridge: Cambridge, 1993.

Allen, Willoughby C. *A Critical and Exegetical Commentary on the Gospel according to St. Matthew.* ICC. Edinburgh: Clark, 1907.

Allison, Dale C., Jr. "Was there a 'Lukan Community'?" *IBS* 10 (1988): 62–70.

Argyle, A.W. "The Greek of Luke and Acts." *NTS* 20 (1974): 441–45.

Aune, David E. "The Significance of the Delay of the Parousia for Early Christianity." In *Current Issues in Biblical and Patristic Interpretation*, ed. G. F. Hawthorne. Grand Rapids: Eerdmans, 1975, pp. 87–109.

"The Problem of the Genre of the Gospels: A Critique of C. H. Talbert's *What is a Gospel?*" In *Gospel Perspectives*, vol. 2, ed. R. T. France and D. Wenham. Sheffield: JSOT, 1981, pp. 9–60.

Prophecy in Early Christianity and the Mediterranean World. Grand Rapids: Eerdmans, 1983.

The New Testament in its Literary Environment. LEC 8. Philadelphia: Westminster, 1987.

Baarlink, Heinrich. *Die Eschatologie der synoptischen Evangelien.* BWANT 120. Stuttgart: Kohlhammer, 1986.

Bacon, Benjamin Wisner. *The Beginnings of Gospel Story*. New Haven: Yale, 1909.

The Gospel of Mark: Its Composition and Date. New Haven: Yale, 1925.

Baer, Heinrich von. "Der Heilige Geist in den Lukasschriften. Zusammenfassende Beurteilung der lukanischen Anschauung vom Heiligen Geiste." In *Das Lukas-Evangelium*, ed. G. Graumann. WF 280. Darmstadt: Wissenschaftliche, 1974, pp. 1–6.

Barclay, William. *The Promise of the Spirit*. London: Epworth, 1960.

Barr, James. "Theophany and Anthropomorphism in the Old Testament." *VTsup* 7 (1960): 31–38.

Barrett, C. K. *The Holy Spirit and the Gospel Tradition*. London: SPCK, 1947.

"The Background of Mark 10:45." In *New Testament Essays*, ed. A. J. B. Higgins. Manchester: Manchester, 1959, pp. 1–18.

Luke the Historian in Recent Study. London: Epworth, 1961.

"Mark 10.45: A Ransom for Many." In *New Testament Essays*. London: SPCK, 1972, pp. 20–27.

New Testament Essays. London: SPCK, 1972.

"The Acts – of Paul." In *New Testament Essays*. London: SPCK, 1972, pp. 86–100.

"Paul's Speech on the Areopagus." In *New Testament Christianity for Africa and the World*, ed. M. E. Glasswell and E. W. Fasholé–Luke. London: SPCK, 1974, pp. 69–77.

Church, Ministry, and Sacraments in the New Testament. Exeter: Paternoster, 1985.

"Paul Shipwrecked." In *Scripture: Meaning and Method*, ed. B. P. Thompson. Hull: Hull, 1987, pp. 51–64.

Acts 1–14. ICC. Edinburgh: Clark, 1994.

"*Imitatio Christi* in Acts." In *Jesus of Nazareth Lord and Christ*, ed. J. B. Green and M. Turner. Grand Rapids: Eerdmans, 1994, pp. 251–62.

Barth, Gerhard. *Der Brief an die Philipper*. ZBKNT 9. Zurich: Theologischer, 1979.

"Matthew's Understanding of the Law." In *Tradition and Interpretation in Matthew*. 2nd ed. Trans. P. Scott. London: SCM, 1982, pp. 58–164.

Bartsch, Hans-Werner. *"Wachet aber zu jeder Zeit!" Entwurf einer Auslegung des Lukasevangeliums*. Hamburg, Bergstedt: Reich, 1963.

"Der Schluss des Markus–Evangeliums. Ein überlieferungsgeschichtliches Problem." *ThZ* 27 (1971): 241–54.

"Der ursprüngliche Schluß der Leidensgeschichte. Überlieferungsgeschichtliche Studien zum Markus–Schluß." In *L'Evangile selon Marc*, ed. M. Sabbe. BEThL 34. Gembloux: Duculot, 1974, pp. 411–33.

Bauckham, Richard. "Synoptic Parousia Parables and the Apocalypse." *NTS* 23 (1977): 162–76.

Bauernfeind, Otto. *Kommentar und Studien zur Apostelgeschichte*, ed. V. Metelmann. WUNT 22. Tübingen: Mohr (Siebeck), 1980 (1939).

"Zur Frage nach der Entscheidung zwischen Paulus und Lukas." In *Kommentar und Studien zur Apostelgeschichte*, ed. V. Metelmann. WUNT 22. Tübingen: Mohr (Siebeck), 1980 (1954), pp. 353–82.

Bavel, T. J. van. "Auferstehung: Grund oder Objekt des Glaubens an Christus?" In *Probleme der Forschung*, ed. A. Fuchs. SNTU 3. Munich: Wien, 1978, pp. 9–23.

Bayer, Hans F. *Jesus' Predictions of Vindication and Resurrection: The Provenance, Meaning and Correlation of the Synoptic Predictions.* WUNT 20. Tübingen: Mohr (Siebeck), 1986.

"Christ-Centered Eschatology in Acts 3:17–26." In *Jesus of Nazareth Lord and Christ*, ed. J. B. Green and M. Turner. Grand Rapids: Eerdmans, 1994, pp. 236–50.

Beare, Francis Wright. *A Commentary on the Epistle to the Philippians*. 3rd ed. BNTC. London: Black, 1978.

Beasley-Murray, George Raymond. "Jesus and the Spirit." In *Mélanges bibliques*, ed. A. Descamps and R. P. A. de Halleux. Gembloux: Duculot, 1970, pp. 463–78.

"Jesus and Apocalyptic: With Special Reference to Mark 14, 62." In *L'Apocalypse Johannique et l'Apocalyptique dans le Nouveau Testament*, ed. J. Lambrecht. BEThL 53. Gembloux, Louvain: Duculot, Louvain, 1980, pp. 415–29.

Jesus and the Kingdom of God. Grand Rapids: Eerdmans, 1986.

Beauchamp, Paul. "Lecture et relectures du quatrième chant du serviteur: D'Isaïe à Jean." In *The Book of Isaiah/Le livre d'Isaïe*, ed. J. Vermeylen. BEThL 81. Louvain: Louvain, 1989, pp. 325–55.

Beck, Brian E. "The Common Authorship of Luke and Acts." *NTS* 23 (1977): 346–52.

"Christian Character in the Gospel of Luke – II." *EpRev* 6 (1979): 86–95.

Berchmans, John. "Some Aspects of Lukan Christology." *Biblebh* 2 (1976): 5–22.

Best, Ernest. *The Temptation and the Passion: The Markan Soteriology.* SNTSMS 2. Cambridge: Cambridge, 1965.

"The Role of the Disciples in Mark." *NTS* 23 (1977): 377–401.

"The Purpose of Mark." *PIBA* 6 (1982): 19–35.

Mark: The Gospel as Story. SNTW. Edinburgh: Clark, 1983.

Bitzer, Lloyd F. "The Rhetorical Situation." *PhRh* 1 (1968): 1–14.

Black, Matthew. "The 'Son of Man' Passion Sayings in the Gospel Tradition." *ZNW* 60 (1969): 1–8.

Bock, Darrell Lane. *Proclamation from Prophecy and Pattern: Lucan Old Testament Christology.* JSNTSS 12. Sheffield: JSOT, 1987.

Luke 1:1–9:50. Grand Rapids: Baker, 1994.

Bode, Edward Lynn. *The First Easter Morning: The Gospel Accounts of the Women's Visit to the Tomb of Jesus.* AnaBib 45. Rome: Pontifical, 1970.

Boobyer, G. H. "Galilee and Galileans in St. Mark's Gospel." *BJRL* 35 (1952–53): 334–48.

Boomershine, Thomas E. "Mark 16:8 and the Apostolic Commission." *JBL* 100 (1981): 225–39.

Boomershine, Thomas E., and Gilbert L. Bartholomew. "The Narrative Technique of Mark 16:8." *JBL* 100 (1981): 213–23.

Boor, Werner de. *Die Apostelgeschichte.* WSB. Wuppertal: Brockhaus, 1965.

Borgen, Peder. "From Paul to Luke: Observations toward Clarification of the Theology of Luke–Acts." *CBQ* 31 (1969): 168–82.

Borse, Udo. "Die Wir-Stellen der Apostelgeschichte und Timotheus." SNTU 10 (1985): 63–92.

Bousset, Wilhelm. *Kyrios Christos: A History of the Belief in Christ from the Beginnings of Christianity to Irenaeus.* Trans. J. E. Steely. Nashville: Abingdon, 1970.

Bovon, François. "Das Heil in den Schriften des Lukas." In *Lukas in neuer Sicht.* Trans. from French by E. Hartmann, A. Frey, and P. Strauss. BTS 8. Neukirchen-Vluyn: Neukirchener, 1985, pp. 61–74.

    Luke the Theologian: Thirty-Three Years of Research (1950–1983). 2nd ed. Trans. K. McKinney. PrinTMS 12. Allison Park, Penn.: Pickwick, 1987.

    Das Evangelium nach Lukas. 1, 1–9, 50. EKK 3/1. Zurich, Neukirchen-Vluyn: Benziger, Neukirchener, 1989.

Bowman, John. *The Gospel of Mark: The New Christian Jewish Passover Haggadah.* SPBib 8. Leiden: Brill, 1965.

Braun, Herbert. "Zur Terminologie der Acta von der Auferstehung Jesu." *ThLZ* 77 (1952): 533–36.

Brawley, Robert L. *Luke–Acts and the Jews: Conflict, Apology, and Conciliation.* SBLMS 33. Atlanta: Scholars, 1987.

Broer, Ingo. *Die Urgemeinde und das Grab Jesu. Eine Analyse der Grablegungsgeschichte im Neuen Testament.* SANT 31. Munich: Kösel, 1972.

Brown, Raymond E. *The Birth of the Messiah: A Commentary on the Infancy Narratives in Matthew and Luke.* New York: Doubleday, 1977.

Brown, Schuyler. *Apostasy and Perseverance in the Theology of Luke.* AnaBib 36. Rome: Pontifical, 1969.

    "'Water-Baptism' and 'Spirit-Baptism' in Luke–Acts." *ATR* 59 (1977): 135–51.

Brox, Norbert. "Lukas als Verfasser der Pastoralbriefe?" *JAC* 13 (1970): 62–77.

Bruce, Frederick Fyvie. "St. Paul in Rome." *BJRL* 50 (1968): 262–79.

    "The Holy Spirit in the Acts of the Apostles." *Int* 27 (1973): 166–83.

    "Is the Paul of Acts the Real Paul?" *BJRLUM* 58 (1975–76): 282–305.

    Philippians. GNC. New York: Harper & Row, 1983.

    "The Acts of the Apostles: Historical Record or Theological Reconstruction?" *ANRW* 2/25/3 (1985): 2569–603.

    "Chronological Questions in the Acts of the Apostles." *BJRLUM* 68 (1985–86): 273–95.

    The Acts of the Apostles: The Greek Text with Introduction and Commentary. 2nd ed. Grand Rapids: Eerdmans, 1986 (1952).

    "Eschatology in Acts." In *Eschatology and the New Testament*, ed. H. Gloer. Peabody: Hendrickson, 1988, pp. 51–63.

    The Book of Acts. 2nd ed. NICNT. Grand Rapids: Eerdmans, 1988.

Bultmann, Rudolf. *The History of the Synoptic Tradition.* 2nd ed. Trans. J. Marsh. Oxford: Blackwell, 1968 (1931).

    Theologie des Neuen Testaments. 9th ed., rev. O. Merk. UTB 630. Tübingen: Mohr (Siebeck), 1984.

Burger, Christoph. *Jesus als Davidssohn. Eine traditionsgeschichtliche Untersuchung.* FRLANT 98. Göttingen: Vandenhoeck & Ruprecht, 1970.

Burkill, T. A. *New Light on the Earliest Gospel: Seven Markan Studies.* London: Cornell, 1972.

Burkitt, F. C. *The Gospel History and Its Transmission.* 3rd ed. Edinburgh: Clark, 1911.

Cadbury, Henry J. "The Purpose Expressed in Luke's Preface." *Exp* 21 (1921): 431–41.

"The Knowledge Claimed in Luke's Preface." *Exp* 24 (1922): 401–20.

"Commentary on the Preface of Luke." In *BC* 2, pp. 489–510.

The Making of Luke–Acts. London: Macmillan, 1927.

The Book of Acts in History. London: Black, 1955.

" 'We' and 'I' Passages in Luke–Acts." *NTS* 3 (1957): 128–32.

"Some Foibles of New Testament Scholarship." *JBR* 26 (1958): 215–16.

"Gospel Study and Our Image of Early Christianity." *JBL* 83 (1964): 139–45.

Caird, George Bradford. *The Gospel of St. Luke.* PGC. London: Black, 1963.

Paul's Letters from Prison (Ephesians, Philippians, Colossians, Philemon) in the Revised Standard Version. NCB. Oxford: Oxford, 1987 (1976).

Campenhausen, Hans von. "The Events of Easter and the Empty Tomb." In *Tradition and Life in the Church.* Trans. A. V. Littledale. London: Collins, 1968, pp. 42–89.

Carroll, John T. *Response to the End of History: Eschatology and Situation in Luke–Acts.* SBLDS 92. Atlanta: Scholars, 1988.

Carson, Donald A. "Redaction Criticism: On the Legitimacy and Illegitimacy of a Literary Tool." In *Scripture and Truth*, ed. D. A. Carson and J. D. Woodbridge. Leicester: IVP, 1983, pp. 119–42, 376–81.

Cassidy, Richard J. *Jesus, Politics, and Society: A Study of Luke's Gospel.* Maryknoll: Orbis, 1978.

Chance, J. Bradley. *Jerusalem, the Temple, and the New Age in Luke–Acts.* Macon: Mercer, 1988.

Chevallier, Max-Alain. "Luc et l'Esprit saint. A la mémoire du P. Augustin George." *RevSciRel* 56 (1982): 1–16.

Clark, Albert C. *The Acts of the Apostles.* Oxford: Clarendon, 1933.

Collange, Jean-François. *The Epistle of Saint Paul to the Philippians.* Trans. A. W. Heathcote. London: Epworth, 1979.

Colson, F. H. "Notes on St. Luke's Preface." *JTS* 24 (1923): 300–309.

Conn, Harvie M. "Lucan Perspectives and the City." *Miss* 13 (1985): 409–28.

Conzelmann, Hans. *Die Mitte der Zeit. Studien zur Theologie des Lukas.* 5th ed. BHTh 17. Tübingen: Mohr (Siebeck), 1964.

"Luke's Place in the Development of Early Christianity." In *SLA*, pp. 298–316.

"Present and Future in the Synoptic Tradition." In *God and Christ*, ed. R. W. Funk. Trans. J. Wilson. JTC 5. New York: Harper & Row, 1968, pp. 26–44.

An Outline of the Theology of the New Testament. Trans. J. Bowden. NTL. London: SCM, 1969.

The Theology of St. Luke. Trans. G. Buswell. Philadelphia: Fortress, 1982.

Acts of the Apostles. 2nd ed. Trans. J. Limburg, A. T. Kraabel, and D. H. Juel. Hermeneia. Philadelphia: Fortress, 1987.

Cosgrove, Charles H. "The Divine δεῖ in Luke–Acts: Investigations into the Lukan Understanding of God's Providence." *NovT* 26 (1984): 168–90.

Couchoud, P.-L. "Is Marcion's Gospel One of the Synoptics?" *HibJ* 34 (1936): 265–77.

Craddock, Fred B. *Philippians.* IBC. Louisville: Knox, 1985.

Luke. IBC. Louisville: Knox, 1990.

Cranfield, C. E. B. *The Gospel according to Saint Mark: An Introduction and Commentary.* CGTC. Cambridge: Cambridge, 1959.

Creed, J. M. *The Gospel according to St. Luke.* London: Macmillan, 1965.

Crehan, J. H. "The Purpose of Luke in Acts." TU 78, *SEv* 2 (1964): 354–68.

Crump, David M. *Jesus the Intercessor: Prayer and Christology in Luke–Acts.* WUNT 49 ss. Tübingen: Mohr (Siebeck), 1992.

"Jesus, The Victorious Scribal-Intercessor in Luke's Gospel." *NTS* 38 (1992): 51–65.

Cullmann, Oscar. *Salvation in History.* Trans. S. G. Sowers. London: SCM, 1967.

Dahl, Nils Alstrup. "Die Passionsgeschichte bei Matthäus." *NTS* 2 (1955–56): 17–32.

"The Story of Abraham in Luke–Acts." In *SLA*, pp. 139–58.

"Form-Critical Observations on Early Christian Preaching." In *Jesus in the Memory of the Early Church.* Minneapolis: Augsburg, 1976, pp. 30–36.

"The Purpose of Luke–Acts." In *Jesus in the Memory of the Early Church.* Minneapolis: Augsburg, 1976, pp. 87–98.

Danker, Frederick W. *Benefactor: Epigraphic Study of a Graeco-Roman and New Testament Semantic Field.* St. Louis: Clayton, 1982.

"Graeco-Roman Cultural Accommodation in the Christology of Luke–Acts." In *Society of Biblical Literature 1983 Seminar Papers,* ed. K. H. Richards. SBLSPS 22. Chico: Scholars, 1983, pp. 391–414.

Luke. 2nd ed. PC. Philadelphia: Fortress, 1987.

Jesus and the New Age: A Commentary of St. Luke's Gospel. 2nd ed. Philadelphia: Fortress, 1988.

"Imaged through Beneficence." In *Reimaging the Death of Jesus,* ed. D. D. Sylva. BBB 73. Frankfurt: Anton Hain, 1990, pp. 57–67, 184–86.

Danove, Paul L. *The End of Mark's Story: A Methodological Study.* BIS 3. Leiden: Brill, 1993.

Deichgräber, Reinhard. *Gotteshymnus und Christushymnus in der frühen Christenheit. Untersuchungen zu Form, Sprache und Stil der frühchristlichen Hymnen.* SUNT 5. Göttingen: Vandenhoeck & Ruprecht, 1967.

Delorme, Jean. "Le salut dans l'évangile de Marc." *LThPh* 41 (1985): 79–108.

Dennison, C. G. "How is Jesus the Son of God? Luke's Baptism Narrative and Christology." *CTJ* 17 (1982): 6–25.

Devoldere, M. "Le prologue du troisième évangile." *NRTh* 56 (1929): 714–19.

Dibelius, Martin. *A Fresh Approach to the New Testament and Early Christian Literature.* London: Nicholson and Watson, 1936.

Studies in the Acts of the Apostles, ed. H. Greeven. Trans. M. Ling and P. Schubert. London: SCM, 1956.

Dietrich, Wolfgang. *Das Petrusbild der lukanischen Schriften.* BWANT 94. Stuttgart: Kohlhammer, 1972.

Dodd, Charles H. *The Apostolic Preaching and its Development: Three Lectures.* London: Hodder & Stoughton, 1944.

"The Fall of Jerusalem and the 'Abomination of Desolation.'" In *More New Testament Studies.* Manchester: Manchester, 1968, pp. 69–83.

Dömer, Michael. *Das Heil Gottes. Studien zur Theologie des lukanischen Doppelwerkes.* BBB 51. Bonn, Cologne: Hanstein, 1978.

Donahue, John R. "Jesus as the Parable of God in the Gospel of Mark." *Int* 32 (1978): 369–86.

Donfried, Karl Paul. "Attempts at Understanding the Purpose of Luke–Acts: Christology and the Salvation of the Gentiles." In *Christological Perspectives*, ed. R. F. Berkey and S. A. Edwards. New York: Pilgrim, 1982, pp. 112–22.

Doohan, Leonard. "Images of God in Luke–Acts," *MilltSt* 13 (1984): 17–35.

Downing, F. Gerald. "Compositional Conventions and the Synoptic Problem." *JBL* 107 (1988): 69–85.

Drane, John W. "Eschatology, Ecclesiology and Catholicity in the New Testament." *ExpT* 83 (1971–72): 180–84.

Drury, John. *Tradition and Design in Luke's Gospel: A Study in Early Christian Historiography.* London: Darton, Longman & Todd, 1976.

Dschulnigg, Peter. *Sprache, Redaktion und Intention des Markus-Evangeliums. Eigentümlichkeiten der Sprache des Markus-Evangeliums und ihre Bedeutung für die Redaktionskritik.* StBB 11. Stuttgart: Katholisches, 1984.

Dumais, Marcel. "Ministères, charismes et Esprit dans l'œuvre de Luc." *EgTh* 9 (1978): 413–53.

"L'évangélisation des pauvres dans l'œuvre de Luc." *SciEs* 36 (1984): 297–321.

Dunn, James D. G. *Baptism in the Holy Spirit: A Re-examination of the New Testament Teaching on the Gift of the Spirit in relation to Pentecostalism Today.* SBT ss 15. London: SCM, 1970.

Jesus and the Spirit: A Study of the Religious and Charismatic Experience of Jesus and the First Christians as Reflected in the New Testament. London: SCM, 1975.

Christology in the Making: An Inquiry into the Origins of the Doctrine of the Incarnation. 2nd ed. London: SCM, 1989.

Dupont, Jacques. "L'utilisation apologétique du VT dans les discours des Actes." *EThL* 26 (1953): 298–327.

"Ascension du Christ et don de l'Esprit d'après Actes 2:33." In *Christ and Spirit in the New Testament*, ed. B. Lindars and S. S. Smalley. Cambridge: Cambridge, 1973, pp. 219–28.

"La portée christologique de l'évangélisation des nations d'après Luc 24,

47." In *Neues Testament und Kirche*, ed. J. Gnilka. Freiburg: Herder, 1974, pp. 125–43.

"Apologetic Use of the Old Testament in the Speeches of Acts." In *The Salvation of the Gentiles*. Trans. J. R. Keating. New York: Paulist, 1979, pp. 129–59.

"La conclusion des Actes et son rapport à l'ensemble de l'ouvrage de Luc." In *Les Actes des Apôtres*, ed. J. Kremer. Gembloux, Louvain: Duculot, Louvain, 1979, pp. 359–404.

"The Salvation of the Gentiles and the Theological Significance of Acts." In *The Salvation of the Gentiles*. Trans. J. R. Keating. New York: Paulist, 1979, pp. 11–33.

The Salvation of the Gentiles: Essays in the Acts of the Apostles. Trans. J. R. Keating. New York: Paulist, 1979.

"Les épreuves des chrétiens avant la fin du monde (Lc 21, 5–19)." In *Etudes sur les Evangiles Synoptiques*. BEThL 70/2. Louvain: Louvain, 1985, pp. 117–27.

Dwyer, Timothy R. *The Motif of Wonder in the Gospel of Mark*. Sheffield: Sheffield, forthcoming.

Dyrness, William. *Themes in Old Testament Theology*. Exeter: Paternoster, 1979.

Easton, Burton Scott. *Early Christianity: The Purpose of Acts and Other Papers*, ed. F. C. Grant. London: SPCK, 1955.

Edmonds, Peter. "Luke's Portrait of Christ." *BibPasBul* 4 (1981): 7–14.

Ehrhardt, Arnold. "The Construction and Purpose of the Acts of the Apostles." In *The Framework of the New Testament Stories*. Manchester: Manchester, 1964, pp. 64–102.

Eichrodt, Walther. *Theology of the Old Testament*, 2 vols. Trans. J. A. Baker. OTL. Philadelphia: Westminster, 1961 (vol. 1), 1967 (vol. 2).

Elliott, J. K. "Does Luke 2:41–52 Anticipate the Resurrection?" *ExpT* 83 (1971–72): 87–89.

Elliott, John H. "A Catholic Gospel: Reflections on 'Early Catholicism' in the New Testament." *CBQ* 31 (1969): 213–23.

Ellis, E. Earle. "Present and Future Eschatology in Luke." *NTS* 12 (1965–66): 27–41.

Eschatology in Luke. FB bs 30. Philadelphia: Fortress, 1972.

The Gospel of Luke. 2nd ed. NCBC. Grand Rapids: Eerdmans, 1981.

Eltester, Walter. "Lukas und Paulus." In *Eranion*, ed. J. Kroymann. Tübingen: Niemeyer, 1961, pp. 1–17.

Enslin, Morton. "ἐφοβοῦντο γάρ, Mark 16:8." *JBL* 46 (1927): 62–68.

"'Luke' and Paul." *JAOS* 58 (1938): 81–91.

"Once Again, Luke and Paul." *ZNW* 61 (1970): 253–71.

Epp, Eldon Jay. *The Theological Tendency of Codex Bezae Cantabrigiensis in Acts*. SNTSMS 3. Cambridge: Cambridge, 1966.

Ernst, Josef. *Die Briefe an die Philipper, an Philemon, an die Kolosser, an die Epheser*. RNT 7. Regensburg: Pustet, 1974.

Das Evangelium nach Lukas. RNT 3. Regensburg: Pustet, 1977.

"Das Jesusbild des Lk." In *Das Evangelium nach Lukas*. RNT 3. Regensburg: Pustet, 1977.

Herr der Geschichte. Perspektiven der lukanischen Eschatologie. StBibS 88. Stuttgart: Katholisches, 1978.
"Das Christusbild des Lukas." In *Lukas. Ein theologisches Portrait.* Düsseldorf: Patmos, 1985, pp. 105–11.
Esler, Philip Francis. *Community and Gospel in Luke–Acts: The Social and Political Motivations of Lucan Theology.* SNTSMS 57. Cambridge: Cambridge, 1987.
Evans, C. F. "The Central Section of St. Luke's Gospel." In *Studies in the Gospels,* ed. D. E. Nineham. Oxford: Blackwell, 1955, pp. 37–53.
"I will go before you into Galilee." *JTS* ns 5 (1964): 3–18.
Resurrection and the New Testament. SBT ss 12. London: SCM, 1970.
Evans, Craig A. *Luke.* NIBC 3. Peabody: Hendrickson, 1990.
Farmer, William Reuben. *The Last Twelve Verses of Mark.* SNTSMS 25. Cambridge: Cambridge, 1974.
Farrer, Austin. *A Study in St. Mark.* Westminster: Dacre, 1951.
Fee, Gordon D. *1 and 2 Timothy, Titus.* GNC. San Francisco: Harper & Row, 1984.
Feiler, Paul Frederick. "Jesus the Prophet: The Lucan Portrayal of Jesus as the Prophet like Moses." Ph.D. Princeton Theological Seminary, 1985.
Feldmeier, Reinhard. "The Portrayal of Peter in the Synoptic Gospels." In M. Hengel, *Studies in the Gospel of Mark.* Trans. J. Bowden. London: SCM, 1985, pp. 59–63.
Feneberg, Wolfgang. *Der Markusprolog. Studien zur Formbestimmung des Evangeliums.* SANT 36. Munich: Kösel, 1974.
Feuillet, André. "La doctrine des Epîtres Pastorales et leurs affinités avec l'œuvre lucanienne." *RevThom* 78 (1978): 181–225.
Fitzmyer, Joseph A. "The Priority of Mark and the 'Q' Source of Luke." In *Jesus and Man's Hope,* vol. 1, ed. D. G. Buttrick. PJPTS. Pittsburgh: PTS, 1970, pp. 131–70.
The Gospel according to Luke, 2 vols. AncB 28. 2nd ed. Garden City: Doubleday, 1981 (vol. 1), 1983 (vol. 2).
"Jesus in the Early Church through the Eyes of Luke–Acts." *ScrB* 17 (1987): 26–35.
Flender, Helmut. *St. Luke: Theologian of Redemptive History.* Trans. R. H. and I. Fuller. London: SPCK, 1967.
Flew, R. Newton. *Jesus and His Church: A Study of the Idea of the Ecclesia in the New Testament.* London: Epworth, 1938.
Flückiger, Felix. "Luk. 21, 20–24 und die Zerstörung Jerusalems." *ThZ* 28 (1972): 385–90.
Flusser, David. "Salvation Present and Future." In *Types of Redemption,* ed. R. J. Z. Werblowsky and C. J. Bleeker. SHR 18. Leiden: Brill, 1970, pp. 46–61.
Fowl, Stephen E. *The Story of Christ in the Ethics of Paul: An Analysis of the Function of the Hymnic Material in the Pauline Corpus.* JSNTSS 36. Sheffield: JSOT, 1990.
France, R. T. "The Servant of the Lord in the Teaching of Jesus." *TynB* 19 (1968): 26–52.
Jesus and the Old Testament: His Application of Old Testament Passages to Himself and His Mission. London: Tyndale, 1971.

"Mark and the Teaching of Jesus." In *Gospel Perspectives*, vol. 1, ed.
R. T. France and D. Wenham. Sheffield: JSOT, 1980, pp. 101–36.

Matthew. TNTC 1. Downers Grove: IVP, 1985.

Franklin, Eric. "The Ascension and the Eschatology of Luke–Acts." *SJT*
23 (1970): 191–200.

Christ the Lord: A Study in the Purpose and Theology of Luke–Acts.
London: SPCK, 1975.

Luke: Interpreter of Paul, Critic of Matthew. JSNTSS 92. Sheffield:
JSOT, 1994.

Friedrich, Gerhard. "Lk 9, 51 und die Entrückungschristologie des
Lukas." In *Orientierung an Jesus*, ed. P. Hoffmann. Freiburg: Herder,
1973, pp. 48–77.

"Ein Tauflied hellenistischen Judenchristen. 1. Thess. 1, 9f." In *Auf das
Wort kommt es an*, ed. J. H. Friedrich. Göttingen: Vandenhoeck &
Ruprecht, 1978, pp. 236–50.

Fuchs, Albert. *Sprachliche Untersuchungen zu Matthäus und Lukas. Ein
Beitrag zur Quellenkritik*. AnaBib 49. Rome: Pontifical, 1971.

Fuller, Reginald H. *The Foundations of New Testament Christology*. New
York: Scribner, 1955.

The Formation of the Resurrection Narratives. London: SPCK, 1972.

Fusco, Vittorio. "Le sezioni-noi degli Atti nella discussione recente."
BibOr 25 (1983): 73–86.

Garland, David E. "The Composition and Unity of Philippians." *NovT* 27
(1985): 141–73.

Gasque, W. Ward. "The Book of Acts in History." In *Unity and Diversity
in New Testament Theology*, ed. R. A. Guelich. Grand Rapids: Eerdmans, 1978, pp. 54–72.

"A Fruitful Field: Recent Study of the Acts of the Apostles." *Int* 42
(1988): 117–31.

A History of the Criticism of the Acts of the Apostles. 2nd ed. Peabody:
Hendrickson, 1989.

Geddert, Timothy J. *Watchwords: Mark 13 in Markan Eschatology*.
JSNTSS 26. Sheffield: JSOT, 1989.

Geldenhuys, Norval. *Commentary on the Gospel of Luke*. NLCNT.
London: Marshall, Morgan & Scott, 1965 (1950).

Gempf, Conrad H. "Historical and Literary Appropriateness in the
Mission Speeches of Paul in Acts." Ph.D. University of Aberdeen,
1988.

George, Augustin. "La prédication inaugurale de Jésus dans la Synagogue
de Nazareth, Luc 4, 16– 30." *BVC* 59 (1964): 17–29.

"Israël dans l'œuvre de Luc." *RevBib* 75 (1968): 481–525.

"L'emploi chez Luc du vocabulaire de salut." *NTS* 23 (1977): 308–20.

"L'eschatologie." In *Etudes sur l'œuvre de Luc*. SouBib. Paris: Gabalda,
1978.

"L'Esprit saint dans l'œuvre de Luc." *RivBib* 85 (1978): 500–42.

Georgi, Dieter. "Der vorpaulinische Hymnus Phil. 2, 6–11." In *Zeit und
Geschichte*, ed. E. Dinkler. Tübingen: Mohr (Siebeck), 1964, pp. 263–93.

Gerhardsson, Birger. *The Gospel Tradition*. ConBib nts 15. Lund: Gleerup,
1986.

Giblet, Jean. "Baptism in the Spirit in the Acts of the Apostles." *OneChr* 10 (1974): 162–71.

Gilchrist, J. M. "The Authorship and Date of the Pastoral Epistles." Ph.D. University of Manchester, 1968.

Giles, Kevin. "Present–Future Eschatology in the Book of Acts (1–2)." *RefTRev* 40 (1981): 65–71; 41 (1982): 11–18.

"Is Luke an Exponent of 'Early Protestantism'? Church Order in the Lukan Writings (1–2)." *EvQ* 54 (1982): 193–205; 55 (1983): 3–20.

"Salvation in Lukan Theology (1–2)." *RefTRev* 42 (1983): 10–16, 45–49.

Glasson, T. F. "The Reply to Caiaphas (Mark XIV.62)." *NTS* 7 (1960–61): 88–93.

Gnilka, Joachim. *Der Philipperbrief.* HThKNT 10/3. Freiburg: Herder, 1968.

Das Evangelium nach Markus. EKK 2/1–2. Zurich, Neukirchen-Vluyn: Benziger, Neukirchener, 1978 (vol. 1), 1979 (vol. 2).

Goodenough, Erwin R. "The Perspective of Acts." In *SLA*, pp. 51–59.

Gooding, David. *True to the Faith: A Fresh Approach to the Acts of the Apostles.* London: Hodder & Stoughton, 1990.

Goppelt, Leonhard. *Theology of the New Testament.* Vol. 2, *The Variety and Unity of the Apostolic Witness to Christ.* Trans. J. Alsup. Grand Rapids: Eerdmans, 1982.

Görg, Manfred. " 'Ich bin mit dir.' Gewicht und Anspruch einer Redeform im AT." *ThGl* 70 (1980): 214–40.

Goulder, Michael D. "Mark XVI.1–8 and Parallels." *NTS* 24 (1978): 235–40.

"Did Luke Know any of the Pauline Letters?" *Pers* 13 (1986): 97–112.

Luke: A New Paradigm, 2 vols. JSNTSS 20. Sheffield: JSOT, 1989.

Graham, Holt H. "The Gospel according to St. Mark: Mystery and Ambiguity." *ATRsup* 7 (1976): 43–55.

Graß, Hans. *Ostergeschehen und Osterberichte.* 2nd ed. Göttingen: Vandenhoeck & Ruprecht, 1964.

Gräßer, Erich. *Das Problem der Parusieverzögerung in den synoptischen Evangelien und in der Apostelgeschichte.* 3rd ed. BZNW 22. Berlin: Töpelmann, 1977.

"Die Parusieerwartung in der Apostelgeschichte." In *Les Actes des Apôtres,* ed. J. Kremer. BEThL 48. Gembloux, Louvain: Duculot, Louvain, 1979, pp. 99–127.

Graudin, A. F. "Jesus as Teacher in Mark." *ConJ* 3 (1977): 32–35.

Green, E. M. B. *The Meaning of Salvation.* London: Hodder & Stoughton, 1965.

I Believe in the Holy Spirit. London: Hodder & Stoughton, 1975.

Green, Joel B. "Jesus on the Mount of Olives (Luke 22.39–46): Tradition and Theology." *JSNT* 26 (1986): 29–48.

"The Death of Jesus, God's Servant." In *Reimaging the Death of the Lukan Jesus,* ed. D. D. Sylva. BBB 73. Frankfurt: Hain, 1990, pp. 1–28, 170–73.

"Good News to Whom? Jesus and the 'Poor' in the Gospel of Luke." In *Jesus of Nazareth Lord and Christ,* ed. J. B. Green and M. Turner. Grand Rapids: Eerdmans, 1994, pp. 59–74.

Grumm, Meinert H. "Another Look at Acts." *ExpT* 96 (1984–85): 333–37.

Grundmann, Walther. *Das Evangelium nach Lukas*. 3rd ed. ThHNT 3. Berlin: Evangelische, 1969.

Guillet, Jacques. "The Holy Spirit in Christ's Life." Trans. D. Armitage. *LumVit* 28 (1973): 31–40.

Gundry, Robert N. "Recent Investigations into the Literary Genre 'Gospel.' " In *New Dimensions in New Testament Study*, ed. R. N. Longenecker and M. C. Tenney. Grand Rapids: Zondervan, 1974, pp. 97–114.

Guthrie, Donald. *New Testament Introduction*. 3rd ed. Downers Grove: IVP, 1970.

New Testament Theology. London: IVP, 1981.

Haefner, Alfred E. "The Bridge between Mark and Acts." *JBL* 77 (1958): 67–71.

Haenchen, Ernst. "Das 'Wir' in der Apostelgeschichte und das Itinerar." *ZThK* 58 (1961): 329–66.

The Acts of the Apostles: A Commentary. Trans. B. Noble, G. Shinn, H. Anderson, and R. McL. Wilson. Oxford: Blackwell, 1971.

Hahn, Ferdinand. *The Titles of Jesus in Christology: Their History in Early Christianity*. Trans. H. Knight and G. Ogg. London: Lutterworth, 1969.

Hamilton, N. Q. "Resurrection Tradition and the Composition of Mark." *JBL* 84 (1965): 415–21.

Hamm, Dennis. "Sight to the Blind: Vision as Metaphor in Luke." *Bib* 67 (1986): 457–77.

Hanson, R. P. C. *The Acts in the Revised Standard Version*. NCB. Oxford: Oxford, 1967.

Harder, Günther. "Das eschatologische Geschichtsbild der sogenannten kleinen Apokalypse Mk. 13." *ThVia* 4 (1952): 71–107.

Harnack, Adolf von. *The Date of Acts and of the Synoptic Gospels*. CTL 33. London: Williams & Norgate, 1911.

Harrison, Everett F. *Introduction to the New Testament*. Grand Rapids: Eerdmans, 1964.

"The Resurrection of Jesus Christ in the Book of Acts and in Early Christian Literature." In *Understanding the Sacred Text*, ed. J. Reumann. Valley Forge: Judson, 1972, pp. 219–31.

Hasler, Victor. "Jesu Selbstzeugnis und das Bekenntnis des Stephanus vor dem Hohen Rat." *SchThU* 36 (1969): 36–47.

Hastings, Adrian. *Prophet and Witness in Jerusalem: A Study of the Teaching of Saint Luke*. New York: Longmans, 1958.

Hawthorne, Gerald F. *Philippians*. WBC 43. Waco: Word, 1983.

Hayes, John H. "The Resurrection as Enthronement and the Earliest Church Christology." *Int* 22 (1968): 333–45.

Hemer, Colin J. "Paul at Athens: A Topographical Note." *NTS* 20 (1974): 341–50.

"Luke the Historian." *BJRLUM* 60 (1977–78): 28–51.

"First Person Narrative in Acts 27–28." *TynB* 36 (1985): 79–109.

The Book of Acts in the Setting of Hellenistic History, ed. C. H. Gempf. WUNT 49. Tübingen: Mohr (Siebeck), 1989.

Hendricksen, William. *Philippians*. London: Banner of Truth, 1973 (1962).

The Gospel of Luke. NTC. Grand Rapids: Baker, 1978.

Hengel, Martin. *Acts and the History of Earliest Christianity.* Trans. J. Bowden. London: SCM, 1979.

"Jesus als messianischer Lehrer der Weisheit und die Anfänge der Christologie." In *Sagesse et religion,* ed. E. Jacob. Paris: France, 1979 (1976), pp. 147–88.

The Atonement: The Origins of the Doctrine in the New Testament. Trans. J. Bowden. Philadelphia: Fortress, 1981.

The Charismatic Leader and His Followers. Trans. J. C. G. Greig. SNTW. Edinburgh: Clark, 1981.

Between Jesus and Paul: Studies in the Earliest History of Christianity. Trans. J. Bowden. Philadelphia: Fortress, 1983.

"Christology and New Testament Chronology: A Problem in the History of Earliest Christianity." In *Between Jesus and Paul.* Trans. J. Bowden. Philadelphia: Fortress, 1983, pp. 30–47.

"Literary, Theological and Historical Problems in the Gospel of Mark." In *Studies in the Gospel of Mark.* Trans. J. Bowden. London: SCM, 1985, pp. 31–58.

"The Gospel of Mark: Time of Origin and Situation." In *Studies in the Gospel of Mark.* Trans. J. Bowden. London: SCM, 1985, pp. 1–30.

"The Titles of the Gospels and the Gospel of Mark." In *Studies in the Gospel of Mark.* Trans. J. Bowden. London: SCM, 1985, pp. 64–84.

The Pre–Christian Paul. Philadelphia: TPI, 1991.

Hiers, Richard H. "The Problem of the Delay of the Parousia in Luke–Acts." *NTS* 20 (1974): 145–55.

Higgins, A.J.B. *Jesus and the Son of Man.* London: Lutterworth, 1964.

Hill, David. *Greek Words and Hebrew Meanings: Studies in the Semantics of Soteriological Terms.* SNTSMS 5. Cambridge: Cambridge, 1967.

Hobbs, Herschel H. *An Exposition of the Gospel of Mark.* Grand Rapids: Baker, 1970.

Hoehner, Harold W. "Why did Pilate hand Jesus over to Antipas?" In *The Trial of Jesus,* ed. E. Bammel. SBT ss 13. London: SCM, 1970, pp. 84–90.

Hofius, Otfried. *Der Christushymnus Philipper 2, 6–11. Untersuchungen zu Gestalt und Aussage eines urchristlichen Psalms.* WUNT 17. Tübingen: Mohr (Siebeck), 1976.

Hooker, Morna D. *Jesus and the Servant: The Influence of the Servant Concept of Deutero-Isaiah in the New Testament.* London: SPCK, 1959.

"Philippians 2:6–11." In *Jesus und Paulus,* ed. E. E. Ellis and E. Gräber. 2nd ed. Göttingen: Vandenhoeck & Ruprecht, 1978, pp. 151–64.

The Message of Mark. London: Epworth, 1983.

"'What doest thou here, Elijah?' A Look at St. Mark's Account of the Transfiguration." In *The Glory of Christ in the New Testament,* ed. L. D. Hurst and N. T. Wright. Oxford: Clarendon, 1987, pp. 59–70.

Horst, P. W. van der. "Can a Book End with *GAR*? A Note on Mark 18:8." *JTS* ns 23 (1972): 121–24.

Hoskyns, Edwyn C. "Adversaria Exegetica." *Theo* 7 (1923): 147–55.

Houlden, J. L. *The Pastoral Epistles: I and II Timothy, Titus.* PNTC. Harmondsworth: Penguin, 1976.

"The Purpose of Luke." *JSNT* 21 (1984): 53–65.

House, P. R. "Suffering and the Purpose of Acts." *JETS* 33 (1990): 317–30.

Howard, Virgil P. *Das Ego Jesu in den synoptischen Evangelien. Untersuchungen zum Sprachgebrauch Jesu*. MThS 14. Marburg: Elwert, 1975.

Hubbard, Benjamin J. "The Role of Commissioning Accounts in Acts." In *Perspectives on Luke–Acts*, ed. C. H. Talbert. PRS 5. Edinburgh: Clark, 1978, pp. 187–98.

Hull, J. H. E. *The Holy Spirit in the Acts of the Apostles*. London: Lutterworth, 1967.

Hultgren, Arland J. "Interpreting the Gospel of Luke." *Int* 30 (1976): 353–65.

    Christ and His Benefits: Christology and Redemption in the New Testament. Philadelphia: Fortress, 1987.

    ed. *New Testament Christology: A Critical Assessment and Annotated Bibliography*. BIRS 12. New York: Greenwood, 1988.

Hunkin, J. W. "St. Luke and Josephus: On the Supposed Evidence for St. Luke's Use of the Writings of Josephus." *CQR* 88 (1919): 89–108.

Hunter, A. M. *Introducing the New Testament*. 3rd ed. London: SCM, 1972.

Hurtado, Larry W. *Mark*. GNC. New York: Harper & Row, 1983.

    "Jesus as Lordly Example in Philippians 2:5–11." In *From Jesus to Paul*, ed. G. P. Richardson and J. C. Hurd. Waterloo, Ont.: Laurier, 1984, pp. 113–26.

    "The Gospel of Mark in Recent Study." *Them* 14 (1989): 47–52.

Jacob, Edmond. *Theology of the Old Testament*. Trans. A. W. Heathcote and P. J. Allcock. London: Hodder & Stoughton, 1958.

Jeremias, Joachim. *The Eucharistic Words of Jesus*. Trans. N. Perrin. NTL. London: SCM, 1966.

    New Testament Theology. Vol. 1, *The Proclamation of Jesus*. Trans. J. Bowden. London: SCM, 1971.

Jervell, Jacob. *Luke and the People of God: A New Look at Luke–Acts*. Trans. D. Juel, J. Andreason, T. Callan, M. Collins, and R. Hock. Minneapolis: Augsburg, 1972.

    "Paul: The Teacher of Israel – The Apologetic Speeches of Paul in Acts." In *Luke and the People of God*. Trans. D. Juel *et al*. Minneapolis: Augsburg, 1972, pp. 153–83.

    "The Divided People of God: The Restoration of Israel and Salvation for the Gentiles." In *Luke and the People of God*. Trans. D. Juel *et al*. Minneapolis: Augsburg, 1972, pp. 41–74.

    "The Problem of Traditions in Acts." In *Luke and the People of God*. Trans. D. Juel *et al*. Minneapolis: Augsburg, 1972, pp. 19–39.

    "The Unknown Paul." In *The Unknown Paul*. Minneapolis: Augsburg, 1972, pp. 52–67.

    "Paul in the Acts of the Apostles: Tradition, History, Theology." In *The Unknown Paul*. Minneapolis: Augsburg, 1984, pp. 68–76.

Johnson, Luke Timothy. *The Literary Function of Possessions in Luke–Acts*. SBLDS 39. Missoula: Scholars, 1977.

    The Writings of the New Testament: An Interpretation. London: SCM, 1986.

The Gospel of Luke. SacPag 3. Collegeville: Liturgical, 1991.

The Acts of the Apostles. SacPag 5. Collegeville: Liturgical, 1992.

Johnson, W. Carter. "The Old Testament Basis for the Doctrine of the Deity of Christ." *GorRev* 6 (1961): 62–79.

Jones, Donald Lee. "The Christology of the Missionary Speeches in the Acts of the Apostles." Ph.D. Duke University, 1966.

"The Title 'Servant' in Luke–Acts." In *Luke–Acts,* ed. C. H. Talbert. New York: Crossroad, 1984, pp. 148–65.

Jonge, Marinus de. *Christology in Context: The Earliest Christian Response to Jesus.* Philadelphia: Westminster, 1988.

Judge, E. A. "The Decrees of Caesar at Thessalonica." *RefTRev* 30 (1971): 1–7.

Kaestli, Jean-Daniel. *L'Eschatologie dans l'œuvre de Luc. Ses caractéristiques et sa place dans le développement du Christianisme primitif.* NSTh 22. Geneva: Labor et Fides, 1969.

Kaiser, Walter C., Jr. *Toward an Old Testament Theology.* Grand Rapids: Zondervan, 1978.

Karnetzki, Manfred. "Die galiläische Redaktion im Markusevangelium." *ZNW* 52 (1961): 238–72.

Karris, Robert J. "The Lukan Sitz im Leben: Methodology and Prospects." In *Society of Biblical Literature 1976 Seminar Papers,* ed. G. MacRae. SBLSPS 10. Missoula: Scholars, 1976, pp. 219–33.

"Poor and Rich: The Lukan Sitz im Leben." In *Perspectives on Luke–Acts,* ed. C. H. Talbert. PRS 5. Edinburgh: Clark, 1978, pp. 112–25.

"Missionary Communities: A New Paradigm for the Study of Luke–Acts." *CBQ* 41 (1979): 80–97.

"Luke 23:47 and the Lucan View of Jesus' Death." In *Reimaging the Death of the Lukan Jesus,* ed. D. D. Sylva. BBB 73. Frankfurt: Hain, 1990, pp. 68–78,187–89.

Käsemann, Ernst. "The Problem of the Historical Jesus." In *Essays on New Testament Themes.* Trans. W. J. Montague. SBT 41. London: SCM, 1964, pp. 15–47.

"Paul and Early Catholicism." In *New Testament Questions of Today.* NTL. London: SCM, 1969, pp. 236–51.

"Kritische Analyse von Phil. 2, 5–11." In *Exegetische Versuche und Besinnungen,* vol. 1. Göttingen: Vandenhoeck & Ruprecht, 1970, pp. 51–95.

Kasting, Heinrich. *Die Anfänge der urchristlichen Mission. Eine historische Untersuchung.* BEvTh 55. Munich: Kaiser, 1969.

Kealy, Sean P. *Mark's Gospel: A History of its Interpretation from the Beginning until 1979.* New York: Paulist, 1982.

Keck, Leander E. "Toward the Renewal of New Testament Christology." *NTS* 32 (1986): 362–77.

Keck, Leander E., and J. Louis Martyn, eds. *Studies in Luke–Acts: Essays Presented in Honor of Paul Schubert.* Philadelphia: Fortress, 1980 (1966).

Kegel, Günter. *Auferstehung Jesu – Auferstehung der Toten. Eine traditions-geschichtlich Untersuchung zum Neuen Testament.* Gütersloh: Mohn, 1970.

Kilgallen, John J. "Persecution in the Acts of the Apostles." In *Luke and*

Acts, ed. G. O'Collins and G. Marconi. New York: Paulist, 1991, pp. 143–60.

Kilpatrick, G. D. "On γραμματεύς and νομικός." *JTS* ns 1 (1950): 56–60.

"The Gentile Mission in Mark and Mark 13:9–11." In *Studies in the Gospels*, ed. D. E. Nineham. Oxford: Blackwell, 1955, pp. 145–58.

"Mark 13:9–10." *JTS* ns 9 (1958): 81–86.

"The Spirit, God, and Jesus in Acts." *JTS* ns 15 (1964): 63.

"Λαοί at Luke 2:31 and Acts 4:25, 27." *JTS* ns 16 (1965): 127.

"The Gentiles and the Strata of Luke." In *Verborum veritas*, ed. O. Bocher and K. Haaker. Wuppertal: Brockhaus, 1970, pp. 83–88.

Kim, Seyoon. *The Origin of Paul's Gospel*. Grand Rapids: Eerdmans, 1982.

Kimball, Charles A. *Jesus' Exposition of the Old Testament in Luke's Gospel*. JSNT 94. Sheffield: JSOT, 1994.

Kingsbury, Jack Dean. *The Christology of Mark's Gospel*. Philadelphia: Fortress, 1983.

Conflict in Luke: Jesus, Authorities, Disciples. Minneapolis: Fortress, 1991.

Kistemaker, Simon J. *Exposition of the Acts of the Apostles*. NTC. Grand Rapids: Baker, 1990.

Klein, Günther. *Die Zwölf Apostel. Ursprung und Gehalt einer Idee*. Göttingen: Vandenhoeck & Ruprecht, 1961.

Knight, George A. F. *Deutero-Isaiah: A Theological Commentary on Isaiah 40–55*. Nashville: Abingdon, 1965.

Knox, John. "On the Vocabulary of Marcion's Gospel." *JBL* 58 (1939): 193–201.

Marcion and the New Testament: An Essay in the Early History of the Canon. Chicago: Chicago, 1942.

"Acts and the Pauline Letter Corpus." In *SLA*, pp. 279–87.

Knox, Wilfred L. "The Ending of St. Mark's Gospel." *HTR* 35 (1942): 13–23.

The Acts of the Apostles. Cambridge: Cambridge, 1948.

Koester, Helmut. *Introduction to the New Testament*. Vol. 2, *History and Literature of Early Christianity*. Philadelphia: Fortress, 1982.

Koet, B. J. "Paul in Rome (Acts 28, 16–31): A Farewell to Judaism?" In *Five Studies on Interpretation of Scripture in Luke–Acts*. SNTA 14. Louvain: Louvain, 1989, pp. 119–39.

Kränkl, Emmeram. *Jesus der Knecht Gottes. Die heilsgeschichtliche Stellung Jesu in den Reden der Apostelgeschichte*. BU 8. Regensburg: Pustet, 1972.

Kratz, Reinhard. *Auferweckung als Befreiung. Eine Studie zur Passions- und Auferstehungstheologie des Matthäus (besonders Mt 27, 62–28, 15)*. StBibS 65. Stuttgart: KBW, 1973.

Kremer, Jakob. "Jesu Verheißung des Geistes. Zur Verankerung der Aussage von Joh 16, 13 im Leben Jesu." In *Die Kirche des Anfangs*, ed. R. Schnackenburg, J. Ernst, and J. Wanke. ErThS 38. Leipzig: St. Benno, 1977, pp. 247–76.

"Weltweites Zeugnis für Christus in der Kraft des Geistes. Zur lukanischen Sicht der Mission." In *Mission in Neuen Testament*, ed. K. Kertelge. QD 93. Freiburg: Herder, 1982, pp. 145–63.

Krodel, Gerhard A. "The Functions of the Spirit in the Old Testament, the Synoptic Tradition, and the Book of Acts." In *The Holy Spirit in the Life of the Church*, ed. P. D. Opsahl. Minneapolis: Augsburg, 1978, pp. 1–46.

Acts. PC. Philadelphia: Fortress, 1981.

Acts. ACNT. Minneapolis: Augsburg, 1986.

Kühschelm, Roman. *Jüngerverfolgung und Geschick Jesu. Eine exegetisch-bibeltheologische Untersuchung der synoptischen Verfolgungsankündigungen Mk 13, 9–13 par und Mt 23, 29–36 par.* ÖBS 5. Klosterneuburg: Österreichisches katholisches, 1983.

Kümmel, Werner Georg. "Das Urchristentum." *ThR* 22 (1954): 138–70, 191–211.

Promise and Fulfilment: The Eschatological Message of Jesus. Trans. D. M. Barton. SBT 23. London: SCM, 1957.

"Futurische und präsentische Eschatologie im ältesten Urchristentum." *NTS* 5 (1958–59): 113–26.

Introduction to the New Testament. 2nd ed. Trans. H. C. Kee. London: SCM, 1975.

Kürzinger, Josef. *Papias von Hierapolis und die Evangelien des Neuen Testaments.* EM 4. Regensburg: Pustet, 1983.

Ladd, George Eldon. "The Christology of Acts." *Found* 11 (1968): 27–41.

A Theology of the New Testament. Grand Rapids: Eerdmans, 1974.

I Believe in the Resurrection of Jesus. London: Hodder & Stoughton, 1976.

Lafferty, Owen J. "Acts 2:14–36. A Study in Christology." *DunwRev* 6 (1966): 235–53.

Lampe, Geoffrey W. H. *The Seal of the Spirit: A Study in the Doctrine of Baptism and Confirmation in the New Testament and the Fathers.* London: Longmans, 1951.

"The Lucan Portrait of Christ." *NTS* 2 (1955–56): 160–75.

God as Spirit: The Bampton Lectures, 1976. Oxford: Clarendon, 1977.

Lane, William L. *The Gospel according to Mark: The English Text with Introduction, Exposition and Notes.* NICNT. Grand Rapids: Eerdmans, 1974.

Larkin, William J., Jr. *Acts.* IVPNTCS 5. Downers Grove: IVP, forthcoming.

Larsson, Edvin. *Christus als Vorbild. Eine Untersuchung zu den paulinischen Tauf- und Eikontexten.* ASNU 23. Uppsala: Almquist and Wiksells, 1962.

Laurentin, René. *Jésus au temple. Mystère de Pâques et foi de Marie en Luc 2, 48–50.* EBib. Paris: Gabalda, 1966.

Laymon, Charles M. *Luke's Portrait of Christ.* Nashville: Abingdon, 1959.

Leaney, A. R. C. *The Gospel according to St. Luke.* 2nd ed. BNTC. London: Black, 1966.

Lemcio, Eugene E. "The Intention of the Evangelist, Mark." *NTS* 32 (1986): 187–206.

The Past of Jesus in the Gospels. SNTSMS 68. Cambridge: Cambridge, 1991.

Lentz, John C. *Luke's Portrait of Paul.* SNTSMS 77. Cambridge: Cambridge, 1993.

Léon-Dufour, Xavier. *Die Evangelien und der historische Jesus*. Aschaffen-burg: Pattloch, 1966.

Resurrection and the Message of Easter. Trans. from French. London: Chapman, 1974.

Lestapis, Stanislas de. *L'énigme des Pastorales de S. Paul*. Paris: Gabalda, 1976.

Lightfoot, J. B. *Saint Paul's Epistle to the Philippians*. London: Macmillan, 1900.

Lincoln, Andrew T. "Theology and History in the Interpretation of Luke's Pentecost." *ExpT* 96 (1985): 204–209.

"The Promise and the Failure: Mark 16:7, 8." *JBL* 108 (1989): 283–300.

Lindars, Barnabas. "Salvation Proclaimed – VII. Mark 10:45: A Ransom for Many." *ExpT* 93 (1981– 82): 292–95.

Lindemann, Andreas. "Die Osterbotschaft des Markus. Zur theologischen Interpretation von Mark 16. 1–8." *NTS* 26 (1980): 298–317.

Lindsey, F. Duane. *The Servant Songs: A Study in Isaiah*. Chicago: Moody, 1985.

Lofthouse, W. F. "The Holy Spirit in the Acts and the Fourth Gospel." *ExpT* 52 (1940–41): 334–36.

Lohfink, Gerhard. *Die Himmelfahrt Jesu. Untersuchungen zu den Himmel-fahrts- und Erhöhungstexten bei Lukas*. SANT 26. Munich: Kösel, 1971.

Die Sammlung Israels. Eine Untersuchung zur lukanischen Ekklesiologie. SANT 39. Munich: Kösel, 1975.

Lohmeyer, Ernst. *Galiläa und Jerusalem.* FRLANT 34. Göttingen: Van-denhoeck & Ruprecht, 1934.

Die Briefe an die Philipper, und die Kolosser und an Philemon. 13th ed. KEKNT 9. Göttingen: Vandenhoeck & Ruprecht, 1964.

Lohse, Eduard. "Lukas als Theologe der Heilsgeschichte." In *Die Einheit des Neuen Testaments*. Göttingen: Vandenhoeck & Ruprecht, 1973, pp. 145–64.

Loisy, Alfred. *Les Actes des Apôtres*. Paris: Nourry, 1920.

L'évangile selon Luc. Frankfurt: Minerva, 1971 (1924).

Longenecker, Richard N. *The Christology of Early Jewish Christianity*. SBT 17. London: SCM, 1970.

"Ancient Amanuenses and the Pauline Epistles." In *New Dimensions in New Testament Study*, ed. R. N. Longenecker and M. C. Tenney. Grand Rapids: Zondervan, 1974, pp. 281–97.

Lubsczyk, Hans. "Kurios Jesus. Beobachtungen und Gedanken zum Schluss des Markusevangeliums." In *Die Kirche des Anfangs*, ed. R. Schnackenburg, J. Ernst, and J. Wanke. ErThS 38. Leipzig: St. Benno, 1977, pp. 133–74.

Lüdemann, Gerd. *Early Christianity according to the Traditions in Acts: A Commentary*. Trans. J. Bowden. London: SCM, 1989.

Mack, Burton L. *A Myth of Innocence: Mark and Christian Origins*. Philadelphia: Fortress, 1988.

The Lost Gospel: The Book of Q and Christian Origins. San Francisco: Collins, 1993.

MacRae, George W. " 'Whom Heaven must receive until the Time': Reflections on the Christology of Acts." *Int* 27 (1973): 151–65.

McRay, John. "Archaeology and the Book of Acts." *CrisTRev* 5 (1990): 69–82.

Maddox, Robert. *The Purpose of Luke–Acts.* FRLANT 126. Göttingen: Vandenhoeck & Ruprecht, 1982.

Magness, J. Lee. *Sense and Absence: Structure and Suspension in the Ending of Mark's Gospel.* Atlanta: Scholars, 1986.

Mahoney, Matthew. "Luke 21:14–15: Editorial Rewriting or Authenticity?" *ITQ* 47 (1980): 220–38.

Malherbe, Abraham J. " 'Not in a Corner': Early Christian Apologetic in Acts 26:26." *SC* 5 (1985–86): 193–210.

Mann, C. S. *Mark: A New Translation with Introduction and Commentary.* AncB 27. Garden City: Doubleday, 1986.

Mansfield, M. Robert. *"Spirit and Gospel" in Mark.* Peabody: Hendrickson, 1987.

Manson, T. W. "The Life of Jesus: A Survey of the Available Material. (3) The Work of St. Luke." *BJRL* 28 (1944): 382–403.

The Sayings of Jesus as Recorded in the Gospels according to St. Matthew and St. Luke. London: SCM, 1949.

Studies in the Gospels and Epistles, ed. M. Black. Manchester: Manchester, 1962.

Manson, William. *The Gospel of Luke.* MNTC. London: Hodder & Stoughton, 1937.

Marshall, I. Howard. "The Christ-Hymn in Philippians 2:5–11." *TynB* 19 (1968): 104–27.

The Work of Christ. Grand Rapids: Zondervan, 1969.

"The Resurrection in the Acts of the Apostles." In *Apostolic History and the Gospel*, ed. W. W. Gasque and R. P. Martin. Exeter: Paternoster, 1970, pp. 92–107.

"The Resurrection of Jesus in Luke." *TynB* 24 (1973): 55–98.

" 'Early Catholicism' in the New Testament." In *New Dimensions in New Testament Study*, ed. R. N. Longenecker and M. C. Tenney. Grand Rapids: Zondervan, 1974, pp. 217–31.

The Origins of New Testament Christology. ICT. Downers Grove: IVP, 1976.

I Believe in the Historical Jesus. Grand Rapids: Eerdmans, 1977.

"The Significance of Pentecost." *SJT* 30 (1977): 347–69.

"Slippery Words: I. Eschatology." *ExpT* 89 (1977–78): 264–69.

Commentary on Luke. NIGTC. Grand Rapids: Eerdmans, 1978.

The Acts of the Apostles. TNTC 5. Leicester: IVP, 1980.

"Pauline Theology in the Thessalonian Correspondence." In *Paul and Paulinism*, ed. M. D. Hooker and S. G. Wilson. London: SPCK, 1982, pp. 173–83.

"Luke and his 'Gospel.' " In *Das Evangelium und die Evangelien*, ed. P. Stuhlmacher. WUNT 28. Tübingen: Mohr (Siebeck), 1983, pp. 289–308.

Luke – Historian & Theologian. 3rd ed. Exeter: Paternoster, 1988.

"In Christ." Paper Presented to the New Testament Postgraduate Faculty, University of Aberdeen, October, 1989.

"The Present State of Lucan Studies." *Them* 14 (1989): 52–56.

"Luke's View of Paul." *SWJT* 33 (1990): 41–51.

"Son of God or Servant of Yahweh? – A Reconsideration of Mark 1.11." In *Jesus the Saviour*. London: SPCK, 1990, pp. 121–33.

"The Development of Christology in the Early Church." In *Jesus the Saviour*. London: SPCK, 1990, pp. 150–64.

"The Development of the Concept of Redemption in the New Testament." In *Jesus the Saviour*. London: SPCK, 1990, pp. 239–57.

The Acts of the Apostles. NTG. Sheffield: JSOT, 1992.

Martin, Hugh. *Luke's Portrait of Jesus*. London: SCM, 1949.

Martin, Ralph P. *Mark – Evangelist & Theologian*. Exeter: Paternoster, 1972.

New Testament Foundations. Vol. 1, *The Four Gospels*. Exeter: Paternoster, 1975.

Philippians. NCBC. London: Marshall, Morgan & Scott, 1982 (1976).

"Salvation and Discipleship in Luke's Gospel." *Int* 30 (1976): 366–80.

Carmen Christi: Philippians ii.5–11 in Recent Interpretation and in the Setting of Early Christian Worship. 2nd ed. Grand Rapids: Eerdmans, 1983.

Martini, Carlo M. "Riflessioni sulla cristologia degli Atti." *SacDoc* 16 (1971): 525–34.

Marxsen, Willi. *Mark the Evangelist: Studies on the Redaction History of the Gospel*. Trans. J. Boyce, D. Juel, W. Poehlmann, and R. A. Harrisville. Nashville: Abingdon, 1969.

The Resurrection of Jesus of Nazareth. Trans. M. Kohl. London: SCM, 1970.

Mattill, A. J., Jr. "The Purpose of Acts: Schneckenburger Reconsidered." In *Apostolic History and the Gospel*, ed. W. W. Gasque and R. P. Martin. Exeter: Paternoster, 1970, pp. 108–22.

"*Naherwartung, Fernerwartung*, and the Purpose of Luke–Acts: Weymouth Reconsidered." *CBQ* 34 (1972): 276–93.

"The Good Samaritan and the Purpose of Luke–Acts: Halévy Reconsidered." *Encounter* 33 (1972): 359–76.

"The Jesus–Paul Parallels and the Purpose of Luke–Acts: H. H. Evans Reconsidered." *NovT* 17 (1975): 15–46.

"The Date and Purpose of Luke–Acts: Rackham Reconsidered." *CBQ* 40 (1978): 335–50.

Luke and the Last Things: A Perspective for the Understanding of Lukan Thought. Dillsboro: Western North Carolina, 1979.

Mattill, A. J., Jr., and Mary Bedford Mattill, comps. *A Classified Bibliography of Literature on the Acts of the Apostles*. NTTS 7. Leiden: Brill, 1966.

Mealand, David L. *Poverty and Expectation in the Gospels*. London: SPCK, 1980.

Meierding, Paul. "Jews and Gentiles: A Narrative and Rhetorical Analysis of the Implied Audience in Acts." Ph.D. Lutheran Northwestern Seminary, 1992.

Mengel, Berthold. *Studien zum Philipperbrief. Untersuchungen zum situativen Kontext unter besonderer Berücksichtigung der Frage nach der*

Ganzheitlichkeit oder Einheitlichkeit eines paulinischen Briefes. WUNT ss 8. Tübingen: Mohr (Siebeck), 1982.

Menoud, Philippe Henri. "During Forty Days (Acts 1.3)." In *Jesus Christ and the Faith.* Trans. E. M. Paul. PittTMS 18. Pittsburgh: Pickwick, 1978, pp. 167–79.

Menzies, Robert Paul. *The Development of Early Christian Pneumatology with Special Reference to Luke–Acts.* JSNTSS 54. Sheffield: JSOT, 1991.

"Spirit and Power in Luke–Acts: A Response to Max Turner." *JSNT* 49 (1993): 11–20.

Merk, Otto. "Das Reich Gottes in den lukanischen Schriften." In *Jesus und Paulus,* ed. E. E. Ellis and E. Gräber. 2nd ed. Göttingen: Vandenhoeck & Ruprecht, 1978, pp. 201–20.

Metzger, Bruce M. *The Text of the New Testament: Its Transmission, Corruption, and Restoration.* 2nd ed. Oxford: Oxford, 1968.

A Textual Commentary on the Greek New Testament: A Companion Volume to the United Bible Societies' Third Edition of the Greek New Testament. 2nd ed. New York: UBS, 1975.

Meye, Robert P. *Jesus and the Twelve: Discipleship and Revelation in Mark's Gospel.* Grand Rapids: Eerdmans, 1968.

Meyer, Eduard. *Ursprung und Anfänge des Christentums,* 3 vols. Stuttgart, Berlin: Cotta'sche, 1921–23.

Michaelis, Wilhelm. "Die sog. Johannes-Jünger in Ephesus." *NKZ* 38 (1927): 717–36.

Die Erscheinungen des Auferstandenen. Basle: Majer, 1944.

Michel, Hans–Joachim. "Heilsgegenwart und Zukunft bei Lukas." In *Gegenwart und kommendes Reich,* ed. P. Fiedler and D. Zeller. StBB. Stuttgart: Katholisches, 1975, pp. 101–15.

Miller, Dale, and Patricia Miller. *The Gospel of Mark as Midrash on Earlier Jewish and New Testament Literature.* SBEC 21. Lampeter, Wales: Mellen, 1990.

Miller, Patrick D., Jr. "'Moses My Servant': The Deuteronomic Portrait of Moses." *Int* 41 (1987): 245–55.

Minear, Paul S. "Luke's Use of the Birth Stories." In *SLA,* pp. 111–30.

"Dear Theo: The Kerygmatic Intention and Claim of the Book of Acts." *Int* 27 (1973): 131–50.

To Heal and To Reveal: The Prophetic Vocation according to Luke. New York: Seabury, 1976.

Moessner, David P. "'The Christ must suffer': New Light on the Jesus–Peter, Stephen, Paul Parallels in Luke–Acts." *NovT* 28 (1986): 250–53.

Lord of the Banquet: The Literary and Theological Significance of the Lukan Travel Narrative. Philadelphia, Minneapolis: Augsburg Fortress, 1989.

Morgenthaler, Robert. *Die lukanische Geschichtsschreibung als Zeugnis. Gestalt und Gehalt der Kunst des Lukas,* 2 vols. AThANT 14–15. Zurich: Zwingli, 1949.

Morris, Leon L. "Luke and Early Catholicism." *JTSA* 40 (1982): 4–16; revision of article by same title in *WTJ* 35 (1973): 121–36.

The Gospel according to St. Luke. 2nd ed. TNTC 3. Grand Rapids: Eerdmans, 1989.

Moscato, Mary A. "Current Theories regarding the Audience of Luke–Acts." *CurTM* 3 (1976): 355–61.

Motyer, J. Alec. *The Prophecy of Isaiah: An Introduction & Commentary.* Downers Grove: IVP, 1993.

Motyer, Stephen. "The Rending of the Veil: A Markan Pentecost?" *NTS* 33 (1987): 155–57.

Moulder, W. J. "The Old Testament Background and the Interpretation of Mark X.45." *NTS* 24 (1978): 120–27.

Moule, Charles Francis Digby. "St. Mark XVI.8 Once More." *NTS* 2 (1955): 58–59.

———. "The Problem of the Pastoral Epistles: A Reappraisal." *BJRL* 47 (1964–65): 430–52.

———. "The Christology of Acts." In *SLA*, pp. 159–85.

———. *The Phenomenon of the New Testament: An Inquiry into the Implications of Certain Features of the New Testament.* SBT ss 1. London: SCM, 1967.

———. "Further Reflexions on Philippians 2:5–11." In *Apostolic History and the Gospel*, ed. W. W. Gasque and R. P. Martin. Exeter: Paternoster, 1970, pp. 264–76.

———. *The Origin of Christology.* Cambridge: Cambridge, 1977.

———. *The Holy Spirit.* MLT. Oxford: Mowbray, 1978.

———. *The Birth of the New Testament.* 3rd ed. London: Black, 1981.

Mounce, Robert H. *Matthew.* GNC. San Francisco: Harper & Row, 1985.

Muhlack, Gudrun. *Die Parallelen von Lukas-Evangelium und Apostelgeschichte.* ThW 8. Frankfurt: Lang, 1979.

Mullins, Terence Y. "Papias on Mark's Gospel." *VigChr* 14 (1960): 216–24.

Munck, Johannes. *The Acts of the Apostles.* AncB 31. 2nd ed., rev. W. F. Albright and C. S. Mann. Garden City: Doubleday, 1967.

Mußner, Franz. "Die Idee der Apokatastasis in der Apostelgeschichte." In *Lex tua veritas*, ed. H. Groß and F. Mußner. Trier: Paulinus, 1961, pp. 293–306.

———. " 'In den letzten Tagen' (Apg 2, 17a)." *BZ* 5 (1966): 263–65.

———. "Die Gemeinde des Lukasprologs." SNTU 6–7 (1981–82): 113–30.

———. *Apostelgeschichte.* NEBKNT 5. Würzburg: Echter, 1984.

Myers, Chad. *Binding the Strong Man: A Political Reading of Mark's Story of Jesus.* Maryknoll: Orbis, 1990 (1988).

Nagata, Takeshi. *Philippians 2:5–11: A Case Study in the Contextual Shaping of Early Christology.* Ann Arbor: UMI, 1981.

Navone, John. *Themes of St. Luke.* Rome: Gregorian, 1970.

Neil, William. *The Acts of the Apostles.* NCBC. Grand Rapids: Eerdmans, 1973.

Neyrey, Jerome H. *Christ is Community: The Christologies of the New Testament.* GNS 13. Wilmington: Glazier, 1985.

———. *The Passion according to Luke: A Redaction Study of Luke's Soteriology.* ThI. New York: Paulist, 1985.

Nickelsburg, George W. E. "Riches, the Rich, and God's Judgment in 1 Enoch 92–105 and the Gospel according to Luke." *NTS* 25 (1979): 324–44.

Nineham, Dennis Eric. *The Gospel of St. Mark*. 2nd ed. PGC. London: Black, 1968.

Nock, Arthur Darby. "Religious Developments from the Close of the Republic to the Death of Nero." In *The Cambridge Ancient History*, vol. 10, ed. S. A. Cook, F. E. Adcock, and M. P. Charlesworth. Cambridge: Cambridge, 1934, pp. 465–511.

"Paul and the Magus." In *Essays on Religion and the Ancient World*, vol. 1, ed. Z. Stewart. Oxford: Clarendon, 1972, pp. 308–30.

Nolland, John. *Luke*, 3 vols. WBC 35. Dallas: Word, 1989–93.

Norris, F. W. "'Christians Only, but not the Only Christians' (Acts 19:1–7)." *RQ* 28 (1985–86): 97–105.

Oberlinner, Lorenz. "Die Botschaft vom Kreuz als die Botschaft vom Heil nach Markus." *BibLit* 61 (1988): 56–65.

O'Brien, Peter T. *The Epistle to the Philippians: A Commentary on the Greek Text*. NIGTC. Grand Rapids: Eerdmans, 1991.

Ogilvie, Lloyd J. *Acts*. CC. Waco: Word, 1988.

Oliver, H. H. "The Lucan Birth Stories and the Purpose of Luke–Acts." *NTS* 10 (1963–64): 202–26.

O'Neill, John Cochrane. "The Use of *KYRIOS* in the Book of Acts." *SJT* 8 (1955): 155–74.

The Theology of Acts in its Historical Setting. 2nd ed. London: SPCK, 1970.

Osborne, Grant R. *The Resurrection Narratives: A Redactional Study*. Grand Rapids: Baker, 1984.

O'Toole, Robert F. "Why did Luke write Acts (Lk–Acts)?" *BTB* 7 (1977): 66–76.

The Christological Climax of Paul's Defense. AnaBib 78. Rome: Pontifical, 1978.

"Luke's Understanding of Jesus' Resurrection–Ascension–Exaltation." *BTB* 9 (1979): 106–14.

"Some Observations on *Anistêmi*, 'I raise', in Acts 3:23, 26." *SciEs* 31 (1979): 85–92.

"Activity of the Risen Jesus in Luke–Acts." *Bib* 62 (1981): 471–98.

"Parallels between Jesus and His Disciples in Luke–Acts: A Further Study." *BZ* 27 (1983): 195–212.

The Unity of Luke's Theology: An Analysis of Luke–Acts. GNS 9. Wilmington: Glazier, 1984.

Outler, Albert C. "Canon Criticism and the Gospel of Mark." In *New Synoptic Studies*, ed. W. R. Farmer. Macon: Mercer, 1983, pp. 233–43.

Page, Sydney H. T. "The Authenticity of the Ransom Logion (Mark 10:45b)." In *Gospel Perspectives*, vol. 1, ed. R. T. France and D. Wenham. Sheffield: JSOT, 1980, pp. 137–61.

Palmer, Darryl W. "The Resurrection of Jesus and the Mission of the Church." In *Reconciliation and Hope*, ed. R. Banks. Grand Rapids: Eerdmans, 1974, pp. 203–23.

"Acts and the Ancient Historical Monograph." In *Ancient Literary Setting*, ed. B. W. Winter and A. D. Clarke. A1CS 1. Grand Rapids: Eerdmans, 1993, pp. 1–29.

Parker, Pierson. "The 'Former Treatise' and the Date of Acts." *JBL* 84 (1965): 52–58.

Parratt, J. K. "The Rebaptism of the Ephesian Disciples." *ExpT* 79 (1967–68): 182–83.

Parsons, Mikeal C., and Richard I. Pervo. *Rethinking the Unity of Luke and Acts*. Minneapolis: Fortress, 1993.

Penna, Romano. "Lo 'Spirito di Gesù' in Atti 16, 7. Analisi letteraria e teologica." *RivBib* 20 (1972): 241–61.

Perlewitz, Lois A. "A Christology of the Book of Acts: Modes of Presence." Ph.D. St. Louis University, 1977.

Perrin, Norman. *The Resurrection Narratives: A New Approach*. London: SCM, 1977.

Pervo, Richard I. *Profit with Delight: The Literary Genre of the Acts of the Apostles*. Philadelphia: Fortress, 1987.

"Must Luke and Acts belong to the Same Genre?" In *Society of Biblical Literature 1989 Seminar Papers*, ed. D. J. Lull. SBLSPS 28. Atlanta: Scholars, 1989, pp. 309–16.

Luke's Story of Paul. Minneapolis: Fortress, 1990.

Pesch, Rudolf. "Die Vision des Stephanus Apg. 7, 55ff., im Rahmen der Apostelgeschichte." *BibLeb* 6 (1965): 92–107,170–83.

Naherwartungen, Tradition und Redaktion in Mk 13. KBANT. Düsseldorf: Patmos, 1968.

"Die Zuschreibung der Evangelien an apostolische Verfasser." *ZKT* 97 (1975): 56–71.

Das Markusevangelium. HThKNT 2/1–2. Freiburg: Herder, 1976 (vol. 1), 1977 (vol. 2).

Die Apostelgeschichte. EKK 5/1–2. Zurich, Neukirchen-Vluyn: Benziger, Neukirchener, 1986.

Peterlin, Davor. *Paul's Letter to the Philippians in the Light of Disunity in the Church*. NovTsup. Leiden: Brill, forthcoming.

Petersen, Norman R. *Literary Criticism for New Testament Critics*. Philadelphia: Fortress, 1978.

Plümacher, Eckhard. *Lukas als hellenistischer Schriftsteller. Studien zur Apostelgeschichte*. SUNT 9. Göttingen: Vandenhoeck & Ruprecht, 1974.

"Wirklichkeitserfahrung und Geschichtsschreibung bei Lukas. Erwägungen zu den Wir-Stücken der Apostelgeschichte." *ZNW* 68 (1977): 2–22.

Plummer, Alfred. *The Gospel according to St. Luke*. ICC. Edinburgh: Clark, 1896.

Pokorný, Petr. "Das Markusevangelium. Literarische und theologische Einleitung mit Forschungsbericht." *ANRW* 2/25/3 (1985): 1969–2035.

The Genesis of Christology: Foundations for a Theology of the New Testament. Trans. M. Lefébure. Edinburgh: Clark, 1987.

Polhill, John B. *Acts*. NAC 26. Nashville: Broadman, 1992.

Popkes, Wiard. *Christus Traditus. Eine Untersuchung zum Begriff der Dahingabe im Neuen Testament*. AThANT 49. Zurich: Zwingli, 1967.

Prast, Franz. *Presbyter und Evangelium in nachapostolischer Zeit. Die Abschiedsrede des Paulus in Milet (Apg 20, 17–38) im Rahmen der lukanischen Konzeption der Evangeliumsverkündigung.* FBib 29. Stuttgart: Katholisches, 1979.

Quinn, Jerome D. "The Last Volume of Luke: The Relation of Luke–Acts to the Pastoral Epistles." In *Perspectives on Luke–Acts*, ed. C. H. Talbert. PRS 5. Edinburgh: Clark, 1978, pp. 62–75.

The Letter to Titus. AncB 35. Garden City: Doubleday, 1990.

Rackham, R. B. "The Acts of the Apostles: A Plea for an Early Date." *JTS* 1 (1899–1900): 76–87.

Rad, Gerhard von. *Old Testament Theology.* Vol. 1, *The Theology of Israel's Historical Traditions.* Trans. D. M. G. Stalker. 2nd ed. New York: Harper & Row, 1962.

Radl, Walter. *Paulus und Jesus im lukanischen Doppelwerk. Untersuchungen zu Parallelmotiven im Lukasevangelium und in der Apostelgeschichte.* EH 23/49. Berne, Frankfurt: Lang, 1975.

Das Lukas–Evangelium. EF 261. Darmstadt: Wissenschaftliche, 1988.

Ramsay, William M. *The Bearing of Recent Discovery on the Trustworthiness of the New Testament.* London: Hodder & Stoughton, 1915.

Ramsey, Michael. *Holy Spirit: A Biblical Study.* London: SPCK, 1977.

Rapske, Brian. *The Book of Acts and Paul in Roman Custody.* A1CS 3. Grand Rapids: Eerdmans, 1994.

Rasco, Emilio. "Hans Conzelmann y la 'Historia Salutis.'" *Greg* 46 (1965): 286–319.

La teologia de Lucas. Origen, desarrollo, orientaciones. AnaGreg 201. Rome: Gregoriana, 1976.

Rau, Gottfried. "Das Markusevangelium. Komposition und Intention der ersten Darstellung christlicher Mission." *ANRW* 2/25/3 (1985): 2036–257.

Rawlinson, A. E. J. *The Gospel according to St. Mark.* 7th ed. WC. London: Methuen, 1949.

Rayan, Samuel. *Breath of Fire – the Holy Spirit: Heart of the Christian Gospel.* London: Chapman, 1978.

Recker, Robert R. "The Lordship of Christ and Mission in the Book of Acts." *RefRev* 37 (1984): 177–86.

Reicke, Bo. "The Risen Lord and His Church: The Theology of Acts." *Int* 13 (1959): 157–69.

"Synoptic Prophecies on the Destruction of Jerusalem." In *Studies in New Testament and Early Christian Literature*, ed. D. E. Aune. NovTsup 33. Leiden: Brill, 1972, pp. 121–34.

"Jesus in Nazareth – Lk 4, 14–30." In *Das Wort und die Wörter*, ed. H. Balz and S. Schulz. Stuttgart: Kohlhammer, 1973, pp. 47–55.

The Roots of the Synoptic Gospels. Philadelphia: Fortress, 1986.

Reploh, K.-G. "Das unbekannte Evangelium. Das Markus-Evangelium in der Theologiegeschichte." *BibKir* 27 (1972): 108–10.

Rese, Martin. *Alttestamentliche Motive in der Christologie des Lukas.* SNTU 1. Gütersloh: Mohn, 1969.

"Das Lukas-Evangelium. Ein Forschungsbericht." *ANRW* 2/25/3 (1985): 2258–328.

Richard, Earl. *Acts 6:1–8:4. The Author's Method of Composition.* SBLDS 41. Missoula: Scholars, 1978.

"Luke: Author and Thinker." In *New Views on Luke and Acts*, ed. E. Richard. Collegeville: Liturgical, 1990, pp. 15–32.

Riddle, Donald W. "The Occasion of Luke–Acts." *JR* 10 (1930): 545–62.

Rigaux, Béda. *The Testimony of St. Mark*. Trans. M. Carroll. Chicago: Herald, 1966.

Témoignage de l'évangile de Luc. Bruges, Paris: Brouwer, 1970.

Dieu l'a ressuscité. Exégèse et théologie biblique. SBFA 4. Gembloux: Duculot, 1973.

Rigg, Horace Abram, Jr. "Papias on Mark." *NovT* 1 (1956–57): 161–83.

Riley, Harold. *The Making of Mark: An Exploration*. Macon: Mercer, 1989.

Preface to Luke. Macon: Mercer, 1993.

Robbins, Vernon K. "The We-Passages in Acts and Ancient Sea-Voyages." *BibRes* 20 (1975): 5–18.

"By Land and by Sea: The We-Passages and Ancient Sea Voyages." In *Perspectives on Luke–Acts*, ed. C. H. Talbert. PRS 5. Edinburgh: Clark, 1978, pp. 215–42.

Jesus the Teacher: A Socio-Rhetorical Interpretation of Mark. Philadelphia: Fortress, 1984.

Robinson, H. Wheeler. *The Christian Experience of the Holy Spirit*. London: Nisbet, 1928.

Robinson, J. A. T. "The Most Primitive Christology of All?" *JTS* ns 7 (1956): 177–89.

Redating the New Testament. Philadelphia: Westminster, 1976.

Robinson, William C., Jr. "The Theological Context for Interpreting Luke's Travel Narrative (9:51ff.)." *JBL* 79 (1960): 20–31.

Der Weg des Herrn. Studien zur Geschichte und Eschatologie im Lukas-Evangelium. Ein Gespräch mit Hans Conzelmann. Trans. G. and G. Strecker. ThF 36. Hamburg-Bergstedt: Reich, 1964.

Roloff, Jürgen. "Die Paulus-Darstellung des Lukas. Ihre geschichtlichen Voraussetzungen und ihr theologisches Ziel." *EvTh* 39 (1979): 510–31.

Die Apostelgeschichte. NTD 5. Göttingen: Vandenhoeck & Ruprecht, 1981.

Ropes, James Hardy. "St. Luke's Preface: ἀσφάλεια and παρακολουθεῖν." *JTS* 25 (1924): 67–71.

Russell, Henry G. "Which was Written First, Luke or Acts?" *HTR* 48 (1955): 167–74.

Sahlin, Harald. *Der Messias und das Gottesvolk. Studien zur protolukanischen Theologie*. ASNU 12. Uppsala: Almquist and Wiksells, 1945.

Sand, Alexander. *Das Evangelium nach Matthäus*. RNT 1. Regensburg: Pustet, 1986.

Sanders, Jack T. *The New Testament Christological Hymns: Their Historical Religious Background*. SNTSMS 15. Cambridge: Cambridge, 1971.

The Jews in Luke–Acts. London: SCM, 1987.

"Who is a Jew and Who is a Gentile in the Book of Acts?" *NTS* 37 (1991): 434–55.

Scharlemann, Martin H. *Stephen: A Singular Saint*. AnaBib 34. Rome: Pontifical, 1968.

Schenk, Wolfgang. "Der Philipperbrief in der neueren Forschung (1945–1985)." In *ANRW* 2/25/4 (1987): 3280–313.

Schille, Gottfried. *Die Apostelgeschichte des Lukas.* 2nd ed. ThHNT 5. Berlin: Evangelische, 1983.

Schmid, Josef. *Das Evangelium nach Markus.* 5th ed. RNT 2. Regensburg: Pustet, 1963.

Schmidt, Thomas E. *Hostility to Wealth in the Synoptic Gospels.* JSNTSS 15. Sheffield: JSOT, 1987.

Schmithals, Walter. *Das Evangelium nach Markus.* ÖTKNT 2/1–2. Gütersloh, Würzburg: Mohn, Echter, 1979.

Das Evangelium nach Lukas. ZBKNT 3/1. Zurich: Theologischer, 1980.

Schnackenburg, Rudolf. *Gottes Herrschaft und Reich. Eine biblischtheologische Studie.* 4th ed. Freiburg: Herder, 1965.

"Christologie des Neuen Testamentes." In *Mysterium Salutis.* 3/1, *Das Christusereignis,* ed. J. Feiner and M. Löhrer. Einsiedeln: Benziger, 1970, pp. 227–388.

Schneckenburger, Matthias. *Über den Zweck der Apostelgeschichte.* Berne: Fischer, 1841.

Schneider, Gerhard. *Verleugnung, Verspottung und Verhör Jesu nach Lukas 22, 54–71. Studien zur lukanischen Darstellung der Passion.* SANT 22. Munich: Kösel, 1969.

Parusiegleichnisse im Lukas-Evangelium. StBibS 74. Stuttgart: Katholisches, 1975.

"Der Zweck des lukanischen Doppelwerks." *BZ* 21 (1977): 45–66.

Die Apostelgeschichte. HThKNT 5/1–2. Freiburg: Herder, 1980 (vol. 1), 1982 (vol. 2).

"Gott und Christus als *KURIOS* nach der Apostelgeschichte." In *Begegnung mit dem Word,* ed. J. Zmijewski and E. Nellessen. BBB 53. Bonn, Cologne: Hanstein, 1980, pp. 161–74.

"Zur Christologie der Apostelgeschichte." In *Die Apostelgeschichte.* HThKNT 5/1. Freiburg: Herder, 1980, pp. 331–35.

Das Evangelium nach Lukas. 2nd ed. ÖTKNT 3/1–2. Gütersloh, Würzburg: Mohn, Echter, 1984.

"Die lukanische Christologie." In *Das Evangelium nach Lukas.* 2nd ed. ÖTKNT 3/1. Gütersloh, Würzburg: Mohn, Echter, 1984, pp. 95–98.

"Urchristliche Gottesverkündigung in hellenistischer Umwelt." In *Lukas, Theologe der Heilsgeschichte.* BBB 59. Bonn, Cologne: Hanstein, 1985, pp. 280–96.

Schreckenberg, Heinz. "Flavius Josephus und die lukanischen Schriften." In *Wort in der Zeit,* ed. W. Haubeck and M. Bachmann. Leiden: Brill, 1980, pp. 179–209.

Schreiber, Johannes. *Theologie des Vertrauens. Eine redaktionsgeschichtliche Untersuchung des Markusevangeliums.* Hamburg: Furche, 1967.

Schubert, Paul. "The Structure and Significance of Luke 24." In *Neutestamentliche Studien,* ed. W. Eltester. BZNW 21. Berlin: Töpelmann, 1954, pp. 165–86.

"The Final Cycle of Speeches in the Book of Acts." *JBL* 87 (1968): 1–16.

Schulz, Siegfried. *Die Stunde der Botschaft. Einführung in die Theologie der vier Evangelisten.* 2nd ed. Hamburg, Zurich: Furche, Zwingli, 1970.

"Mark's Significance for the Theology of Early Christianity." In *The Interpretation of Mark*, ed. W. Telford. IRT 7. London: SPCK, 1985, pp. 158–66.

Schürmann, Heinz. "Die vorösterlichen Anfänge der Logientradition. Versuch eines formgeschichtlichen Zugangs zum Leben Jesu." In *Traditionsgeschichtliche Untersuchungen zu den synoptischen Evangelien*. KBANT. Düsseldorf: Patmos, 1968, pp. 39–69.

Das Lukasevangelium. 1, 1–9, 50. 2nd ed. HThKNT 3/1. Freiburg: Herder, 1982.

Schütz, Frieder. *Der leidende Christus. Die angefochtene Gemeinde und das Christuskerygma der lukanischen Schriften*. BWANT 89. Stuttgart: Kohlhammer, 1969.

Schweizer, Eduard. *Lordship and Discipleship*. Revision of German 1st ed. (1955). SBT 28. London: SCM, 1960.

"Anmerkungen zur Theologie des Markus." In *Neotestamentica et Patristica*. NovTsup 6. Leiden: Brill, 1962, pp. 35–46.

Erniedrigung und Erhöhung bei Jesus und seinen Nachfolgern. 2nd ed. AThANT 28. Zurich: Zwingli, 1962.

"Eschatologie im Evangelium nach Markus." In *Beiträge zur Theologie des Neuen Testaments*. Zurich: Zwingli, 1970, pp. 43–48.

The Good News according to Mark. Trans. D. H. Madvig. London: SPCK, 1971.

"Towards a Christology of Mark?" In *God's Christ and His People*, ed. J. Jervell and W. A. Meeks. Oslo: Universitetsforlaget, 1977, pp. 29–42.

Luke: A Challenge to Present Theology. London: SPCK, 1980.

The Holy Spirit. Trans. R. H. and I. Fuller. London: SCM, 1980.

"Zur lukanischen Christologie." In *Verifikationen*, ed. E. Jüngel, J. Wallmann, and W. Werbeck. Tübingen: Mohr (Siebeck), 1982, pp. 43–65.

The Good News according to Luke. Trans. D. E. Green. Atlanta: Knox, 1984.

Scott, Ernest F. *The Spirit in the New Testament*. London: Hodder & Stoughton, 1923.

Seccombe, David Peter. "Luke and Isaiah." *NTS* 27 (1981): 252–59.

Possessions and the Poor in Luke–Acts. SNTU series B 6. Linz: 1982.

Segbroeck, Frans van, comp. *The Gospel of Luke: A Cumulative Bibliography 1973–1988*. BEThL 88. Louvain: Louvain, 1989.

Seidensticker, Philipp. *Die Auferstehung Jesu in der Botschaft der Evangelisten. Ein traditionsgeschichtlicher Versuch zum Problem der Sicherung der Osterbotschaft in der apostolischen Zeit*. StBibS 26. Stuttgart: Katholisches, 1967.

Senior, Donald. "The Struggle to be Universal: Mission as Vantage Point for New Testament Investigation." *CBQ* 46 (1984): 63–81.

Sherwin-White, A. D. *Roman Society and Roman Law in the New Testament*. Oxford: Oxford, 1963.

Silva, Moisés. *Philippians*. WEC. Chicago: Moody, 1988.

Simon, Marcel. *St. Stephen and the Hellenists in the Primitive Church*. London: Longmans, 1958.

Siotis, Markus A. "Luke the Evangelist as St. Paul's Collaborator." In

Neues Testament und Geschichte, ed. H. Baltensweiler and B. Reicke. Zurich, Tübingen: Theologischer, Mohr (Siebeck), 1972, pp. 105–11.

Smalley, Stephen S. "The Christology of Acts." *ExpT* 73 (1962): 358–62.

"The Christology of Acts Again." In *Christ and Spirit in the New Testament*, ed. B. Lindars and S. S. Smalley. Cambridge: Cambridge, 1973, pp. 79–93.

Smith, James. *The Voyage and Shipwreck of St. Paul*. 4th ed. London: Longmans, 1880.

Spencer, F. Scott. *The Portrait of Philip in Acts: A Study of Roles and Relations*. JSNTSS 67. Sheffield: JSOT, 1992.

Squires, John T. *The Plan of God in Luke–Acts*. SNTSMS 76. Cambridge: Cambridge, 1993.

Stählin, Gustav. "Τὸ πνεῦμα 'Ιησοῦ (Apostelgeschichte 16:7)." In *Christ and Spirit in the New Testament*, ed. B. Lindars and S. S. Smalley. Cambridge: Cambridge, 1973, pp. 229–52.

Stanley, David M. "The Conception of Salvation in Primitive Christian Preaching." *CBQ* 18 (1956): 231–54.

Stanton, Graham N. *Jesus of Nazareth in New Testament Preaching*. SNTSMS 27. Cambridge: Cambridge, 1974.

"Luke and the People of God." Paper presented to the Divinity Faculty, University of Aberdeen, February, 1991.

Steck, Odil Hannes. *Israel und das gewaltsame Geschick der Propheten. Untersuchungen zur Überlieferung des deuteronomistischen Geschichtsbildes im Alten Testament, Spätjudentum und Urchristentum*. WMANT 23. Neukirchen-Vluyn: Neukirchener, 1967.

Stein, Robert H. "A Short Note on Mark xiv.28 and xvi.7." *NTS* 20 (1974): 445–52.

Luke. NAC 24. Nashville: Broadman, 1992.

Stemberger, Günter. "Galilee – Land of Salvation?" In W. D. Davies, *The Gospel and the Land*. Berkeley: California, 1974, pp. 409–38.

Sterling, Gregory E. *Historiography and Self-Definition: Josephus, Luke–Acts and Apologetic Historiography*. NovTsup 64. Leiden: Brill, 1992.

Stock, Augustine. *The Method and Message of Mark*. Wilmington: Glazier, 1989.

Stolle, Volker. *Der Zeuge als Angeklagter. Untersuchungen zum Paulusbild des Lukas*. BWANT 102. Stuttgart: Kohlhammer, 1973.

Stonehouse, Ned B. *The Witness of Luke to Christ*. London: Tyndale, 1951.

Origins of the Synoptic Gospels: Some Basic Questions. London: Tyndale, 1964.

Stott, John R. W. *The Message of Acts: To the Ends of the Earth*. BST. Leicester: IVP, 1990.

Strecker, Georg. "Redaktion und Tradition im Christushymnus Phil. 2:6–11." *ZNW* 55 (1964): 63–78.

Streeter, Burnett Hillman. *The Four Gospels: A Study of Origins Treating of the Manuscript Tradition, Sources, Authorship, and Date*. London: Macmillan, 1924.

Strobel, August. "Schreiben des Lukas? Zum sprachlichen Problem der Pastoralbriefe." *NTS* 15 (1968–69): 191–201.

Stuhlmacher, Peter. "Existenzstellvertretung für die Vielen. Mk 10, 45 (Mt 20, 28)." In *Werden und Wirken des Alten Testaments*, ed. R. Albertz, H.-P. Müller, H. W. Wolff, and W. Zimmerli. Göttingen: Vandenhoeck & Ruprecht, 1980, pp. 412–27.

Summers, Ray. *Jesus, The Universal Savior: Commentary on Luke*. Waco: Word, 1972.

Swete, Henry Barclay. *The Holy Spirit in the New Testament: A Study of Primitive Christian Teaching*. London: Macmillan, 1909.

Sylva, D. D. "The Cryptic Clause ἐν τοῖς τοῦ πατρός μου δεῖ εἶναί με in Lk. 2:49b." *ZNW* 78 (1987): 132–40.

Synge, F. C. "Mark 16.1–8." *JTSA* 11 (1975): 71–73.

Tajra, Harry W. *The Trial of St. Paul: A Juridical Exegesis of the Second Half of the Acts of the Apostles*. WUNT 35. Tübingen: Mohr (Siebeck), 1989.

Talbert, Charles Harold. *Luke and the Gnostics: An Examination of the Lucan Purpose*. Nashville: Abingdon, 1966.

"An Anti–Gnostic Tendency in Lucan Christology." *NTS* 14 (1967–68): 259–71.

"The Redaction Critical Quest for Luke the Theologian." In *Jesus and Man's Hope*, vol. 1, ed. D. G. Buttrick. PJPTS. Pittsburgh: Pittsburgh, 1970, pp. 171–222.

Literary Patterns, Theological Themes and the Genre of Luke–Acts. SBLMS 20. Missoula: Scholars, 1974.

"The Concept of Immortals in Mediterranean Antiquity." *JBL* 94 (1975): 419–36.

"Shifting Sands: The Recent Study of the Gospel of Luke." *Int* 30 (1976): 381–95.

Reading Luke: A Literary and Theological Commentary on the Third Gospel. New York: Crossroad, 1982.

"Discipleship in Luke–Acts." In *Discipleship in the New Testament*, ed. F. F. Segovia. Philadelphia: Fortress, 1985, pp. 62–75.

Tannehill, Robert C. "The Mission of Jesus according to Luke IV 16–30." In *Jesus in Nazareth*, ed. W. Eltester. BZNW 40. Berlin: de Gruyter, 1972, pp. 51–75.

The Narrative Unity of Luke–Acts: A Literary Interpretation, 2 vols. FF. Philadelphia: Fortress, 1986 (vol. 1), 1990 (vol. 2).

Tasker, R. V. G. *The Gospel according to St. Matthew*. TNTC 1. London: Tyndale, 1963.

Tatum, W. Barnes. "The Epoch of Israel: Luke I–II and the Theological Plan of Luke–Acts." *NTS* 13 (1966–67): 184–95.

Taylor, Vincent. "The Spirit in the New Testament." In *The Doctrine of the Holy Spirit*. London: Epworth, 1937, pp. 41–68.

The Atonement in New Testament Teaching. London: Epworth, 1940.

The Formation of the Gospel Tradition. 2nd ed. London: Macmillan, 1949.

The Gospel according to St. Mark: The Greek Text with Introduction, Notes, and Indexes. London: Macmillan, 1952.

The Person of Christ in New Testament Teaching. London: Macmillan, 1958.

The Passion Narrative of St. Luke: A Critical and Historical Investigation. SNTSMS 19. Cambridge: Cambridge, 1972.

Thompson, G. H. P. *The Gospel according to Luke.* NCB. Oxford: Clarendon, 1972.

Thornton, Claus-Jürgen. *Der Zeuge des Zeugen. Lukas als Historiker der Paulusreisen.* WUNT 56. Tübingen: Mohr (Siebeck), 1991.

Thornton, T. C. G. "To the End of the Earth: Acts 1:8." *ExpT* 89 (1977–78): 374–75.

Thüsing, Wilhelm. *Erhöhungsvorstellung und Parusieerwartung in der ältesten nachösterlichen Christologie.* StBibS 42. Stuttgart: Katholisches, 1969.

Die neutestamentlichen Theologien und Jesus Christus. Vol. 1, *Kriterien aufgrund der Rückfrage nach Jesus und des Glaubens an seine Auferweckung.* Düsseldorf: Patmos, 1981.

Per Christum in Deum. Vol. 1, *Gott und Christus in der paulinischen Soteriologie.* 3rd ed. NTAb 1/1. Münster: Aschendorffsche, 1986.

Tiede, L. David. *Prophecy and History in Luke–Acts.* Philadelphia: Fortress, 1980.

"Acts 1:6–8 and the Theo-Political Claims of Christian Witness." *WW* 1 (1981): 41–51.

Torrey, C. C. *The Composition and Date of Acts.* Cambridge, Mass.: Harvard, 1916.

Townsend, John T. "The Date of Luke–Acts." In *Luke–Acts,* ed. C. H. Talbert. New York: Crossroad, 1984, pp. 47–62.

Trites, Allison A. "The Importance of Legal Scenes and Language in the Book of Acts." *NovT* 16 (1974): 278–84.

The New Testament Concept of Witness. SNTSMS 31. Cambridge: CUP, 1977.

Trocmé, Etienne. *Le "Livre des Actes" et l'histoire.* EHPhR 45. Paris: France, 1957.

Trompf, G. W. "The First Resurrection Appearance and the Ending of Mark's Gospel." *NTS* 18 (1972): 308–30.

Turner, M. M. B. "Jesus and the Spirit in Lucan Perspective." *TynB* 32 (1981): 3–42.

"The Spirit of Christ and Christology." In *Christ the Lord,* ed. H. H. Rowdon. Leicester: IVP, 1982, pp. 168–90.

"The Spirit and the Power of Jesus' Miracles in the Lucan Conception." *NovT* 33 (1991): 124–52.

"The Spirit of Christ and 'Divine' Christology." In *Jesus of Nazareth Lord and Christ,* ed. J. B. Green and M. Turner. Grand Rapids: Eerdmans, 1994, pp. 413–36.

Tyson, Joseph B. *The Death of Jesus in Luke–Acts.* Columbia: South Carolina, 1986.

Unnik, W. C. van. "The 'Book of Acts' the Confirmation of the Gospel." *NovT* 4 (1960–61): 26–59.

"Once More St. Luke's Prologue." *NT* 7 (1963): 7–26.

"Der Ausdruck ἕως ἐσχάτου τῆς γῆς (Apostelgeschichte 1:8) und sein alttestamentlichen Hintergrund." In *Sparsa collecta,* vol. 1. NovTsup 29. Leiden: Brill, 1973, pp. 386–401.

"L'usage de σώζειν 'Sauver' et des dérivés dans les évangiles synoptiques." In *Sparsa collecta*, vol. 1. NovTsup 29. Leiden: Brill, 1973, pp. 16–34.

Vielhauer, Philipp. "On the 'Paulinism' of Acts." In *SLA*, pp. 33–50.

Geschichte der urchristlichen Literatur. Einleitung in das Neue Testament, die Apokryphen und die apostolischen Väter. deGrLe. Berlin: de Gruyter, 1975.

Vincent, Marvin R. *The Epistles to the Philippians and to Philemon.* ICC. Edinburgh: Clark, 1897.

Volger, Friedrich. "Zu Luk. 1, 4." *NKZ* 44 (1933): 203–205.

Voss, Gerhard. *Die Christologie der lukanischen Schriften in Grundzügen.* SNT 2. Bruges, Paris: Brouwer, 1965.

" 'Zum Herrn und Messias gemacht hat Gott diesen Jesus' (Apg 2, 36). Zur Christologie der lukanischen Schriften." *BibLeb* 8 (1967): 236–38.

Vriezen, Theodorus Christiaan. *An Outline of Old Testament Theology.* 2nd ed. Trans. from Dutch. Oxford: Blackwell, 1970.

Wagner, Guy. "Le scandale de la croix expliqué par le chant du Serviteur d'Isaïe 53. Réflexion sur Philippiens 2/6–11." *EThR* 61 (1986): 177–87.

Wainwright, Arthur W. *The Trinity in the New Testament.* London: SPCK, 1962.

Walasky, Paul W. *"And so we came to Rome": The Political Perspective of St. Luke.* SNTSMS 49. Cambridge: Cambridge, 1983.

Walker, William O., Jr. "Acts and the Pauline Corpus Reconsidered." *JSNT* 24 (1985): 3–23.

Weatherly, Jon. "The Jews in Luke–Acts." *TynB* 40 (1989): 107–17.

Jewish Responsibility for the Death of Jesus in Luke–Act. JSNTSS. Sheffield: JSOT, forthcoming.

Weeden, Theodore J. "The Heresy that Necessitated Mark's Gospel." *ZNW* 59 (1968): 145–58.

Mark – Traditions in Conflict. Philadelphia: Fortress, 1971.

Wehnert, Jürgen. *Die Wir-Passagen der Apostelgeschichte. Ein lukanisches Stilmittel aus jüdischer Tradition.* GThA 40. Göttingen: Vandenhoeck & Ruprecht, 1989.

Weiser, Alfons. *Die Apostelgeschichte.* ÖTKNT 5/1–2. Gütersloh, Würzburg: Mohn, Echter, 1981 (vol. 1), 1985 (vol. 2).

Weiss, Johannes. *The History of Primitive Christianity*, vol. 1. Trans. F. C. Grant, A. H. Forster, and P. S. Kramer. London: Macmillan, 1937.

Wenham, John. *Redating Matthew, Mark and Luke: A Fresh Assault on the Synoptic Problem.* Downers Grove: IVP, 1992.

Westermann, Claus. *Isaiah 40–66: A Commentary.* Trans. D. M. G. Stalker. OTL. London: SCM, 1969.

White, R. E. O. *The Answer is . . . the Spirit.* Edinburgh: Saint Andrew, 1979.

Luke's Case for Christianity. Harrisburg, Pa.: Moorehouse, 1987.

Wikenhauser, Alfred. "Das Christusbild der Apostelgeschichte." In *Die Apostelgeschichte.* RNT 5. Regensburg: Pustet, 1961, pp. 126–32.

Die Apostelgeschichte. RNT 5. Regensburg: Pustet, 1961.

Wilckens, Ulrich. *Die Missionsreden der Apostelgeschichte. Form- und traditionsgeschichtliche Untersuchungen.* 3rd ed. WMANT 5. Neukirchen-Vluyn: Neukirchener, 1974.

"Interpreting Luke–Acts in a Period of Existentialist Theology." In *SLA*, pp. 60–83.

Resurrection, Biblical Testimony to the Resurrection: An Historical Examination and Explanation. Trans. A. M. Stewart. Edinburgh: St. Andrew, 1977.

Wilcock, Michael. *The Message of Luke: The Saviour of the World.* BST. Downers Grove: IVP, 1979.

Wilcox, Max. *The Semitisms of Acts.* Oxford: Clarendon, 1965.

Williams, C. S. C. "The Date of Luke–Acts." *ExpT* 64 (1952–53): 283–84.

The Acts of the Apostles. 2nd ed. BNTC. London: Black, 1964.

Williams, David John. *Acts.* GNC. New York: Harper & Row, 1985.

Williams, R. R. *The Acts of the Apostles.* TBC. London: SCM, 1953.

"Church History in Acts: Is it Reliable?" In *Historicity and Chronology in the New Testament.* London: 1965.

Willimon, William H. *Acts.* IBC. Atlanta: Knox, 1988.

Wilshire, L. E. "Was Canonical Luke Written in the Second Century? – A Continuing Discussion." *NTS* 20 (1974): 146–53.

Wilson, Stephen G. "Lukan Eschatology." *NTS* 16 (1969–70): 330–47.

The Gentiles and the Gentile Mission in Luke–Acts. SNTSMS 23. Cambridge: Cambridge, 1973.

Luke and the Pastoral Epistles. London: SPCK, 1979.

Windisch, Hans. "Jesus und der Geist nach synoptischer Überlieferung." In *Studies in Early Christianity*, ed. S. J. Case. New York: Century, 1928, pp. 209–36.

Winn, Albert C. "Elusive Mystery: The Purpose of Acts." *Int* 13 (1959): 144–56.

Winter, Paul. "Lc. 2, 49 and Targum Yerushalmi." *ZNW* 45 (1954): 145–79.

Wolff, Hans Walter. *Jesaja 53 im Urchristentum.* 4th ed. MSB 223. Gießen: Brunnen, 1984.

Wood, H. G. "The Priority of Mark." *ExpT* 65 (1953–54): 17–19.

Wren, Malcolm. "Sonship in Luke: The Advantage of a Literary Approach." *SJT* 37 (1984): 301–11.

Wright, N. T. "Adam in Pauline Christology." In *Society of Biblical Literature 1983 Seminar Papers*, ed. K. H. Richards. SBLSPS 22. Chico: Scholars, 1983, pp. 359–89.

"ἁρπαγμός and the Meaning of Philippians 2:5–11." *JTS* ns 37 (1986): 321–52.

"Jesus Christ is Lord: Philippians 2.5–11." In *The Climax of the Covenant.* Minneapolis: Fortress, 1991.

Wuellner, Wilhelm H. *The Meaning of "Fishers of Men."* NTL. Philadelphia: Westminster, 1967.

Yates, J. E. "The Form of Mark 1.8b: 'I baptize you with Water; He will baptize you with the Holy Spirit.'" *NTS* 4 (1957–58): 334–38.

The Spirit and the Kingdom. London: SPCK, 1963.

Zahn, Theodor. *Introduction to the New Testament*, 3 vols. Trans. M. W. Jacobus, C. S. Thayer, J. M. Trout, W. A. Mather, L. Hodous, E. S. Worcester, W. H. Worrell, and R. B. Dodge. Edinburgh: Clark, 1909.

Ziesler, John A. "Luke and the Pharisees." *NTS* 25 (1979): 146–57.

"The Name of Jesus in the Acts of the Apostles." *JSNT* 4 (1979): 28–41.

Zimmerli, Walther. *Old Testament Theology in Outline*. Trans. D. E. Green. Edinburgh: Clark, 1978.

Zimmerli, Walther, and Joachim Jeremias. *The Servant of God*. 2nd ed. Trans. H. Knight. SBT 20. London: SCM, 1965.

Zmijewski, Josef. *Die Eschatologiereden des Lukas-Evangeliums. Eine traditions- und redaktionsgeschichtliche Untersuchung zu Lk 21, 5–36 und Lk 17, 20–37*. BBB 40. Bonn, Cologne: Hanstein, 1972.

INDEX OF ANCIENT SOURCES

INDEX OF SUBJECTS